Jerome Rothenberg

Associate Professor of Economics
Department of Economics
Northwestern University

THE MEASUREMENT OF

SOCIAL WELFARE

GREENWOOD PRESS, PUBLISHERS
WESTPORT, CONNECTICUT

Library of Congress Cataloging in Publication Data

Rothenberg, Jerome, 1924-
    The measurement of social welfare.

    Reprint of the ed. published by Prentice-Hall,
Englewood Cliffs, N. J.
    Bibliography: p.
    1. Welfare economics.   I. Title.
[HB99.3.R66 1973]   330.15'5   73-5207
ISBN 0-8371-6872-4

Originally published in 1961
by Prentice-Hall, Inc., Englewood Cliffs, New Jersey

Reprinted with the permission
of Prentice-Hall, Inc.

Reprinted by Greenwood Press, Inc.

First Greenwood reprinting 1973
Second Greenwood reprinting 1976

Library of Congress catalog card number 73-5207

ISBN 0-8371-6872-4

Printed in the United States of America

To My Parents

Preface

In this book, *The Measurement of Social Welfare*, I have examined the possibilities for a useful, rather than merely a formally correct, welfare economics. I have focused on the question of what the fundamental criterion of *social welfare* must be like in order that a welfare analysis based on it be especially relevant to guide policy decisions. Three characteristics seem appropriate. First, the standard must be internally consistent. Second, it must enable us to compare a large proportion of the policy alternatives before use. Third, it must be compatible with relevant values prevailing in the community.

The point of departure of the study is the finding by Arrow that if the standard be fashioned to reflect a particular interpretation of "rational" evaluation and in addition bear the kind of correspondence to the values of the individuals in the community which we call consumer sovereignty, then the standard will necessarily be internally inconsistent. This finding has had a strong impact, largely in convincing economists that almost nothing in the way of practical help can be expected from welfare economics. Very little of the immersion of economists in matters of public policy in recent years has been significantly informed by the formal corpus of welfare theory. This book is partly an attempt to see exactly how restrictive Arrow's finding is, and how best to by-pass it so as to form a useful analytic apparatus.

Part I sets forth the basic problem and examines Arrow's analysis and implications in some detail. Parts II, III, and IV examine a wide variety of approaches in the welfare literature in order to discover how useful are the criteria of choice which they generate. The approaches falling under the rubric, "New Welfare Economics," are analyzed, as well as approaches which introduce varying degrees of cardinality into individual utility indicators, including two chapters on approaches based on the Von Neumann-Morgenstern expected utility hypothesis. In addition, approaches resting on specific group uniformities in individual preferences and on group value judgments concerning interpersonal comparability of social welfare impact, are analyzed. These sections of the book provide an extensive, reasonably complete survey of the welfare literature of the past twenty-five years. They incidentally provide as well an extensive survey of the non-normative field of utility and decision theory. The discussion is self-contained throughout, leading from an elementary statement of each approach to more difficult material.

The analyses of Parts II, III, and IV examine welfare criteria primarily with regard to their internal consistency and power in application. Part V, however, deals with the relevance of welfare criteria to the values prevailing in the community. Its approach is to ask whether individual systems of values can be "aggregated" or their differences "resolved." Is there any sense in which we can speak meaningfully of a community's representative values? Findings in allied sciences like anthropology, sociology, and social psychology suggest that within "going societies" there exist values which are pervasively accepted, which are strategic in that they form a matrix from which most other values in the community flow, and which tend to support what seem to be the crucial characteristics of the community. Such values would seem to fulfill the meaning of a social value criterion. Chapter 13 presents the refutable hypothesis that such sets of values are empirically discoverable in "going societies" and examines their properties. Finally, it explores the implications for welfare theory if such values are adopted to formulate the criterion of social welfare. The treatment of Part V therefore represents a novel departure in welfare economics. My argument is that this new direction deserves serious attention. With more work it could provide a significant advance toward building a dependable bridge between positive economic theory and the evaluation of public policy.

This Preface has spoken entirely of welfare *economics*. I believe the book has considerably wider relevance than to economics alone, however. In many respects the logical structure of a bridge between pure theory and policy recommendation does not depend on the specific subject matter of theory and policy. Moreover, other social sciences are as closely concerned with a criterion of *social welfare* as is economics. The analyses of the book ought to have much the same relevance to these disciplines as to economics itself.

I especially appreciate the generous and substantial aid to this work in its early stages by Professors Albert G. Hart and William S. Vickrey.

To Kenneth J. Arrow and William Baumol go my deep thanks for their kind encouragement and valuable comments.

To my wife go words that I shall not say here.

JEROME ROTHENBERG

Contents

ix

PART III. CARDINAL ANALYSIS

Part I

THE PROBLEM OF

SOCIAL CHOICE

CHAPTER 1

The Welfare Function:

Its Role in Welfare Economics

1-1. The Nature of Welfare Economics

Welfare economics is that part of economics where such words as "good" and "bad," "ought" and "ought not," hopefully banished from the realm of positive economics, reappear to serve as guides for public policy. It is an applied science, in the same way that medicine is an applied science. Medicine gathers together pertinent information from anatomy, physiology, pharmacology, bacteriology, psychology, physical chemistry, and other disciplines in terms of a single purpose: to combat illness in man; or, to put it in a positive way, to further human health. Welfare economics, similarly, gathers together the pertinent theoretical relationships from positive or "pure" economics in terms, typically, of a single end: the economic welfare of the community. The various prescriptions of welfare economics, whether in concrete form bearing on real issues of the day, or in the highly abstract form of "optimum conditions," have meaning only with respect to the particular end or set of ends being considered.

This is not to say that all welfare economists always are thinking of the same end toward which to prescribe. For one thing, it is not at all clear what dividing line — if any — should be set up between policy evaluations and recommendations ostensibly aimed at limited special goals, and other policy evaluations and recommendations ostensibly aimed at the goal of the welfare of the group. In other words, our very definition of "welfare economist" is notoriously ambiguous. There is a presumption that no public policy (in the widest sense of the term) is oriented toward social diswelfare, and even tyranny or the most special pleading is often explicitly or implicitly justified as being "good" for the whole group. At the very least, the special pleaders implicitly assume either that fulfillment of their "local" goals can be accomplished with no diminishment of welfare elsewhere, or else, if some welfare diminishment elsewhere is unavoidable, that it will be "less than" the increase in welfare attendant upon realization of their goals. Some knowledge about which goals should properly be allowed to refer to the welfare of the community as a whole and which should not can be obtained as fruits of welfare analysis itself, but I suspect that much the greater part must be sought in semantic rules of thumb, ethical beliefs, etc.

A second reason for diversity in the ends predicated is that even where economists explicitly adapt their analysis to the goal of social welfare, their conception of this goal usually differs.[1] As will become obvious shortly, these differing conceptions are possible because the end to which an analysis is adapted is not *empirically given to* the investigator; it is instead *postulated by* the investigator. It is a definition and, as such, can be chosen at will. They have in fact been chosen at the varying wills of economists.

The structure of welfare analysis would appear to be the following. We assume that our end is given by some set of assertions E. Now, starting from our existing state of the world S, we consider the whole set of possible public policies P — interpreting this broadly to include various kinds of structural reorganizations as well as the more narrowly understood government actions. Each of these policies, if introduced, would have consequences in that it would determine some future state or sequence of states of the world. We are able to predict this future state or sequence with more or less uncertainty by making use of the empirical theories of pure economics which can be put into the form as follows. *If* some change P_r is made in an existing state of things, *then* the following will occur.[2] Each policy can now be considered as a means to reaching a particular state — its predicted consequences. We are interested in comparing these various states with one another in terms of the degree to which they fulfill the assumed welfare end. We do this by ordering the states in these terms.[3]

---

[1] In this work I shall be using "social welfare," "welfare of the community" and "group welfare" — where "group" is not otherwise restricted — as interchangeable terms. Omission of the qualifying *"economic"* before these terms will be explained briefly below.

[2] The degree of uncertainty in the predictions, and one's confidence in them, of course, depend on the scope and power of the pertinent theories and on the degree to which they have been verified. This is accepted as data by the welfare economist.

[3] If we are significantly unable to predict a single state outcome for each policy, but only a penumbra of states, with perhaps some notion of the likelihood with which the various portions of the penumbra may occur, then our analysis really requires ordering such whole penumbras. This problem is formally identical with the problem treated in the chapter on "expected utility."

This ordering of states[4] is logically equivalent to an ordering of the corresponding public policies in terms of the degree to which *they* fulfill the assumed welfare end.[5] With this ordering we are able to make recommendations about good and bad public policies; we are able to suggest which policies ought to be introduced and which ought not to be introduced.

Another way of looking at the same structure is to start from the assumed end and the prevailing state and then seek to "reform" those structural characteristics of the prevailing state which seem undesirable. This means that the economist would implicitly be considering a subset of alternative policies with certain localized scope and comparing them in terms of the desirability (with respect to the assumed end) of their consequences.

Let us say now that we have performed our analysis and made our policy recommendations to an authority with power to implement them. What is the status of these recommendations? Clearly, they may be rejected. It is of great importance to understand on what grounds they may be rejected, or, for that matter, accepted. To clarify this, let us note the elements of the structure just described.

(1) The subjects referred to by the analysis (i.e., the individuals, or groups, or systems of groups).

(2) The set of assertions E defining the welfare end.

(3) The particular set of alternative policies P whose ordering is the basis for policy recommendations.

(4) The set of state of the world consequences S of the policies P.

(5) The scientific laws L relating each P_r to a corresponding S_r.

(6) The criterion C by which the state of the world outcomes are ordered in terms of the degree to which they fulfill the welfare end E.

Whether the authority, or indeed, anyone, should accept a particular set of recommendations would seem to depend on two questions:

(A) Is the analysis on which the recommendations are based accurate?

(B) Is the analysis relevant?

The first question refers to portions of the analysis which can be characterized as true or false. It relates to the quality of the inductive and deductive reasoning in the analysis. If it is granted that the laws of positive economics are accepted as data in welfare economics, then the only element in the analysis which has refutable content is the one which states that the particular specified P is actually the total set of alternative policies which

---

[4]Or penumbras.

[5]This is true so long as any valued aspects of the policies themselves, i.e., aside from their "consequences" (conceived narrowly), are included in the specification of the resulting state. In other words, this is true if the consequences are construed broadly.

can be considered.[6] The accuracy of the given analysis, then, would involve the validity of the assertion of P, the absence of logical error (inconsistency), and, to some extent, the accuracy with which the analytic concepts are identified with empirically observable entities.[7]

However, it is easy to see that our acceptance or rejection of the analysis does not depend solely, or even, perhaps, largely, on its accuracy. All this means is that, even when referring to things in the real world, a particular policy recommendation follows *if E*, and *C*, and the pertinent economic laws are accepted. Verification of the latter is, we know, clearly possible in principle. But E and C are not elements about which it can be said that they are true or false. One is a definition, the other an operating rule. They can never be proved or disproved by observation.[8] So, acceptance of them involves something else. When we remember that in common usage the maximum fulfillment of social welfare is really only another term for "desirable goal of public policy," we see that giving some specific content to E and C means offering a particular notion of the desirable goal of public policy. So E and C are value judgments. A necessary condition to accepting any policy recommendation is to accept the value judgments embedded in its derivation. (This is the gist of the "relevance" question above.) The crucial value judgments here are those defining the end toward which policy should be directed and the criterion by which one can evaluate states of the world in terms of this end. There are value judgments connected with the remaining elements of the analysis as well.

This does not fully answer the question raised concerning acceptance by the authority. What value judgments will *he* accept? This will be considered in a later chapter. At this point, however, it may be suggested

---

[6]Three points deserve elaboration:

(1) If economic laws are not deemed as givens to welfare economics, then their content also is empirically refutable. But this does not change the conclusion made in the text below. If the responsibility for verifying economic laws is more conventionally placed outside of welfare economics, then we may still reject a welfare analysis employing what we believe to be faulty theories; only our rejection would then be based on the relevance of the analysis, instead of on its accuracy.

(2) To demonstrate that given P implies S, P is the only other refutable content of the analysis. We may symbolize its logical structure as follows: P, and if (E and C), and if (P implies S), and if (E and C and S implies $R(S)$, i.e., the particular ordering of S), and if (P and S and $R(S)$ implies $R(P)$, i.e., the corresponding ordering of P), then $R(P)$. Except for the assertion of P the sentence would be a tautology, in other words, without any other empirical content.

(3) P is refutable because, for example, a policy alternative not included in P may be discovered.

[7]The process of identification has some nonrefutable but valuational aspects as well.

[8]I can never prove, for example, that some E is not what one ought to mean by social welfare. Only solid *empirical* discoveries about the (metaphysical?) "purpose" of human life can open the door to an interpretation of this kind of statement as being true or false.

that we should expect the degree of his acceptance to reflect the extent of general agreement or disagreement among the population. We can therefore expect, as a result, a hierarchy of "useful" welfare analyses, each of them accurate but differing over their relevance. It should be emphasized again that the evaluation of relevance is a value judgment.[9] Also the evaluation of relevance involved in the authority's attitude is a value judgment, although of a special and complicated sort.

This book is almost exclusively concerned with this hierarchy of usefulness of different kinds of welfare analysis. We focus on the question of which specification of E and C gives the most useful analysis or, less austerely, which specifications are likely to prove more useful, which less useful. In the light of our own delineation, it is an open question whether this book should be considered part of welfare economics, especially since some of the materials dealt with are usually deemed to reside outside of the field of economics as a whole. In an important sense this is a *meta*-welfare economics, for it examines the foundations of public policy in general. The policy alternatives dealt with by no means need to be "economic policies." It is hoped, therefore, that this book will have relevance for those branches of all the social sciences where recommendations about public policies or even normative evaluations about different "states of affairs," are an important or regular feature.

1-2. Value Judgments and the Economic Welfare Function

The analysis of the last section emphasizes the dependence of welfare conclusions on value judgments embedded in the analysis. This dependence was subject to some confusion during the 1930's, in large measure arising out of criticisms made by Lionel Robbins. His *An Essay on the Nature and Significance of Economic Science*, published in 1932,[10] argued strongly that value judgments made by economists are out of place in scientific — objective — analysis. If they must be dealt with at all, they should be handled descriptively by accepting the values of the community as observational data.

---

[9]For example, the following are nonrefutable, but debatable value judgments: a welfare analysis that concerns only a small subset of peculiar individuals is irrelevant, as is an analysis which defines welfare as revealable by the number of pencils carried by an individual, or an analysis in which only four or five out of thousands of possible policies are evaluable. These are not useful welfare analyses.

I think we ourselves would think of the reasonableness of our judgments here in terms of the extent of probable agreement with them.

[10]London: Macmillan.

In the face of this, Kaldor, Hicks, and others sought to isolate a value-free, purely objective kernel of welfare economics.[11] The orientation of their efforts was named the New Welfare Economics, and its chief fruit centered around the use of the so-called "Compensation Principle."[12] It was later pointed out that the procedures of the New Welfare Economics did not dispense with ethical assumptions (such as consumer sovereignty, and indifference of resources in different uses).[13] But the analytic techniques of this "school" were not such that the assumptions could be clearly isolated. Moreover, the same was found to be true of other welfare analyses such as those of Pareto, Marshall, Barone, Pigou, Lerner, and Kahn.[14] Although ethical assumptions were embedded, they were not obvious — to the point of misleading examination of the analysis; they were not localized, so that their effects on the analysis could be isolated; and the analyses were ill-adapted to additions or subtractions of sets of such assumptions.

It was Abram Bergson, by his introduction of the concept of the Economic Welfare Function, who solved these problems and achieved a notable isolation and clarification of the function of value judgments in welfare economics.[15] The Economic Welfare Function was ideally suited to the formalization of any set of value assumptions within a welfare analysis, and to the compact tracing out of their implications.

Bergson began by postulating an undefined relationship between the welfare of the community and variables like "the amounts of each of the factors of production, other than labor, employed in the different production units, the amounts of the various commodities consumed, the amounts of the different kinds of work done, and the production unit for which this work is performed by each individual in the community during that period of time."[16]

---

[11]See for example N. Kaldor, "Welfare Propositions in Economics," *Economic Journal,* Vol. XLIX (1939), 549-552; J. R. Hicks, "Foundations of Welfare Economics," *Economic Journal,* Vol. XLIX (1939), 696-712; M. Reder, *Studies in the Theory of Welfare Economics* (New York: Columbia University Press, 1947).

[12]This will be examined in detail in Chapters 3 and 4.

[13]W. J. Baumol, "Community Indifference," *Review of Economic Studies,* Vol. 14, No. 1 (1946-1947), 44-48; Abram Bergson, "A Reformulation of Certain Aspects of Welfare Economics," *Quarterly Journal of Economics* (February, 1938), 310-334; Paul A. Samuelson, *Foundations of Economic Analysis* (Cambridge: Harvard University Press, 1947), Chapter VIII. Also see Chapters 3 and 4 below.

[14]Pareto, *Cours d'Economie Politique* (Lausanne, 1897); Marshall, *Principles of Economics* (1895); Enrico Barone, "The Ministry of Production in a Socialist State," *Collectivist Economic Planning* (ed. Hayek), originally appeared in *Giornale degli Economisti* (1908); A. P. Lerner, "The Concept of Monopoly and the Measurement of Monopoly Power," *Review of Economic Studies* (October, 1934), and *Economics of Control;* R. F. Kahn, "Some Notes on Ideal Output," *Economic Journal,* Vol. XLV (March, 1935), 1-35. For an elegant demonstration of this, see A. Bergson, *op. cit.*

[15]*Ibid.*

[16]*Ibid.,* 311.

(1) $\qquad W = W(x_1, y_1, a_1{}^x, b_1{}^x, a_1{}^y, b_1{}^y, \ldots ,$
$\qquad\qquad x_n, y_n, a_n{}^x, b_n{}^x, a_n{}^y, b_n{}^y, C^x, D^x, C^y, D^y, r, s, t, \ldots)$

where x_1, y_1 are quantities of the (assumed) two kinds of consumer's goods consumed by individual i; $a_1{}^x, b_1{}^x, a_1{}^y, b_1{}^y$ are the amounts of the (assumed) two kinds of labor performed by individual i in the production of commodities x and y respectively (each commodity is assumed to be produced in a single production unit); C^x, D^x, and C^y, D^y are the amounts of the (assumed) two kinds of nonlabor resources employed in the production of x and y respectively; $r, s, t, \ldots$ are other unspecified factors influencing welfare.[17]

Bergson then makes the important assumption that, while interrelationships between what can be considered the "noneconomic" factors $r, s, t, \ldots$, and the "economic" factors x, y, a, b, etc. are certainly to be expected (e.g., "A sufficient diminution of x_i and y_i may be accompanied by an overturning of the government"[18]), the range of values taken by these economic factors in typical welfare studies (in other words the relevant set of policies P) is not sufficiently large to affect significantly the institutional fabric represented by $r, s, t, \ldots$. This is not an unusual assumption; on the contrary, it is the general operating assumption of most theoretical studies in economics.[19] But it makes possible "a partial analysis" of welfare, namely, that we can examine changes in welfare proceeding from changes in "economic" magnitudes alone, *as though* all other variables remained constant.

This gives us, from Eq. (1), an "Economic Welfare Function," viz.

(2) $\qquad E = E(x_1, y_1, a_1{}^x, b_1{}^x, a_1{}^y, b_1{}^y, \ldots ,$
$\qquad\qquad x_n, y_n, a_n{}^x, b_n{}^x, a_n{}^y, b_n{}^y, C^x, D^x, C^y, D^y, \mid r, s, t, \ldots).$[20]

The conception of the Economic Welfare Function must be clearly understood. It does not refer to some "economic welfare" defined in such terms as the Cannan concept of the "more material side of human happiness." In this latter kind of interpretation, there is a real possibility of divergence between economic welfare and welfare in general. This kind of concept of economic welfare suggests the existence of an "economic welfare," a "spiritual welfare," an "artistic welfare," etc., and of corresponding groups of individual ends classified as "economic," "spiritual," "artistic," etc., to which groups of means classified as "economic," etc., minister respectively. The total welfare of the individual according to this view is

---

[17]*Ibid.*, 311. The simplifying assumptions can of course be dropped; they were adopted to keep the notation within manageable bounds.

[18]Bergson, *loc. cit.*

[19]The notable exceptions are to be found in works on the process of economic development like those of Marx, Veblen, and Schumpeter.

[20]Bergson, *op. cit.*, 311.

some combination of these separable welfares, perhaps a simple summation.[21]

This fragmentation of individual well-being cannot be accepted in the light of modern psychological understanding of personality as an integrated system. Just as the individual obtains no unique degree of satisfaction from consuming a single commodity irrespective of what other commodities are contained in his standard of living, so too his evaluation of a whole commodity bundle is not independent of the existing social structure, political policies, etc., which form his total environment. And conversely, political decisions, family relationships, civic responsibilities, are never evaluated outside of the particular economic opportunities in the environment. This is an extension of the notion of commodity relatedness to the whole behavior pattern of each individual.[22]

Bergson's Economic Welfare Function refers to something quite different. The individual's well-being does depend on the total environment, and changes anywhere in the environment will affect his welfare. The Economic Welfare Function simply traces the effects on the individual's welfare of changes occurring in one part of the environment, the other portions remaining unchanged. The term "economic welfare," therefore, signifies not a separate kind of welfare, but influences on the individual's one and only welfare which happen to be localized in changing economic events. Since we shall be referring to this single notion throughout the present work, we may drop the qualifying "economic" without misunderstanding.

From the welfare function E (not to be confused with my earlier abbreviation of the community's postulated ends) we may obtain those conditions required to secure a maximum social welfare. Mathematically, this involves setting $dE = 0$, subject to whatever constraining relationships are held to exist among the various determining variables. At this stage, the constraining relationships are transformation (or production) functions, *empirically* relating units of output forthcoming with different, most efficient combinations of inputs. Since the assumption permitting us to work with E instead of W is empirically verifiable [Eq. (1)], the optimum conditions derived at this stage "are the general conditions for a position of

---

[21]See the criticisms of this kind of welfare concept in Lionel Robbins, "Robertson on Utility and Scope," *Economica*, New Series Vol. XX, No. 78 (May, 1953), 105-107. Robbins advocates the Pigovian definition of economic welfare in terms of "accessibility to the measuring rod of money" (*Economics of Welfare*) as avoiding his strictures, but somewhat similar criticisms can be applied to Pigou's concept as well.

[22]This interrelatedness between the economic and noneconomic refers to how an individual *judges* his environment. It is not the same as the interrelatedness cited in the text above where economic *events* influence the course of non-economic *events*, and conversely. This last refers to what determines what the individual's environment *will be*.

maximum economic welfare for any Economic Welfare Function . . . ."[23]
In effect, they involve no value judgments whatever. (The noneconomic
factors r, s, t, . . . , can never be *completely* constant over relevant changes in
the economic factors. The operating assumption that what minor variations do occur have trivial effects on the welfare of the community is a value
judgment.) For this reason, it will be informative to reproduce them.

There are three groups. The first deals with the consumption of
consumer's goods by the various individuals.

$$(3) \quad \begin{cases} \dfrac{\partial E}{\partial x_i} = \dfrac{\partial E}{\partial x_k} = mp \\[2ex] \dfrac{\partial E}{\partial y_i} = \dfrac{\partial E}{\partial y_k} = mq \end{cases}$$

for all i, k, and some p, q, and m (and, to generalize beyond two commodities, for all x, y).

The change in social welfare resulting from the consumption of a
marginal increment of any given good must be the same for all individuals,
and, moreover, this must be proportional to the price of the commodity
(the same proportion for all goods).

The second group deals with the provision of labor services in production.

$$(4) \quad \begin{cases} \text{(a)} \quad -\dfrac{\partial E}{\partial a_i{}^x} = \dfrac{\partial E}{\partial a_k{}^x} = mg^x \\[2ex] \text{(b)} \quad -\dfrac{\partial E}{\partial a_i{}^y} = \dfrac{\partial E}{\partial a_k{}^y} = mg^y \\[2ex] \text{(c)} \quad -\dfrac{\partial E}{\partial b_i{}^x} = \dfrac{\partial E}{\partial b_k{}^x} = mh^x \\[2ex] \text{(d)} \quad -\dfrac{\partial E}{\partial b_i{}^y} = \dfrac{\partial E}{\partial b_k{}^y} = mh^y \end{cases}$$

for the same m as above, for all i, k, and for some g^x, h^x, g^y, h^y (and, to
generalize beyond two types of labor, for all a, b).

The change in social welfare resulting from the rendering of a marginal
increment of a given type of labor to produce a certain commodity must be
the same for all individuals, and, moreover, this must be proportional to the
negative of the wage for that type of work (the same proportion must hold
for all kinds of work as for all commodities above).

The third group deals with production and is in two parts.

$$(5) \quad \begin{cases} \dfrac{p\,\partial x}{\partial A^x} = g^x, \quad \dfrac{p\,\partial x}{\partial B^x} = h^x \\[2ex] \dfrac{q\,\partial y}{\partial A^y} = g^y, \quad \dfrac{q\,\partial y}{\partial B^y} = h^y \end{cases}$$

---

[23]Bergson, *op. cit.*, 315–316.

and

$$(6) \quad \begin{cases} m\left(\dfrac{p\,\partial x}{\partial C^z} - \dfrac{q\,\partial y}{\partial C^y}\right) = -\left(\dfrac{\partial E}{\partial C^z} - \dfrac{\partial E}{\partial C^y}\right), \\[2mm] m\left(\dfrac{p\,\partial x}{\partial D^z} - \dfrac{q\,\partial y}{\partial D^y}\right) = -\left(\dfrac{\partial E}{\partial D^z} - \dfrac{\partial E}{\partial D^y}\right). \end{cases}$$

The first part says that the increased social welfare of the extra goods produced by a marginal increment in any given type of work must be offset by the decrease in welfare due to that increment of work being rendered. The second part says that, for any shift of a marginal unit of nonlabor resources from the production unit producing one commodity to the production unit producing another commodity, the increased social welfare resulting from the shift must be offset by the decrease in welfare resulting from the adjustment.[24]

The usefulness of the welfare function E is that we may now introduce any set of (consistent) value assumptions we choose (these have the function of restricting the shape of the function), and we shall easily be able to trace its effect on the optimum conditions.

To illustrate, let us introduce some value judgments which are assumed in most welfare studies.

---

[24]*Ibid.*, 314-315.   To see more clearly the reasoning involved in the last group, consider the first part.

$$p = 1/m \cdot \partial E/\partial x_i \text{ for all } i, \text{ so } p = 1/m \cdot \partial E/\partial X,$$

and by similar reasoning,

$$q^z = 1/m \cdot \partial E/\partial A^z.$$

Substituting in the first equation of (5), we obtain

$$\partial E/\partial X \cdot \partial X/\partial A^z = -\partial E/\partial A^z.$$

For the second part, substituting for mp and mq in (6) we obtain,

$$\frac{\partial E}{\partial X} \cdot \frac{\partial X}{\partial C^z} - \frac{\partial E}{\partial Y} \cdot \frac{\partial Y}{\partial C^y} = -\left(\frac{\partial E}{\partial C^z} - \frac{\partial E}{\partial C^y}\right).$$

Any advantages arising out of the change in relative production (the left side of the equation) must be offset by net disadvantages resulting from the shift and concerning the direct welfare effects (abstracting from effects through production changes) of having more nonlabor resources in one line, less in another — like more factory smoke (the right side of the equation).

Bergson points out that the derivation of (5) involved dividing out m from the equations; hence, it implied the value assumption that $m \neq 0$. This is a *value* assumption because

$$m = \partial E/\partial x_i \div p = \partial E/\partial y_i \div q,$$

i.e., in the optimum situation, m is the extra social welfare obtained by any individual's spending an extra unit of money on any commodity. It is a very weak assumption. It simply assumes that social welfare is in some way affected by economic activities. Without it there is obviously no welfare economics.

1. Nonlabor resources employed in indifferent uses. "A shift in a unit of any factor of production, other than labor, from one production unit to another would leave economic welfare unchanged, provided the amounts of all other elements in welfare were constant."[25] In other words, "factory smoke," etc., are assumed to have no effect on social welfare.

The sense of this assumption is that $\partial E/\partial C^x - \partial E/\partial C^y = 0$. So, Eq. (6) becomes:

$$\text{(7)} \qquad \frac{p\,\partial X}{\partial C^x} = \frac{q\,\partial Y}{\partial C^y} \quad \text{and} \quad \frac{p\,\partial X}{\partial D^x} = \frac{q\,\partial Y}{\partial D^y}$$

(equal marginal value productivities), or

$$\text{(8)} \qquad \frac{p}{q} = \frac{\partial Y}{\partial C^y} \div \frac{\partial X}{\partial C^x} = \frac{\partial Y}{\partial D^y} \div \frac{\partial X}{\partial D^x}$$

(ratio of marginal productivities in any two uses must be the same for all nonlabor resources).

2. Consumer sovereignty. "Individual's preferences are to 'count'."[26] Any change which leaves everyone indifferent has the same level of social welfare; a change by which one person is better off while everyone else is indifferent represents an increase in social welfare; a change by which one person is worse·off while everyone else is indifferent represents a decrease in social welfare. In other words, this assumption decentralizes the evaluation of alternatives so that each individual first orders various alternatives and so that these orderings become the determining variables of social welfare.

Thus, the effect is to convert E into $E = E(U^1, U^2, \ldots, U^n)$. Now, from the two equations in Eq. (3), we obtain

$$\text{(9)} \qquad \frac{\partial E}{\partial x_i} \bigg/ \frac{\partial E}{\partial y_i} = \frac{p}{q} = \frac{\partial E}{\partial x_k} \bigg/ \frac{\partial E}{\partial y_k}.$$

Consumer sovereignty means that x_i, a_i, etc. are not the proximate determining variables of E, but affect E only insofar as they affect each U^i. So, since

$$\frac{\partial E}{\partial x_i} \bigg/ \frac{\partial E}{\partial y_i} = \frac{\partial E}{\partial U^i} \cdot \frac{\partial U^i}{\partial x_i} \bigg/ \frac{\partial E}{\partial U^i} \cdot \frac{\partial U^i}{\partial y^i} = \frac{\partial U^i}{\partial x_i} \bigg/ \frac{\partial U^i}{\partial y_i} = \frac{\partial y_i}{\partial x_i} \bigg|\; U^i \text{ constant}$$

(the marginal rate of substitution of Y for X) and

$$\frac{\partial E}{\partial x_k} \bigg/ \frac{\partial E}{\partial y_k} = \frac{\partial U^k}{\partial x_k} \bigg/ \frac{\partial U^k}{\partial y_k} = \frac{\partial y_k}{\partial x_k} \bigg|\; U^k \text{ constant.}$$

Eq. (9) becomes

$$\text{(10)} \qquad \frac{\partial y_i}{\partial x_i} \bigg|\; U^i \text{ constant} = \frac{\partial y_k}{\partial x_k} \bigg|\; U^k \text{ constant} \quad \text{for all } i, k.$$

---

[25] *Ibid.*, 316.
[26] Samuelson, *Foundations of Economic Analysis*, 223.

3. Equal distribution of "Shares." "If the shares of any ith and kth individuals were equal, and if the prices and wage rates were fixed, the transfer of a small amount of the share of i to k would leave welfare unchanged."[27] To put it differently: for given prices and wage rates, any departure from equal shares will bring about a social welfare decrease; any closer approximation to it will bring about a social welfare increase.[28]

Defining the share of individual i as

$$S_i = px_i + qy_i - g^x a_i{}^x - h^x b_i{}^x - g^y a_i{}^y - h^y b_i{}^y$$

(the amount of money by which the value of i's consumption of goods exceeds his wages), the assumption says

(11) $$dE = \frac{\partial E}{\partial m_i} \cdot dm_i + \frac{\partial E}{\partial m_k} \cdot dm_k = 0$$

for $m_i = m_k$, $dm_i = -dm_k$, and given p, q, g^x, g^y, h^x, h^y.

It can be shown that Eq. (11) is equivalent to Eq. (3) and is therefore to be interpreted as the form which Eq. (3) takes under this assumption.[29]

1-3. Welfare Analysis and the Economic Welfare Function: a Program

Let us return now to our schematization of welfare economics. The ultimate purpose in undertaking a welfare analysis has been claimed to be the attempt to evaluate different policy alternatives. This, we have seen, necessitates specifying the ends in terms of which the alternatives are to be evaluated and a criterion or rule for performing these comparisons on the alternatives in question. The Economic Welfare Function combines both these specifications, the restrictions on its form expressing both the ends specified and the comparison rule.

We may now state the problem of the present work. In terms of our welfare function, what kinds of decisions on ends are necessary and sufficient in the light of the real world to enable us to derive social orderings of the relevant alternatives? Are there difficulties in the way of successfully employing an empirically specified welfare function to make concrete policy recommendations? Lastly, but in many ways most important of all, assuming that we have succeeded in restricting the welfare function so as to

---

[27]Bergson, *op. cit.*, 321.

[28]This rule does not in fact enable a *complete* ordering of distributions, since not all redistributions of money incomes among a large group of persons can be uniquely characterized in terms of direction with respect to equality of shares. Lorenz functions, sum of mean deviations, variance, etc., give contradictory readings; the choice of any one as a criterion of equality is arbitrary.

[29]Bergson, *loc. cit.*, fn. 8.

obtain a social ordering, and this ordering has enough empirical content for us to make concrete policy recommendations — with what justification do we expect authorities to heed *our* recommendations instead of recommendations derived from some entirely different welfare function? In other words, how do we go about prescribing that *one* set of decisions on ends which will make the welfare analysis derived therefrom *uniquely* qualified to make recommendations in a given community?

Bergson has a suggestion to make on this.

> In general, any set of value propositions which is sufficient for the evaluation of all alternatives may be introduced [into the welfare function], and for each of these sets of propositions there corresponds a maximum position. The number of sets is infinite, and *in any particular case the selection of one of them must be determined by its compatibility with the values prevailing in the community the welfare of which is being studied.* For only if the welfare principles are based upon prevailing values, can they be relevant to the activity of the community in question . . . . The determination of prevailing values for a given community . . . [is] a proper and necessary task for the economist.[30]

To point up the problem, a particular set of value assumptions on ends which is sufficient to enable us to derive a complete ordering of alternatives is that presented in the last section: (1) indifference in nonlabor resource use, (2) consumer sovereignty, and (3) a rule by which to evaluate income distributions (equal shares). How could we get to know about its "compatibility with the values prevailing in the community"? Does the procedure which might be used to make this discovery consist of observation or another less proximate set of value judgments?

As I indicated above, I do not believe this problem to be trivial. If ever we intend welfare economics to be a fruitful source of concrete recommendations about good and bad, about policies which ought to be introduced and policies which ought not, we must be able to give our analysis this uniquely relevant empirical content. Otherwise, we are simply playing with deductive chains: "if you want this, do this; if you want that, do this other; if you want a third, do something else; if . . . "; etc. And if we stake our usefulness on being asked for a particular chain we may have to prepare many more than we shall need — a highly uneconomical prospect. Or, alternatively, we may be able to predict who will ask, and which chain will be chosen, and on what justification. But perhaps the choice will be unwarranted — or the chooser. This we can never know without some solution to the problem I am posing here.

In the next chapter I shall examine the attempt by Kenneth Arrow to throw light on this problem. The conclusion of Arrow's study indicates a

---

[30]Bergson, *op. cit.*, 323. Italics mine.

substantial barrier to its solution. In succeeding chapters, therefore, I shall examine a variety of welfare formulations in the recent literature with a view toward breaking through the barrier. In the last part of this book I shall suggest an alternative formulation of the problem which gives promise of yielding tolerable results after some additional effort in that direction. Each of the approaches presented will be evaluated both from the point of view of its analytic effectiveness and of its practical usefulness when appropriately adapted for application to the real world. Given a work of the present orientation, the latter type of evaluation is important in its own right. In addition, however, it is especially necessary here in order to achieve proper perspective. The approach which I shall present ultimately for sympathetic consideration exists at the present time in so skeletal a form as to make a serious test of theoretical definitiveness out of the question. It would therefore be misleading to evaluate treatments in the literature solely on an austere formal level while craving the reader's indulgence for more lenient informal evaluation of a novel approach. Neither the weaknesses *nor* the strengths of the newer approach could be properly appreciated thereby.

As this preview indicates, I intend the present work as a tentative step forward on a difficult road. I do not see this as definitive either in retrospect or prospect.

CHAPTER 2

A Paradox on Social Welfare:

Kenneth Arrow and the General

Possibility Theorem

In Chapter 1 it was shown that a welfare analysis consisted of tracing implications from a set of value judgments, the most notable of which was the postulation of a particular schema of ends whose fulfillment is deemed desirable. We saw that the welfare function is an analytic tool which is especially convenient for making explicit the special set of value judgments involved in any such analysis and in enabling their implication to be examined. We posed two problems. First, what sets of values can, in the context of actual behavior, lead to useful social orderings? Second, how do we choose that particular set of values which will give rise to the most useful social ordering for a given community?

The substantial contribution to welfare economics by Kenneth Arrow is directed precisely to these questions.[1] His innovation in analysis and presentation by using the methods of symbolic logic, and the very high level of abstraction his contribution incorporates, is at one and the same time a danger and an opportunity. On the one hand, there is the great ease with which one can misunderstand the argument; on the other, there is the possibility of making valid interpretations on more than one level.

---

[1]*Social Choice and Individual Values* (New York: John Wiley & Sons, Inc., 1951).

With due regard for both dangers I shall at first briefly repeat Arrow's argument without much discussion, and then raise some of the pertinent issues more fully.

2-1. The General Possibility Theorem

(1) The alternatives of choice in Arrow's analysis are social states.

The most precise definition of a social state would be a complete description of the amount of each type of commodity in the hands of each individual, the amount of labor to be supplied by each individual, the amount of each productive resource invested in each type of productive activity, and the amounts of various types of collective activity, such as municipal services, diplomacy and its continuation by other means, and the erection of statues to famous men.[2]

(2) "It is assumed that each individual in the community has a definite ordering of all conceivable social states, in terms of their desirability to him."[3]

(3) We are ultimately interested in the derivation of a social ordering of these social states. In line with the analysis of the last chapter, we should like to proceed by means of an explicit rule relating individual orderings to the social ordering. In Arrow's terminology, this "rule" is called the Social Welfare Function. We shall see that this "rule," like Bergson's Economic Welfare Function, combines an assertion about ends with a criterion for judging alternatives in terms of these ends. At a later point, I shall compare this function more fully with Bergson's function. Arrow's exact definition of the Social Welfare Function is as follows: "By a social welfare function will be meant a process or rule which, for each set of individual orderings . . . for alternative social states (one ordering for each individual), states a corresponding social ordering of alternative social states.[4]

(4) We shall now introduce the value judgments by which Arrow would restrict the Social Welfare Function. Let me preface this with a brief explanation of the terminology used.

When comparing any two alternative social states (x and y), a given individual can say whether he prefers x to y, y to x or is indifferent between them. Say our individual is individual i. xP_iy means i prefers x to y; yP_ix means he prefers y to x; xI_iy means he is indifferent between the two. In addition to these symbols of relationship, Arrow combines preference and indifference in a "weak" relationship xR_iy or yR_ix (x is either preferred to or indifferent with y; i.e., y is not preferred to x, or y is either preferred to

---

[2]*Ibid.*, 17.
[3]Arrow, *loc. cit.*
[4]*Ibid.*, 23.

or indifferent with x; x is not preferred to y). This single relation R can be substituted completely for both P and I. Thus, $xP_iy = xR_iy$ and not yR_iy; $xI_iy = xR_iy$ and yR_ix.

The individual is assumed as a matter of *fact* to have an ordering of alternatives which fulfills these conditions.

(A) For all x and y, xR_iy or yR_ix (including, of course, both) — *connexity* of R_i.

(B) For all x, y, and z, xR_iy and yR_iz implies xR_iz — *transitivity* of R_i.[5]

Thus, a complete ordering of alternatives can be conceived as comprising a set of comparisons between all possible alternative pairs. A complete ordering is symbolized by R_i (or sometimes T_i, or R'_i, etc.). When the relations R, P and I appear without subscripts they refer to a specific *social* comparison or the *social* ordering rather than to a specific comparison or ordering of any one individual.

(5) The value judgments imposed on the social welfare function are as follows.

Condition 1. "Among all the alternatives there is a set S of three alternatives such that, for *any* set of individual orderings $T_1, \ldots, T_n$ of the alternatives in S, there is an admissible set of individual orderings $R_1, \ldots, R_n$ of all the alternatives such that, for each individual i, xR_iy if and only if xT_iy for x and y in S."[6]

An admissible set of individual orderings is one "for which the Social Welfare Function defines a corresponding social ordering" such that R is both connex and transitive.[7]

Condition 1 asserts, in effect, that among all the alternatives there are at least three such that all logically possible individual orderings of these three are admissible, i.e., are orderings for which the social welfare function is required to render a choice. We may express this concisely by saying that there is at least one "free triple" among all admissible alternatives. For every other triple of alternatives, the social welfare function may — but may not — be required to choose only among a few of the logically possible sets of orderings. The purpose of the condition is to ensure that the Social Welfare Function will not be made trivial by being restricted to choices in only a few highly selected sets of possible individual preferences. It may seem as though the requirement of only one free triple does not ensure very

---

[5]*Ibid.*, 13. In an appendix to Chapter 7, and in Chapter 10 I shall examine the justification for assuming that individual orderings are complete (*all* alternatives ordered) and transitive. My conclusions indicate that we currently possess no strong evidence to warrant *dropping* these assumptions. The arguments of the following chapters will not, as far as we now know, be damaged by their inclusion.

[6]*Ibid.*, 24.

[7]Arrow, *loc. cit.*

much.[8] Actually, it accomplishes more than it appears to at first sight. It prevents the use of any single general principle by which admissible sets of orderings can be selected out of the set of all logically possible sets of orderings. For example, a device such as that requiring individual i's ordering of every alternative pair to be the opposite of individual j's would be excluded.

Condition 1 is therefore stipulating "that, for some sufficiently wide range of sets of individual orderings the social welfare function gives rise to a true social ordering."[9] This is essentially stating the problem itself, namely, that a unique social ordering be in some sense derivable from a reasonably wide range of individual orderings ("all social choices are determined by individual desires").[10] The additional requirement, that this ordering have the properties of connexity and transitivity, is deemed by Arrow to be indissoluble from the problem. If R is not connex, then there are some admissible alternatives for which no social choice is rendered. We have only a partial ordering, with some social states not comparable to others. If R is not transitive, then we have no unique ordering at all. The comparison between some x and z will differ depending on whether it was deduced from intermediate comparisons or based on direct confrontation. Moreover, if R is intransitive, so too is P.[11] Also the intransitivity of P,

---

[8]We shall see shortly, that this does in fact ask too little of the welfare function — too little, that is, to generate the conclusion for which Arrow's work is celebrated.

[9]*Ibid.*, 25.

[10]*Ibid.*, 29.

[11]That the transitivity of the connex relation R implies the transitivity of P can be shown as follows. By the definition of R and P, P is equivalent to not-R. So our proof will show that the transitivity of any connex relation R implies the transitivity of not-R.

Assumption 1: Transitivity. For all x, y, z

$$(xRy), \text{ and } (yRz) \text{ implies } xRz. \tag{1}$$

Assumption 2: Connexity. For every x, y,

$$xRy, \text{ or } yRx. \tag{2}$$

Definition 1. $xPy = \text{not-}yRx.$ (3)

(actually $xPy = xRy$ and not-yRx; but (2) enables the shorter form).

Now assume not-R is intransitive; namely, for some x, y, z, (xPy) and (yPz) implies zRx.

$$\tag{4}$$

We shall show that (4) leads to a contradiction. Substitute (3) in (4):

$$\text{not-}(yRx) \text{ and not-}(zRy) \text{ implies } zRx \text{ for some } x, y, z \text{ fulfilling (4);} \tag{5}$$

$$\text{not-}(yRx \text{ and } zRy) \text{ implies } zRx \text{ for this } x, y, z. \tag{6}$$

Now, substitute (1) in (6):

$$\text{not-}(zRx) \text{ implies } zRx \text{ for this } x, y, z. \tag{7}$$

Hence, the assumption that there exists some x, y, z such that assumption (4) holds, leads to a contradiction. There is no x, y, z such that, given (1), (2) and (3), assumption (4) holds. Thus, not-R, or P, is transitive.

such that for some x, y, z, xPy, and yPz, but zPx, means that this x, y, z cannot be ordered. Consequently, these properties are considered by Arrow as an index of the rationality of social choice.[12]

Condition 2. "Let $R_1, \ldots, R_n$ and $R'_1, \ldots, R'_n$ be two sets of individual ordering relations, R and R' the corresponding social orderings, and P and P' the corresponding social preference relations. Suppose that for each i the two individual ordering relations are connected in the following ways: for x' and y' distinct from a given alternative x, $x'R'_iy'$ if and only if $x'R_iy'$; for all y', xR_iy' implies xR'_iy'; for all y', xP_iy' implies xP'_iy'. Then, if xPy, $xP'y$."[13]

Arrow's own paraphrase of this is:

> The social welfare function is such that the social ordering responds positively to alterations in individual values, or at least not negatively. Hence, if one alternative social state rises or remains still in the ordering of every individual without any other change in those orderings, we expect that it rises, or at least does not fall, in the social ordering.[14]

This condition contains much of the content of the assumption of consumer's sovereignty. In conjunction with Condition 4 Arrow does, in fact, refer to it as such, though a difference between his and Bergson's treatment of individual orderings induces him to call the two conditions "citizen's" sovereignty.[15] I shall discuss this difference below, as well as its formal adequacy for Arrow's purposes.

Condition 3. "Let $R_1, \ldots, R_n$ and $R'_1, \ldots, R'_n$ be two sets of individual orderings and let $C(S)$ and $C'(S)$ be the corresponding social choice functions. If, for all individuals i and all x and y in a given environment S, xR_iy, if and only if xR'_iy, then $C(S)$ and $C'(S)$ are the same."[16] $C(S)$ and $C'(S)$ refer to the most preferred alternative chosen out of the set of available alternatives.

Arrow calls this condition "The Independence of Irrelevant Alternatives." Briefly, it means that the selection of the socially most preferred alternative from a set of alternatives depends only on the ordering of these

---

[12]The requirement that preferences be consistent, so that a given choice between some x and y will always result in the same preference being accepted, is implicitly also assumed as a question *of fact* for individuals, and as a postulated condition for social choice. In a later chapter, for experimental purposes I shall consider a definition of preference and indifference in stochastic terms, i.e., in terms of proportions of particular responses in a large sequence of similar choice situations. Under such a definition, the notion of consistency disappears. Transitivity does not disappear under a stochastic treatment. Transitivity may, by the way, be considered a characteristic of rational choice, along with consistency, but is not itself to be identified with rationality.

[13]*Ibid.*, 26.

[14]*Ibid.*, 25.

[15]Actual equivalence to consumer's (or citizen's) sovereignty would be yielded by a slightly stronger form of Condition 2. *Ibid.*, 30, fn. 4.

[16]*Ibid.*, 27.

alternatives and not on the existence of, or ordering of, alternatives outside this set. His paraphrase of Condition 3 is:

> If we consider two sets of individual orderings such that for each individual his ordering of these particular alternatives in a given environment is the same each time, then we require that the choice made by society from that environment be the same when individual values are given by the first set of orderings as they are when given by the second.[17]

An example given by Arrow of a choice mechanism which violates this condition is voting by rankings of alternatives. Each individual gives rank numbers to various alternatives. Say there are three voters and four candidates. First choice is given the number 1, second choice the number 2, etc. The numbers voted for each candidate are added. The candidate with the lowest score wins. Table 1 shows two possible outcomes.

TABLE 1

Voter	Situation 1 Alternative				Situation 2 Alternative			
	x	y	z	w	x	y	z	w
1	1	2	3	4	1	–	2	3
2	1	2	3	4	1	–	2	3
3	3	4	1	2	3	–	1	2
Ranks	5	8	7	10	5	–	5	6

In the first situation, when all four candidates are "available," x is the winner. In the second situation, where candidate y is no longer "available" (in the running), s and z are tied for first place, even though the individual orderings for the available x, z, and w are the same as in the first situation.[18]

Arrow considers Condition 3 a necessary property of rational choice: "irrelevant" opportunities should not influence choices among relevant opportunities. On the level where it is most intuitively reasonable, it says, for example, that modern (non-Faustian) man should make his choice of a wife between two women on the basis of which of the two he prefers and not be unduly influenced by the fact that what he would really prefer is Helen of Troy.

Condition 4. "The Social Welfare Function is not to be imposed . . . . A Social Welfare Function will be said to be *imposed* if, for some pair of distinct alternatives x and y, xRy for any set of individual orderings $R_1, \ldots, R_n$, where R is the social ordering corresponding to $R_1, \ldots, R_n$."[19]

---

[17]*Ibid.*, 26-27. In Arrow's treatment, individual orderings are deemed to reflect individual "values" instead of individual "tastes." This distinction, as well as its source, will be discussed in a later section of this chapter.

[18]*Ibid.*, 27.

[19]*Ibid.*, 28.

To paraphrase: "When the social welfare function is imposed, there is some pair of alternatives x and y such that the community can never express a preference for y over x no matter what the tastes of all individuals are, even if all individuals prefer y to x; some preferences are taboo."[20]

Therefore, the condition asserts that for every pair of distinct alternatives x and y, there is at least one set of individual orderings — even if only the unanimous preference of y over x — for which yPx.[21]

Evidently imposition violates citizen (or consumer) sovereignty. As indicated above, this condition, along with Condition 2, is meant to bear the approximate content of an assumption of citizen sovereignty. The function of this condition is to exclude the possibility of "external" control over a society's choice.

Condition 5. "The Social Welfare Function is not to be dictatorial . . . . A Social Welfare Function is said to be *dictatorial* if there exists an individual i such that, for all x and y, xP_iy implies xPy regardless of the orderings $R_1, \ldots, R_n$ of all individuals other than i, where P is the social preference relation corresponding to $R_1, \ldots, R_n$."[22]

The social choices are determined solely by the preferences of the single individual. Since in a sense, individual i is a citizen (or consumer) of the community, violation of Condition 5 is not strictly a violation of consumer's sovereignty. But in the context of our — and Arrow's — investigation, a dictatorial Social Welfare Function would be a trivial solution. In a more general sense, therefore, we may consider Condition 5 part of a general requirement for citizen's sovereignty.

To summarize these value judgments, they represent, in Arrow's view, simply the assumptions of citizen's sovereignty and rationality in a general form.

(6) Arrow develops the logical implications of the five value judgments just discussed and finds them to be contradictory. The content of this conclusion is termed the General Possibility Theorem, and follows.

General Possibility Theorem. "If there are at least three alternatives which the members of the society are free to order in any way, then every Social Welfare Function satisfying Conditions 2 and 3 and yielding a social ordering satisfying Axioms I and II must be either imposed or dictatorial."[23]

---

[20]Arrow, *loc. cit.*

[21]Actually, this means that there is at least one set for which not-xRy. Because of connexity, not-xRy implies yRx and not-xRy, which together imply yPx.

[22]*Ibid.*, 30.

[23]*Ibid.*, 59. The existence of three freely orderable alternatives which will still give rise to a social ordering satisfying Axioms I and II (connexity and transitivity of the social ordering relation R) is Condition 1. The derivation of the theorem comprises the whole of Chapter 5, 46-60.

A simple example of the difficulty is given by the so-called "Paradox of Voting." Envisage a collective preference scale arrived at by majority vote.

> Let A, B, and C be the three alternatives, and 1, 2, and 3 the three individuals. Suppose individual 1 prefers A to B and B to C (and therefore A to C), individual 2 prefers B to C and C to A (and therefore B to A), and individual 3 prefers C to A and A to B (and therefore C to B). Then a majority prefer A to B and a majority prefer B to C. We may therefore say that the community prefers A to B and B to C. If the community is to be regarded as behaving rationally, we are forced to say that A is preferred to C. But in fact a majority of the community prefers C to A. So the method just outlined for passing from individual to collective tastes fails to satisfy the condition of rationality, as we ordinarily understand it.[24]

We shall give a sketch of Arrow's proof of the General Possibility Theorem.[25] We introduce the notion of a decisive set. A set of individuals is decisive for alternative x over y (where x and y are distinctive) if x is socially preferred to y whenever everyone in the set prefers x to y. This means that the unanimous choice of this set prevails socially even if everyone else in the whole population prefers y to x. Arrow's proof consists of two parts. First, applying himself to the alternatives of a free triple, he proves that if an individual is decisive for any alternative against any other, then he is decisive in the choice between *every* pair of alternatives: he is a dictator. Since this is forbidden by Condition 5, no individual can be decisive on any issue. Second, he considers decisive sets in a free triple of alternatives, i.e., sets of individuals who are decisive on some paired comparison in the triple. Since in any free triple unanimity by the total population is always an admissible set of orderings, and unanimity always determines social choice, at least one decisive set can always be found.[26] Arrow selects that decisive set which contains the fewest persons. By the first part of the proof, this number will always be at least two. Split the decisive set into two parts, containing respectively one person and the remainder of the decisive set. Then, for this free triple he proves both that "the existence of the decisive set is self-contradictory" and that its non-existence implies that unanimity is not decisive, thereby violating Conditions 2 and 4.[26] Thus, all five conditions cannot be met simultaneously.

---

[24]*Ibid.*, 3.

[25]*Ibid.*, 51-59. See also Julian Blau, "The Existence of Social Welfare Functions," *Econometrica*, Vol. 25, No. 2 (April, 1957), 302-13; and William Vickrey, "Utility, Strategy, and Social Decision Rules," *The Quarterly Journal of Economics*, Vol. LXXIV, No. 4 (November, 1960), 509-10.

[26]By Condition 4 there is always some set of individual ordering such that xPy. Now, let everyone who previously preferred y to x or were indifferent in this first set come to prefer x to y. We have unanimous preference for x over y. If xPy under the first set then, by Condition 2, xPy under the change to unanimity. See below for a generalization of this.

[26]Blau, *op. cit.*, 311.

Alternatively, since Conditions 1 through 3 are mutually compatible, any Social Welfare Function satisfying Conditions 1 through 3 must be either imposed or dictatorial.

The crucial portion of the first part can be shown as follows. x, y, and z are alternatives in a free triple. Assume that individual A is decisive for x against y. Now we shall prove that A is decisive for x against z. Since A is decisive for x against y, xP_Ay. Decisiveness means that xP_Ay implies xPy. This holds even if yP_ix for all i other than A. Consider some set of individual orderings in which everyone other than A does prefer y to x, and in addition, prefers y to z, but prefers z to x, i.e., the unanimous (less A) preference ordering yzx. Let A's ordering be xyz. Then everyone — including A — prefers y to z. So yPz. Since xPy and yPz, transitivity of social preference (Condition 1) requires that xPz. But A is the only one who prefers x to z — everyone else prefers z to x. Yet, the social choice is for x over z. Any change in others' preferences in favor of x against z will not make the social ordering go adverse to x (by Condition 2). So xP_Az is a sufficient condition for xPz. A is decisive for x over z.

To indicate A's decisiveness for x against y and z most clearly, we have shown A standing out against the rest of the population in both comparisons. But the comparison between y and z are not constrained by this decisiveness. Let us consider a set of orderings in which preferences for y and z are reversed. Again, yP_ix and zP_ix for all i other than x. But now zP_iy for all i. Since z is unanimously preferred to y, zPy. So, xPy, zPy. We are no longer forced to conclude xPz simply on grounds of the transitivity of social preference (Condition 1). We may have either xPz or zPx. Since zP_ix for all i other than A, it seems reasonable to suppose that there might be a Social Welfare Function which judged thereby zPx — nothing apparently prevents it (of course, nothing apparently prevents such a function from judging xPz either). Suppose zPx. Now, compare our results with these two different sets of orderings. In the first, xPz. The change to the second involves a change in individual orderings between y and z — and hence a change in the social ordering of the two — but no change in orderings between x and z. Yet, without a change in individual orderings between x and z, we have a change in the social ordering to zPx. This violates Condition 3. Since the social ordering xPz in the first is unambiguous — being forced by unanimity and transitivity (Conditions 2 and 1), while the second was not, it is the second ordering which is disallowed. Thus, despite all but A preferring z to x and the fact that it is not forced by transitivity, the Social Welfare Function is constrained by Condition 3 from judging zPx. Only xPz is allowed.[27] These are the crucial cases. If we examine every other conceivable set of orderings, applying Condition 3 in

---

[27] I am indebted to Martin Bailey for clarifying this last point.

the same way, we shall discover that whenever A prefers x to y and z, the social choice is for x against the others. A is decisive for both comparisons. Following much the same analysis we can prove the "spread" of A's decisiveness to all paired comparisons.

The second part of the proof, briefly, is as follows. Having chosen the smallest decisive set (V_1) over the free triple x, y, z, and partitioned it into V', composed of one member, and V_2, composed of the remainder of the decisive set, Arrow considers a set of orderings such that xP_iy and yP_iz for the member of V' (i.e., xyz), zP_ix and xP_iy for all i in V_2 (zxy) and yP_iz and zP_ix for all i in the remainder of the population (V_3) (yzx). By the assumed decisiveness of V_1, xPy. Now, yP_iz for all i not in V_2. Suppose zPy. Then V_2 is decisive for z against y. This is inconsistent with the fact that V_1 $(= V' + V_2$, with V' containing one member) is the smallest decisive set for any paired comparison among x, y, and z. Thus, zPy is not allowed, and y must be socially preferred to z. But then, by transitivity, xPz. However, xP_iz only for the single member of V', everyone else preferring z to x. Thus, V' is decisive for x against z, again providing a contradiction not only with the method of selecting V_2, but also with the first part of the proof that stipulates that no one individual be decisive on any issue. This completes the proof that Conditions 1 through 5 cannot be satisfied simultaneously.

Julian Blau has shown that the Possibility Theorem is in fact false under the conditions as stated. He cites the following counterexample.[28] Let there be four alternatives: a set X, comprising x, y, z, and a set W, comprising the single alternative w; also let there be two or more individuals, A, and everyone else, O. Let x, y, z be a free triple, but all individuals are constrained as to how they may order w with the rest.[29] Everyone must place w either higher or lower than all of the rest. Moreover, while A is free to choose between these two possibilities, O must make the opposite of A's choice. Thus, x, y, z is the only free triple allowed since w can never appear *between* any two of the other alternatives in the ordering of any individual. The Social Welfare Function specified makes A decisive on all choices within the free triple (X) but decides the position of w by majority rule.

The dictatorship of A in the free triple would disqualify such a Social Welfare Function, if it were not for the fourth alternative and the constraints placed on its ordering which guarantee, when there are more than two individuals, that A can never be decisive on all issues. Besides, A's decisiveness in the free triple prevents anyone else from being a dictator. It can easily be seen that all five conditions are satisfied. A's decisiveness

---

[28]Blau, *op. cit.*, 304.

[29]Actually, X may contain an indefinite number of alternatives, such that all triples within X are free for A and O.

makes the social ordering of the free triple fulfill all the conditions placed on individual orderings. Changes in anyone else's orderings in X do not induce changes in the social ordering of X. So they do not conflict with Condition 2.

Moreover, by the nature of the limitations on the set of admissible orderings, w cannot be the rising alternative envisioned by Condition 2, and no one of x, y, or z can rise above w without taking the other two with it, thereby again removing it from relevance to Condition 2 (since under Condition 2 only one alternative changes). All social orderings are possible with appropriate individual orderings (Condition 4). When w is involved, majority rule does not lead to intransitivities because in every triple to which it is applied two of the alternatives are constrained in such a way that they can be treated as a single alternative. Thus, there are always in effect only two alternatives being compared. So transitivity is never called into question. Majority rule is acceptable.

The exception to Arrow's theorem comes about because of near-dictatorship and the highly restrictive limitations on orderings concerning w. But if, following Blau, we add complexity to the example, we see that other factors may frustrate the Possibility Theorem as well.[30] Let us add alternative v. The same limitations are applicable on admissible orderings of X and w. In addition, A is free to order v anywhere with respect to X and w (except, as before, no alternative can be placed between any of the alternatives of X). O (i.e., all others) are constrained as follows. If A prefers X to v, v is O's most preferred alternative; if A prefers v to X, v is O's least preferred alternative. The Social Welfare Function again makes A decisive on X, makes X and w the most and least preferred alternative sets with the choice between them based on majority rule, and places v always between them.

Consider two instances. (1) A's ordering is Xwv, O's is vwX, the social ordering wvX. (2) A: wvX, O: Xwv, social ordering, Xvw. This Social Welfare Function fulfills Conditions 1 through 5. There seems to be a violation of Condition 2 in that, moving from (1) to (2), w rises above v for O while remaining unchanged for A. Yet w falls below in the social order although it was preferred to v in (1). However, considering the limitations in admissible orderings, w does not rise alone relative to v. V is constrained to fall relative to both w and X. So, Condition 2 does not strictly apply to this particular change in preferences. There also seems to be a violation of Condition 4, since v can never be socially most preferred. But v can be preferred to *either* w or X and vice versa. These possibilities exhaust all the requirements of nonimposition. Fulfillment of the other conditions can be seen by inspection.

---

[30]*Ibid.*, 305.

This example "works" partly because of the limitations on the domain of admissible orderings and partly on the disqualification of Condition 2 in many possible value changes. It is clearly in the spirit of Arrow's conditions that the "perverse" fall of w in the social ordering when it rose in O's ordering should be considered a violation of consumer's sovereignty. Condition 2 can be strengthened to bring this about. Blau presents the following modification. His paraphrase of Condition 2 is: "Let $R = (R_1, \ldots, R_n)$ be a n-tuple of ballots. Suppose that a certain alternative α is raised on some or all of the individual ballots, but no other change is made, thus producing a new n-tuple $R' = (R'_1, \ldots, R'_n)$. Then, for any β, if $\alpha P \beta$ then $\alpha P' \beta$."[31] He strengthens this to: "Condition 2' (monotonicity): Let α and β be any two alternatives. Let $\tau = (T_1, \ldots, T_n)$ be an n-tuple of partial ballots listing only the individual choices between α and β. (By Condition 3, which we assume, the social ordering of α and β is then determined.) Suppose that α is raised on some or all of the individual partial ballots, thus producing a new n-tuple $\tau' = (T'_1, \ldots, T'_n)$. If $\alpha P \beta$ then $\alpha P' \beta$."[32] Blau refers to 2' as monotonicity because it disallows changes in individual orderings from having inverse changes in the social ordering. Blau refers to Arrow's Condition 2 as "quasi-monotonicity" because it fails to rule out such inverse effects when more than one "linked" alternative moves up in individual orderings. If we substitute Condition 2' for 2, the second example fails to fulfill all five conditions (but not the first example).

The second example is interesting because it reveals some strange properties. Since V is socially preferred to w, despite the fact that everyone prefers w, we have a welfare function which violates unanimity rule. We indicated above that Conditions 2 and 4 together imply that unanimous choice is always socially decisive — *for any paired comparison within a free triple.* Now we see that Conditions 2 and 4 do not imply unanimity rule when the domain of admissible orderings is stringently limited. Second, Arrow's conditions are seen not to be in Blau's term, "hereditary." That is, if a Social Welfare Function satisfies Conditions 2 through 5 on the total set of alternatives, it does so on any subset of alternatives.[33] We see, however, that while Conditions 3 and 4 are hereditary (since their fulfillment on the whole set implies their fulfillment on all subsets), Conditions 2 and 5 do not. In both examples, if we restrict alternatives to X, the welfare function is dictatorial. In the second example, considering only w and ν, the welfare function violates Condition 2.

These properties of Arrow's conditions seem out of spirit with their intention. Since they are absent for any free triple of alternatives, they can

---

[31]*Ibid.*, 303.
[32]*Ibid.*, 305.
[33]*Ibid.*, 305.

be dispelled from the total set by requiring that all conceivable triples of the total set of alternatives be free.[34] If all possible orderings are admissible, then Conditions 2 and 4 are equivalent to unanimity rule; moreover, all conditions are hereditary. Condition 2 is hereditary because there are no linked alternatives. Condition 5 is hereditary by part 1 of Arrow's proof: an individual decisive on one issue is decisive on all.

If we substitute Condition 2 by 2' (monotonicity) and amend Condition 1 to require that all triples be free (in Blau's terminology, that the domain of admissible orderings is "universal"[35]), then the modified set of conditions is one which cannot be fulfilled by any social welfare function. Blau proves — indeed, it should be intuitively clear from our discussion that such proof would be easy — a new Possibility Theorem very close in spirit to Arrow's.[36]

How much damage is done to the Possibility Theorem by Blau's counterexamples? The completeness of the theorem is of course destroyed. Blau's examples give one type of successful restriction on admissibility; it is open to the ingenuity of others to seek additions. This particularistic assaying was just what Arrow's theorem was thought to have ended. A scholar is free to feel that he is not bound by any real stricture without having first sought and failed. In this sense, Arrow's theorem may have lost a substantial part of its influence in channeling further research. In contrast, Blau's "successful" welfare functions are themselves nearly irrelevant for the practical applicability of welfare economics. His functions are almost completely dictatorial. The problem of social choice for all free triples is solved by dictatorship.

The case is even stronger for pessimism. Blau's suggested modifications of Arrow's conditions are well within the spirit of Arrow's intention. The tightening of monotonicity has at least as much intuitive persuasiveness as a reasonable characterization of rational democratic choice, as does the

---

[34]We note that Arrow's proof always dealt with the free triple required by Condition 1. His proofs were valid for the alternatives of that triple. Arrow took for granted that the proofs generalized to all other alternatives in the total set.

[35]Blau, *op. cit.*, 305.

[36]*Ibid.*, 309-13. The proof is, in fact, quite similar to Arrow's. Blau characterizes the two parts of the proof as showing (1) that the conditions require that all Social Welfare Functions be neutral, and (2) that the class of nondictatorial sets was additive. "A Social Welfare Function is neutral if every set E of individuals is decisive on all issues, or if its opposition (the rest of society) is decisive on all issues, or if neither set is ever decisive . . . the social welfare function treats alternatives (but not necessarily people) in a neutral manner" (p. 311). Additivity of nondictatorial sets means that if two sets of individuals are nondictatorial, then the two sets together are nondictatorial as well. Since neutrality implies that no individual may be dictatorial we can prove, by mathematical induction, that the total population — unanimity — is nondictatorial. This contradicts Conditions 2 and 4.

Vickrey suggests a modification of Condition 1 (which he terms the "range" condition) very similar to Blau's (*op. cit.*, 509, 513-516). As in Blau, a Possibility Theorem can be proven for the new set of conditions (which differ somewhat for Conditions 2 through 5 as well) that closely retains the spirit of Arrow's.

original condition. The requirement that *all* triples be free does admittedly seem to have a different impact than Arrow's. It appears to be asking much more of the welfare function. But this appearance may be deceptive. We remarked above that Arrow's Condition 1, whether by accident or design, precludes any limitation on orderings from a single principle or complex of principles which apply to all triples.[37] Blau's counterexamples work because they call on ordering principles that apply to only a few alternatives instead of all. Unless many alternatives are affected by these "partial" principles, however, the question of social choice remains essentially unsolved for the great mass of issues. If many alternatives are included, in contrast, the intuitive sense of the limitations is probably not very different from the organizing force of principles which restrict orderings on all issues. In short, accepting both of Blau's suggested modifications probably does not do much violence to the intuitive appeal of Arrow's characterization of acceptable Social Welfare Functions. But we then have an Impossibility Theorem whose impact differs very little from that of Arrow's.

In what follows, we shall accept Blau's modifications, investigating the possibility of a useful welfare economics within the context of a theorem that states that no Social Welfare Function can be formulated which simultaneously fulfills apparently reasonable conditions. We recognize the difference between this and Arrow's position at least to this extent: if we should find a particular formulation which fulfills Arrow's original conditions but not the modified ones, we shall nonetheless judge our quest to have been essentially successful.

2-2. *Tastes versus Values*

The first issue that must be clarified in interpreting Arrow's conclusion concerns the specific restrictions, alluded to above, which Arrow places on the individual orderings of social state alternatives. It will be remembered that in our discussion of the Bergson Economic Welfare Function we made no direct reference to the character of the determining variables (the individual utility functions) introduced by means of the assumption of consumer's sovereignty. We did, however, symptomatically interpret the optimum welfare conditions in a way which discloses Bergson's own explicit intention on this score. In Bergson's treatment, each individual's utility (or preferences) depends solely on the commodities he himself obtains, and not on commodities going to others.[38] In Arrow's treatment, however, this

---

[37]Such as "single-peakedness," to be discussed in Chapter 11.

[38]We may recollect that Conditions (3) were of the form $\partial E/\partial x_i = \partial E/\partial x_k$. In drawing the implications of consumer sovereignty as applied to these conditions we proceeded as follows:

restriction is not assumed. Since the orderings are observable, and, in principle they include subsets of alternatives which differ only in regard to commodities going to others, the question of whether or not these orderings depend solely on an individual's own consumption or are dependent upon others' consumption as well, is a question of fact — it is subject to empirical verification. Be this as it may, Arrow simply assumes that individuals can and do order social states on whatever basis they are in fact ordered.

The context of Arrow's schema, however, would seem to *require* a broader notion than Bergson's. "Some of the components of the social state, considered as a vector, are collective activities . . .; such problems as the division of the national income between public and private expenditure . . ."[39] *could not* be evaluated by an individual solely in terms of his own consumption. Furthermore it is undeniable that individuals do have attitudes about such problems. Moreover, we are also convinced that they have attitudes toward different broad patterns of wealth distribution — toward questions, for example, like who should be given public relief. These attitudes may be characterized as ethical judgments. They reflect the *values* of these individuals. If one is asked to express his preferences with respect to different possible economy-wide outcomes, it is hard to believe that he would not consult these values since *they* assert for him the kind of world — the kind of things happening to different people — which he considers desirable or undesirable. The very statement of Arrow's problem, therefore, would seem to call forth evaluations of social states on grounds in addition to what each individual himself obtains.

On the basis of these considerations Arrow introduces the following distinction which he credits to Milton Friedman.

> In general, there will, then, be a difference between the ordering of social states according to the direct consumption of the individual and the ordering when the individual adds his general standards of equity (or perhaps his standards of pecuniary emulation). We may refer to the former ordering as reflecting the *tastes* of the individual and the latter as reflecting his *values*. The distinction between the two is by no means clear-cut. An individual with aesthetic feelings certainly derives pleasure from his neighbor's having a well-tended lawn. Under the system of a free market, such feelings play no direct part in social choice; yet psychologically they differ only slightly from the pleasure in one's own lawn. Intuitively, of course, we feel that not all the possible preferences which an individual might have ought to count; his preferences for matters which

---

$$\frac{\partial E}{\partial x_i} = \frac{\partial E}{\partial U^i} \cdot \frac{\partial U^i}{\partial x_i} \quad \text{and} \quad \frac{\partial E}{\partial x_k} = \frac{\partial E}{\partial U^k} \cdot \frac{\partial U^k}{\partial x_k}.$$

The omission of all terms such as $(\partial E/\partial U^k) \cdot (\partial U^k/\partial x_i)$ and $(\partial E/\partial U^i \cdot (\partial U^i/\partial x_k)$ implicitly assumes that each U^i is a function of x_i, y_i alone and not

$$U^i = U^i(x_1, x_2, \ldots, x_n, \quad y_1, y_2, \ldots, y_n).$$

[39] Arrow, *op. cit.*, 18.

are 'none of his business' should be irrelevant. Without challenging this view, I should like to emphasize that the decision as to which preferences are relevant and which are not is itself a value judgment and cannot be settled on an a priori basis.[40]

Arrow's conclusion, despite the important qualification he makes, suggests that Bergson's and his treatments differ in that their respective assumptions of "consumer's" and "citizen's" sovereignty refer to different parts of any individual. The first refers to a person's *tastes* and the second to his *values;* it is expected that "in general, there will, then, be a difference between" orderings of social states based on the two.

I think this overstates the difference between what is essentially involved. I think it can be shown by elaborating upon Arrow's qualifications that what distinguishes the two treatments is not that they refer to different kinds of behavior but that they represent responses to different questions (or situations).

The assumption of consumer's (or citizen's) sovereignty in welfare economics signifies that an individual's preferences between alternative situations discloses his hypothetical well-being under each of them. Let us first consider why the consumption of a particular commodity bundle *by* an individual is relevant to his well-being.

Some commodities minister directly to biological needs of the organism. But many commodities are directed toward needs which are derived from the social context of the individual. They are, in effect, means by which the individual hopes to induce certain desirable behavior toward himself by others, or means by which the individual will approve of his own behavior in terms of the social norms which he accepts. Even under the latter motivation, self-approval according to the social code is often based upon an envisaged approval (particular behavior toward one) by others. Consuming these commodities, then, is tantamount to expecting a certain relationship with specified or generalized "others." It is a putting forth of specific social signals. Automobiles, clothing, jewelry, and housing, are examples. This motivation is not only important in commodities satisfying so-called "derived needs," it is also an element — and often a determining one — in choices among commodities satisfying "elemental needs." I suggest, therefore, that an individual's attitudes toward goods which he himself consumes is in no sense independent of his attitudes toward the relationship broadly conceived of others to him (including, of course, what he considers desirable or undesirable states of affairs).

If the well-being of a given individual in terms of his own consumption depends importantly on the actions of others in this general sense, then it is surely conceivable that the actions of others which are embodied in their

---

[40]*Ibid.*, 18.

consumption of particular commodities (i.e., the putting forth of their own signals) can affect the well-being of the given individual, even without a change in his consumption. If, then, we should find that individuals do in fact express important consideration about others' consumption (such that, for example, he would prefer increased consumption for some other person at the expense of his own consumption — charity; or, he would prefer to change his own consumption pattern when others change theirs — fashion), then these so-called "external relations" in consumption (or external economies and diseconomies) influence the same "welfare" of a person as does his own consumption. Furthermore, evaluation by the individual of both alternative consumption standards for himself and whole social states are based on the same attitudes of the total personality. They are based on the same set of individual *values*.[41]

I suggest, therefore, that orderings of a given set of alternatives are the same whether based on "tastes" or on "values." It makes no sense to say to an individual: first, order these alternatives on the basis of your "tastes," then on the basis of your "values." If he is asked to order alternatives in terms of their desirability to him, he has only one evaluative schema by which to do so.[42]

It is perfectly obvious that, notwithstanding all this, Bergson's and Arrow's restrictions *are* different. But the difference now can be seen to reside elsewhere than in different kinds of rankings. If we accept my argument, in what sense should we speak of a ranking of social states based on individuals' own consumption? Such a ranking appears meaningful if we understand it to mean an ordering by a given individual of social state alternatives which differ from one another as far as the commodity bundles going to that individual are concerned but not as far as commodity bundles going to other individuals. The individual is evaluating different possible changes in his consumption patterns under the assumption that everyone else's consumption pattern remains unchanged Thus, we have a partial analysis since all alternatives in which the consumption pattern of others change are excluded.[43]

---

[41]The importance of external relations in consumption has been cogently argued by James S. Duesenberry, *Income, Saving and The Theory of Consumer Behavior* (Cambridge: Harvard University Press, 1949); and William J. Baumol, *Welfare Economics and the Theory of the State* (Cambridge: Harvard University Press, 1952). It is, indeed, the cornerstone of their analyses. For a formal model employing these relations, see Gerhard Tintner, "A Note on Welfare Economics," *Econometrica*, Vol. 14, No. 1 (January, 1946), 69-78.

[42]It follows from this that the question of which preferences are "relevant" and which are "none of his business" means something different than Arrow's passage suggests. I shall deal with this question in my discussion of the "irrelevant alternatives" condition in Chapter 5.

[43]We have here a formal resemblance to partial derivatives.

Under this conception, we may interpret the assertion to the effect that the introduction of the individual's "general standards of equity . . . or . . . his standards of pecuniary emulation" makes a difference on his ordering, as the perfectly consistent notion that the individual's ordering of commodity bundles going to himself will not be unique. It will differ when these bundles are contemporary with one set of given bundles going to others from when the same bundles are contemporary with a different set of bundles going to others.

Is Bergson's position necessarily tied to this rather severe restriction on individual orderings, referred to here as "tastes"? It can easily be shown that if external consumption relations are as important as I have here suggested, Bergson's approach cannot usefully maintain this restriction. Arrow's position, moreover, can be painlessly substituted.

Assume they *are* important. Now, the introduction of consumer's sovereignty into Bergson's Economic Welfare Function requires that the social choice among alternatives be determined by individual preferences toward these same alternatives. These alternatives are very similar to Arrow's social states. Under Bergson's assumption, they can be ordered by each individual on the basis of the commodities going to him alone. This implies that he is indifferent to all alternatives in which he obtains the same commodity bundle, regardless of what commodities go to others. All the available alternatives can be ordered by all individuals if this procedure is followed.

Another way of looking at this is to take each person's ordering not of social states but of commodity bundles going to himself. Each social state can then be *synthesized* as the simultaneous distribution of a given commodity bundle to each individual. Under the Bergson assumption, the set of individual evaluations of the social state will be nothing but the individual valuations of each *separate* commodity bundle.

Neither procedure is valid under our assumption of external consumption relations. The first is unwarranted because, in general, alternatives will *not* be indifferent simply because they give the individual the same commodities. This was the point made above. The second only apparently avoids the outright contradiction. The individual evaluation of a given commodity bundle is not invariant but depends upon what others get. A particular evaluation by any individual therefore implies for each individual that some one of a particular limited subset of distributions to others has been assumed. A social state can be synthesized out of the separate bundles of the various individuals only if they are all mutually consistent, i.e., only if they are all reciprocally members of each other's limited subset of consistent "external" distributions. Noncontradictory sets of individual evaluations are, of course, conceivable, but they can be disclosed only by examination of each individual's external relations — in effect, by individual orderings of all social states *when external relations are admitted!* This is exactly Arrow's procedure.

Nothing in the conception of the Economic Welfare Function, or of consumer's sovereignty, prohibits the inclusion of individual orderings on the basis of values.[44] The preceding demonstration shows that, if my assumption of fact is correct, they are required to save this formulation of social choice from self-contradiction. I suggest, therefore, that the Bergson restrictions on individual orderings may be dropped when interpreting the Economic Welfare Function.[45] I do not believe that this does violence to Bergson's own intentions since he avowedly adopts these and other simplifications for expositional convenience rather than as ultimate analytic commitments. Bergson's analysis, then, can apparently be reinterpreted advantageously to refer to the same variables as does Arrow's.

One consequence of this is that in the rest of the present work we shall be employing the Arrow notion of individual orderings of social states exclusively. Consequently, we shall find little need to distinguish "tastes" from "values" and shall use them interchangeably except where noted. In the exceptional instances, "tastes" will refer to individual preference scales which are *in fact* independent of others.

Another consequence is that we must be extremely careful about drawing the distinction between those individual preferences which ought, and those which ought not, "to count." Our analysis strongly suggests that there is little or no qualitative difference — in terms of an individual's own satisfaction (or happiness) — between preferences which some outsider would judge to be that individual's "own business" and those which the outsider would judge to be none of his business.

Of course, some may object that an individual has far less competence in deciding what some other person ought to have than in deciding what he himself ought to have, and on this basis the distinction should be maintained. This consideration seems fundamentally to involve as criterion, not whether certain preferences refer to the evaluating individual himself or to some outsider, but whether the preferences are "well-informed." Insight and knowledge would appear to be the by-words. But on these grounds, many people are willing to argue that the values of some individuals regarding *their own way of life* are promulgated out of ignorance and faulty insight. Psychoanalysts, the clergy, reformers of many stripes, have, in a real sense, their *raison d'etre* in criticizing the personal values of large subsets of the population. If only informed preferences are to count, some

---

[44]Their inclusion would change the optimum conditions by introducing terms like $\partial u^i / \partial x_k$.

[45]Arrow calls these the "individualist assumptions." Arrow shows, by the way, that the Possibility Theorem applies even under these assumptions. Cf. Chapter VI, 61-73.

individuals are likely to be disenfranchised on the basis of the values relating to their own way of life (in addition to children and the institutionalized). This is a substantial modification of consumer's sovereignty. The real character of this modification becomes apparent when it is understood that the degree of "informedness" of anyone's preferences is not a matter of *fact* (such that a measuring procedure could in principle be set up whose judgments would command universal acceptance). Different individuals will differ in their judgments about the informedness of a given set of values, primarily because they will have different notions about the extent to which different knowledge is relevant. In this context, "relevance" reflects the values of the judges themselves. Judgments about the informedness of preferences are in considerable measure *value judgments*. Although there are instances where the judgment that certain preferences are uninformed could probably gain general agreement, these instances are not apt to be numerous. Consequently, any particular spelling-out of the intended distinction on grounds of informedness is apt to be unrewardingly arbitrary for use in welfare economics.

If a distinction must be made about preferences which should and should not count, a better case can apparently be made for "accepting" all individual preferences as discovered (even though, undoubtedly, individuals often *misunderstand* their own true preferences), and *weighting* the influence of different preferences in the determination of social choice according to their *intensity*. This will be amplified in Chapter 5.

2-3. *Changes in Tastes (Values)*

In his full review of Arrow's book, I. M. D. Little seriously questions the relevance of Arrow's conclusion.[46] Arrow's function is not the same as Bergson's. So his negative findings have nothing to do with welfare economics. According to Little, "Bergson's welfare function was meant as a 'process or rule,' which would indicate the best economic state as a function of a changing environment (i.e., changing sets of possibilities defined by different economic transformation functions), *the individuals' tastes being given*.[47] But Arrow conceives of a Social Welfare Function in which individual tastes — in the sense of rank ordering — do change, and which, in fact, establishes a relationship between the social judgments under different individual rankings. Thus, one of the "conditions of correspondence" — to use Little's term — which Arrow requires the Social Welfare Function to fulfill is meaningless if tastes are given. Little is

---

[46]"Social Choice and Individual Values," *Journal of Political Economy,* Vol. LX, No. 5 (October, 1952).

[47]*Ibid.,* 423. Italics Little's.

referring to Condition 2. His paraphrase of this condition is: "If one possibility rises or remains still in the order of every individual, then cet. par., it must not fall in the collective order."[48] Thus, claims Little, "Arrow's result has no bearing on the possibility or impossibility" of the Bergson function.[49] And later he asserts ". . . that Arrow's work has no relevance to the traditional theory of welfare economics, which culminates in the Bergson-Samuelson formulation," allowing, though, that it might have advantages of its own.[50]

I believe Little's judgment is too sweeping. It reveals a narrowness in interpreting the Bergson formulation which would severely hamstring any welfare analysis based upon this foundation. Little may well have confused the surface assumptions of typical working procedure with the deeper and more implicit assumptions involved in the very formulation of the Social Welfare Function. In any event, I submit that Arrow's conception is not essentially different from the Bergson-Samuelson formulation on this score.

Let us attempt to derive the Arrow Social Welfare Function from the Bergson Economic Welfare Function.

(1) Take the Bergson welfare function (under consumer's sovereignty) as modified in the last section.

$$(1) \quad E = E[U^1(x_1^1, x_2^1, \ldots, x_n^1; x_1^2, \ldots, x_n^2; \ldots; x_1^m, \ldots, x_n^m),$$
$$U^2(x_1^1, x_2^1, \ldots, x_n^1; x_1^2, x_2^2, \ldots, x_n^2; \ldots; x_1^m, \ldots, x_n^m) \ldots,$$
$$U^m(x_1^1, \ldots, x_n^m)]$$

showing a rule for combining the utility function of the different members of the community to obtain an index of social welfare. (Subscripts refer to the kind of good or service, including productive services calculated as negative commodities; superscripts refer to the individual possessing the commodity.)

Define each social state A_r as the matrix

$$(2) \quad \left\{ \begin{array}{cccc} x^1{}_{1A_r} & x^1{}_{2A_r} & \cdots & x^1{}_{nA_r} \\ x^2{}_{1A_r} & x^2{}_{2A_r} & \cdots & x^2{}_{nA_r} \\ \cdot & & & \\ \cdot & & & \\ x^m{}_{1A_r} & \cdots & & x^m{}_{nA_r} \end{array} \right\}$$

expressing a particular distribution of goods and services to the various members of the community. (Subscript A_r reflects this particular distribution.)

(2) We may now define social preference and indifference.

---

[48]*Ibid.*, 422.
[49]*Ibid.*, 423.
[50]*Ibid.*, 425.

For any A_r and A_s, we can compare E_r with E_s

for $E_{A_r} > E_{A_s} \rightarrow A_r P A_s$ (A_r is socially preferred to A_s)
          $E_{A_r} < E_{A_s} \rightarrow A_s P A_r$ (A_s is socially preferred to A_r)
          $E_{A_r} = E_{A_s} \rightarrow A_r I A_s$ (A_r and A_s are socially indifferent)

(3) The central problem of welfare economics in the Bergson treatment is to maximize E subject to technological constraints. But the technological constraints will differ with different environments, and each set of constraints makes attainable a different set of social states. Thus, the maximization problem will, in general, require comparisons between different combinations of the total number of social states — every A_r will conceivably be compared with every A_s. So it is possible to derive a social preference ranking of the social states from the Bergson Social Welfare Function, and this ranking is relevant to the central problem of welfare economics. It is of the form:

(3) $$[R] = \begin{bmatrix} R_{A_1} \\ R_{A_2} \\ \cdot \\ \cdot \\ \cdot \\ R_{A_h} \end{bmatrix} = R(U^1, U^2, \ldots, U^m)$$ (where the vector R represents the social ranking of the h social states)

(4) Each individual's utility index can similarly be transformed into a preference scale simply by ranking, for each individual i,

$$U^i(A_1), U^i(A_2), \ldots, U^i(A_h)$$

Thus, we obtain for the ith individual:

(4) $$[R^i] = \begin{bmatrix} R_{A_1}{}^i \\ R_{A_2}{}^i \\ \cdot \\ \cdot \\ \cdot \\ R_{A_h}{}^i \end{bmatrix} = R^i[U^i(x_1{}^i, x_2{}^i, \ldots, x_n{}^i; x_1{}^1, x_2{}^1, \ldots, x_n{}^1; \ldots; x_1{}^m, \ldots, x_n{}^m)]$$

and finally, combining Eqs. (3) and (4), we obtain

(5) $$(R) = f(R^1, R^2, \ldots, R^m)$$

(where R^i is the ranking of social states by the ith individual).

But this is exactly Arrow's Social Welfare Function — a rule for deriving a social preference scale from the preference scales of the individual members of the community.

As was pointed out in step 3 above, this particular transformation of the Bergson welfare function is useful in that the central problem of welfare economics requires a social ranking of social states. Such a ranking, then, is certainly not irrelevant for welfare economics. But Eq. (5) clearly reflects the dependence of the transformed Social Welfare Function (R) on possible changes in R^i. It is certainly not true, as Little says:

> If tastes change, we may expect a new ordering of all the conceivable states; but we do not require that the difference between the new and the old ordering should bear any particular relation to the changes of taste which have occurred. We have, so to speak, a new world and a new order; and we do not demand correspondence between the change in the world and the change in the order.[51]

The conceivable changes in taste (expressive only of changes in rankings — the problem differs if we have cardinal measurement of utility or differentiation of preference intensities) help to make explicit the nature of the rule by which individual choices are weighted and combined.[52] The function (5) treats the whole preference scales of the several individuals as its arguments. (This differentiates this function from one whose variables are rank numbers. Such a scale would not be compatible with the exclusion of cardinal preference elements.)[53]

For the purpose of delineating the nature of the Social Welfare Function, only the following properties of hypothetical changes in tastes are required for the content of Condition 2. First, the social weighting of some A_r at rank k in a given individual's scale is the same as that of some A_s, if A_s were at rank k for the same individual. In other words, social states are treated symmetrically, and only their ranking in particular preference scales is relevant to social choice. Second, an alternative A_i is ranked socially higher only if it ranks higher in the preference scales of the various individuals. Third, the combinatorial rule is not itself a function of tastes.[54]

Surely the function $E = E(U^1, U^2, \ldots; U^n)$ expresses in less overt form these same rules for combining individual choices which $(R) = f(R^1, R^2, \ldots, R^n)$ makes somewhat more explicit. That their rigorous statement involves positing hypothetical changes in tastes should not blind one to their presence in an analytic system which is typically employed under the working assumption of constancy of tastes.

If it is true, as Little says, that "we do not require that the difference between the new and the old ordering should bear any particular relation to the changes of taste which have occurred," then indeed we *have* no unique rule of combining individual choices into a social preference scale — we have no determinate Social Welfare Function.

---

[51]Little, *op. cit.*, 423-424.
[52]For a discussion of this, see Chapters 6-10 below.
[53]This will be seen especially in Chapter 7.
[54]This will be qualified later in the present work (Chapter 13).

Little is consistent in the position he expresses here when he attacks the reasonableness of Arrow's Condition 2. After illustrating Condition 2 by a situation in which one individual's tastes change, he continues: "Could not . . . (individual) A's change of taste as between (social states) y and z justify a higher weighting of his first choice . . .?"[55] This might be interpreted in two ways. First, A's change of tastes between y and z might be felt to throw light on the resulting *intensity* of his preference for x over y and z. For example, his new ranking of y and z "makes clear" that x is preferred to both y and z by more than was previously realized, and therefore x *deserves* a higher weighting in the Social Welfare Function.[56] This introduces cardinal preference notions which may not be deemed admissible into welfare economics; moreover, it seems clear from the context that this is not Little's intent. If restricted to ordinal considerations alone, Little's position would seem to be that the Social Welfare Function is a combinatorial rule, which rule itself is a function (unspecified) of tastes. The rule changes whenever anyone's tastes change, or whenever the composition of the underlying population changes. The same rule cannot be used in comparing the social welfare judgments under two hypothetically different preference rankings by a single individual. Are we willing to restrict welfare analysis to so narrow a gauge, e.g., requiring a new basic function each time some advertising project converts one or two consumers to a different brand? I believe we are thinking of a rule more invariant than that. In a later chapter I will indeed argue that the social judgment rule is a function of certain tastes (*really* values), but that *these* "tastes" can *realistically* be assumed unchanging within the time scale employed in traditional economic analysis.[57] The total skepticism of Little's conception whereby *any* change in *any* tastes *might* require a new rule yields welfare economics little breathing space.

An objection somewhat similar to Little's might be raised against my interpretation here. It is generally believed that we are unable to compare the welfare of an *individual* in two different situations where his tastes are different (let alone the situation of two different people with different tastes). Yet, social welfare comparisons depend on individual welfare comparisons. How then can we substantiate Arrow's claim to be able to make social comparisons with different tastes when the component individual comparisons are deemed meaningless?

The issue of welfare comparisons under changing tastes is an important one, and I have made suggestions elsewhere as to how to give meaning to

[55]Little, *op. cit.*, 425.
[56]Cf. Chapters 6 through 10, especially Chapter 8.
[57]Chapter 13.

such comparisons.[58] But that issue need not be significant here. As I interpret it, Arrow's formulation of the Social Welfare Function asserts that, for any set of individual orderings of the alternative social states, there is a corresponding social ordering. For a different set of individual orderings, there is a different social ordering. For example, under the first set of rankings, social state A is preferred to B; under the second, B is preferred to A. The relationship between the change in individual orderings and the change in the social orderings derives simply from the assumption that the combinatorial "rule" itself is independent of the individual orderings. But we are nowhere required to say whether social welfare has *risen* or *fallen* by a change from A to B concurrent with the change in orderings. Comparison between A and B is defined only for the given set of orderings, not for the process of change in those orderings. It is true enough that the usefulness of the Social Welfare Function, as so interpreted (like Little's function), depends on the persistence of particular sets of orderings over time. In particular, if tastes change with every change in social states, welfare comparisons between historical situations may be impossible.[59] But contrary to Little's conception of the Social Welfare Function, the Arrow Social Welfare Function *is defined* for every new set of orderings, even if tastes change frequently.

2-4. *The Social Welfare Function and*
The Economic Welfare Function

The two previous sections have delineated a close correspondence between the Bergson Economic Welfare Function and the Arrow Social Welfare Function. It strongly suggests that we may, for the problem of this work, interpret the Possibility Theorem as applying to both. In effect, this means that we may take the Bergson function as a Social Welfare Function. Arrow's demonstration then means that all Economic Welfare Functions which incorporate a particular set of value judgments on ends (Arrow's five conditions) will render contradictory social orderings. Arrow's five value judgments are inconsistent. The Possibility Theorem, when viewed in this light, is seen to be a carrying forth of one aspect of Bergson's investigative program: with what sets of value judgments can we construct noncontradictory welfare functions, and with what sets can we not? The whole emphasis of this viewpoint is on the examination of the properties of different sets of value judgments for welfare analysis. It is not concerned with the "possibility" (or "impossibility") of a welfare function as such.

---

[58]"Welfare Comparisons and Changes in Tastes," *American Economic Review* (December, 1953), reprinted with modifications as the Appendix to this chapter.

[59]But see the Appendix to this chapter.

Thus, Arrow's conclusion, on this interpretation, represents a contribution to the first question raised in Chapter 1, namely, Under what circumstances can a consistent welfare function be constructed?

But the Possibility Theorem also throws light on our second question. By what means is a uniquely appropriate welfare function determined? Let us return to our illustration of this problem made in Chapter 1. A certain person has constructed a welfare analysis on the basis of a set of value assumptions about ends which he finds desirable. On the basis of this analysis, he makes certain policy recommendations to the "authorities," i.e., he presents a certain ordering of alternatives. Similarly, everyone else in the community presents corresponding policy recommendations derived from a welfare analysis based on value judgments which he deems appropriate. We thus have a set of individual orderings of alternatives, each representing a different welfare function. Which ordering should the authorities accept? Or, if not a single ordering, what combination of orderings should they accept?

We see that the statement of this problem is formally identical with what we considered under our first interpretation. If the uniquely appropriate ordering is to be somehow chosen from among those presented, then we are simply asking to know by what rule it is to be so chosen. What is the functional relationship between the uniquely appropriate welfare ordering (let us call it the social ordering) and the individual orderings?

We might go much further beyond formal resemblance if the individual orderings of this schema were the same as those under the first interpretation. Without wishing to suggest a conclusive answer, they do not appear to be the same. The orderings under the first interpretation were meant to answer this hypothetical question posed to each individual: What are your preferences among alternatives in terms of *your* well-being? The orderings under the second are meant to answer this hypothetical question: What are your preferences among alternatives in terms of what you believe to be the well-being of the community? No doubt the two sets of orderings have much in common. As has been pointed out earlier, the individual's values are the criteria of his well-being *because* they evaluate the desirability of different social states. It would be easy, in fact, to define away the problem: a state which an individual feels is best for the community is *necessarily* one which he would *like to see* come about, therefore, one which *he* prefers.

There does seem to be one difference, however, which in practice may or may not be important. Under the first, the individual is being asked which alternative *he* would most prefer, but he is not being asked about how he would like to see a decision actually made to determine policy. Under the second, he is being asked what public policy he thinks ought to be adopted. An illustration should clarify in what way these differ. A poker player may decide that, all other things being equal, he would most prefer to win ten out of fifteen hands. Yet, he may further decide that, within wide limits, he would prefer whatever actual outcome occurred through the working of the rules of poker. In the latter decision, he nonetheless expects that the outcome will, in some respect, depend on his own preferences about hands he would like to win. The second interpretation, then, is one where the individual is asked to indicate not his choice of social states but his choice of Bergson Economic Welfare Functions. This statement is, of course, the very point of departure of the present interpretation. The important conclusion made here is that it does not automatically *reduce* to the first interpretation. Since, for some persons, their values, with regard to choice of welfare functions, may be relatively independent of their ordering of social states, their choice of functions may well imply a different ordering of social states than when this choice is excluded.

Of course, the set of individual orderings in a Bergson function need not differ from this derived set. We can guarantee that the two will be identical by means of a formal device. We simply introduce into the Bergson function those value judgments which suffice to determine the uniquely appropriate aggregating function as well as the resultant ordering. The former judgments are, as we have suggested, themselves some function of individual values. Therefore, their introduction really involves imposing further restrictions on the original set of individual values and on the rule for combining them. Having done so, the new set will now be identical with the derived set under the second interpretation, for the simple reason that the two *interpretations* of social choice are now formally equivalent under these conditions.[60]

In terms of operations on Bergson functions, therefore, the second interpretation is concerned with the implications of imposing sets of value judgments which uniquely determine the function. These sets are completely embodied as restrictions on individual orderings and a rule for combining them. Arrow's five conditions now refer to the means of deriving a unique Social Welfare Function on the basis of individual recommendations. The Possibility Theorem asserts that these means will not suffice to derive a unique function with the properties of the determining functions.[61]

We may express this symbolically. Consider Eq. (5) in the last section.

(5) $$R = f(R^1, R^2, \ldots, R^n).$$

Our second interpretation claims that what is being chosen is some E. In other words,

---

[60]It is to be emphasized that this function, and hence these restrictions, are in principle empirically observable. Consequently, identity is assured only if they represent the same empirical generalization upon which the derived values are based.

[61]Namely, giving rise to a complete and transitive ordering of alternatives.

(6) $R = f^*[g[R^{1*}(E_1\{u^1, u^2, \ldots, u^n\}, E_2, \ldots, E_r), R^{2*}, \ldots, R^{n*}] \mid$
$$A_1, \ldots, A_h] = f(R^1, R^2, \ldots, R^n)$$

and

(7) $$g[R^{1*}, R^{2*}, \ldots, R^{n*}] = \overline{E}(u^1, \ldots, u^n);$$

so

(8) $$R = f^*(\overline{E} \mid A_1, \ldots, A_h).$$

The Possibility Theorem concerns Eq. (7). Since each E_b is assumed, with given specifications of individual orderings, to give rise to a complete and transitive ordering of alternatives, the Possibility Theorem asserts that the restrictions on g do not suffice to choose one of the E_b. Moreover, if Conditions 2 through 5 are maintained, $\overline{E}$ does not give rise to a transitive ordering of alternatives.

2-5. The Nature of Solutions to the Paradox

Under both interpretations of the Possibility Theorem which we have considered, the solution of the paradox would seem to reside in one or both of the following measures.

(1) Relax one or more of Arrow's conditions.

(2) Impose additional restrictions on the individual orderings.

Relaxation of Arrow's Conditions

The "reasonableness" of any one condition need not be the same under the two interpretations. Under both, Condition 1 essentially sets forth the basic problem — derivation of a complete and transitive social ordering of social states for a sufficiently wide range of individual orderings. The requirement for a wide range of admissible orderings would apparently be more secure under the first, however, since, as I shall argue in a later chapter, while individual choices among social states may, in fact, differ appreciably from one individual to the next, individual choices among welfare functions are less apt *in fact* to differ appreciably.

Conditions 2, 4, and 5 essentially set forth and specialize the requirement for both interpretations that the social choice be truly dependent on individual orderings. In Chapter 12 we shall consider an argument that Condition 5 (nondictatorship) is "unreasonable" under the second, but not the first, interpretation.

Condition 3 is meant to specify a supposed property of "rational" choice. In later chapters we shall consider an argument that it is "unreasonable" on grounds which can logically be applied to both interpretations but which seem to have far greater practical relevance with respect to the first.

Use of the terms "reasonable" or "unreasonable" are, of course, at this stage of the enquiry, ambiguous. I hope to rectify this in the succeeding discussions. Indeed, one of the chief goals which future chapters will have is to clarify the grounds on which these terms can be applied.

Imposition of Additional Restraints on Individual Orderings

We have examined the assumptions characterizing individual orderings at various places in the present chapter. In sum, no restrictions have been placed on them, other than to require that they be complete and transitive orderings of the whole set of "available" social state alternatives. In later chapters we shall discuss introducing additional assumptions. These are largely attempts to give individual preference scales cardinal significance. In this connection, it is important to note that the mere introduction of these restrictions on individual orderings leaves the analysis unchanged since the effect of one of the conditions on the welfare function itself (namely Condition 3, independence of irrelevant alternatives) is to require that only ordinal properties of individual preferences be consulted. Consequently, in this particular instance the additional restrictions will be considered as part of an argument to relax Condition 3; in general, solutions sought in the direction of respecifying the individual ordering variables are not independent of the structure of the welfare function itself (as indeed, our exposition of the two interpretations in the last section testified).

2-6. A Bergson Solution: Consensus and the Social Welfare Function

I shall leave to future chapters a systematic examination of restrictions on individual orderings. But a brief consideration of one particular set of additional restrictions appears to be appropriate at this time. It may be remembered that in chapter 1 I introduced three sets of value judgments into the Bergson welfare function by way of illustrating the usefulness of that function as an analytic tool. They were, essentially: (1) an assumption of socially indifferent occupations for nonlabor productive inputs, (2) consumer sovereignty, and (3) the desirability of equal shares. What is important about these assumptions is that Bergson deals with them as a set which is sufficient to render a complete social ordering — a set which will enable the choosing of a unique optimum social state or subset of social states. Neglecting the first assumption (which is not, in fact, a necessary condition for deriving an optimum subset), and treating Arrow's Conditions 1 and 3 as essentially asserting the problem of finding a social optimum.

Arrow's restrictions boil down roughly to consumer's sovereignty.[62] Will the addition of a general agreement on the distribution of money income suffice to give us an acceptable social ordering?

Let us introduce agreement on income distribution. What form will it take in our schema? It will take the form of each individual's expressing preferences about different distributions of money income to the various individuals. This accounts for our consideration of it in a section devoted to additional restrictions on individual orderings. But a particular distribution of money to different individuals is not a unique distribution of commodities to different individuals. It is not a social state. So we are not by this means really restricting individual orderings of social states.[63]

A particular distribution of money incomes could mean a particular distribution of commodities only if a particular set of prices were given, since we should then be able to predict how each individual, given his tastes, would spend his income. Prices do not, however, appear in the Social Welfare Function (except in the special cases irrelevant here, where individual *preferences* — not purchases! — are a function of prices, like Veblen's snob appeal[64]). But this stricture may be avoided if we are able to predict prices as an endogenous outcome of factors which are included in the Social Welfare Function. This will be possible, given the set of available social states, if the form of the Social Welfare Function includes a model of the economic system. The set of technologically possible social states gives us a production transformation locus for the society. This, together with the given set of individual tastes *and* an initial distribution of money incomes, determines for every market structure a distribution of commodities.[65]

This circumvention enables us to map a distribution of money income roughly onto a corresponding social state. The value judgment about distribution therefore gives an ordering of these social states on the basis of the conformance of their initial relative distribution of income to the scale established by the ethical agreement on distribution. Its restriction on some given individual's ordering is to require this individual's choice of that social state where, subject to the *relative* budgetary restriction imposed by the value agreement, each individual — including himself — obtains what he most prefers.[66] It must be emphasized again that this restriction has

---

[62]We are using "consumer" and "citizen" interchangeably after reinterpreting Bergson's individual orderings as "values." See above.

[63]Cf. Samuelson, *Foundations of Economic Analysis*, 225; Arrow, *op. cit.*, 72.

[64]Cf. Leibeinstein, "Bandwagon, Snob & Veblen Effects in the Theory of Consumer's Demand," *Quarterly Journal of Economics*, Vol. LXIV, No. 2 (May, 1950), 183-207.

[65]See Chapter 13, footnote 24, for qualifications on the uniqueness of the outcome.

[66]Absolute budgetary limitations, of course, have no place in the Social Welfare Function, since the Social Welfare Function concerns preferences rather than opportunities. This distinction holds even though preferences are sometimes influenced by opportunities — especially past opportunities.

content only so long as a unique set of prices is implied; its content changes with anyone's change in tastes or with a change in technical possibilities (or a change in market structure).

To continue, every individual chooses the sole social state derived in this manner. The ethical rule on distribution together with consumer sovereignty are thus seen to be restrictions which choose a unique welfare function and a unique state for a given set of tastes. The actual state is chosen by being synthesized out of the separate commodity bundles chosen by individuals for themselves with the given budgetary limitation. But this state will be a consistent synthesis only if each individual's own "optimum" purchases are not regretted as soon as he discovers about the purchases of others. In other words, if consumers' preferences for their own consumption patterns are influenced by others' patterns, it may not be possible to synthesize a logically consistent social state, since their preferences *cum* attitudes vis-à-vis others may be incompatible.[67] This kind of external consumption relation is not a matter of equity, since equity has already been accounted for in the agreement on distribution. It is, rather, a relatedness involving the specific composition of others' consumption patterns: e.g., fashions.[68]

However, let us for the moment disregard this possibility and assume that a consistent social state has been chosen. Now let tastes change.[69] The assumed restrictions will result in a new social state being chosen by this same method. In fact, the social state which is chosen will change for every change in individual tastes.

As a result of a similar examination Arrow concludes:

> Therefore, the given ethical system is a rule which defines the social state chosen from a given environment as a function of the tastes of all individuals. If, for a given set of tastes, the environment varies, we expect that the choices will be consistent in the sense that the choice function is derivable from a social weak ordering of all social states. Thus, [this] ethical scheme . . . has the form of a rule assigning a social ordering to each possible set of individual orderings representing tastes. . . . [It] is

---

[67] As in a game of strategy without a saddle-point, there will be no equilibrium. I am, of course, abstracting from another potential source of incompatibility, namely, the effects on the level of economic activity of different relative distributions of money income.

[68] As an example, take two women, each of whom is anxious to be in the forefront of clothing styles with respect to the other. If neither can predict the other's new wardrobe, a reciprocal confrontation will typically result in each wishing she had bought something different. And even if both can make good predictions about the other's choice, neither wants to make a final adjustment until the other has chosen. This is formally identical to the theory of oligopoly when conjectural variation functions do not intersect.

[69] I mean "tastes" in the narrowest sense, especially since we have assumed away the difficulty of the last paragraph.

mathematically isomorphic to the social welfare function under individualistic assumptions.[70]

And Arrow demonstrated that such a function is also subject to the Possibility Theorem.[71] Such a welfare function cannot be constructed satisfying Conditions 1–5.

Arrow's identification is not strictly correct. A change in the available alternatives will not necessarily give rise to the consistency of choices referred to by Arrow, because it will often reflect a situation under which a new set of prices prevails. To explain, assume we have a certain set of available states, out of which — with the resulting set of prices — some alternative A_1 is chosen over others, including some A_2.

Now, if the available set changes, so that A_1 and A_2 are still available, but in such a way that the relative prices of different commodities remain unchanged, then we should indeed expect that A_2 will not now be chosen over A_1 since with unchanged prices A_1 and A_2 still mean to the community what they meant before the available set changed. If, however, the change in available alternatives is accompanied by a change in relative prices, then A_1 and A_2 signify different distributions of commodities among the population. There is no reason to expect that A_1 need be preferred to A_2 under this quite different comparison.

The importance of this complication is that, in the real world, changes in the set of available alternatives typically occur through circumstances — like changes in the quantity or quality of certain resources, or in the state of technological knowledge — under which relative prices are likely to change. The range over which we should expect equivalence between an Arrow Social Welfare Function and this model embodying general agreement on income distribution is therefore not large. They are equivalent, for given tastes, where relative prices remain unchanged, i.e., where resources and technology are constant. Only here, therefore, does the Possibility Theorem apply. But this limited applicability should not delude us into believing that outside this range the model under consideration provides a satisfactory Social Welfare Function. Quite the contrary. It does even worse than the general Arrow-type function. For it does not even guarantee that social choices will be consistent.

The restrictions added to individual orderings by way of a general agreement on relative income distribution do not enable us to construct a Social Welfare Function satisfying Arrow's conditions.

We must not be misled by this conclusion, however. The failure of this Bergson Social Welfare Function to satisfy either Arrow's conditions or the condition of consistent choice need not be fatal to its usefulness. If it were really a fact that all individuals agreed on a rule for evaluating different

---

[70]Arrow, *op. cit.*, 72.
[71]Actually this is a corollary, but the result is the same.

distributions of relative money income (or at least agreed on the best distribution), *and* agreed on a rule — free market choice for consumers — for converting money distributions into commodity distributions, this would imply a set of individual values such that the community would make a unanimous selection of both an optimum social state and an optimum Social Welfare Function.[72] No economist seeking a concept of social choice could afford to overlook such actual consensus. We should, indeed, be strongly tempted to identify this consensus as social choice not only because we may feel that the welfare of a group of individuals cannot be understood without reference to their own values, but also because the greater the consensus in the group about desirable and undesirable states of affairs, the more arbitrary is any evaluation which differs appreciably from the generally accepted one.[73] Logically speaking, this identification can be wrought most simply by introducing as a postulate the assumption of consumer sovereignty: social values should be a reflection of individual values. To accept this consensus as social choice means to select the implied Social Welfare Function — *without having to introduce any additional value judgments:* Any condition not implied by acceptance of the consensus, whether Arrow's Condition 1, the condition of consistent choice, or some other, is simply irrelevant.

This is an important conclusion. Arrow's conditions, reducing broadly to consumer's sovereignty and a particular version of rationality, can be interpreted as intending a statement of those minimum properties which presumably "everyone" would expect a criterion of social welfare to possess. A criterion which failed to possess these properties would apparently be generally thought not to merit serious consideration.

(1) Our current knowledge about the culture-boundedness and plasticity of human nature, unmitigated by any *objective* delineation of human adaptability limits, makes us wary of postulating an individual or social welfare apart from the values of the individuals concerned.[74] The assumption of consumer's sovereignty expresses this appropriately cautious scientific attitude. Since the facts do not convincingly warrant more, the assumption can apparently be generally accepted *within the context of scientific method*. (It does not preclude disagreement from a different context — e.g., from a nonrefutable religious faith.)

(2) A persuasive case can, I think, be made for the contention that what

---

[72]Abstracting from the problem discussed above concerning continued disequilibrium of market outcomes.

[73]Since the Bergson agreement implicitly selects a welfare function along with its choice of social states, a *unanimous* agreement strictly implies that the economist *must* necessarily adopt this Social Welfare Function, because his own agreement is included in the unanimity. This is, of course, trivial.

[74]See also the discussion on "informed" and "uninformed" preferences in Section II above.

we usually mean by irrational behavior on the part of an individual is behavior which that individual would regret after being enlightened (about facts alone). Irrational choice is, in this sense, a kind of mistaken choice.[75] It is intuitively sound that a concept of social choice which gives rise to irrational choice be disdained. The choices do not represent welfare since they are *mistaken* in the meaningful sense that they would have been different if people knew *better* (if they knew the *facts* of the case).

The conclusion that we may choose a criterion of social welfare that makes all or part of these apparently reasonable requirements irrelevant, calls for further expatiation about the consensus identified as social choice. The agreement on distribution of money income is irrational in an important sense — irrational for every individual who is a party to the agreement — if this is the extent of the agreement; since if nothing in the agreement restricts the relative prices of commodities, a given distribution of money income can mean a wide range of distributions of these commodities which can be purchased for any possible set of prices. The agreement in this case is not, practically speaking, an agreement on social state outcomes.[76] This agreement alone does not warrant identification with a criterion of social welfare. But if the agreement extends to the "rule" for converting a money distribution to a social state, this makes all the difference. For now it is not solely the chosen social state which is valued but also the decision-making "rule." Although the ordering of social states may be irrational (from the point of view of Arrow's conditions), and if this ordering derives from a highly valued decision-making rule, there may well be no regrets about the outcome. If we interpret each alternative of choice as including a decision-making rule (the Social Welfare Function) as well as a "policy," then what I am suggesting is that the actual consensus concerning a decision-making rule may well give rise to a rational ordering of alternatives (in terms of Arrow's conditions). In this broadened sense, the economist's

---

[75]A typical definition of rationality is given by Dahl and Lindblom: "An action is rational to the extent that it is correctly designed to maximize *net* goal achievement . . . given the goals in question and the real world as it exists." *Politics, Economics and Welfare* (New York: Harper & Brothers, Publishers, 1953), 38. An action would appear to be irrational because of "unintended" ignorance about available alternatives, or about the consequences of different alternatives, or about the nature of one's goals, or else due to a logical error in comparing. To bypass this impossibly difficult problem of trying to judge the rationality of someone's action by re-creating the entire choice situation — alternatives, consequences, ends — a first approximation to such judgment would appear to be whether the individual approves of, or regrets, his action after having been given selected information bearing upon the nature of the environment (the available alternatives), the most pertinent causal relationships (the consequences of different actions), conscious and unconscious wants (the system of ends), and information about logical analysis, like arithmetic, etc. This information is not valuative.

[76]In Chapter 5 we shall consider the situation under which, at each level of "total output" there exists a consensus about the ordering of the possible distributions of commodities or "real income," rather than merely of money income.

selection of an actual value consensus to represent social choice need not be independent of Arrow's conditions.[77] Choices (assuming our broadened definition of "alternative") which would be widely regretted if more information were forthcoming, do not reflect social welfare no matter how widespread the supporting consensus.

Bergson's schema throws into highlight, then, a third direction in which we may seek to solve the problems of the present work. We may attempt to discover an actual similarity (or solidarity) of attitudes in social groups which will both logically suffice to choose among social states and for which the choices appear to possess some valid claim to reflect welfare.

More concretely, however, it cannot honestly be said that the hypothetical consensus which we have described above is a consensus which we should actually expect to discover in the real world. We have interpreted it as calling for unanimous (or perhaps only nearly unanimous) ordering of different distributions of welfare. These different distributions of welfare are intended to refer to a given total output of the various commodities — a given commodity bundle.[78] For any two such distributions some persons are better off in one, other persons in the other. The agreed-upon evaluation of each pair of distributions evidently can weigh the gains to one group with the losses of the other group. If these interpersonal comparisons of utility[79] (or welfare) are subject to widespread agreement for each total commodity bundle, it is hard to see why *exactly the same kind of interpersonal judgments* is not subject to similar agreement when we compare a distribution representing one total commodity bundle with a distribution representing a different commodity bundle. The assumption of a given commodity bundle actually has no effect on the kind of consensus being hypothesized. To assert that we might expect to find agreement on the evaluation of different relative distributions but not on the evaluation of different absolute distributions is highly artificial. But if we drop this artificial restriction, then we are envisaging unanimous or near unanimous agreement on the ordering of *all* social state alternatives. We should hardly expect to locate any such agreement in modern civilization.

The Bergson schema, in short, is not a practical resolution of our difficulty. But the approach is highly suggestive. We may seek a criterion of social choice for a certain community by attempting to discover there an actual value consensus which seems relevant to welfare.

---

[77]Except that, of course, this selection represents in Arrow's terms the imposition of a set of special restrictions on individual orderings — a violation of Condition 1.

[78]Abstracting, as before, from effects on the level of activity. Such effects make my thesis stronger.

[79]More accurately, interpersonal "evaluations" of utility. The distinction will be elaborated in later chapters.

2-7. Prospect

Arrow's concept of the Social Welfare Function can be interpreted to include the Bergson Economic Welfare Function. In the remainder of our enquiry, therefore, we may proceed in terms of the Social Welfare Function without loss of scope.

In this chapter we have seen that our twin questions as to the construction of consistent Social Welfare Functions and unique social choice among these functions, may be more difficult to resolve as a result of the Possibility Theorem. An apparently reasonable set of value judgments turns out to be incompatible for either purpose. As was outlined in the preceding section, there are certain avenues which may be explored in order to bypass these difficulties. These will be considered in the remainder of the present work. In the next chapter I shall begin by examining the procedures of the New Welfare Economics, with a view toward discovering how the mainstream of welfare analysis resolves the queries set forth in our study. In Parts II, III, and IV I shall explore the implications of imposing certain additional restrictions on individual orderings, with or without relaxation of Arrow's Condition 3. As was noted above, these will have their greatest practical relevance in terms of constructing consistent Social Welfare Functions. But they will not be without import for the problem of choosing among functions. In Part V I shall address myself for the most part to this second problem. After examining a suggestion to relax the nondictatorship condition (Condition 5), I shall develop the outlines of a conception of Social Welfare Function which essentially bypasses Arrow's conclusions and is not without some promise of resolving both queries in a manner consistent with the needs of actual policy recommendations.

APPENDIX

Welfare Comparisons and Changes in Tastes

It has frequently been noted that the "New Welfare Economics" operates on the working assumption that tastes do not change, or alternatively, that if they change, welfare comparisons are meaningless. This assumption has, of course, been given explicit attention in index number theory and in welfare theory proper, but it has not until quite lately received much emphasis in the recent upsurge of interest in welfare economics associated with such names as Arrow, Little, Samuelson, Baumol, and Scitovsky.

Professor Sidney Schoeffler, in an interesting paper whose point of departure, like that of this book, is Arrow's book, examines the whole question of changes in tastes and the ability to make welfare judgments.[1] In addition, he advances two methods by which welfare judgments might be made in a setting in which individual tastes change frequently.

The main purpose of this Appendix is to offer a modification of one of Schoeffler's suggested comparison methods which I think might justifiably increase the frequency of the unambiguous responses it can render.

The framework within which Schoeffler advances his suggestions may be briefly sketched as follows. Consider an individual at two periods of time. At t_0 the social state (the matrix showing the distribution of all goods and services, the political situation, the Social Welfare Function, etc.) is A, at t_1 it is B. If the individual's tastes are unchanged, he can say with consistency both at t_0 and t_1 whether he prefers A to B, B to A, or is indifferent towards both of them. He therefore can say at t_1 whether or not he is better off than at t_0; and his answer will be the same as when he is asked at t_0 where he would be better off (i.e., if B were expected to exist at t_1).

Similarly, every other individual in the community can be conceived of as capable of making the same comparison. On the basis of these individual comparisons, a social comparison can be conceived of which "reflects" these individual comparisons.[2] On the basis of the rule for deriving the social from the individual comparisons, we can say that society at t_1 is better off, worse off, or as well off, as at t_0.

But this last comparison and all the comparisons on which it is based depend on the tastes of the various individuals being unchanged at the two moments in time. If tastes change, then some individual might well say at t_1 that he prefers B to A while at t_0 he might say that he prefers A to B. Which statement is correct? The economist claims to be unable to find out. He characterizes the comparisons as meaningless. Thus, Schoeffler says, "It is meaningless . . . for the reader to ask himself whether he is more or less happy now than he was at four years old."[3] And the social comparisons based on them he similarly characterizes as meaningless.

We may summarize the above into the terminology of Social Welfare Functions: Expressing tastes solely in terms of individual orderings of the alternative social states, the social welfare function is a rule by which we derive a social ordering corresponding to each set of individual orderings.[4] The social ordering is a function of the several individual orderings. Given

---

[1]"Note on Modern Welfare Economics," *American Economic Review* (December, 1952).

[2]Neglecting Arrow's "Possibility Theorem" which states in this context that if the social comparisons are asked to fulfill certain apparently reasonable conditions of correspondence with the individual comparisons, then no method of arriving at such social comparisons exists.

[3]Schoeffler, *op. cit.*, 883.

[4]More complicated functions typically imply cardinal properties of utility. See Chapters 6 through 10.

a particular set of individual orderings, we obtain a particular social ordering, and so long as this particular set of individual orderings remains unchanged, we can compare the welfare of any individual or of the group itself under various actual alternative social states. If any of the individual orderings change, we will have a new set of orderings and can obtain a new social ordering, whereby, so long as the new orderings remain unchanged, we may from this single new vantage point make actual welfare comparisons between alternative social states. But when these orderings change, comparison of the affected individuals' or of the group's welfare under a social state when one set of orderings prevailed with the social state when another set of orderings prevailed, is meaningless. Under the circumstances envisaged by Schoeffler, moreover, any change in the environment changes with it some individual orderings. A given set of orderings will prevail for one social state only, and when this state changes to the one with which it is to be compared, the set of individual orderings will also have changed. So it seems that we are left with no consistent criterion for making *any* actual comparisons.[5]

Professor Schoeffler suggests that, even under the transitoriness of individual orderings, unambiguous welfare conclusions can sometimes be drawn with a slight modification in the definition of welfare change. His proposed treatment resembles Scitovsky's famous double criterion for judging changes in social welfare under alterations affecting income distribution. An individual is to compare social states A and B. Consider his comparison on the ordering which prevailed under both of the social states. Thus, for example, if he preferred A when A existed in fact and also after the change to B, then the change to B decreased his welfare. Similarly, if he preferred B both before and after the change to B, then he benefited from the change. If he preferred A before the change and B after, then Schoeffler defines the change as "welfare-neutral." If he preferred B before the change and A after, then Schoeffler defines the change as "welfare-abortive." These last two concepts mean essentially that only ambiguous conclusions can be drawn.

The crucial aspect of this method seems to me to be that pre-change and post-change orderings are symmetrically weighted in deriving welfare conclusions. This is very likely an unobjectionable device for posing the general case. However, I would suggest that there is an important subset of all cases where individual orderings change when a lack of symmetry might

---

[5]Anticipatory comparisons are, of course, possible, whereby *hypothetically* different social states are compared with the prevailing state. These comparisons, however, are without practical importance for our present purposes since an alternative state conceived of cannot come into existence without changing some individual's ordering and making his original judgment inconsistent.

be appropriate, and might, indeed, enable unambiguous welfare conclusions to be given more frequently than with symmetry.

One of the most important reasons for individual orderings to change is the accumulation of experience with old and new commodities which the consumer gains. Experimentation with familiar goods and services ordinarily enables the consumer better to evaluate how they satisfy him — enables him *more accurately* to order them *in accordance with unchanged underlying propensities.* Similarly, experience with new commodities does not ordinarily signify changes in the personality make-up of the consumer, but it does give him an opportunity not previously possessed to establish a consumption pattern closer to his essentially unchanged criterion of what is desirable.

Professor Schoeffler implicitly recognizes this phenomenon when he points out that "a person's attitude toward goods is determined in large measure by the assortment of goods which is *at present* in the visual field of the individual."[6] Attitudes toward goods are determined largely by one's experience of them — all other aspects of the personality unchanged. Georgescu-Roegen devotes substantially the whole of his admirable article, "The Theory of Choice and the Constancy of Economic Laws," to the implications of this factor for demand theory.[7]

So, in the light of experience with various commodities, a consumer's orderings of social states will change. But because these changes are the results of learning, they are irreversible. Consider the model formulated by Schoeffler. Any action (or policy) which changes the social state will in general bring about also a change in some individual orderings. We desire to draw welfare conclusions about the change from state A to state B. Under state A, individual i's ranking is R'_i, by which he prefers B to A; under B, it is R''_i, by which he prefers A to B. Schoeffler, treating R'_i and R''_i symmetrically, draws the conclusion that the change is "welfare-abortive" (an ambiguous conclusion). Can we *meaningfully* lessen the ambiguity? I suggest so.

If the change from R'_i to R''_i represents the clarification, the learning from experience about different types and combinations of commodities, then:

(1) A change back from state B to state A would not result in a similar change from R''_i to R'_i.

(2) A would have been preferred by the i'th individual over B both after and before the change if he had known more about B before the change; and this is testified to by our expectation that, in the event of a change back to B, he would probably still prefer A thereby enabling us to

---

[6]Schoeffler, *op. cit.*, 882. Italics mine.
[7]*Quarterly Journal of Economics*, Vol. LXIV (February, 1950), 125-138.

render in that event an unambiguous welfare conclusion that welfare is greater at *A* than at *B*.

Can we not, with this illustration in mind, feel justified in dropping the double ordering perspective when changes in orderings reflect trial and error approximations to an unchanged underlying predispositional scale? Our procedure, where justifiable, would be simply to evaluate the given change in terms of what Schoeffler calls the *ex post* ordering alone (R''_i in our illustration), and would thereby enable us to draw unambiguous welfare conclusions.

Two related problems present themselves. First, how can one empirically tell when a particular change in some individual's orderings fulfills the characteristics described here? To be sure, no ordering change is due solely to clarification. All education changes the individual in some way. But modern psychology promises an ability in the not too distant future to limn empirically the major orientation patterns of an individual, and consequently to enable us to trace significant changes in these patterns. Certainly, it can not be expected that even in this near future we shall be able to separate out different kinds of changes in orderings with more than rough proximateness. But this may well provide a tolerable margin in actual empirical applications. It cannot be honestly contended that there is a much greater degree of correspondence between our present demand theory and the real world.

For our immediate purposes, however, is the psychologists' suggestion that basic personality patterns do exist, and that they remain relatively stable through substantial portions of a person's adult lifetime. If we can accept for economic analysis the notion that the changes in orderings meriting multiple perspective weights are only those changes which reflect significant personality reorientations, then we can realistically assume "tastes" (as these basic orientations) to be constant for a much wider range of economic problems than has heretofore been possible.

The second issue raised is allied to the first, and is very important. Why *should* economists identify tastes only as these basic orientations? Granted, where actually erroneous expectations account for some orderings, changes which reflect only a correction of such errors (let us call them "correctional changes") may appropriately be treated as approximations toward equilibrium within a stochastic conception of consumer behavior. There are, however, other changes in orderings which neither substantially represent trial and error revisions ("correctional changes") nor changes in basic personality orientations ("personality changes"). These represent moderately different ways of looking at various — even familiar — commodities; and they would seem to be exactly what economists have always referred to by the concept of "changes in tastes." Economists *have not*, in the past, restricted the concept solely to "personality changes." What justification is there now for such a restriction? If there is no justification, and one attempts actually to apply the schema presented here, then is it possible empirically to differentiate between corrective changes, which we would not want to consider changes in tastes, and those intermediate changes, which we would want to consider changes in tastes? Finally, if we cannot in fact make this distinction but would nevertheless like to use the schema analytically, then would not this practically involve dispensing with the concept of consumer equilibrium, since what would then be considered "equilibrating" changes might actually continue indefinitely without any apparent tendency to converge?

I cannot give definitive answers to these questions. But I should like to suggest what kind of answer seems appropriate at this time.

(1) There is justification in restricting the concept "changes in tastes" to "personality changes" (and thus, identifying "tastes" with basic personality orientation). This justification consists in the desirability of subsuming much of the intermediate class of ordering changes under the "corrective" category. We speak of changes in tastes representing analytic discontinuities because they supposedly represent evaluative discontinuities for the individuals concerned. But the consumer typically does not feel such discontinuities when only minor ordering changes occur. He acts with most of them as though he had "learned better." This strongly resembles the characteristic of corrective changes. Evaluative discontinuity takes place when there is a significant change in perspective — when the consumer has experienced the change in basic personality orientation to which I have referred above as "personality change." In a real sense, then, all nonpersonality changes can usually be lumped together and simply treated as partaking more or less of the character of equilibrating adjustments in the light of experience. For concrete applications, where it may be desirable to exclude ordering changes which partake "too little" of the character of "corrections," an arbitrary cut-off point can be established to suit the nature of the particular problems at hand.

(2) If the procedure outlined in paragraph (1) should prove unacceptable, and it be desirable that "intermediate" changes be included as changes in tastes, then the concrete cut-off point mentioned above, where the change partakes "too little" of the character of correction (interpreted now more narrowly than above), assumes great analytic importance. Since the degree of "littleness" here is probably a continuum, the cut-off point will be arbitrary. But within this limitation, it seems reasonable to expect that at least a rough classification is possible by observation of consumer behavior. Interviewing studies, for example, would seem an appropriate tool for throwing light on this, since how the consumer describes his ordering change is evidence as to what kind of change it is. Reversibility or irreversibility of the ordering changes might be suggested as a useful

index for classifying. Whatever the empirical means used, however, no substantial difficulties in principle suggest themselves why it should not be possible to come observationally close to any specified domain of the concept of correctional change — so long as that very domain can be operationally defined. The burden, indeed, would seem to be on the critic to say exactly what he means by the "intermediate" category.

(3) Assuming that we do lump correctional with "intermediate" ordering changes, whether deliberately [as paragraph (1) argues], or inadvertently [as might occur if the argument of paragraph (2) were groundless], what becomes of the concept of equilibrium? A number of economists even now are convinced that application of consumer demand theory to real world statistical observations requires interpreting the theory stochastically. A stochastic model postulates randomly distributed deviations from equilibrium over time, to reflect the trial and error behavior of consumers in seeking equilibrium. Thus, according to this view, already current, the equilibrating process is not thought of as one of instantaneous adjustment but rather as one requiring perhaps considerable duration. It is by no means self-evident that by including "intermediate" changes as part of the random component we should be appreciably increasing the duration of the adjustment path, and thereby watering down the equilibrium concept.

It might be argued, in fact, that the proposed treatment of ordering changes strengthens rather than weakens the equilibrium concept. When "intermediate" changes are treated as changes in tastes, their supposed frequency means that before a consumer ever reaches one equilibrium he is imposing on himself the need to begin adjusting to a new one. Without the "feedback" of successfully realized equilibria to serve as incentive and guide for the consumer, the very meaning of adjustment becomes suspect, and, in any case, prediction becomes hazardous for the economist in a system where initial conditions change more rapidly than full adjustment to old conditions can be attained. If conservation of the equilibrium concept be a legitimate methodological criterion — and of course it may not be — then lumping "intermediate" with purely correctional ordering changes would seem to possess this saving grace in at least as great a measure as existing stochastic theory.

To summarize the argument, I have, in effect, advanced a new definition of "tastes," under which it would be appropriate to draw unequivocal welfare conclusions, even under those situations defined by Schoeffler as involving "changes in tastes." Some empirical and methodological implications of the new definition have been briefly explored. It is hoped that the seemingly important analytic advantages sketched here will merit deeper examination of this approach by others.

Part II

ORDINAL ANALYSIS

CHAPTER 3

The Compensation Principle:

The Payment of Compensation

3-1. Introduction

The compensation principle has been much discussed in welfare economics. Its ostensive aim is to help make possible welfare comparisons between alternative social states. Are the comparisons which can be made under the compensation principle sufficient to construct a social ordering of alternatives? If a social ordering can be constructed, will it be subject to Arrow's Possibility Theorem? Can the compensation principle serve as the foundation for a useful welfare analysis? The conclusion of this chapter is that the compensation principle cannot appreciably aid in the construction of a useful Social Welfare Function.

The compensation principle really subsumes under it two different kinds of analysis. The form in which it was first advanced, and in which it is still held, with modifications, by supporters of the principle, is one in which the *possibility* of "adequate compensation" is determining.[1] The form in which it has been interpreted by a number of its critics is one

---

[1] In addition to the works of Kaldor, Hicks, and Reder cited in Chapter 1, I might mention the work by E. J. Mishan, "The Principle of Compensation Reconsidered," *The Journal of Political Economy*, Vol. LX, No. 4 (August, 1952); and that by M. J. Bailey, "The Interpretation and Application of the Compensation Principle," *The Economic Journal*, Vol. LXIV, No. 253 (March, 1954).

in which not the possibility but the actuality alone of "adequate compensation" is determining.[2]

In its early formulation by Kaldor and Hicks, the principle was employed to broaden the range of situations in which welfare comparisons could be made despite the restrictive assumptions of the New Welfare Economics. Most restrictive of all, of course, was the assumption that interpersonal comparisons of utility were inadmissible. Conclusions of the New Welfare Economics were to be based on the fewest possible controversial value judgments; they were to be, insofar as possible, value-free. Interpersonal comparisons of utility were not deemed to possess a positive content; they were felt, rather, to reflect value judgments about different distributions of real income and, as such, merit no place in "scientific" economic analysis.[3]

As a result of this assumption, welfare comparison between two social state alternatives was impossible if some individuals in the group preferred (i.e., would be better off in) one state while other individuals preferred the other state. If such mixed responses existed, then there was no "objective" way to compare the welfare improvement that would be experienced by one group in changing from one state to the other, with the welfare deterioration that would be experienced by the other group in making the change. Allowable comparisons could be made only if there were no opposite responses. Hence, the following Paretian definition of economic welfare change was employed:[4]

(1) Alternative *A* has a higher group welfare than alternative *B* if and only if every member of the group is at least as well off, and if at least one person is better off, in *A* than in *B*. The opposite is true for *B* having a higher group welfare than *A*.

(2) Alternative *A* has the same group welfare as alternative *B* if and only if every member of the group is as well off in *A* as in *B* and as well off in *B* as in *A*.

It will be noted that comparison between alternatives calling forth mixed responses is not defined. Such alternatives are, in effect, simply declared not comparable. Since we certainly expect that such pairs of alternatives exist (and, indeed, comprise probably the bulk of all pairs in

---

[2]See the discussion of the compensation principle in Baumol, "Community Indifference"; Samuelson, *Foundations of Economic Analysis*, especially 249-252; Arrow, *Social Choice and Individual Values*, Chapter IV; Tibor Scitovsky, "A Note on Welfare Propositions in Economics," *Review of Economic Studies*, Vol. 9 (November, 1941), 77-88; I.M.D. Little, *A Critique of Welfare Economics* (Oxford: Oxford University Press, 1949).

[3]Lionel Robbins, *The Nature and Significance of Economic Science*.

[4]Hicks, "Foundations of Welfare Economics"; Lange, "The Foundations of Welfare Economics," *Econometrica*, Vol. 10, No. 3 (July-October, 1942), 215-228.

the real world), this procedure is tantamount to permitting only a partial social ordering of alternatives.

The compensation principle in its original form was expressly designed to give meaning to comparison between members of such pairs — and thereby to permit a complete ordering of alternatives — by specifying a procedure that could transform the given mixed situation into case 1 or 2. Thus, as is familiar, given alternatives *A* and *B* and the, for simplicity, two-person group, with individual 1 better off under *A* and individual 2 better off under *B*, we can make *B* comparable to *A* by generating a new situation *C* out of, say, *A* which *can* be compared to *B* under case 1 or 2. The transformation is accomplished by lump-sum redistributions of commodities between the members of the group.[5] Any situation derivable from another by lump-sum redistributions is apparently assumed to have the same potential welfare level, since the real income of the community seemingly depends on the bundle of real goods produced rather than on any one distribution of it.

If now, *C* is such that everyone would be at least as well off as in *B*, while some are better off than in *B*, then *C* has a higher welfare level than *B*, and consequently, *A* has a higher welfare level than *B*, since *A* has the same commodity bundle. Summarizing the procedure, *A* has a higher welfare level than *B* if it *would be possible* to generate a new situation by lump-sum redistributions of the goods and services in *A* such that no one is worse off in the new situation while some are better off, than in *B*.

Two features of this procedure deserve notice. First, the equivalence of *A* and *C* upon which the demonstration rests implies, strictly speaking, either: (1) that a given commodity bundle has the same group welfare level, no matter what the distribution of welfare; or (2) that group welfare is a function of two independent variables — "level of production" and "distribution of welfare" — and the compensation procedure concerns itself solely with the effect on group welfare of changes in the "level of production" alone.

The first interpretation implies, of course, that the distribution of welfare has no effect on the group welfare level. This conclusion is not seriously held by economists today. It is the second interpretation which is accepted. However, while most economists believe that distribution "matters," many feel it is not for the economist to claim that his tools make possible an "objective" measurement of the effect of distribution on welfare.

The problem is not that the distribution of welfare cannot be measured. It can be measured suitably for the purpose. Although a cardinal nomenclature is not to be expected, ordinal mappings are in principle possible,

---

[5]*Lump-sum* distributions are wanted so as presumably to leave economic incentives unaffected.

such that each distribution is a point in m-dimensional space, each dimension representing values of an arbitrary monotone index of one individual's utility (or welfare) level. A particular form of this is Samuelson's utility possibility locus.

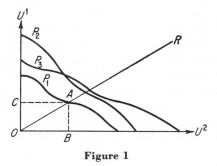

Figure 1

Figure 1 illustrates some utility possibility curves for the simple case of two individuals. Points along each curve, P_1, P_2, P_3, reflect lump-sum redistributions of a given particular commodity bundle, a different bundle involved for each curve. The redistributions are characterized as follows: any point A on some P_1 is determined as the highest possible value of U^1 which can be obtained by redistributing the commodity bundle pertinent to P_1 between individuals 1 and 2, so that the index of welfare for individual 2 is OB. Given the relevant commodity bundle, a level of OB is attainable by a number of different possible redistributions. OC is the highest utility index for individual 1 which is attainable from any of that number. The procedure is symmetrical for the individuals involved: thus OB is also the highest value of U^2 attainable with given commodity bundle and given U^1. All points on the various utility possibility curves are similarly determined. It might be pointed out that each curve is simply the transformation of a contract curve (with given total quantities of the several commodities) onto a different plane.

In this diagram, I noted that each point was a separate welfare distribution. It might be thought that although each absolute distribution of welfare must be represented by a single point, the same relative distribution will be revealed in a number of points — such that, for example, differences in the welfare level of one individual are accompanied by proportional differences in the same direction in the welfare levels of the other individuals (like the line OR in Figure 1). This is not so. In order to be valid, we would have to be able to define relative distribution of welfare. This we cannot do because we have no unique cardinal indices of individual welfare. The U^1, U^2, ... U^m dimensions measure only arbitrary monotonic indices of individual welfare. Monotonicity is not restriction enough to make invariant the quotient between the index values for any two individuals over all the allowable transformations of their respective indices.[6]

---

[6]What would be required to keep the quotient invariant (this quotient, after all, is the factor of proportionality) is individual utility indices unique up to proportional transformations — only the unit of measurement being arbitrary — in other words, ratio scales. (cont.)

Not only can distribution of welfare be measured, in the sense above, but different absolute distributions can be ordered by any individual. If it is assumed that each individual orders welfare distributions on the basis only of what he himself receives, then the U^i values of his own utility index alone represent this order. Similarly, whatever external relations in consumption are introduced — including where individual "values," rather than merely "tastes," are consulted — the U^i values attached to points in the space comprise the individual ordering of distributions.

The problem, then, is neither measurement *per se*, nor the possibility of individual ordering. It is rather, the possibility of obtaining a *social* ordering of welfare distributions. Contrast the social ordering of production with that of welfare distribution. "Production" changes involve similar or at least neutral changes on the part of the group. It is not hard for economists adopting individualist assumptions (and minimizing the importance of external consumption relations) to hold that the members of the group would choose between the alternatives unanimously. In contrast, such comparisons between different welfare distributions of the same commodity bundle, i.e., socially choosing the best point on a generalized utility possibility locus, would not involve unanimous choice between alternatives, any one of which is better for some individuals and worse for others. So, for these latter situations, due to the interdiction against the economist making interpersonal comparisons of utility, there is no way for him to compare the advantages to some individuals of changing from A to B with the disadvantages to others. He can apparently compare "production levels" "objectively," since the group tells him unanimously its choice; he can apparently not compare welfare distributions "objectively," since the group responds heterogeneously, and he has no indubitable additional resources to tell him how to reconcile this heterogeneity.

The second characteristic of this formulation to notice is that compensation does not actually have to be paid in order to achieve an improvement. It is enough to establish the desirability of an alteration in the social state that adequate compensation *could* be paid.

This has important consequences. Let us say that it is discovered that altering the social state from A to B will result in a situation in which those who benefit from the change could compensate those who suffer from the change so that no one would be worse off than in A, and at least one person would be better off. Can we conclude that if the change is made but the "adequate" compensation, although possible, is not actually performed, the community will be in fact better off? A number of critics, including Baumol, Little, Samuelson and Arrow, have sharply answered no.[7] Altera-

---

The argument given here is the same as that of Arrow, "Little's Critique of Welfare Economics," *American Economic Review*, Vol. XLI, No. 5, 928.

[7] See the bibliography mentioned in footnote 2 of this chapter.

tions which would improve welfare *if* accompanied by compensation need not lead to improvement if compensation is omitted. A simplified example will help to elucidate this familiar conclusion.

Assume that the alteration being considered is the introduction of a new invention. If it is introduced, it will enable the innovating firm to cut production costs appreciably and undersell its competitors. The resulting social state *B* will find the single immensely wealthy stockholder of the innovating firm with a small percentage increase in money income, and a large number of significantly poorer persons — displaced workers, bankrupt competitors, etc. — with large percentage decreases in money income. If the beneficiary of the innovation were to make gifts to the sufferers with the increase in his money income,[8] he might have enough, due to the increased productivity brought about by the innovation, to succeed in raising all those in question to at least their previous income level while retaining some increase for himself.[9] In this case, we would conclude that the welfare of the community was greater at *B* than in its previous state. But if no such gifts were made, would we still be willing to conclude that a welfare improvement had taken place? We might, with greater reason, conclude the opposite.

Under what circumstances would it be possible to draw welfare conclusions in the absence of actual compensation? Only if the computed necessary compensations for different individuals (in whatever form they occur: money, a particular commodity or commodity bundle, etc.) indicated something comparable about their well-being.

Assume an outcome with one gainer and one loser. The gainer could be taxed up to $100 and still remain at least as well off in the new state as formerly (i.e., before the change). The loser would require at least $99 compensation to be as well off as he formerly was. Clearly, adequate compensation could be paid. If paid, the new state would be preferable to the old. If not paid, we might still be willing to declare the new state preferable if we knew that the sacrifice of $100 by the one was a greater sacrifice of welfare than the sacrifice of $99 by the other. For this would indicate that under the change, the gainer gained more welfare than the loser lost; on balance, there had been an increase in the welfare of the group.

Involved here is, of course, the twofold assumption: (1) that for each individual the level of his welfare is a linear function of the level of his income (since equal changes in income must give rise to equal changes

---

[8]Or, what comes to the same thing, if the government were to tax his gains and use the proceeds to make payments to the others.

[9]I am assuming here, for simplification, that individuals are indifferent in choosing between occupations. To relax this assumption in the example here requires that the gifts be sufficient not only to achieve former income levels but also to compensate for having to take less desirable jobs — including, perforce, involuntary unemployment!

in the level of welfare) and (2) that every individual's welfare is the same function of his income level, except for an additive constant.[10]

But even this assumption will not suffice if it is deemed (by the evaluator) that changes in some persons' well-being should be *weighted* more heavily than changes in others'. Thus, the economist might not be willing to conclude that a group welfare increase had taken place in the example just given if the loser were originally much poorer than the gainer — even if the gainer should have gained more individual welfare than the loser lost.

The qualification is, of course, an intrusion of considerations about welfare distributions. It suggests, and at a later stage the suggestion will be deepened, that it may not be desirable, or even possible, to isolate "level of production" from "distribution of welfare" by the procedure given above. But even without this qualification the necessary twofold assumption has been open to criticism. In order that the marginal utility of income for each individual be defined equal, whatever the level of income and whichever the individual, we are restricted to the same linear welfare indicator (except for a zero point) for all individuals in the group. Thus, not only are we forced to postulate individual utility indicators unique up to cardinal measurement, but also a singularly over-simple notion of interpersonal comparisons of utility. On both counts, we may phrase the chief objection as asserting that we just do not possess anything like the information needed to restrict

---

[10]The compensation procedure can be defined for non-money commodities — some single commodity, or some specified combination of commodities (a "commodity bundle"). Such alternate procedures are not interchangeable with that described in the text, and they are less satisfactory than using general purchasing power. In any particular situation, the compensation outcome (whether the sum of gains in compensation units exceeds or falls short of the sum of losses) would depend not only on the distribution of real income gains and losses, as when money is the compensation unit, but also on the distribution of tastes for the particular compensation commodity. The decision could easily differ from that obtained with a money unit. Thus, as an example, say the alteration of social state involves improvement in cheese production. There follows transferring land out of vegetable production and into cheese production, greater cheese output and lower cheese prices, smaller vegetable output and higher prices. Now, if cheese is the commodity in which compensation must be paid, the increased output of cheese may not be sufficient for the cheese lovers adequately to satisfy the vegetable lovers and yet maintain a higher welfare level themselves since the vegetable lovers will require a great deal of compensation in cheese while the extra satisfaction of the cheese lovers comes only insofar as they are able to consume extra cheese. It is quite conceivable that if compensation were rendered in money instead, the outcome would be reversed.

The thesis of this footnote is valid, of course, only for models in which practical difficulties of universal barter are recognized. In models of greater generality, where such difficulties are neglected, every commodity represents general purchasing power. Therefore, a unique compensation result will be forthcoming whatever the commodity in which compensation is paid.

our choice of welfare indicators to those precsribed here. The compensation procedure is, to use Arrow's term, too "arbitrary."[11]

As a result largely of this criticism, the rationale of the compensation principle has been reformulated in two alternative directions.[12] The possibility of adequate compensation (i.e., more dollars of compensation could be paid than needed to be received, positive payments exceed negative payments, hence, a positive algebraic total) now is taken to mean not that welfare is improved by the change but that *it could be* improved. The calculation of total algebraic compensation no longer measures *actual* welfare changes but only *potential* welfare changes. The arbitrary choice of welfare indicators can be abandoned. And if compensation is actually made, then a potential improvement becomes an actual improvement.

One of the diverging positions has retained emphasis on actual welfare increases and decreases. Consequently, the analysis of this position requires that compensation be paid. The other position employs the concept of potential welfare increases and decreases; the analysis of this position is concentrated on calculating whether or not adequate compensation could be paid.

3-2. The Payment of Compensation: A Unanimity Social Welfare Function[13]

The position largely taken by critics of the compensation principle is that only the analysis which deals with actual welfare changes is sensible. Consequently, they declare that compensation must be paid in order that the analytic conclusions be meaningful.

Will the social comparisons generated by this version of the compensation principle enable us to construct a social welfare function which fulfills Arrow's conditions? Let us examine the nature of the decision process involved. It will be remembered that there are two elements in the process:

---

[11]*Social Choice and Individual Values*, 39. In the passage cited, Arrow suggests an alternative compensation procedure whose basis may be somewhat better supported by empirical evidence than the assumption of constant marginal utility of income. In brief, it is that, not the sum of positive and negative absolute dollars of compensation be calculated, but the sum of the positive and negative compensating fractions of income be calculated. For this procedure, the indicativeness of the algebraic total requires that individual utility be a linear function of the logarithm of income. This is, of course, consistent with the Weber-Fechner laws of psycho-physical perception, Bernoulli's concept of moral expectation, etc. Cf. Harold T. Davis, *The Theory of Econometrics* (Bloomington, Indiana: The Principia Press, 1941), Chapter 3, especially 74-75.

[12]Hicks, "The Foundations of Welfare Analysis"; Samuelson, *Foundations of Economic Analysis*, Chapter VIII; Arrow, *Social Choice and Individual Values*, Chapter IV.

[13]The terminology of the distinction I am making, "the payment of compensation," and "the possibility of compensation," is from Arrow, *Social Choice*, 34 and 38.

(1) Definition of the admissible comparisons which can be made,

(2) A rule for converting choice situations for which comparisons are inadmissible into situations for which choice is admissible.

The following are the only admissible comparisons:

(1) State A is socially preferred to state B if every member of the group prefers A to B[14] (and similarly for B preferred to A);

(2) State A is socially preferred to state B if no member prefers B to A while at least one member prefers A to B (and similarly for B preferred to A);

(3) State A is socially indifferent with state B if every member of the group is indifferent between A and B.

Consequently, comparison in a situation in which some members prefer A and some prefer B is not admissible. Such situations, however, can be transformed into those admitting of comparison. The transformation procedure, as will be remembered from the discussion above, is the following:

(1) All distributions of a given commodity bundle among the group represent the same level of production insofar as group welfare is concerned and differ only with respect to the distribution of welfare;

(2) Any one distribution of welfare at a given level of production can be transformed into any other distribution of welfare attainable at the same level of production by means of some combination of positive and negative lump-sum compensations.

The structure of group choices generated from this procedure can be seen by examining the utility possibility diagram below (Figure 2): P_1, P_2, P_3 and P_4 are utility possibility curves, each reflecting a particular commodity bundle (a flow of goods and services within a specific time period). Let us start at distribution A on P_1. A certain alteration will give rise to B. Since individual 1 is better

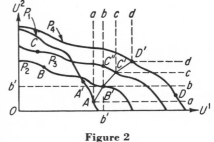

Figure 2

off in A while 2 is better off in B, no comparison between them is admissible. But if a particular compensation were made by 2 to 1, the situation B' would be forthcoming, and B' is preferred to A by both 1 and 2.[15] Hence the change is unanimously supported if compensation is paid — it improves welfare.

---

[14]In my previous terminology this reads: state A possesses a higher level of group welfare if every member of the group has a higher level of individual welfare in A than in B.

[15]In Scitovsky's terms, we could say that the gainer (2) could bribe the loser (1) into "voting" for the change.

Similarly, if we were to reverse the change starting at B', the situation A' would be reached. This can be made comparable with B' by compensation bringing us back within the rectangle $b'b'$ (to perhaps A) where everyone is worse off than at B'.[16]

We may proceed further. The change from B' to C will be advantageous if combined with compensation bringing about C', since C' is unanimously preferred to B'. Moreover, C' is unanimously preferred to A. Likewise, changing C' to D will be advantageous if combined with compensation bringing about D'. D' is unanimously preferred to C', B' and A.

Inspection indicates that the ordering of admissible alternatives is transitive, since every "higher" alternative is to the northeast of all "lower" alternatives. Each possible ordering is a unanimity ordering based on a particular initial distribution of welfare.[17] How well does this ordering serve as a foundation for a useful Social Welfare Function?

(1) The ordering violates Arrow's Condition 1. Take as an example the two-person group where individual 1's ordering of three alternatives is ABC (A preferred to B and C, B preferred to C) and individual 2's ordering is CBA. Both individual orderings are admissible; yet, by the compensation principle, no social ordering can be given: the alternatives are defined as non-comparable. Only a partial ordering, not a complete ordering, can be derived from this unanimity function.

We may technically secure compatibility with Condition 1 by introducing the concept of admissibility of alternatives. Then, only alternatives which are part of admissible sets of alternatives are admissible. And admissible sets are those all members of which, when plotted onto a utility possibility space of (m-dimensions for an m-membered group), are values of a single-valued *vector* function of some scalar parameter alpha, with the elements of the vector $U_1, U_2, \ldots$, each being non-decreasing functions of the parameter alpha, but not necessarily continuous functions. There will, of course, be an infinite number of such sets.[18] (In Figure 2, A, B', C', D' are values of one such function.) No other violation of Condition 1 is involved, since the order achieved in any admissible set is transitive.

(2) Condition 2 is obviously fulfilled; there is a positive association between individual preference and social preference, by the very definition of social welfare change employed. For example, in the terms of Condition 2, we may refer back to Figure 2. Let alternative I be represented as the

---

[16]This reverse change will always be consistent with the original change so long as the utility possibility curves are not upward sloping to the right. This possibility will be examined further in the text below.

[17]See the Appendix for an additional model.

[18]This is somewhat similar to a modification suggested by Arrow for the kind of analysis where only the possibility of compensation is calculated (*Social Choice*, 42). Arrow's suggestion, however, was an attempt to make the procedure fulfill Condition 3 rather than, as here, Condition 1.

situation given by A; alternative II by B'; and alternative III by C'. Then alternative III is socially preferred to alternative II and II preferred to I. Now let II rise in the order of individual 2, with no other ordering change occurring. II can now be represented by C''. C'' is evidently socially preferred to A. So II has not fallen in the social order.

(3) Condition 3 is also fulfilled. The procedure makes no welfare comparisons between alternatives like A and B[19] but only A and B', and the comparison between A and B' is independent of what other alternatives are available and of this ordering. (It will be seen in the next section that where compensation is not actually paid, and comparison of pairs like A and B is admissible, the ordering *is* dependent on other alternatives, e.g., on the position of B' with respect to A.)

(4) Condition 4 is obviously fulfilled by the definition of admissible welfare comparisons.

(5) Condition 5 is fulfilled. No one individual's ordering determines the social ordering regardless of the ordering of others.[20]

3-3. Evaluation

We have seen that, when appropriately interpreted, the unanimity Social Welfare Function constructed on the basis of the compensation principle fulfills Arrow's conditions for an acceptable Social Welfare Function. It is not subject to the Arrow "Possibility Theorem." If it is an acceptable function, is it also a useful function? My own opinion is that it is not. It possesses some important shortcomings. Of the four that I shall discuss, the first is a matter of fundamental principle; the second is a technical weakness; and the rest are practical difficulties.

The first, and most important shortcoming of the compensation analysis is its ability to order only alternatives within a given admissible set.

What is the frame of reference within which we can evaluate the analysis as a whole? Presumably, it may be interpreted primarily as a device by which observers can rate the changing social scene. Or it may be viewed as a tool with which to make recommendations for public policy. Surely the first is inappropriate since very few undisturbed consecutive social states are likely to prove comparable by compensation definition. The distribution of welfare is constantly changing over time; it is this very fact that led to the promulgation of the compensation procedure — an attempt to make a larger range of real alternatives comparable.

---

[19]Of course, the procedure does compare production between A and B.

[20]There is an element of dictatorship in a unanimity social welfare function. The group decision cannot differ from the evaluation of any member of the group. Each individual has an absolute veto over the social ordering. Consequently, although the ordering of any one individual is not sufficient, it is necessary to determine the social order.

It is, or course, the public policy purpose which is envisaged in a schema which gives weight to redistribution of income that could come about only through government action. But then, the analysis must be judged grossly deficient on this ground as well, for it renders only puny help indeed. Given an initial contemporary situation, it specifies from the totality of alternatives a set of worse states, a large set of better states and, perhaps, even a final sub-set of best states. It cannot stipulate from this subset a single best state. But far more important, it cannot assert that there is no state *outside* the ordered sets which is better than any state *within* the ordered sets. So it cannot even recommend that *any* of the alternatives which it has ordered should be chosen. This difficulty would be lessened if the population believed that government action must be restricted to choice from among admissible alternatives. But they clearly do not. Each recognizes that his own well-being is to some extent dependent on the distribution of income. And probably every government action in history has changed in some way or other their distribution among the population. And why should it not be so? Why should government be restricted only to actions which change everybody's well-being in the same (or neutral) direction, when the smallest decision made by a single individual in the market place, however lightly undertaken, can bring about the forbidden redistribution which hurts one person and helps another? If this kind of restriction were in force, government action might have to shift helplessly for every such individual decision.

There is a further irony. Basic both to Arrow's theorem and to the compensation approach is the assumption that existing individual preference scales are sacrosanct data. It is these preferences, however and whenever they might have been formed, and however and whenever they might be changed, that must be consulted. They must not be criticized or by-passed, and public policy must certainly not be deliberately undertaken to bring about changes in them. Yet numerous individuals daily try their utmost in the market to change the preferences of others, and many of them are specialized to do just this. There cannot be a very strong consensual value judgment in our society that current preferences are sacrosanct.

The justification for insisting that asymmetrically stringent restrictions be placed on public policy is not hard to discern. As in the market, the several interests of the population find representation in the political decision-making of a representative democracy. Again as in the market, this representation is not "perfect." Yet government action is considered coercive in a way that is not true of market action (although there is much to the argument that the difference is one of degree only). So it is understandable that there should be a greater felt need to safeguard the under-represented against political exploitation than against market exploitation.

The second defect is a technical property of the analysis. In the formulation above we proceeded on the implicit assumption that each individual's welfare, or, what we treated as the same thing — each individual's preferences[21] — were based only on what he himself consumed. From this assumption we derived downward sloping utility possibility functions (i.e., negative first derivatives). It scarcely needs amplifying that this assumption imposes a significant limitation on the analysis. Much recent literature has stressed the great importance of external economies and diseconomies in consumption.[22] It may well be held that the fundamental issues of welfare economics are meaningless if such relationships are excluded. Not only such relatively direct impact as soot nuisance, "keeping up with the Joneses," etc., but also the perhaps more indirect but very lively interest in alternative income distributions, testify that each individual's ordering of social states is strongly influenced by the distribution of goods and services to others as well as to himself. And, of course, what is especially important for welfare analysis, is that individuals are not always able to express their feelings with regard to others' consumption in their own market behavior.[23]

What is the consequence to the compensation analysis if these external relations are introduced? Each consumer's ordering is now a function of commodities going to everyone else as well as to himself. It will now be possible for the utility possibility function in any of its two-dimensioned projections to be upward sloping for at least part of its length.

In the simplest case of two individuals we may find utility-possibility curves like those of Figure 3. P_1P_1 illustrates a situation in which 1's well-being is a function of his own consumption, while 2 is affected by his own and also by 1's consumption (he has external economies). When 2 receives only a small portion of the given commodity bundle, while 1 gets most of it, their well-being is competitive (hence the

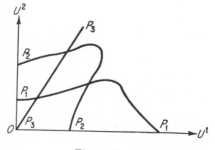

Figure 3

---

[21]Modern psychology, as well as "ancient" religion, testifies to the potential chasm yawning between the two concepts. The distinction is also important in some of the literature of welfare economics. See, e.g., John M. Clark, *Alternative to Serfdom* (New York: Alfred A. Knopf, Inc., 1948), Chapter 2; various of the writings of Frank H. Knight, like *The Ethics of Competition* (London: Allen & Unwin, 1935); *The Economic Order and Religion* (New York: Harper & Brothers, Publishers, 1945); *Freedom and Reform* (New York: Harper & Brothers, Publishers, 1947); *The Economic Organization* (New York: Augustus M. Kelley, 1951).

[22]For example, Duesenberry, *Savings, Income and The Theory of Consumer Behavior;* Arrow, *Social Choice and Individual Values;* W. J. Baumol, *Welfare Economics and The*

downward portion in the right half); but once 2 has received a certain substantial share (the farthest remove on the bulge) any further redistribution in his favor at 1's expense will make *both* 1 and 2 worse off, since part of his satisfaction comes from 1's consumption of certain goods and services.[24] P_2P_2 illustrates a situation in which the well-being of each depends on the consumption of both. This may be thought of as stemming from strong external economies in particular commodities for both (as, for example, the satisfaction derived by each from the use of telephone service), or, even more appropriately, as the influence on their well-being of attitudes about equitable distribution of income. Redistributions in either direction away from the (for simplification) mutually regarded most desirable distribution of income result in diminished welfare for both.[25]

Theory of the State. Duesenberry and Baumol emphasize the effects of others' specific consumption patterns and general standard of living on one's own consumer evaluations; Arrow generalizes these effects by emphasizing not only others' consumption vis-a-vis one's own, but also one's interest in the distribution of goods and services between one "outsider" and another: in short, one's values — equity, etc. — as well as one's tastes.

[23]See the discussion of this in Chapter 2, Section II.

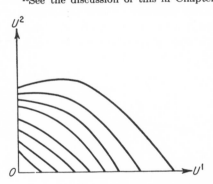

[24]Of course the external economics will typically involve particular kinds of commodities, and they will depend on the absolute standard of living achievable by both as well. Thus, the more realistic illustration is as follows: For small commodity bundles these may be only competitive relations. Only as larger and larger commodity bundles are involved, will the indirect or vicarious pleasures 2 derives from 1's consumption begin to offset his need for direct, personal consumption.

It should be noted that P_1P_1 is a double-valued function of U^2 but a single-valued function of U^1. This is, of course, a reflection of the lack of symmetry in the evaluative functions of the two individuals. Double-valued functions do violence, it is true, to the definition of the functions as indicating, for a given value of one, the maximum achievable value of the other. This is identical with the definitional distortion involved in production-possibility curves possessing rising positions as a result of production complementarity. Cf. Graaff, *op. cit.*, 49, fn. 2.

[25]Here, too, as with P_1P_1, the external economies are typically functions of the size of the relevant commodity bundle. Distributional ethics of the sort viewed here would appear to be most deeply engrained in our kind of economy where the bundle is large; although where uncertainty is great and morale low, an unusually small bundle (e.g. in deep depressions) might also be approached with those attitudes by members of the community, as a kind of insurance against worse loss. "If I favor equitable treatment for the other man when he is harder hit than I, then if it should happen that I become hard hit — and the present circumstances clearly make that now seem possible — I will be taken care of too." Or: "Unless these unfortunates are treated especially well now, when they are so desperate, they may be driven to desperate acts which would topple me to their level."

If the simplifying assumption of both — or, in the general case, all — individuals

P_3P_3 illustrates the extreme case in which (1) both individuals determine their well-being on income distribution grounds alone, or (2) both are exactly agreed as to their ordering of income distributions. It is not hard to suggest that this is a highly unlikely set of circumstances.

In addition to these cases dealing with external economies between two or more individuals, there are cases in which the positive slope arises from external *diseconomies*, but only when there are at least three individuals! One such type is reported by Graaff.[26] Consider a three-person economy with one generalized commodity, "riches." Individual 1's well-being is independent of 2 and 3 and vice versa; 2's and 3's well-being are dependent on one another's consumption as well as on their own. The dependency is that of external diseconomy, when 2, for example, obtains more riches, 3's well-being diminishes. Now, the partial derivative of 2's (or 3's) utility with respect to 1 - 3's (or 2's) utility held constant, will be positive (i.e., the slope in the 1 - 2 plane will be upwards) since when a small amount of riches is redistributed from 1 to 2, 1 is worse off. And to prevent 3 from being worse off as a result of 2's increase, a further redistribution from 2 to 3 is necessary. It is clearly possible that 2 will end up worse off than before the first redistribution because (1) he will have left only slightly more than originally or perhaps even less, and (2) 3 is now better off. So the well-being of 1 and 2, and of 1 and 3 may move in the same direction.

The implication of these external relations for the Compensation Principle is to blur the significance of the value judgments on which it is based. Take the following example: $P_1 P_1$ and P_2P_2 are two utility-possibility curves. (See Figure 4.) A (on P_1P_1) is the initial situation. We are considering an alteration whereby we will move to B. We may, by means of compensations, reach B'. Then, by the Compensation Principle, we are

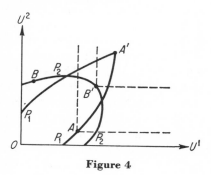

Figure 4

better off under the change and the redistribution. Is this consistent? Starting from B' let us undo the alteration. Conceivably we may not return to P_1P_1 but now to a new distribution A'. B' is better than A but worse than A'. Thus, the alteration with compensation is better than no

---

agreeing on the most desirable income distribution be dropped, then in the typical case of each considering the most desirable distribution where he gets more than in the other's (or others') ideal distribution, the effect will be to flatten the rising portions of the curve. When these ideals are significantly dispersed, the rising portions tend to disappear entirely.

[26]de V. Graaff, *op. cit.*, 49, fn. 2.

alteration without redistribution but worse than no alteration with redistribution.

Clearly the example shows, if anything, that there should be a redistribution from A to A'. But where does the Compensation Principle assert that it may draw inferences about income distributions? Certainly it seems valid, in the example just given, because the participants expressed themselves unanimously about the alternative distributions. But if we admit that attitudes about income distribution are determinants of individual utility functions and introduce such functions into an analysis which ostensibly can separate distribution from production, then how do we know when our analytic conclusions include or exclude distributional considerations? If our analysis includes them, as in such circumstances (i.e., external consumption relations) I think it must, and in an essentially hidden way, then what is the justification for the explicit definitional exclusion of other distributional considerations such as led to our formulation of admissible sets of alternatives?

It might be objected that in the example of Figure 4 the market mechanism itself would have brought about the redistribution from A to A' — that A could never have been an equilibrium position; so that additional planned redistribution contravening the market mechanism would not even have had to be considered. In such a case, my argument above would be weakened. The objection is certainly correct if both these conditions hold: (1) that there are no restrictions on the freedom to deal on the market, and (2) that there are only two individuals comprising the economy.

Violation of the first condition might obviously prevent attainment of an equilibrium position. The second condition, fulfillment of which makes the objection of no force in the real world, is explained as follows. In a two-person economy, A cannot be an equilibrium because 1 and 2 know that they can both be made better off by a redistribution of goods between them *and* that a single exchange transaction will suffice to achieve this improvement (thus, if the redistribution involves more of a certain commodity for 2, less for 1, this can be accomplished simply by 1 *giving* 2 the pertinent goods). However, in a three-person economy, assume that in the state currently prevailing, all can be made better off together but only by individuals 1 and 2 decreasing their consumption for the benefit of individual 3. At the same time, there are external *dis*economies in the relationship between 1 and 2 (i.e. in the prevailing state). In this situation, neither 1 nor 2 will singly donate to 3's consumption unless each knows that the other will too. But neither can be sure that the other will follow suit, since each benefits by the other's relative disadvantage. To achieve the required redistribution would require an advance voluntary agreement between 1 and 2 or some institutionalized agency whereby the full scope of the action would be enforced upon all and, because presumably understood, complied with by all. This latter is, of course, a welfare schematization of the function of the state.[27]

The failure of automatic market adjustment toward this kind of equilibrium is grossly increased as the number of members in the community increases, since, besides the purely strategic problems, the very knowledge about these mutual interrelationships which is necessary to achieve optimal behavior (i.e., optimal distributions) becomes more and more difficult to come by in the growing complexity of the system. In the real world, it is certainly conceivable that states analogous to A should be market outcomes.

A third shortcoming of this version of the Compensation Principle is the difficulty of calculating the required compensations. One method would be to discover the actual individual preference scales of the population. This would have to be done with a high degree of accuracy, because even moderate individual errors, if systematic, can cumulate to substantial errors on the community-wide level. The investigators would certainly have to know something about the kinds of errors which are likely to be made, and their probable direction and magnitude. Moreover, the whole confusing problem of changes in the structure of individual preference scales over time would have to be faced and solved.[28] Lastly, to serve any useful purpose whatsoever, this entire task must not command a disproportionate amount of manpower.

It would certainly appear that these requirements cannot be met — perhaps not one of them can — on the strength of the current level of econometric achievement.

An alternative method would be to bypass the need for discovering entire preference scales, and concentrate only on obtaining estimates of necessary compensation. Two sorts of procedures come to mind. One would be analogous to certain contemporary personality projective tests in psychology or to procedures used in psychological scaling of attitudes. The other would be a formalization of a procedure whereby the members of the community made declaration of what compensation they required (positive or negative). Both types, but especially the latter, would be subject to significant motivational distortion. Moreover, the problem of insuring consistency of response is a major one. And the requirements for the necessary degree of accuracy, even when the two procedures are combined,[29] would seem to exceed current experimental prowess in psychology.

---

[27]Cf. Baumol, *Welfare Economics and The Theory of the State* (Cambridge: Harvard University Press, 1952), especially Chapter 11. It is also an explanation of the point made above, that consumers' external preferences cannot always be expressed on the market.

[28]See the Appendix to Chapter 2.

[29]Combination would possess real methodological advantage.

A third method would be to forsake the attempt to determine individual compensation and estimate instead the average probable compensation (positive or negative) for individuals in different selected categories such as income, size of family, region of residence, occupation, etc. Since individual compensation depends in principle on individual, or realistically, on family, tastes (or values), and since these individual preferences are not abstractable into the few status categories that would be involved without an unknown error, this method would give only very rough aid for the purpose at hand. Essentially, this same procedure has been advocated by Little to aid in formulating public policy. Yet Little would employ this method to throw light on income distributions as well.[30] Indeed, it is surely academic to insist that such crude measurement of what is claimed to be objectively measurable, namely, level of production, is qualitatively more objective than rough judgments about the consensus ordering of income distributions. If necessary compensations be measured in this fashion, the whole "scientific" restraint of the Compensation Principle would seem to be beside the point.

A fourth difficulty with this version of the Compensation Principle is that, since compensation must actually be paid, an administrative means must be found to make bounties and levy taxes which can actually achieve redistribution to any point of a given possibility locus. Samuelson has thrown doubt on the belief that this is unproblematical.[31]

First, he notes that peculiar characteristics of individual indifference maps may result in an equilibrium which is unstable so that changes in the disposable income of these individuals by means of taxes or subsidies will bring about movements away from the desired optimum position (i.e., the position aimed at by the compensation procedures).

Second, the lump-sum collections and payments are meant to affect individual activities only insofar as they affect disposable incomes, and each individual is expected to readjust to his new situation by unrestricted trading on the market at prevailing fixed prices. But in an economy where price discrimination (such as all-or-none offers, sliding scales, etc.) is pervasive, "lump-sum allowances may not suffice to reach the optimum point."[32] It may parenthetically be pointed out that in the real world where oligopolistic markets are important, the demand readjustments resulting from compensation may have unpredicted consequences.[33]

---

[30]*Critique of Welfare Economics*, Chapter 4; Arrow, "Little's Critique of Welfare Economics."

[31]*Foundations of Economic Analysis*, 247-249.

[32]Samuelson, *loc. cit.*

[33]It should be noted that Samuelson's objections are formulated for the context of an economy which has fulfilled all the optimum conditions of production and exchange, so that everyone is on a generalized contract locus derived from the *various* points of the production frontier, i.e., on the production possibility function. Compensation procedures are designed in his treatment to reach the single preferred income distribution

Last, and most important, it may not be practical to construct a lump-sum compensation procedure.[34] If the techniques for calculating the necessary individual compensation (positive or negative) be precise and accurate, then payments to or collections from individuals can be overtly tied to circumstances of the social state alteration — discrete, unique, historical circumstances; and, so long as measures like secrecy about the detailed principles of calculation (and as to how much so-and-so pays or receives) prevent motivational distortions in the present or future proceedings, other incentives need not be affected. But if, as is likely, these techniques are imperfect, then the taxes and bounties will not be associated solely with past, non-repeated, non-predictable circumstances, and the element of current adjustment to a new manipulable situation will enter, thus affecting marginal judgments. Such effects on incentives (for work, for consumption of particular commodities, etc.) mean that the process of redistribution of a given commodity bundle will itself bring about a new commodity bundle, so that we move onto a different utility-possibility function. This possibility is especially likely if lump-sum redistributions are required frequently.

---

on this particular utility possibility locus (derived not from a single commodity point but for the entire transformation function). Our treatment, however, is concerned at this point with movements along a utility possibility locus which reflects contract curve redistributions of *any single* commodity bundle. Only optimum exchange conditions are assumed fulfilled — so that we are on *some* contract locus — since this is required by the very definition of the utility possibility function.

In Samuelson's economy, the optimum is assumed to have been achieved in spite of, or with the aid of, the indifference map curvatures and price discrimination of the first two objections. It is doubtful, however, whether pervasive oligopoly structures under private control are compatible with the optimum as employed by Samuelson.

[34]My formulation of this objection differs from Samuelson's because of the difference in purpose envisaged for the redistribution. See last note.

CHAPTER 4

The Compensation Principle:

The Possibility of Compensation

4-1. The Possibility of Compensation

As was noted above, there are really two versions of the Compensation Principle. We have discussed the first, under which actual welfare changes are its analytic grist. In this second, it is the concept of potential welfare change which is central. As initially conceived by Kaldor and Hicks, a potential increase in welfare would occur in the situation where, as a result of some new element operating in the economy (e.g., a change in public policy, an innovation, etc.), social state A is changed into B, B differing from A in that some individuals are better off and some worse off, and by the gainers paying the losers compensation a new situation B' could be achieved such that no one is worse off than in A, while at least someone is better off. Unlike the previous version, where our comparison would be simply between A and B' (i.e., welfare improvement due to the change *plus* compensation), our comparison here is between A and B. B is said to be "potentially better" than A because it would take only a lump-sum redistribution of the goods and services in B (i.e., a movement along the same utility-possibility curve) to bring about an actual welfare improvement.

As we noted above, the analysis here is quite sharply distinguishing between the commodity bundles at A and B and the distribution of income at A and B. Commodity bundles can be ordered; relative income distributions can not. Calling B "potentially better" than A, therefore, is asserting that (1) B has a "bigger" commodity bundle than A — a higher level of production; and (2) there is a method whereby we can, but need not, change the welfare distribution of B's commodity bundle without in any other way affecting the bundle so that the higher production at B can be shown to be capable of giving rise to an actual increase in welfare. Whereas our previous version of the Compensation Principle compared absolute distributions in particular, we are here in effect comparing commodity bundles — levels of production. We are really saying that a particular *change* is good or bad, since it is the change that alters its commodity bundle and this, regardless of the welfare distribution which results.[1]

It must be understood that the need to assure oneself that adequate compensation is possible does not stem from belief that the welfare distribution at B may be inferior to that at A and must be improved in order that the welfare change be unambiguous. This notion is a more recent one and leads to further modifications. (I shall examine two attempts along these lines in the next chapter.) The possibility of compensation is important only because no objective meaning is given to judgments about actual welfare changes when, in the sense used here, the relative distributions are different. Compensation guarantees that the two situations can be made comparable, and, if made comparable, that situation possessing the higher level of production would manifest its superiority.

Given this definition of potential welfare change, the totality of alterna-

---

[1]Insofar as the change is accompanied by actual compensation, the change increases actual welfare, so the final state is actually better — preferred — to the initial state. Where compensation is not paid, the final state does not improve actual welfare but only potential welfare: it is not "preferred" to the initial state, in the sense of our correspondence between actual welfare changes and "preference". Thus, the preference counterparts of potential welfare changes do not really apply to the terms of our social welfare functions or to Arrow's Conditions. On the other hand, these terms *can* be applied to alternative *policies* applied to an initial condition. If we are willing to assert that, of any two policies, the one which leads to the higher potential welfare is always preferred, then choices among policies will conform to our discussion of social choice. We shall indicate below why we believe such an assertion should not be made; but assuming for the present that the assertion is warranted, we may note that, strictly speaking, the social welfare function formulated by its use violates Arrow's Condition 3. The Compensation Principle operates by aggregating the money (or commodity) equivalents of individual welfare changes between an initial and a final state. These are indicative, not only of the fact that each individual prefers one state to the other, but also of the degree of difference in well-being between the two — i.e., of preference intensities. Thus, we can imagine two situations which have identical sets of individual partial orderings of the initial and final states. Everyone who prefers the former to the latter in the first situation prefers it in the second, and vice versa. Yet it is clearly possible that overcompensation can be paid in the first but not in the second. The social orderings will differ then in the two situations, yet the individual orderings are the same. (I am indebted to M. J. Bailey for this point.) We do not consider this as sufficient to disqualify the potential welfare approach, since we shall argue in Chapter 6 that the exclusion of preference intensity from social choice via Condition 3 is not especially reasonable. We argue that Condition 3 can be modified to admit preference intensities while still excluding true irrelevancies.

tives can be ordered with respect to it. Thus, the statement, B is potentially better than A, C is potentially better than B, etc., means that the gainers in C could more than compensate the losers by shifting from either A or B, that gainers could compensate losers in shifting from A, etc. This involves an enormous advantage over the compensation version discussed in the last section.[2]

But are these orderings consistent? It was Scitovsky who first pointed out that they are not, even for comparison between two alternatives.[3] Thus, take the example of A, B, and B'. B is potentially better than A because those who gained as a result of the change from A to B could more than compensate those who lost as a result of the change. But now if we start at B, possessing a different distribution of welfare, we may find that undoing the original change will also be potentially better. Those who gain by undoing the change can more than compensate those who lose. In other words, a particular change is good, but undoing the change is also good.

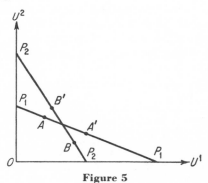

Figure 5

Formally, this state of affairs can be illustrated by means of utility-possibility curves. See Figure 5. P_1P_1 and P_2P_2 are utility-possibility curves which intersect between A and A' (or between B and B'). Let A represent the initial state. Now the alteration brings about situation B. But a redistribution of the goods at B could be undertaken that would give rise to B', which is better than A. So B is potentially better than A. Now, starting at B,[4] the undoing of the alteration will result in A again. But there is a redistribution of the goods and services at A that would give rise to A', which is better than B. So A is potentially better than B.

Why does this inconsistency arise?

E. J. Mishan, in an interesting article,[5] makes clear the source of the incongruity. Briefly, it stems from utilizing different income distributions in the states serving as frame of reference for the welfare comparisons. As a

---

[2]Let us call that the "payment" version in contrast with the present "possibility" version.

[3]"A Note on Welfare Propositions in Economics," *Review of Economic Studies*, Vol. 9 (November, 1941), 77-88.

[4]B is the hypothetical terminal state after the alteration, since the redistribution to B' does not have to be performed.

[5]"The Principle of Compensation Reconsidered," *Journal of Political Economy*, Vol. LX, No. 4 (August, 1952), 312-322.

simple example of the effect of the initial income distribution on welfare conclusions, consider the following extension of the cheese-vegetable example presented above. The output of cheese is increased, that of vegetables decreased. In order that the new situation be potentially better than the old, the cheese lover must be able to compensate the vegetable lover. Much depends, of course, on the quantitative details of the output change in relation to the exact structure of the preference maps of the two individuals, but a great deal of the answer is given by the initial distribution of increase between the two individuals. Thus, if the cheese lover is very wealthy relative to the vegetable lover, the amount of money which he would be willing to give up without becoming worse off than before the change would in all likelihood be substantial (low marginal utility of income), whereas because every dollar possesses far more significance for the vegetable lover, only a small amount of money would suffice to compensate him for the loss of vegetable output. In such a situation, the probability that adequate compensation could be paid is high. However, let the vegetable lover be rich and the cheese lover poor. The vegetable lover will now require many dollars of compensation, while the cheese lover's gain now signifies for him an equivalence of far fewer dollars. In this situation, there is a much lower probability that adequate compensation could be paid. Thus, different initial income distributions can result in different welfare conclusions, all other aspects of the situations being identical.

In a more complex way in the real world,[6] this kind of influence is at the base of Scitovsky's inconsistency. In Figure 5 the possibility of adequate compensation, when changing from A to B, depended on the referential welfare distribution at A, whereas the possibility of adequate compensation, when changing back from B to A, depended on the different referential distribution at B. In a real sense, the respective welfare judgments are not comparable, for when the real income distributions are different, a different portion of the preference maps of the various members of the community is involved. In effect, the social judgments are derived from "different" populations.

Scitovsky's suggestion, of course, was that only in the absence of inconsistency could one assert that a welfare change had occurred. His double test was simply to examine the possibility of compensation in both directions. At the pre-change distribution could the prospective gainers bribe the prospective losers into supporting the change? At the post-change distribution could the prospective losers bribe the prospective gainers into opposing the change? If the answers are "yes" and "no" respectively, the change will bring about a potential increase in welfare; if "no" and "yes,"

---

[6]The common equilibrium marginal rates of substitution between each pair of commodities, on which the possibility of compensation depends, differ at different points on the generalized contract locus.

the change will bring about a decrease. If "yes" and "yes," or "no" and "no," Scitovsky proposes that pre-change and post-change states be declared indifferent.[7]

Scitovsky's procedure is satisfactory so long as alternative welfare distributions cannot meaningfully be ordered within the same framework as that of production levels. But the emphasis in investigations employing the concept of the Social Welfare Function[8] and in the book by Little,[9] on judgments about alternative welfare distributions themselves, means that, in principle, the analytic structure of welfare economics must henceforth organize choice in terms of both variables. Since our typical choosing concern has heretofore been on whether or not to make alterations that would change commodity bundles,[10] only the income distributions pertinent to this calculation have been introduced (e.g., in Figure 5, those prevailing at A, A', B and B'). So only contradictions arising from this small sub-set of the totality of possible distributions have needed to be considered. But if now, other distributions along a utility possibility curve can be considered for desirable redistribution apart from changes in commodity bundles, then the very conception of what is being compared when a commodity-change alteration *is* involved, must be broadened accordingly. Referring again to Figure 5, the question that the relation "potential welfare change" puts to us is: How does the entire set of possible contract curve redistributions in P_1P_1 compare with that in P_2P_2? We must compare utility-possibility curves as a whole. In slightly different terminology, potential welfare change asks us to compare one prospect matrix with another.

Accepting this broadened conception, it is easy to see why Scitovsky's test is inadequate. Consider Figure 6. Since P_1P_1 and P_2P_2 do not intersect between A and A' (or B and B') the alteration which transforms A into

---

[7]Actually, the last two possibilities are essentially different. The former involves the inconsistency in question while the latter need not. If "no" and "no" reflect a situation in which at the initial distribution the prospective losers could bribe the prospective gainers and at the terminal distribution the gainers could bribe the losers, then the inconsistency applies. But if the situation is one where neither gainer nor loser could bribe the other at either distribution, then no inconsistency is involved. This latter might be called a case of "true" potential indifference, in contrast to the indifference category which signifies only non-comparability. Arrow has noted a suggestion by Scitovsky that this would be the state of affairs if the two alternative states were both general equilibrium optima in the Pareto sense: "Little's Critique," 929, fn. 15.

[8]Bergson, "A Reformulation of Certain Aspects of Welfare Economics," *Quarterly Journal of Economics* (1939); "Socialist Economics," *A Survey of Contemporary Economics;* and Lange, "Foundations of Welfare Economics."

[9]Little, *op. cit.*

[10]Redistributions in terms of money incomes will change commodity bundles since they change demand conditions throughout the economy, thereby giving rise to a new output pattern equilibrium; but redistributions in goods and services out of a given commodity bundle will not result in a changed commodity bundle unless the redistribution itself has an influence on tastes.

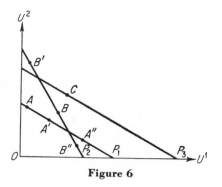

B would be judged potentially advantageous. But if distributions of welfare closer to *A″* and *B″* were considered socially desirable, the alteration would have resulted in a welfare deterioration. There is no unambiguous potential welfare increase between P_1P_1 and P_2P_2. Similarly, neither is there between P_2P_2 and P_3P_3 (since they intersect). But a movement from P_1P_1 to P_3P_3 does involve an unambiguous potential

Figure 6

welfare increase, because for *every* initial and terminal distribution of welfare gainers could reimburse losers, and not conversely.[11]

How may we derive a true social ordering of alternatives by means of the relation "potential welfare change"? It is quickly seen that such an ordering will not be possible unless we make a further modification.

Referring back to Figure 6, let us consider the social ordering of the "prospect-matrices" indicated therein, namely, P_1P_1, P_2P_2 and P_3P_3. P_1P_1 and P_2P_2 intersect; consequently, by the Scitovsky usage, they are socially indifferent. Similarly, P_2P_2 and P_3P_3 intersect; they are indifferent. If our procedure gave rise to a true (transitive) ordering, we could assert that P_1P_1 and P_3P_3 were indifferent. But we know by inspection that P_3P_3 represents a welfare improvement over P_1P_1. This contradiction comes about by defining intersecting functions as indifferent. It would seem clearly wiser to treat intersecting functions as non-comparable.

Adoption of this rule enables derivation of the following true ordering of "prospect-matrices."[12] Of any two non-intersecting utility-possibility loci (they may coincide for part of their range), that locus for which at least part extends to the northeast of the other represents the greater potential social welfare. This ordering has a very strong resemblance to the unanimity Social Welfare Function of the last section. Indeed, it reflects a double-unanimity restriction. From the vantage point of *every distribution* attainable in either prospect-matrix (a given commodity bundle), *every person* is as well off (or better off) in the one prospect-matrix than in the other.

We may now enquire under what circumstances utility-possibility loci will intersect and under what circumstances they will fail to intersect. Our description of the source of the Scitovsky paradox revealed that when the alteration in social states was such that the output of one commodity or of a group of commodities increased while that of another commodity or group

---

[11]See Chap. 5.1 for a discussion of Little's procedure.
[12]The rule is generalizable to *m*-individual groups.

of commodities decreased, the possibility that gainers could compensate losers depended on the distribution of income. As we might expect, this paradox will not arise when only one commodity is involved, or, when all commodities either increase or decrease together (although not necessarily in any fixed proportion).

If there is only one commodity, and the alteration is such that output of this commodity increases, then the level of production in the final state B is unambiguously greater than in initial state A. Every level of welfare for, say, individual 1, will represent a particular quantity of the total output of our single commodity. In state B, every time we give him a certain quantity — so that he reaches a certain utility level — we have a larger quantity left to give to individual 2 than we had in state A. So 2 can achieve a higher utility level than in state A for every level reached by individual 1. For every welfare distribution the utility-possibility locus on which B is situated is higher than the locus on which A is located.

If there is more than one commodity, and all increase or decrease, then, again representing the initial state by A (Figure 6), let us construct the new utility-possibility locus. We can enable either individual to reach a particular level of utility in the new situation by giving him the same combination of commodities as previously. But now we have more of all commodities remaining to give to the other individual. This is true for every level of one individual's utility. So for all welfare distributions, both (or all, in the general case) persons can be made better off. Here too we have an unambiguous increase in production and potential social welfare.

If there is more than one commodity and some commodities increase while others decrease, then there is in general no unambiguous production increase and no unambiguous potential welfare change. Let us again reconsider our cheese-vegetable example. In state A let the commodity bundle consist of five units of cheese and five of vegetables. In state B let the bundle consist of eight units of cheese and two of vegetables. Now assume that individual 1 is a cheese lover and individual 2 a vegetable lover. Table 2 describes, in order of 1's decreasing utility level, four pairs of commodity distributions to 1 and 2 which result in the same utility level for 1 in one prospect-matrix as in the other.

TABLE 2

| | Output in A | | | | Output in B | | | |
| | 1 | | 2 | | 1 | | 2 | |
Utility level of 1	Ch.	V	Ch.	V	Ch.	V	Ch.	V
4	5	4	0	1	8	0	0	2
3	4	5	1	0	7	1	1	1
2	0	2	5	3	0	2	8	0
1	1	1	4	4	1	1	7	1

In each instance, the B-bundle combination which enables 1 to achieve the same level of utility as with the A bundle is assumed to have been chosen so as to maximize the attainable utility level for 2.

Now compare the utility levels attainable by 2 with the two bundles for given levels attained by 1. Corresponding to 1's utility levels 4 and 3, individual 2 is clearly better off with B-bundle. Corresponding to 1's utility level 2, individual 2 has gained three units of cheese but lost three units of vegetables. Since he is a vegetable lover, we may assume that his marginal rate of substitution of cheese for vegetables is greater than 1; he requires more than 1 extra unit of cheese to compensate for the loss of 1 unit of vegetables. Consequently, he is worse off with the B bundle than with the A bundle. Corresponding to 1's utility level 1, 2 again has had to give up vegetables for cheese in the ratio of one to one, and thus (since this is close to eight cheese, zero vegetables) is worse off with the B-bundle than with the A-bundle.

To summarize, at some distributions, the utility-possibility locus passing through A is higher than that passing through B; at other distributions it is lower.[13] The intersection is a consequence of a heterogeneous change in the commodity bundle and a diversity of tastes among the population. In the absence of different tastes, the first factor alone would not suffice to bring about intersection. Whatever the change in output, the utility-possibility locus would be symmetrical, so if any member of the population gained where another member continues to obtain a given utility level, the second will similarly gain at the mirror image of that distribution where the first individual obtains the given utility level.

The fact is, in the general case, that when there are different tastes in the population, a heterogeneous change in the commodity bundle affects the different members of the community unequally. The weighting of these individuals in the making of the social choice (in the sense of their willingness to compensate or their need to receive compensation will differ for different distributions of welfare. Thus, in the example given here, for those distributionswhere the gainer is "rich," he is more than able to compensate the loser; for those distributions where he is "poor," he is unable to make adequate compensation to the loser.

It is, of course, possible to conceive of situations in which different tastes and a heterogeneous output change are present, but the relevant loci fail to intersect. One such situation could be constructed where the output of cheese increased appreciably while that of vegetables decreased only

---

[13]My example really described only portions of the locus of U^2 as a single-valued function of U^1. This will be identical with the locus of U^1 as a single-valued function of U^2 where there are no strong external relations in consumption. My demonstration is incomplete where the locus has an upward slope; but the argument of this part will still hold.

very slightly, *and* the vegetable lovers had only a slight preference for vegetables as against cheese. But these situations are, in a real sense, fabricated; they require just the right combination of a specific output change with a specifically restricted set of preference maps. Their exceptionality does not call for a serious attempt at working them into general necessary and sufficient conditions for unambiguous potential welfare changes. We typically proceed in our welfare analyses making no restrictions at all about the relevant indifference maps (other than convexity). We mean our analyses to hold for all kinds of maps. Since any heterogeneous output change can be made to yield intersecting loci by the appropriate specification of indifference maps, the exception noted here is not general enough to qualify theorems of the desired generality.

We may summarize our investigation with the following necessary and sufficient condition for an unambiguous potential welfare change:[14]

---

[14]Alternative necessary and sufficient conditions for the non-intersection of utility-possibility functions may be somewhat more general than the foregoing suggests. It is worth noting one interesting set of specifications based on restrictions on the community's preference maps alone and independent of the particular change in commodity bundles involved. I refer to the argument of W. M. Gorman's "Community Preference Fields," *Econometrica*, Vol. 21, No. 1 (January, 1953), 63-80. The pertinent condition is that the preference scale of each individual be such that all "personal Engel curves are parallel straight lines for *different* individuals at the *same* prices." (p. 63) Thus, whatever the distribution of income and tastes, "an extra unit of purchasing power . . . [will] be spent in the same way no matter to whom it is given." (p. 64) This is a strong restriction. Indeed, Gorman indicates that if we but assume that the admissible indifference system for any one individual starts at the origin (instead of at some minimal "living standard" in the positive orthant), then the condition above requires that all tastes be identical.

We noted in our text above that intersection of utility-possibility functions is due to the differential weighting of different tastes at different income distributions. The rationale of Gorman's treatment, in oversimple terms, would seem to be to make each individual's tastes independent of his income level.

This means that if, with a given distribution of income, a given production-possibility function, and a given set of prices, a particular commodity bundle is purchased (chosen), then, no matter how we radically alter the distribution of income while keeping prices unchanged, the same bundle will be purchased. This will occur because anyone losing purchasing power will curtail his expenditures in the proportions given by the slopes of the income-consumption curves, whereas anyone gaining purchasing power will expand his expenditures in exactly the same proportions, whatever his income level or tastes. Consequently a revealed preference type of procedure for the community as a whole will enable us to derive a unique system of community indifference curves independent of income distribution, or, what is the same thing, a non-intersecting set of utility-possibility curves. Thus, assume that bundle *A* reveals itself to be preferred by the community to bundle *B* for a particular distribution of income. Then the condition above guarantees that *A* will reveal itself to be preferred to *B* for all distributions of income (since the revealed-preference procedure concerns bundles actually purchased by the community).

An additional result of the system is that if we choose for each individual the particular (cardinal) utility indicator mathematically compatible with the analysis, we find that each utility-possibility curve possesses a unique constant summation of individual utilities. Since our paraphrase above suggested that changes in income distribution envisaged transfers of a certain fixed amount of purchasing power (i.e., lump-sum compensations), the utility significance of every dollar must be equal for every individual

(1) Potential welfare increases when the production of all commodities increases;

(2) Potential welfare decreases when the production of all commodities decreases;

(3) Potential welfare changes ambiguously when the production of some goods increases while the production of other goods decreases.

From a practical point of view, this criterion is of great importance because it provides us with the only feasible means of calculating when potential welfare changes do or do not occur. The other obvious method, direct calculation of the possibility of compensation, aside from its computational difficulties, is inappropriate, since in order to insure that the relevant utility-possibility curves never cross, an infinite number of possibilities would have to be computed, each at a different distribution.

In order to facilitate this evaluative task, it will be advantageous to retranslate our analysis into production-possibility (or transformation) diagrams.

Consider Figure 7. An entire "prospect-matrix" becomes a single point expressing the size of the commodity bundle (the axes X and Y measure objective quantities of commodities X and Y respectively; here too we may generalize to more than two commodities algebraically). Thus, prospect B represents a potential welfare increase over prospect A.

So far we have suggested that welfare comparisons under this ver-

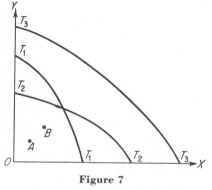

Figure 7

(therefore, this includes constant marginal utility of income, linear utility functions, etc. See the discussion of this in the text above.)

In addition to the notable restriction imposed on individual preference scales, Gorman's formulation contains other difficulties from our point of view. Gorman's proofs employ operations on cardinal interpersonally comparable individual utility indices. These indices are deduced "so as to have the property that their sum defines a collective demand function under his special (purely behavioristic and therefore ordinal) assumptions about consumption." (Personal communication from Kenneth J. Arrow) Thus, cardinal utility functions with particular properties can be inferred from assumptions about market behavior. (We shall find the same phenomenon below when we discuss the expected utility hypothesis in Chapters 9 and 10). The reasonableness of the functions so inferred depends on the reasonableness — accuracy — of the behavioral assumptions. Their apparent artificiality in the present instance makes the utility indices suspect.

Finally, two eccentric implications of the analysis are the exclusion of inferior goods and the fact that if any individual fails to consume some amount of every commodity, the consumption of each neglected commodity by every other member of the community must be independent of the income of each! Only further narrowing modifications succeed in undoing these results.

sion of the Compensation Principle are comparisons between different prospects in the sense of points A and B.[15] But it is mistaken to believe that the prospect adequately summarizes all the possibilities of a given social state. For the community, possessing as it does a given vector of productive resources and a given state of technological knowledge, the commodity bundle which it produces at a certain time is not the only one which can possibly be produced. Consequently, when we are concerned with social state alterations which involve changing the very production possibilities of the economy, we must broaden our notion of what the alternatives of choice are. Each alternative will be the whole set of commodity combinations which the economy can produce with its given resources and technological knowledge — or, bearing in mind our criterion, the frontier of these possibilities, the production-possibility (transformation) function of the economy.

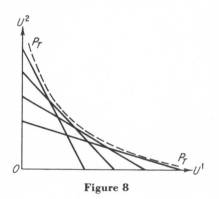

Figure 8

Every transformation function can be translated into a utility-possibility curve, as exemplified in Figure 8. Each point on the transformation curve gives rise to a different utility-possibility curve, each drawn as a solid line. (They all intersect, since no one represents more of all commodities.) The envelope curve (dotted line P_t) touching their northeastern-most reaches is the locus representing the transformation function. It can be interpreted as that locus indicating, for each utility level of one individual, the maximum utility which can be attained for the other person out of all the possible output combinations and their distributions available to the economy. De V. Graaff refers to it as the "Welfare frontier."[16]

When we are faced with choice between two different Welfare frontiers, we must still be aware that decisions about optimum welfare distributions are left open. So the only unambiguous potential welfare changes which can be asserted in this kind of choice situation is, again utilizing our criterion about output bundles, where the frontiers do not intersect; one production transformation function is wholly enclosed by the other (including con-

---

[15]The ordering derivable from this relation is formally analogous to that derivable from the payment version. Here we define admissible sets of prospects in exactly the same manner as we previously defined admissible sets of alternatives. Comparison as to potential welfare is defined only between prospects which are members of the same admissible set.

[16]J. de V. Graaff, *Theoretical Welfare Economics* (Cambridge: Cambridge University Press, 1957), 59-60.

gruent ranges). Thus, in Figure 7, the choice between T_1 and T_2 does not involve an unambiguous potential welfare change; the choice between T_1 and T_3 or T_2 and T_3 does; T_3 is potentially better than either T_1 or T_2.[17]

Having broadened our notions of what welfare comparisons may entail, it behooves us to ensure the accuracy of the criterion which will generate a social ordering. In reconsidering the compensation principle, E. J. Mishan proposes the following theorem: "As between two bundles producible with the given resources of the economy, the one which fulfills the optimum conditions of production and exchange is, by the compensating principle, unambiguously superior to the suboptimal bundle. . . . The principle of efficient resource allocation . . . is never self-contradictory in the sense of intersecting utility-possibility loci." [18]

This theorem, which was first made explicit, as far as I know, by J. de V. Graaff,[19] suggests that it is possible to narrow our ordering beyond that established by the criterion above. We may pick out a single point on the transformation function as potentially better than all the others. Unfortunately, deeper examination discloses that this possibility is illusory.

In the discussion to follow, I shall refer to Mishan's Figures 5 and 6, pages 320 and 322. The first of these enables us to compare the welfare levels of points fulfilling the optimum conditions and those which do not. It represents the juxtaposition of a transformation curve and a set of alternative community indifference curve mappings, as constructed by Mishan. See my Figure

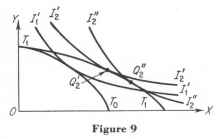

Figure 9

9. Every commodity bundle (i.e., every point in the XY plane) can generate an infinite number of community indifference curve mappings. A different map is generated from the given point for every different original distribution of welfare specified. For each mapping, every indifference curve represents all the different commodity bundles for which everyone is equally well off at some particular welfare distribution. Succeeding indifference curves in a given mapping represent commodity bundles belonging to the same admissible set of bundles; in other words,

---

[17]The entire argument about translating utility-possibility functions into commodity points owes much to Samuelson, "Evaluation of Real National Income," *Oxford Economic Papers* (January, 1950); see also F. M. Bator, "The Simple Analytics of Welfare Maximization," *American Economic Review*, Vol. XLVII, No. 1 (March, 1957), 22-59.

[18]"The Principle of Compensation Reconsidered," *The Journal of Political Economy*, Vol. LX, No. 4 (August, 1952), 321 and 313.

[19]"On Optimum Tariff Structures," *Review of Economic Studies*, Vol. XVII, No. 1 (1949), 47-52.

they are commodity bundle sets such that, specifying an initial distribution achievable with the original bundle, each bundle in a "higher" set enables everybody to obtain a higher (or unchanged) utility level than they can obtain with bundles in "lower" sets.

With Figure 9 we interpret the Mishan theorem as saying that given an initial welfare distribution such that I'_2 is a member of a compatible community indifference map (tangent to the transformation function T_1T_1 at Q'_2), moving away from Q'_2 to any other bundle involves a loss of welfare: Q'_2 gives the highest level possible (the common marginal rates of substitution in consumption equals the common marginal rate of transformation). Given a different initial welfare distribution, such that now I''_2 is a member of a compatible map (tangent to the transformation function at Q''_2) and I'_2 is no longer, then Q''_2 is the best commodity bundle achievable.

As a corollary, considering suboptimal transformation curve T_1T_0 as well as optimal curve T_1T_1:

> . . . for all conceivable community indifference maps, an indifference curve which is tangent to the suboptimal production curve will be below the indifference curve which is tangent to the optimal production curve . . . because any indifference curve which is tangent to the suboptimal production curve must intersect the optimal production curve and we have just shown that any intersecting indifference curve will always have above it an indifference curve, consistent with it, which is tangent to the optimal production possibility curve.[20]

To what kind of social ordering of social state alternatives will this theorem give rise? We can formulate the problem in this way: Can Mishan's analysis enable us to order commodity bundles in such a way that a "higher" bundle generates a utility-possibility curve which is higher than a "lower" bundle for all possible contract curve distributions of welfare? In particular, optimal bundles must generate higher utility possibility loci than suboptimal bundles.

I suggest that Mishan's analysis cannot fulfill this requirement. The crux of the difficulty seems to be:

(1) Social ordering requires comparisons between specific alternative commodity bundles;

(2) Unambiguous potential welfare changes require uniform comparisons for all conceivable contract curve distributions of welfare;

(3) No specific single commodity bundle fulfills the optimum conditions of production and exchange for *all* relevant welfare distributions.

To illustrate, let us compare Q'_2 with Q''_2 in Figure 9. Given one initial welfare distribution, Q'_2 will fulfill the optimum conditions (it will represent the point of tangency between an indifference map consistent with the particular welfare distribution and the community's transformation curve)

---

[20]Mishan, *op. cit.*, 321–322.

but Q''_2 will not. So, for this distribution, Q'_2 gives rise to greater welfare than does Q''_2. However, for a particular different initial welfare distribution Q''_2 will be the optimum situation while Q'_2 now will not. Hence, for this second distribution, Q''_2 is better than Q'_2. Evidently their utility-possibility curves intersect, and there is no unambiguous potential welfare change between them.

Now, for appropriate initial welfare distributions, many other points in the transformation curve can fulfill the optimum conditions. Indeed, as Mishan's article lucidly explains, the optimum conditions can be fulfilled for every point along the transformation curve whose marginal rate of transformation equals the common marginal rate of substitution of consumers at some contract curve distribution of welfare. One should expect that in the typical case a large number of production possibilities could theoretically be optimal. So for these, Mishan's theorem gives us no aid in establishing a social ordering.

But the instances which remain unresolved are even more widespread than the preceding would indicate. For Mishan's theorem cannot even tell us that a bundle on the transformation curve is always superior to one inside it. Thus, consider Figure 10.

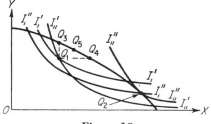

Figure 10

We desire to compare Q_1 with Q_2 (which is on the transformation curve). It is certainly conceivable that there should be an initial welfare distribution such that the indifference map generated from Q_1 includes I'_i and I''_i. By this mapping Q_1 reflects a higher welfare than Q_2. Consequently, Q_2 does not reflect a higher welfare than Q_1 for *all* welfare distributions. So the utility-possibility curves intersect, and a movement from Q_1 to Q_2 does *not* involve an unambiguous potential welfare improvement. (Parenthetically, it may be remarked that if Q_2 were the optimal bundle this would indicate that the relevant welfare distribution must be such as could not generate an indifference map by which Q_1 is better than Q_2. The appropriate map in this case would include the curves I'_i and I''_i — by which Q_2 is better than Q_1.)

In Figure 10, the only bundles on the transformation curve which are known to be unambiguously better than Q_1 (without further information from the pertinent generalized contract locus) are those between Q_3 and Q_4, such as Q_5. But this comes not from Mishan's theorem but from our own criterion. Moreover, this characteristic is not even the peculiar property of bundles on the transformation curve, since all bundles within the $Q_1Q_3Q_4$ sector are similarly unambiguously better than Q_1.

Mishan's analysis is not, thereby, incorrect in the context of his own purposes. But his purposes are somewhat different from our own. It is rather important that we understand the difference. Mishan can be interpreted as saying, not that one *social state* is unambiguously better than another at every conceivable distribution of both, but that one *social policy* is unambiguously better than another at every conceivable initial distribution. Start with any arbitrary initial distribution of a commodity bundle that exists when the economy diverges from Pareto optimality. Now consider the policy of securing the marginal equivalences of Pareto optimization. Compare the new state achieved with the original one. By lump-sum compensation the new state can be made to dominate the old, but the old state cannot by lump-sum compensation be made to dominate the new. The new policy, in this sense, unambiguously increases potential welfare. The same judgment holds for every conceivable initial distribution of the commodities in the original state. For each, the optimum state achieved by the new policy will be different, as indicated above, but by lump-sum compensation can be made to dominate the initial state (but not vice versa). Under these circumstances it is surely reasonable to consider the new policy an improvement.[21]

Such an orientation is not wrong. Indeed, since we are interested in ordering alternative social states for the purpose of ordering alternative social policies it seems at first sight the truly apposite approach. There are, however, reasons for rejecting this in favor of our present approach.

First, in each pair of policies we compared, one represented the policy that would achieve the conditions necessary for a general (Pareto) optimum. The argument was that any point on the welfare frontier could, by lump-sum transfers, dominate any point off the frontier. How easy is it to formulate a policy which will carry the community from some initial suboptimal position to a position on the frontier? Not easy at all. Any contemporary situation is likely to diverge from the frontier and for a variety of reasons. More than one condition necessary for the general optimum is likely to be violated at any time.[22] A policy designed to correct this must be highly complex. It must, of course, be based on highly accurate knowledge of exactly where the optimum conditions are violated.

___

[21]The same position is taken in M. J. Bailey, "The Interpretation and Application of the Compensation Principle," *The Economic Journal*, Vol. LXIV, No. 253 (March, 1954), 39-52. Bailey makes more explicit than Mishan that it is alternative *policies* that are to be compared, and that the movement toward the Pareto optimum occurs whatever the starting distribution and does not entail Scitovsky-type inconsistencies. However, he does not treat so explicitly as Mishan comparisons between different commodity bundle outcomes of alternative policies, placing primary analytic focus on different distributions of the same commodity bundle.

[22]For a detailed demonstration of these two assertions, see Pigou, *The Economics of Welfare;* Little, *A Critique of Welfare Economics*, Chapters 8 through 10; and de V. Graaff, *Theoretical Welfare Economics*, Chapters 2 through 4, and 6 through 8.

One cannot assume, for example, that this would in fact be a pristine optimal world if simply one organization, say government, just stopped interfering with the natural course of things. Divergence from optimality stems from many sources. Furthermore, knowledge about the exact nature of the divergence is enormously hard to come by. The exact effect of particular taxes on incentives, the effect of various types of oligopolistic market patterns on prices-outputs-qualities of commodities, the extent of the "coercion" of worker's preferences about leisure versus commodities entailed in the pervasive existence of standard work-weeks — all these and others affect the nature of the divergence of some actual state from the welfare frontier, and all are questions to which positive economic theory gives no confident answer.

The problem is even more difficult than this would suggest. The violations of the optimal conditions listed above, and those typically listed by Little and by most writers in the field of public finance, anti-trust policy, etc., involve relationships which have their full force in market transactions. But there is another type of violation that, like an iceberg, shows only to a small degree, if at all, in the market. This involves the existence of external economies and diseconomies in both production and consumption.[23] When a consumer consumes a commodity, his consumption sometimes affects, favorably or adversely, the well-being of other consumers in ways not connected to the effect of his purchase in relative prices or relative supplies. When a producer produces a commodity, his action sometimes affects the ability of other producers to produce their commodities or affects the well-being of consumers in ways other than through the effects of his purchases and sales on relative supplies. Market prices as allocative signals do not reflect these external effects, so that the market is led to allocate resources without taking into account welfare-influencing factors. Here, then, is an area where we do *not* expect the market to work optimally if everyone does nothing but turn his back nor interfere. Exactly the contrary is true. Explicit extra-market action is required. But action calls for knowledge of where these external effects are important. Such knowledge is extremely difficult to come by, short of crude rule-of-thumb estimates, and in addition, consumption externalities modify the optimum conditions so as to call for interpersonal comparisons of utility, which is anathema to the approach we are considering.[24]

---

[23]On this, see especially Pigou, *op. cit.*, Part 2, Chapters 9 and 10; Baumol, *Welfare Economics and the Theory of the State;* de V. Graaff, *op. cit.,*; and The Committee on Public Finance, *Public Finance*, Chapter 2: "The Role of Government in a Market Economy," by Nelson McClung, Jerome Rothenberg, and Angel Rugina (New York: Pitman Publishing Corp., 1959).

[24]In the absence of external effects, a brief paraphrase of the first-order conditions for the General Optimum is:

(1) For all consumers of any two commodities including negative commodities:

i.e., providing productive services, the marginal rate of substitution between them must be equal:

$$\frac{\partial u^\alpha/\partial x_i{}^\alpha}{\partial u^\alpha/\partial x_j{}^\alpha} = \frac{\partial u^\beta/\partial x_i{}^\beta}{\partial u^\beta/\partial x_j{}^\beta}$$

for all individuals α, β, and all commodity pairs i, j (where superscripts denote individuals and subscripts denote commodities).

(2) For all producers of any two commodities, the marginal rate of production transformation between them must be equal:

$$\frac{\partial t^\alpha/\partial x_i{}^\alpha}{\partial t^\alpha/\partial x_j{}^\alpha} = \frac{\partial t^\beta/\partial x_i{}^\beta}{\partial t^\beta/\partial x_j{}^\beta}$$

for all firms α, β, ..., and all commodities i, j, ... (where $\partial t^\alpha/\partial x_i$ is the marginal cost of X_i for firm α).

(3) For any two commodities the common marginal rate of substitution must equal the common marginal rate of transformation:

$$\frac{\partial T/\partial X_i}{\partial T/\partial X_j} = \frac{\partial u^1/\partial x^1{}_i}{\partial u^1/\partial x^1{}_j} = \frac{\partial u^2/\partial x_i{}^2}{\partial u^2/\partial x_j{}^2} = \cdots \frac{\partial u^n/\partial x_i{}^n}{\partial u^n/\partial x_j{}^n}$$

for all commodities i, j, ... and all individuals $1, 2, \ldots n$ (where $\dfrac{\partial T/\partial X_i}{\partial T/\partial X_j}$ = the common marginal rate of transformation between i and j, as in (2) above).

None of these equations requires making interpersonal comparisons of utility.

When external effects are present the above conditions are modified to the following:

(1)′

$$\frac{\partial W/\partial x_i{}^\alpha}{\partial W/\partial x_j{}^\alpha} = \frac{\partial W/\partial x_i{}^\beta}{\partial W/\partial x_j{}^\beta} = \cdots \quad \text{for all consumers } \alpha, \beta, \ldots$$

Since α's consumption of X_i, X_j have welfare effects on other consumers (some favorable, some unfavorable), the net effect in social welfare must somehow be calculated. This can only be done via an explicit social welfare function $W = W(U^1, U^2, \ldots U^n)$. But such a net effect requires comparing — indeed aggregating! — these several effects to different individuals, thereby entailing interpersonal comparisons of utility. This condition states that the ratio of total welfare effects — the marginal *social* rate of substitution (equal to the marginal private rate when no external effects exist, but in general not equivalent here) — between two commodities be equal for all individuals consuming them both.

(2)′

$$\frac{\partial T/\partial X_i}{\partial T/\partial X_j} = \frac{\dfrac{\partial t^\alpha}{\partial x_i{}^\alpha} + \sum_{\theta \neq \alpha} \dfrac{\lambda^\theta}{\lambda^\alpha} \dfrac{\partial t^\theta}{\partial x_i{}^\alpha}}{\dfrac{\partial t^\alpha}{\partial x_j{}^\alpha} + \sum_{\theta \neq \alpha} \dfrac{\lambda^\theta}{\lambda^\alpha} \dfrac{\partial t^\theta}{\partial x_j{}^\alpha}} = \frac{\dfrac{\partial t^\beta}{\partial x_i{}^\beta} + \sum_{\theta \neq \beta} \dfrac{\lambda^\theta}{\lambda^\beta} \dfrac{\partial t^\theta}{\partial x_i{}^\beta}}{\dfrac{\partial t^\beta}{\partial x_j{}^\beta} + \sum_{\theta \neq \beta} \dfrac{\lambda^\theta}{\lambda^\beta} \dfrac{\partial t^\theta}{\partial x_j{}^\beta}}$$

for all firms α, β, θ, ...

Each summation term expresses the effect that one firm's production of a particular commodity has on the production (or costs) of all other firms. Since these can be summated in physical (value) terms, no resort is needed to an explicit welfare function. Of course, the system really includes external effects on consumers as well, e.g., the familiar smoke nuisance (menace?). In general, therefore, we would have to include terms like in (1)′, thus again necessitating interpersonal utility comparisons. Each fraction in (2)′ represents the marginal *social* rate of transformation (when external effects are present, not necessarily equal to marginal private rates).

(3)′ Equality between (1)′ and (2)′ for any two commodities.

It should be clear that $\partial W/\partial X_i{}^\alpha$ or $\sum_{\theta \neq \alpha} \dfrac{\lambda^\theta}{\lambda^\alpha} \dfrac{\partial t^\theta}{\partial x_i{}^\alpha}$, not being directly reflected in market transactions, necessitate exceedingly complicated calculations, some of which, indeed, are ruled out in the present approach. (See de V. Graaff, *op. cit.*, Appendices to Chapters 2 through 4; also Little, Chapters 8 through 9; plus a large literature on the New Welfare Economics. For an additional source on external effects see G. Tintner, "A Note on Welfare Economics," *Econometrica*, Vol. XIV (1946), 69-78.

The moral of this first point is that we are neither likely, in practice, to be located at the welfare frontier nor to be confronted with policies which are accurately designed to take us there. So the analysis which tells us that the optimum is better than the suboptimum is not often relevant unless it can also tell us which of any two suboptimal positions is preferable.

We are most often likely to be comparing policies which lead to suboptimal states. Can traditional analysis help? Bailey, in the article cited, argues that it can. He offers as example that we can not only unambiguously judge between excise tax and head tax but also between excise tax at higher rate and excise tax at lower rate. His conclusion is, in effect, that the greater the distortion of the free market (i.e., the nature of the divergence from optimality in Bailey's example) the greater the welfare loss.[24] There may be policy pairs for which it is possible to determine which policy represents the greater divergence from optimality. But this is apt to be rare. We have already remarked that any realistic contemporary situation is likely to diverge from optimality in many respects — more than one optimum condition will be violated, and in complicated ways. In such a situation, adoption of a policy which improves conformity with any one of the violated conditions, e.g., by decreasing monopoly in one industry, or even secures complete fulfillment of such a condition, will not necessarily increase social welfare (defined in terms of vector dominance). In the previous set of violations, some violations may have tended to offset others. If one of these is abolished, the net divergence of the remaining set may increase. By this type of analysis, the only way to guarantee formally that there will, in fact, be an improvement in welfare is to move toward fulfilling all conditions simultaneously.

This conclusion suggests that only if we compare policies which differ from one another monotonically in all violations of optimality will we be likely to obtain unambiguous evaluations. If the policies differ non-monotonically, i.e., one does not decrease every divergence from optimality more than the other, then one will be likely to be better for one initial distribution, the other better for a different distribution. Their utility-possibility curves will intersect. Monotonicity in this sense is an extremely stringent requirement. For example, all policy pairs, in which at least one member deals with fewer than the total number of deviation directions, fail to satisfy it. Except in the rare case where the excise tax in question is the only violation of the optimum conditions, even Bailey's example, where one policy abolishes a particular violation while the other preserves it, fails to satisfy monotonicity. When there are many conditions violated, rectifying any one of these violations does not necessarily improve welfare.[25] So here

---

[24]Bailey, *op. cit.*, 45-47.
[25]Samuelson, *Foundations of Economic Analysis.*

again we suggest that unambiguous judgments can be obtained in only a very small number of instances. Of course, if the successful instances represent choices among the best alternatives, it is immaterial whether or not comparisons between uninteresting policy pairs can be unambiguously resolved. In terms of our critique, however, it is likely that the not overly restricted class of alternatives selected for judgment in the final rounds will represent rectifications in a variety of directions and hence will probably pair up non-monotonically with one another. Only pairs composed of these final contestants pitted against very poor policies are likely to be monotonic. Such guidance is not very helpful.

There is a third limitation of the present approach. Up to now we, and the literature we have considered, have acted as though the welfare frontier were a given, and different policies simply "landed" farther away from or nearer to it. The position and shape of the frontier depends upon consumer tastes, the state of technology and the amounts and qualities of available resources. In point of fact, a sizeable proportion of public policies actually adopted or seriously considered affect, indeed, were deliberately fashioned to affect, the frontier. Policies are designed to develop or improve resources and technical methods, to spread information; success in these directions sometimes, predictably, changes tastes as well. To insist that these dynamic elements be excluded from a critique of welfare theory is to insist that a crucial aspect of the usefulness of the field be repudiated a priori. We prefer to allow that policies often have such dynamic effects.

If we compare two policies which cause changes in the welfare frontier, or even where only one has such effects, we will typically be unable to make unambiguous judgments. Assume for the moment that we could reach whatever frontier is brought about. Even a comparison of respective optima on different frontiers will be ambiguous because few policy-induced changes in the frontier make one frontier entirely contained in the other. The frontiers will intersect: For some initial distributions policy A gives the better frontier equilibrium, for other distributions B gives the better.[26] The situation is even less hopeful where the respective frontiers are unlikely to be reached by policy. All the complexities cited in our previous argument hold, and in addition is the necessity to compare degree of deviations from different and possibly intersecting frontiers. Restrictions on pairs of alternatives for which useful comparisons could be made would be onerous.

Finally, if we waive all these objections, so that we can assume that our

---

[26]As an example, a government subsidy to develop new coffee-producing resources is likely to be ranked higher than one to promote growth in walnuts if most of the community's income is in the hands of coffee-lovers; the reverse will be true if most of the income is in the hands of walnut-lovers. Notice that such policies are obviously biased in favor of some individuals at the expense of others. This is true in varying degree for many public policies.

most relevant choices will be between policies that promote or sustain divergences from the optimum and policies that bring us to the optimum, we are still not without problems. Our whole discussion is in the context of hypothetical, but not actual compensation. Thus, for any given initial distribution the two policies in any pair will give rise to states, neither of which dominates the other (of course, actual compensation could transform the state on the frontier to a dominating one). Although the New Welfare Economics deems it in principle unscientific to formulate "objective" or widely accepted criteria for comparing different distributions, our discussion of values versus tastes argues that individuals nonetheless feel that their well-being depends upon the configuration of commodities to the whole population; they evaluate alternative social states in terms of what goes to others as well as what comes to themselves. Suppose that we are comparing the suboptimal consequence (S_A) of "non-optimal" policy A with the optimal consequence (S_B) of "optimal" policy B at some given initial distribution. It does not violate any of Arrow's conditions or the assumptions of the New Welfare Economics that S_A should be unanimously preferred to S_B. Thus, by Arrow's Conditions 2' and 4, as well as by the Paretian definition, S_A will be socially preferred to S_B. So policy B could not be "better" than policy A at every distribution. Indeed, by stretching the improbable but by no means impossible, the consequence of S_A might be preferred unanimously to the corresponding consequence of S_B at every initial distribution. Policy B will be "worse" than policy A.

We need not consider such rarities alone. Suppose that there exists in fact a Social Welfare Function that we would be willing to call acceptable.[27] Our acceptance would not be inconsistent with the New Welfare Economics, since the latter can be interpreted as being willing to make some of the same value judgments as comprise welfare function, but not all. Then it would not be at all rare to discover that, in terms of this welfare function, the consequence of "non-optimal" policy A would be socially preferred to the corresponding consequence of "optimal" policy B for some initial distributions, the reverse preference holding at other distributions. Only for special welfare functions or for special pairs of optimal–non-optimal policies would we obtain unambiguous judgment in favor of the optimal policy.

In sum, if distributional considerations are important to the population but welfare evaluations are going to be made explicitly excluding them, then, at the least, such evaluations beg the question of how relevant is the welfare criterion "level of production."[28] At the worst, if an acceptable Social Welfare Function exists which compares social states by going

---

[27]Our argument in later chapters will attempt to persuade the reader that an acceptable function need not — in fact, ought not to — satisfy all of Arrow's conditions, the most promising candidates for violation being Conditions 1 and 3.

[28]We shall have more to say about this below.

beyond the Paretian value assumption, the evaluations of the present form of the Compensation Principle may be falsified.[29]

To conclude this critique, if we attempt to employ general equilibrium analysis by interpreting the alternatives of choice directly as public policies, we are likely to find that the analytic apparatus will give unambiguous, consistent judgments in only a very limited number of cases. The requirement that the comparison between policies be uni-directional for all starting points is highly restrictive. It suggests that the simpler procedure would be to try to compare individual social states instead of policies. This has been the approach we have been following. It is·true that we find this approach extremely limiting as well. But the criticisms we have made of the policy comparison approach do point in the direction of comparing social state pairs. It is instructive therefore, to follow such a path and examine the limitations of that approach.

We may proceed, then, under the assumption that the justified social ordering is generated from the criterion we derived above. Does this ordering fulfill Arrow's conditions? At bottom, our procedure is a unanimity Social Welfare Function, since "admissible" transformation curve comparisons are defined in terms of "admissible" commodity bundle comparisons, which in turn are defined as a set of unanimity comparisons for points on different utility-possibility curves. The parallel discussion of the unanimity Social Welfare Function generated by the payment version may be essentially repeated here.

By appropriately defining admissible alternatives[30] we obtain transitive orderings fulfilling Condition 1. The derivation of these alternatives from utility-possibility curves fulfills Condition 2. Since our alternatives are not single social states as in the original Kaldor-Hicks formulation but rather entire utility-possibility curves or envelope functions of sets of such curves, the social ordering is independent of irrelevant alternatives. Lastly, my remarks in the last section about dictatorship and imposition apply identically. Our present version of the Compensation Principle also gives rise to an acceptable social welfare function.

4-2. Evaluation

The usefulness of the function derived in the last section is severely limited. There is one basic difficulty. Only admissible alternatives can be ordered.

---

[29]Always assuming, of course, that the optimal policy is not always to be supplemented either by status quo compensation or by lump-sum transfers to achieve improved distributions.

[30]Members of sets of *commodity points* for which each set is the values of a single-valued function of commodities $X_1, \ldots X_{n-1}$ (continuous or discontinuous), the function restricted only in that all first derivatives are positive or zero. Derived from this is the concept of admissible transformation functions as members of sets of such functions in each set of which members nowhere intersect.

And admissibility is restricted far more substantially here than in the payment version. Many of the alternative social states admissible under the payment version are part of inadmissible utility possibility functions under the present version. The ability to order only situations in which the actual production of all goods and services changes in the same direction is extremely limiting. The restriction on comparison between transformation functions, so that only when it is *possible* to produce more of all goods (or more of some and the same amount of all others) or less of all goods (less of some and the same amount of all others) is it possible to talk about potential welfare changes in technology, may have somewhat more frequent relevance to events in the real world. But it is open to the additional, incredibly difficult task, of actually measuring changes in transformation functions. Next to this, the measurement problem connected with comparison between commodity bundles is modest.

Both kinds of comparisons fare even worse in contrast to the payment approach. Under the latter, all alternatives can be, in principle, transformed into admissible alternatives. Under the possibility approach, however, no procedure is available by which analogous transformations can be performed. It is this fact that is especially damaging to comparisons between commodity bundles, since there are situations in which more of all kinds of commodities *could* be produced than in some base period but are not in fact produced. Almost without exception, technological change results in heterogeneous output changes, since the technological possibility of greater production of all goods will be offset by the more or less *specialized* economic advantages attainable with the change, these differentials which make it pecuniarily worthwhile to expand activities in one direction *at the expense of* activities in other directions.

The sharply restricted range of comparisons available with the possibility version of the Compensation Principle stems from the attempt under this approach to isolate "objective" production changes from "subjective" or at least as yet unresolvable changes in distribution. The latter treatments do not consider welfare comparisons "objectively" meaningless, but they do insist upon introducing them separately. It is undoubtedly true that production changes can be unambiguously defined as uniformly directioned changes in the output of all goods, but what purpose is served by information about such changes? Given an initial social state, we may recommend that any of a number of commodity bundles will bring about a potential welfare increase, but we do not specify a single best commodity bundle; nor do we assert anything about what distributions of the bundles referred to will *actually* increase welfare. One might in fact ask: If there is no mechanism by which social evaluation of distributions is rendered, then of what use to the community is the (rather trivial) information about *potential* welfare changes, since potential changes can be converted into actual changes only by the "addition" of some social decision about distribution? It is no answer to suggest that each individual will "add" his own decision about distribution, because this leaves us again with only a set of individual value scales and no suggestion as to how these will in fact be articulated to form a social judgment. We are back near the *beginning* of our problem.

What is still more disastrous is that our ordering of commodity bundles not only cannot enable us to choose bundle and distribution from within the ordered set, but, because distributional considerations are excluded, we cannot assert that there is no bundle outside the ordered set which, for whatever distribution of that bundle, will be better than any bundle within the ordered set. On the basis of what the Compensation Principle tells us, we do not know whether the best actual welfare is achievable from a bundle within the ordered set or not. So we cannot advise that the social choice be restricted to the bundles ordered. We construct an ordering and refrain from telling what it can be used for.

The difficulty stems from trying to separate production from distribution. Much of the recent literature decries this attempt.[31] We obtain no unambiguous welfare meaning from any particular collection of commodities in a world of many persons where tastes and values differ. The "total" value of any such collection depends on its distribution. And even the attempt to compare any two collections from a non-welfare point of view will not be independent of distribution.

> In a world of more than one commodity, there is no unequivocal meaning to comparing total production in *any* two social states save in terms of some standard of value which makes the different commodities commensurable; and usually such a standard of value must depend on the distribution of income.
>
> In other words, there is no meaning to total output independent of distribution.[32]

Yet even if the analytic procedure of separating production from distribution were justified, it would serve no purpose. The separation is not devised for its own sake; there is no gain in obtaining pure ranking of production and relative distribution. Our ultimate purpose is to order social states in their entirety. In other words, we plan to recombine them anyway. Consequently, recognition that the initial extraordinarily difficult separation is epistemologically unjustified, together with the conviction that individuals are in fact influenced in their ordering of social states by considerations about income distribution, would seem to call for an analytic

---

[31]Samuelson, *Foundations;* Arrow, *Social Choice;* also "Little's Critique."

[32]Arrow, *Social Choice,* 39-40. Of course, comparison which will be independent of income distribution can be made between two collections of commodities, if our collections are admissible bundles — i.e., more of all commodities in one collection than in the other.

schema whereby we derive social orderings of absolute welfare distribution — social states themselves — directly from similar social orderings of absolute welfare distributions by the members of the community. This is meaningful and in principle enables comparisons between all social states. There are no restrictions on the admissibility of social state alternatives.[33]

To summarize, the whole notion of potential welfare change as change in the level of production is dubious. If we assume that welfare distributions affect the social ordering of social states but profess to know nothing about such distributions, then our measures of potential welfare change tell us very little. If we recognize the effect of distribution and introduce choices between distributions into the analysis, then we do better to dispense with potential welfare and make direct comparisons between absolute distributions.[34] Only if we deny that a social ordering of real alternatives is in any way dependent upon the distribution of welfare, is the analysis of production levels especially useful. And even here, I might remark, *potential* welfare is superfluous, since it is no longer potential welfare but actual welfare that is being measured.

---

[33]But such schemes are, of course, subject to Arrow's Possibility Theorem. For amplification, see the Note appended to this chapter.

[34]This over-all evaluation of the Compensation Principle is, of course, based on the tacit assumption that a procedure for discovering social comparisons between absolute distributions can be found which is not subject to even more serious difficulties than the Compensation Principle. If this is not so, then although its limitations still stand, the Compensation Principle might nonetheless prove the most serviceable tool we have.

CHAPTER 5

Mixed Approaches:

Production and Distribution

In this chapter we shall discuss three approaches that recognize the limitations inherent in a criterion limited to unanimity or level of production. All three explicitly consider distribution, the first two admitting social orderings of different distributions, the third evoking an empirical generalization about the distributional impact of a sequence of production changes. They are, respectively, the approaches of I. M. D. Little, Franklin M. Fisher, and J. R. Hicks.

5-1. Little

We turn first to the approach followed by I. M. D. Little in his *A Critique of Welfare Economics.*[1] Little attempts to retain the Scitovsky criterion *along with* the assumption that "relative" real income distributions can be evaluated. Briefly, his approach is to compare an initial position — which, because of its asymmetric treatment in the analysis, is to be interpreted as a true starting situation — with an altered state possessing a different level of production and different welfare distributions, and a redistribution of the initial state, possessing the same relative distribution as in the altered state, without a change in production. To illustrate the aforementioned asymmetry, no redistribution of the altered state is envisaged in the comparison. In order that a decision be

---

[1] I am heavily indebted in this treatment to Arrow, "Little's Critique of Welfare Economics," *American Economic Review* (1949), 923-34.

made to change the prevailing state, the proposed movement must attain
an improved welfare distribution. If, in addition, the proposed alteration
will give us an increased level of production as well as the improvement
in distribution, i.e., at the terminal distribution losers cannot bribe the
gainers to oppose the move (non-fulfillment of the Scitovsky criterion),
we should make the alteration. If not, i.e., at the terminal distribution
losers *can* bribe gainers to oppose the change, then make only the redistribution.

Little's own formulation does not translate into our utility-possibility
diagrams without modification. It is marred by, from the point of view of
this analysis, certain eccentricities:

(1) The initial position possesses asymmetrical properties which bias
decisions in its favor.

(2) The existence of better or worse distributions can be determined
only by comparing the initial state with the altered state possessing a
different level of production. Hence, comparisons are envisaged between
different relative welfare distributions at different real income levels. The
meaningfulness of this procedure has been questioned in Chapter 3. And
this would also leave in doubt the meaning of those redistributions of the
original bundle possessing the *same* distribution as that of the alteration.

We *may*, however, translate into our terminology by dropping these
characteristics. All redistributions of a given commodity bundle are
conceivable and can be socially ordered and this result applied to redistribution of the terminal bundle as well as the initial bundle. Further, we
loosen the requirement for production comparisons between *equal* distributions simply to comparisons between distributions in which everyone is
better off (or neutrally affected), or worse off. Now, referring to Figure 6,
Little's position asserts that B is preferred to A if some A' can be formed by
lump-sum redistribution from A such that (1) A' is distributionally better
than (i.e., socially preferred to) A, and (2) every one is better off in B than
in A'. Schematically: the shift from A to A' is good, from A' to B is good,
so A to B is better than A to A'. Since we have abandoned the analytic
asymmetry which would give special emphasis to A, we may also conclude
that B is better than A if some B' can be formed by lump-sum redistribution
from B such that (1) B' is distributionally better than B and (2) everyone is
better off in B' than in A. The first employs the Scitovsky criterion
supplemented by an evaluation of different distributions; the second
employs the Kaldor-Hicks criterion similarly supplemented.

If the evaluation of the distributional change is in the opposite direction
to the production change, no decision can be made since evaluations about
production level cannot be compared with evaluations about distribution.
This appears to be an unwarranted restriction on the analysis.

Little assumes that alternate relative distributions of welfare can be socially ordered. Also different levels of production can be ordered. To what purpose are these orderings introduced into welfare analysis? Not to derive twin hierarchies in which the respective element of each is a different fragment of the various social states. This would neither enable us to evaluate the passing scene nor to give counsel about public policy. Rather, we are trying to order social states in their entirety. But for this task, we see that by Little's criterion all those alterations in which the distributional change runs counter to the production change cannot be evaluated. This limitation derives solely from Little's artificial cleavage between production level and distribution. If both elements can be separately ordered, which itself is problematical,[2] then certainly social states as a whole can be ordered.

Indeed, our supposed separate ordering of relative distributions is really an ordering of social states. If different redistributions of a given commodity bundle can be socially ordered, even though they do involve some individuals being better off and some worse off, then the restriction of these comparisons being made for a given commodity bundle is, from our present point of view, not really a restriction at all. Total social well-being is not invariant for any given bundle but will vary with different redistributions. It therefore hardly seems useful to pretend that it is the invariance of the commodity bundle that makes social ordering possible.

But the ability to order social state alternatives directly and exhaustively accomplishes that which the compensation principle in its various forms only indirectly and incompletely (and questionably) attempts.

One final point. By admitting ordering of alternative distributions into the analysis, and refusing to make welfare decisions unless production and distribution move in the same direction, Little makes his analysis refer to actual not potential welfare changes. Thus, B in the example cited from Figure 6, is *actually* better than A if both production and distribution are improved over A. Similarly, the whole ordered chain of alternatives which can be constructed — since the relation "better than," as defined by the procedure, is transitive — will similarly refer to an ordering of actual welfare levels.

Yet a strange difficulty is encountered. Suppose we were to apply Little's procedure to the comparison between A'' and B' (Figure 6). The distribution at B'', which can be reached from B' by a lump-sum redistribution, is better than at B'. In A'' everybody is better off than in B''. So by the theorem, A'' is better than B'. We should expect to obtain the same result with the B' distribution. Thus, the distribution at A'' is better than at the redistribution A. But now this A is worse for everybody than B'. There is in fact no redistribution of the A'' bundle by which everyone is

---

[2]See above, and our discussion of the second approach in this section.

better off than at B'. So the reverse comparison (analogous to the Kaldor criterion, when B' is the initial position) cannot be made. This is, of course, the familiar Scitovsky paradox; but we have previously met it in the attempt to measure consistent *potential* welfare changes: we meet it here as part of an attempt to measure actual welfare changes.

5-2. Fisher

The second approach is one that has been presented by Franklin M. Fisher.[3] This approach, like Little's, focuses on the question of which alternatives are better or worse than, or indifferent to, a given "initial" alternative, but it avoids most of the defects of Little's treatment. Like Little, Fisher distinguishes between income (or production) and distribution; but he characterizes distribution explicitly in terms of commodities, not "real income." Income represents particular total bundles of commodities. Different incomes at the same given distribution are simply points on a given radial projection, i.e., every individual receives the same multiple of the amount he had of each commodity in the initial position, thereby maintaining for him a constant percentage of each commodity. Fisher assumes that for each level of income (i.e., a given commodity bundle) there are value judgments which give social orderings of the various possible relative distributions of that income.

The central focus is to consider some initial total distribution of commodities, a social state, and to partition the space of social states so as to indicate which set of social states is socially preferred to it, which are "inferior to it," and which are indifferent. This is accomplished in three stages. The first stipulates the familiar ambiguous partition which results when we accept only unanimity as our value judgment (the Pareto optimal analysis of the present chapters). We have seen that no alternative for which at least one individual is worse off while others are better off than in the initial state can be compared with the initial state. In commodity distribution space, only points in the northeast (positive) and southwest (negative) orthant with respect to the initial position can be compared with the initial position.

The second stage extends the set of comparable alternatives to the different distributions of the level of income represented in the initial state. This is accomplished by supplementing Pareto optimality with a value judgment which renders a social ordering of the different possible distributions of the same income. Redistributions of the same income which are

---

[3] "Income Distribution, Value Judgments, and Welfare," *The Quarterly Journal of Economics*, Vol. LXX (August, 1956), 380-424; and Peter B. Kenen, and Franklin M. Fisher, "Income Distribution, Value Judgments, and Welfare: A Correction," *The Quarterly Journal of Economics*, Vol. LXXI (May, 1957), 322-24.

worse than the initial distribution represent inferior social states, redistributions which are better represent preferred social states. Indifference is defined similarly.

The third stage makes even more alternatives, indeed, if the procedure be extended indefinitely, the entire space, comparable with the initial state. It introduces value judgments which establish the minimum changes in income which would be required to make the initial state socially indifferent to some particular redistribution of the initial income level. This extends comparability in the following way. The only alternatives which are not yet comparable with our initial state represent different income levels. Consider one of these (A_1) at a higher income level than the initial state (A_0). Now compare A_1 with that social state (A_{01}) possessing the same income level as A_1 and the same distribution as A_0. If A_1 is socially preferred to A_{01}, in other words, A_1 represents the better distribution, then A_1 is perforce socially preferred to A_0. If A_{01} is preferred to A_1, then A_1 may nonetheless be preferred to A_0 if the increase in income more than offsets the worsening of distribution. Employing the procedure of the third stage, we determine the smallest decrease in income from A_{01} which is necessary to give us a social state that is socially indifferent with A_1. Call this state A_{01}^1. Now compare the income levels of A_0 and A_{01}^1. If A_{01}^1 represents a higher income, the income change from A_0 to A_1 is more than enough to offset the worsening of distribution: A_1 is preferred to A_0. If A_{01}^1 represents a lower income, the increase from A_0 to A_1 is not sufficient to offset the worsening of distribution: A_0 is preferred to A_1. If the two incomes are equal, the income change exactly offsets the distribution change: A_1 and A_0 are socially indifferent. [Actually, Fisher uses an inversion of this procedure. Instead of constructing an intermediate position with the same distribution as A_0 and the same income of A_1, he constructs one with the same income as A_0 and the same distribution as A_1, call this A_{10}. If A_{10} is preferred to A_0, and A_1 represents a higher income than A_0, A_1 is preferred to A_0. Where these comparisons are mixed, a similar procedure to that of the text is employed. The results in the two approaches are the same. Fisher employs the second approach because this shows somewhat more clearly the implications for the Compensation Principle of the existence of distributions which are preferable to that of the initial state.]

The same procedure can be used when the income level of A_1 is lower than A_0. Form A_{01}; determine whether the distribution and income changes are in the same or opposite preference direction; and, if opposite, form A_{01}^1 and compare the income levels of A_{01}^1 and A_0. If the distributions at A_{01} and A_1 are judged equally good, then of course, A_{01}^1 is identical with A_{01}, so the comparison between A_1 and A_0 depends entirely on their relative income levels.

Fisher is interested in such a partition of the distribution space for the purpose of extending the range of circumstances under which we can argue that policies that increase the level of income also increase actual welfare, without any need for compensation to be paid to damaged individuals. An alteration that increases income will increase *actual* welfare without compensation if it improves distribution as well; or, while worsening distribution, if the increase in income more than offsets the worsening of distribution. [4]

For the purposes of the present work we must go further. We are not interested in a three-fold partition of the space only, for this tells us only that an indefinitely large number of alternatives are better than some initial state. We are interested in knowing which, for each set of attainable alternatives, is the best alternative, i.e., which is the best possible alteration of the initial state. [5] Thus, we must similarly partition the space with respect to every possible point. This in the limit, enables us to derive a social ordering of all available alternatives. The graphic counterpart of this procedure can be seen as follows. In commodity space, our total partitioning gives us a set of unique nonintersecting community indifference functions, which de V. Graaff calls "Bergson frontiers," [6] each function

---

[4] Actually, Fisher's analysis includes additional variables, but these are beyond the scope of our present concern.

[5] This is not a trivial emendation. In the spirit of Fisher's discussion we ask: is B better than initial position A? If so, move to B. Is C better than B? If so, move to C. This continues, presumably, until a "best" position is reached. But unless we presume either that the same set of alternatives is forever available or that, if it changes, it changes independently of alternatives actually chosen, our sequence of choices will influence available alternatives. If G was, at time t_0 the *best* choice, but we in fact chose B, then C, etc., "in the direction of" G, we may never reach the path of subsequently unfolding possibilities promised by choosing G at t_0. Choice between B and G at t_0 will be in a strict sense exclusive: choice of one *precludes* choice of the other.

The crucial question is whether the set of available alternatives can be treated as independent of the temporal sequence of actual choices. We can make it so by the formal device of defining each social state at t_0 as a whole path of successive opportunities into the indefinite future. Aside from extraordinary cumbersomeness, this makes choice at t_0 completely exclusive. If I choose B, I am forever barred from choosing G. Defining social states as distributions — and hence opportunities — for only a short period in the future seems to make inescapable that actual choices in the present will affect future attainable alternatives. A given social state determines the pattern of saving, the directions in which profitable business opportunities are to be found; consequently, it determines the direction in which new inputs and new technologies will be sought and existing inputs be improved, and the resources available for expansion and technological change. It determines, in short, factors which strongly influence future attainable states.

Thus, our approach in this book, where at a given time we seek the *best* alteration of the existing situation (including, of course, the possibility of a policy of no change), is not necessarily equivalent to an approach which concentrates on whether a given state is better or worse than the existing state.

[6] J. de V. Graaff, *Theoretical Welfare Economics* (Cambridge: Cambridge University Press, 1957), 48-50. See also Paul A. Samuelson, "Social Indifference Curves," *The Quarterly Journal of Economics*, Vol. LXX, No. 1 (February, 1956), 1-22.

indicating production combinations which are socially indifferent if optimally distributed. Superimposition of a social (commodity) transformation function, indicating maximal production possibilities, that is, the set of non-dominated output bundles, suffices to determine which attainable output combination, and hence, working backward again via our distribution value judgments, which social state is best.

It should be clearly understood that the social ordering derived by employing Fisher's model does not represent an achievement for the New Welfare Economics, despite the fact that Fisher's method increases the range of choices over which actual welfare comparisons can be made without the need for compensation. Extension in comparability is achieved solely as a result of introducing value judgments about income distribution — the very thing the New Welfare Economics was developed to avoid. Income changes are sufficient to establish actual welfare changes only where we have determined that the accompanying distributional changes are either advantageous or only insufficiently disadvantageous. Although his emphasis on the distinction between income and distribution is in the spirit of the New Welfare Economics, Fisher's model is essentially an improved variant of the distribution consensus approach of Bergson, which we considered in Chapter 2. The improvement resides in expressing distribution preferences directly in terms of commodities rather than indirectly through money income.

To what extent does this approach advance our search for a useful theory of welfare economics? The key rests in the value judgments about distribution. We have seen above that any such judgment involves interpersonal comparisons of utility. Moreover, if Fisher's social partition is to be accomplished, at least one such value judgment must be "socially accepted." Thus, the model's achievement is relevant to our quest only if there exists some socially accepted method of making the interpersonal comparisons of welfare entailed in social preferences about distribution. Does the fact that these interpersonal comparisons refer to distributions of the same income level make them different in kind from the interpersonal comparisons envisaged in the general statement of the problem of the social welfare function? We have already argued that they are not. Again, it must be emphasized that the distinction between distribution and income level·is neither clear nor essential. We suggest now in addition that it is not especially useful. If we are correct, then Fisher's model, instead of solving the problems posed in Chapter 2, is in effect simply restating them in different form.

We have argued above that our "income" measurements, and the welfare significance, of any commodity bundle, depend on its distribution. It may nonetheless be true that one can usefully separate out income and distribution by concentrating on commodity bundles themselves and not on money value measurements. We may speak of income changes only in terms of (commodity) vector comparisons. One bundle is bigger than another only if all components of the first are bigger than the comparable components of the second.[7] Distributions are defined as indicated — *independently of income level* — as distribution matrices, each matrix expressing the percentage of each commodity going to each individual. Then the ordering of social states is the resultant of two components, preferences for income levels and preferences for distributions. Social preferences for different income sizes are given simply by the fundamental assumption of economic scarcity: more is preferred to less. Distribution preferences are given by distribution value judgments.

The distinction between income and distribution achieves a useful simplification if (1) pure distribution value judgments are simpler than judgments about social states; (2) distribution value judgments are not more problematic than judgments about social states and income changes are easy to measure; or (3) it is easier to construct (or discover) judgments of the former type which command general agreement than judgments of the latter type. We argue that none of these is true.

Distribution value judgments, like judgments about social states, entail interpersonal comparisons of welfare. Yet the former would be the simpler if they were in fact pure, i.e., if individuals typically evaluated different distributions irrespective of the level of income represented in the alternatives. If distribution is indeed *evaluatively independent* of income, then distinguishing the two is analytically efficient. But distribution is not typically independent of income in this respect. This is even asserted by Fisher.[8] Consider some principle which might form the basis of a distribution value judgment, for example: "The rich 'as all the pleasure while the poor man gets the blame." Here the condemnation of wide differences in income gets much of its moral steam from the fact that the lower end recipients are poor. If total income were much higher, so that the same income differences could be associated with lower recipients being fairly well-to-do, far less of the condemnation would be likely to remain.

In an example given by Fisher,[9] total income is so small that equal distribution would give each a less-than-subsistence diet, thereby guaranteeing the death of everyone. Unequal distribution is necessary in order that anyone survive, the minimum degree of inequality for any given number to survive being a function of the level of income, the size of the population and the commodity needs for survival. So certain degrees of inequality are preferred to equality and to other degrees of inequality.

---

[7]Somewhat more loosely we may define "bigger" analogous to "dominant," so that we require only that some components be larger and none smaller.

[8]Fisher and Kenen, *op. cit.*

[9]*Ibid., op. cit.*, 384, n. 7.

Again, as the income level changes the social ordering of distributions changes. For high income level the subsistence argument rules out only a few extreme degrees of inequality, but certainly not equality.

This is, indeed, the general case. The two examples above suggest that relative distributions are not entirely evaluated as ends in themselves but also partly as means toward more ultimate ends, e.g., survival or minimum standards of living compatible with dignity. Other value judgments are conceivable, involving ends like large-scale philanthropic activities in the arts, rapid economic growth through a high rate of total saving, discouragement of ostentatious consumption, etc. The relative ability of different distributions to achieve these different goals is to some extent, and the relative desirability of these goals themselves is to a much larger extent, a function of the total level of income. On these grounds we should certainly expect the social ordering of distributions to be a function of income level.

One final point. For each individual the relatedness of different commodities is a function of his income. Thus, a poor man is likely to consider a new residence as a strong substitute for a new car. A rich man is more likely to consider them complementary. Sport shoes and dress shoes, similarly, are likely to be close substitutes for a poor man, close complements for a rich man. These are ground for believing that individuals evaluate allocations of commodities to others to some extent not simply as undifferentiated amounts of income, but as particular patterns of consumption (each of which they think may be differentially satisfying to different recipients). Assume this is important and that we are comparing distributions A and B at income levels 1 and 2. We rank A better than B at level 1 largely because the consumption pattern allocated to some group G_1 in B is peculiarly awkward. At income level 1 too many of the commodities are substitutes; not enough are complements. At income level 2, G_1 receives the same multiple (greater than 1) of all the commodities of the first situation. But now, at his higher income level, more of the commodities are complements, fewer are substitutes; the over-all consumption pattern is less awkward. A member of G_1 experiences a greater increase in satisfaction than if he had been given comparable amounts of general purchasing power in both situations. Since at income level 2 there is, in this loose sense, a disproportionate improvement for the members of G_1, we might be willing to rate B better than A at level 2. Thus, inasmuch as commodity relatedness is important in evaluating different distributions, individual orderings of distributions, and hence social orderings, will be affected by the level of income involved.

We should not pretend that we have demonstrated that distribution orderings change violently for small changes in income. Indeed, most of our discussion suggests the opposite: only substantial changes in income are likely to bring about important changes in the relative evaluation of distributions. Nonetheless, even this damages the notion that a few simple criteria in pure distributional ethics will enable one to deduce an ordering for the whole space (or even the relevant range) of alternatives. A system of criteria which is complex enough to be compatible with the interdependence of distributional ethics and income is likely to be much the same as would be needed to order the space of alternatives without first distinguishing between income and distribution.

The second possible advantage of the distinction between income and distribution, namely, the ease of measuring income, is, of course, historically the chief reason for the distinction. In the New Welfare Economics the existence of generally approved distribution value judgments is discounted: Distributional comparisons are deemed by nature controversial. But the total value of output is asserted to be positively associated with movements of the economy toward a Pareto optimum, in which case changes in such total value are evaluatively non-controversial. Either everyone is in fact better off, or some are better off without anyone being worse off, when total value increases. Then the whole analytic apparatus of general equilibrium theory is available to indicate the circumstances under which the value of output increases or decreases, and these value changes carry implicit unanimity value judgments. In this view, the distinction between output and distribution is useful because it makes relevant to social welfare comparisons a powerful tool for judging in at least one dimension of the problem. Without even having to know beforehand what social state would result, one could recommend a policy consistent with achievement of a Pareto optimum and know that it would increase output. Our discussion of point 1 above suggests that if pure distribution value judgments are as complex as social state judgments, and distribution is evaluatively important, then the ability to predict the income consequences of different policies is not per se of much use. But this ability is useful if distribution is an unimportant consideration in over-all social state evaluations, or if distribution judgments are frequently or inherently clouded.[10]

It is crucial to the appreciation of Fisher's system that we understand that "level of income" in his system is *not* equivalent to "total value of output" (or "production")[11] in the New Welfare Economics. A given "total value of output" can signify a variety of different commodity combinations, since commodities can be substituted for one another without affecting total value by adhering to substitution ratios given by relative prices. Each level of income in Fisher's model, in contrast, is a unique commodity vector. The propositions of general equilibrium theory apply

---

[10]Not simply controversial. Controversiality means differences in tastes, and it is the function of the Social Welfare Function to render social judgments in the *presence* of differences in tastes.

[11]What we called "income" before considering Fisher's Model.

to the former, but they do not apply to the latter. The increase in the value of output which comes about by adjusting the last group of markets where marginal rates of social transformation diverged from their respective marginal rates of substitution[12] does not generally involve an increase in the quantity of all commodities or even an increase in some with no decrease in others. Generally, some commodities increase, but others decrease, less than in proportion to relative prices.

If commodity changes under Pareto optimal readjustments are heterogeneous in this way, then they will not generally be preferred to initial states for every possible distribution of income. But this repeats our previous discussion of potential welfare in Chapter 4. Under the concept of income as total *value* of output, the level of income is not independent of its distribution, since different distributions determine different relative prices and hence different value sums. It is the strength of Fisher's model that, by his treatment of income as a commodity vector, the level of income *is* independent of distribution. But this makes the familiar conditions for general optimum of much slighter relevance for predicting the relative income levels of different policies.

A final remark is in order to clarify this critique. We have acknowledged that the income-level-distribution distinction makes general equilibrium theory and the Pareto optimum unusually relevant to welfare analysis. The argument that such a distinction be rejected in favor of direct orderings of social states does not mean that general equilibrium analysis, or even the Pareto optimum, have no use in welfare economics. Quite the contrary. If the practical alternatives of choice in welfare economics are in fact public policies, and these are evaluated in terms of the social states to which they lead, then there must be some method of determining the social state consequences of each policy. This absolutely essential task is the function of positive economic theory, with especial reference to general equilibrium theory.

Furthermore, assume that in the course of gauging the social state opportunities achievable through the available policies, one sub-set is found which dominates the rest of the set in the sense that: (1) for every point not in the sub-set there is at least one point in the sub-set for which either everyone is better off, or some are better off without anyone else being worse

---

[12]Assuming away the complication that if aggregate social transformation or community indifference functions are, atypically, concave rather than convex, then the general optimum is achieved where total value of output is minimized rather than maximized. See Francis Bator, "The Simple Analytics of Welfare Economics," *American Economic Review*, Vol. XLVI, No. 1 (March, 1957), 45-53; de V. Graaff, *Theoretical Welfare Economics*, 66-70 (being careful, as Graaff is not, to interpret his analysis in terms of *aggregate*, not individual, concavities); Jerome Rothenberg, "Non-convexity, Aggregation and Pareto Optimality," *The Journal of Political Economy*, Vol. LXVIII, No. 5 (October, 1960) 435-468.

off; and (2) for no point in the sub-set is it true that there is another point in the sub-set such that everyone is better off, or some are better off without anyone being worse off. Then there would be overwhelming agreement that no point outside the dominating sub-set be considered further as the best state. Final social choice would be made only from among the points of the dominating sub-set. This sub-set is, of course, a Pareto optimum. Where it is attainable in its entirety, all final choices will be restricted to it in this more general approach as well as in an approach distinguishing income level from distribution.

This Pareto optimum should not, however, be identified with *the* Pareto optimum which results from the satisfaction of the familiar marginal equivalences, assuming given factor endowments, technology, and tastes. As we indicated in the last chapter, among the public policies open to government are some which have the effect and usually the deliberate intent to change resources and technology (and even tastes). The dominating sub-set here represents portions of several alternative welfare frontiers of the more familiar data-fixed type. The policies necessary to reach this optimum need not be the same as what would be required in the purely static analysis.

This is not the situation we confronted in Chapter 4. There, on the one hand, we spoke of pairs of points where neither in fact dominated the other, and, although some lump-sum transfers could make one dominate the other, other such transfers would reverse the dominance. On the other hand, we spoke of a static Paretian frontier where the relevant choices were between sub-sets of sub-optimal points on the one hand (different degrees of different divergences from optimality), and a single, nondominating point on the frontier on the other. That the latter type of such choice was preliminary to the further choice among the several points *on* the frontier was not envisaged because of a suppression of explicitly distributional considerations.

We have argued so far that pure distribution value judgments are no less complex than judgments about social states as a whole, and that there is little to be gained by being able to speak about income level abstracted from its distribution (when income is defined in terms of commodity vectors). Nonetheless, even if the income-level-distribution distinction has no analytic advantages, it would have the advantage of being easier to talk about or work with if criteria for ordering distributions were easier to formulate or discover than criteria for ordering social states. Are they in fact easier?

Fisher gives us little aid in this. He does not deal with how we construct or find widely approved distributional criteria. The only criterion with moral thrust that he employs explicitly is strict equalitarianism. This scarcely commands general approval, however. Fisher deals with certain structural properties of value judgments, like local "single-peakedness,"

which we shall discuss at length in Chapter 9 in different context, but these
are more relevant to a one-commodity than to a multi-commodity world.
In general, his use of distribution criteria is hypothetical: he sets almost no
concrete restrictions on these criteria. [The tone of this is not fair to Fisher.
It is our purpose here to emphasize the concrete substance of value judg-
ments· The emphasis in Fisher's paper, however, is different. The central
problem for him is to examine the implications of certain structural characteristics which are likely to be widely required as reasonable properties of
all acceptable families of value judgments. This is a task somewhat analogous to Arrow's. Although we are here primarily concerned with the fact
that it is distribution value judgments which are examined, and though
some of these characteristics apply most appropriately to distribution,
Fisher's work is suggestive for the more general types of value judgment
as well.]

Considering our reasons for believing that the income-distribution
distinction has little analytic usefulness, we know no theoretical reason why
distributional criteria should be formulated by moral observers in precedence to criteria for evaluating total social states. Admittedly, humans
classify and abstract as tools to organize all huge cognitive tasks, but
classification for its own sake is useless. A particular classification will
serve no purpose if it merely translates the complexity of the original
problem into new terms without increasing its tractability. This is not to
say that concrete anthropological investigation may not disclose instances
where distributional criteria are in fact formulated and generally approved in precedence to more general evaluative criteria. It is only that, by
not in any essential way lessening the complexity of the over-all evaluative
tasks, we guess that there is no presumption that empirical investigation
will disclose such precedence.

To conclude, Fisher's model does not substantially simplify the task
which we have formulated in Chapters 1 and 2.

5-3. Hicks

We turn now to an approach of quite a different kind. It says that although
distributional matters are important, in matters of practical policy they
ought to be excluded. This is not the full position taken by J. R. Hicks or of
any one else in the literature that I know of. But as part of his total position, Hicks made an early influential statement of this attitude.[13] We shall
be speaking primarily of this one analytical segment, rather than of his
whole position. Consequently, to avoid making our discussion a caricature

---

[13]"The Rehabilitation of Consumer's Surplus," *Review of Economic Studies* (1940-41).

of the Hicks position, we shall present Hicks' own paragraph on the subject, thereby indicating not only the segment in which we shall be further concerned, but also its relationship to the rest of Hicks' approach and the tone of the whole.

> If the economic activities of a community were organised in the principle of making no alterations in the organisation of production which were not improvements in this sense [i.e., such that compensation could be paid], and making all alterations which were improvements that it could possibly find, then, although we could not say that all the inhabitants of that community would be necessarily better off than they would have been if the community had been organised on some different principle, nevertheless there would be a strong probability that almost all of them would be better off after the lapse of a sufficient length of time. Substantially, that is the creed of classical economics; if the "improvements" are properly defined, it would appear to be a creed that is soundly based. But it is a creed which asks a great deal of human patience, more patience than is characteristic of the twentieth century, even of the economists of the twentieth century; more patience, perhaps, than we ought to ask. Yet even if we cannot wait for this long run, our criterion still has something to offer. When any considerable improvement, in our sense, is made, it ought to be possible actually to give compensation, out of the gains of the gainers, to cover the losses of the losers. It is true that some of the institutions which would be necessary to effect such compensation would themselves have a harmful effect upon production, so that reluctance to wait for the slow operation of the law of averages may have a less favourable effect in the long run than the first policy would do; but even so there will be much to be gained from due attention to the criteria of productive improvement. These criteria stand, whether distributional considerations are being given much or little weight.[14]

The principle that concerns us here is that every policy which promises to increase income in the sense of total value of outputs, i.e., every policy which has the property that prospective gainers could completely compensate prospective losers and still be better off by the policy, should be adopted without paying compensation and, in the long run, everyone will (probably) in fact be better off than if a different principle had been followed. In the terminology of Chapter 4, if every policy that increases *potential welfare* is adopted, with a long enough sequence of such adoptions, we should expect to see *actual welfare* increased by more than with any other type of sequence of adoptions. Potential welfare changes are being explicitly related to actual welfare changes. This is a mixed approach. Distributional considerations are present, but on a different level of discourse than in the other approaches of the present chapter. In those approaches, delineating the particular distributions which result from par-

---

[14]Hicks, *loc. cit.*, 111. A similar position, somewhat more restrained, is found in Harold Hotelling, "The General Welfare in Relation to Problems of Taxation and Railway and Utility Rates," *Econometrica*, Vol. 6, No. 3 (July, 1938), 267-268.

ticular policies was unproblematic, but their relative desirability was in question. In this approach it is the delineation of distributions which result from bundles of policies that is central, while their relative desirability is not called in question. This approach does not provide a separate criterion to enable us to recognize maximum social welfare but rather an empirical strategy for achieving it. The criterion it presupposes is the Pareto optimum.

Each policy selected gives rise to a change (increase) in income and a change in distribution. Assume that the uncompensated distribution change typically makes some persons better off and some worse off. The income change is declared to be good. But it is not true in the present approach that the distributional change is declared to be bad. Indeed, distributional changes are not declared to be either bad or good. This stems from the belief, noted earlier, that pure distributional comparisons are intrinsically controversial and hence not susceptible of generally approved judgments. So the averaging-out mechanism envisaged is not one of good distributional changes offsetting bad. It is a process by which enough policies are carried out so that the formal requirements for comparability of social states are likely to have been met under the Pareto optimum criterion of welfare improvement. Each policy generally creates gainers and losers. Averaging out occurs with a given sequence of policies if, for every individual, the total of gains resulting from policies which benefit him exceeds the total of losses from policies which harm him. The present approach asserts then, that an actual sequence of policies chosen solely because they are income increasing over an appropriately sufficient time will: (1) in fact average out in this sense, so that all individuals are better off by the sequence than in the initial position, and (2) increase welfare by more than any sequence of policies chosen with regard to a different strategy over the same period.

It is instructive to try to suggest conditions under which an income-increasing sequence will average out. Let us speak of the gainers of any policy as the policy's "gain directions," the losers as its "loss directions." Now, if we assume that the income-increasing potential of policies is independent of their gain and loss directions, then in a sequence of such policies gain and loss directions will be random variables. A given individual has as much likelihood to gain as to lose if we choose any one policy of the sequence at random. Secondly, in every policy, gainers gain more than enough to compensate losers (but, of course, no compensation takes place). Loosely speaking, gains are greater than losses. Thus, every individual has an equal probability of winning or losing from any policy, but the expected amount of gain is greater than the expected amount of loss; so the expected value to him of the whole sequence of policies is positive; he expects to be better off on balance.

Unfortunately, this demonstration is faulty in a way which seems inevitable from the nature of the conclusion. We cannot really infer from the possibility of compensation in any policy that expected gains for a certain individual are larger than expected losses *for the same individual*. The possibility of compensation (for simplicity, in a two-person world) establishes only that a combination gain for one person — loss for the other — can be converted to a smaller gain to the first and either small gain or no loss to the other. To say that a gain to individual *A* on one policy will offset a loss to the same person on another policy because the loser can generally be compensated *on the same policy* by the gainer, is to suggest that *A* stands in the same relationship to *B* when *A* is a loser as *B* stands to him when *A* is a gainer. But every possibility of compensation represents a special relationship between the utility effects of particular commodity transfers between two individuals with different preference systems. The implicit equivalence of situations implies at the least some tacit assertions about relative marginal utilities of income or, more generally, interpersonal comparisons of utility. But assertions of this type are strongly rejected by this approach. The situation in a multi-person world is even more complicated, and assertions of the same forbidden type are required to infer the conclusion. Averaging out does not seem capable of being established on a strict statistical basis consistently with the ordinal analysis of the New Welfare Economics, even if one makes the strong assumption that the income-increasing potential of policies is independent of their gain and loss directions.

Our argument suggests that the Hicksian conclusion follows not so much from a theorem of statistical theory as from an article of faith. From an appeal to the principle of equal ignorance, if the value of output is constantly increasing over time and each individual has an equal likelihood to have gained rather than lost from each policy, it seems reasonable to suppose that almost everyone would have gained. In a one-commodity world this would be an extremely reasonable article of faith. In a multi-commodity world, where an increase in "income" means a heterogeneous change in different commodities, it is not nearly so reasonable. Little declares that "it would be, at best, wishful thinking" to expect averaging out from such frequency distributional considerations.[15]

There is a further problem connected with averaging out. Hicks' sequence of policies is envisaged as occurring over a "sufficient length of time" — a long run. If this long run is as long as one may reasonably guess would be necessary to approximate averaging out in the sense above, then it is highly likely that tastes would have changed in the population; and, indeed, the very composition of the population might have changed

---

[15]*Critique of Welfare Economics*, 2nd ed., 94.

significantly through births and deaths. The New Welfare Economics provides no procedure for making welfare comparisons when tastes change and certainly none for comparing the welfare of different populations. Thus, it is more than patience that is required to make us believe that a sequence of income-increasing policies will increase welfare; it is interpersonal comparisons of utility.[16,17]

Our objections so far have tended to cast doubt on whether policy sequences of the sort mentioned by Hicks can be expected to be better empirically than an initial position in terms of the criterion of dominance.[18] There is a second aspect to this strategy, however. Hicks asserts that it will increase welfare by more than any other; it is the best strategy. Suppose we construct a different strategy (call it PP_A)[19] such that while over the same period some policies chosen may be the same as in Hicks' strategy (PP_H), at least some will be different. Now, let us first compare them both with the initial position in terms of dominance. Let us assume that the state reached by $P\dot{P}_H$, S_H, is better than the initial state, S_0. But it is certainly not incompatible with the nature of PP_A that the point reached, S_A, should also be better than S_0. Thus, both, in these terms, are "good" strategies. Compare S_H with S_A. This *can* be said about the comparison: S_H may dominate S_A but S_A may not dominate S_H (this derives from the Pareto optimal properties of PP_H). We may, however, select a PP_A such that S_H does not dominate S_A.[20] There will in general be many such strategies. Since neither dominates the other, no judgment can

---

[16]*Ibid.*

[17]Both Hicks in our quoted paragraph, and Little (p. 95), suggest that in the implementation of the strategy actual compensation should probably be paid where "significant" changes in distribution would otherwise take place. This *might* have the effect of decreasing the length of time over which the uncompensated sequence would be required to average out, thereby avoiding the full force of this objection. Similarly, if "significant" were interpreted loosely, so that compensation were frequently resorted to, the averaging-out process might be relatively unimportant, uncompensated distributional changes being considered unimportant enough so that welfare changes could be defined in these instances solely in terms of income changes.

Both these cases raise the problems connected with payment of actual compensation (which we discussed in Chapter 3) without fully resolving the problems of the present strategy. In both cases, for example, interpersonal comparisons may sometimes be involved in deciding which distributional changes ought to be compensated; in the second case such comparisons are implied as well by the assumption that some distributional changes are too small to cumulate large enough over the sequence to affect social welfare. Finally, the original assumption of randomness of gains and losses with respect to income-increasing potential need not carry over to "significance" of distributional change. Thus, selective elimination of "large" changes from the uncompensated sequence need not improve its averaging-out potential, may, indeed impair it.

[18]Everyone will at least be as well off, some better off, compared with the initial position.

[19]PP signifies "policy path."

[20]Certainly PP_H is a better strategy than all those which give rise to terminal states dominated by S_H.

be made between the two strategies unless we are willing to make interpersonal comparisons of utility. This is of course the familiar dilemma. Suppose we are willing to make such comparisons, namely, to judge between different total distributions. Nothing whatever in our construction guarantees that S_H will invariably rank higher than S_A under such comparisons. All we can make is the assertion in familiar spirit that although Hicks' strategy is better than some, it is not necessarily the best of all. To discover whether it is in some given situation best of all would require that we resort to the very kind of enquiry which Hicks' strategy was devised to obviate.

We have interpreted Hicks' proposal strictly. Suppose we consider it somewhat more loosely as stipulating a reasonable strategy, justified by the necessary compromises due to ignorance, uncertainty of the future, and the controversiality of most value judgments other than that of Pareto optimality. Does it provide a tolerably good rule of thumb for guiding social improvement over time?

In the present, more informal context we may admit that, although it does not follow logically from the premises of the strategy, we have a fair expectation that almost everyone *will* be better off at the end of a protracted sequence of compensation-approved policies than at the beginning. But there are some difficulties that lessen the attractiveness of this strategy from a practical point of view.

First, for a rule of thumb it is not especially easy to apply. We have already noted the considerable problems involved in calculating whether or not compensation could be paid for any given policy. We may, of course, water down the principle by requiring that only roughly approximate potential gains and losses be calculated, for example the gains and losses of major "groups." As indicated above, this marks a major compromise of the whole approach since it admits a subtle form of interpersonal comparisons of utility and worth. By treating individuals as members of groups, identified only in terms of impersonal indices, it implicitly argues a similarity of welfare impact for all individuals with similar index readings. In addition, it renders judgment that some gains or losses are large enough, some too small, to "matter."

Our objection here is not that a simple, powerful procedure can be found which represents a smaller retreat, but rather that, if one is willing implicitly to make evaluations about some relative distributions (which is what is implied by the "group index" procedure), then there probably remains little justification for being unwilling to make evaluations about other relative distributions. Indeed, the interpersonal comparisons involved in the former are likely to be more *ad hoc*, less coherent, than many of those which adherents of the New Welfare Economics have criticized. The latter pretend to be based upon characteristics that are believed to affect in the most enduringly profound way the well-being of the individual. The former, in contrast, collects in groups those individuals who are likely to be grossly affected in a similar way by the *particular policy* in question. Since the major bunchings of (non-pecuniary) effects of different types of policies will typically involve different aspects of individual personality, employment of the group classification which most efficiently simplifies the calculation of a compensation for each policy will result in a set of inter-personal comparisons with no systematic ethical foundation. A sacrifice of computational ease by adopting one or at most a few group classifications to be applied to all policies would be required to lessen this danger.

Second, relations among alternatives are more complicated than Hicks' statement would indicate. It is, for example, inappropriate to attempt to implement *all* policies for which potential overcompensation exists. Some policies are mutually exclusive. When one has chosen A, one has in effect chosen not-B, not-C, etc. One cannot implement both a policy which uses a particular piece of land as reservoir for a new dam *and* one which uses the same land to grow wheat. Yet either policy might well allow potential overcompensation. Other pairs of policies may not be logically incompatible but are strongly competitive, in the sense that the presence of each substantially interferes with what is desirable in the other. Either member of such a pair might allow potential overcompensation when the other member is *not* present, but not otherwise.

This seems at first sight a minor complexity. Unfortunately, its most obvious resolution further erodes the austerity of the approach regarding interpersonal comparisons of utility. It seems reasonable to choose between two exclusive, or only highly substitutive, policies, both of which permit potential overcompensation and neither of which dominates the other, on the basis of which policy permits the greater potential over-compensation. By a series of such choices, we may build up a sub-set of compensation-approved policies which prevail over competing compensation-approved policies. Can we infer from this procedure that the chosen sub-set is socially preferred to all other compensation-approved policies on ordinal Paretian grounds? We can not. Our analysis in Chapter 4 should make clear why this is so. The possibility of potential overcompensation is established in terms of money values of gains and losses. Suppose policy A permits larger overcompensation relative to the status quo than does policy B. This means only that the money value of net gains in A exceeds that in B, and such can certainly be true without A dominating B. Thus, it need not be the case that A is socially preferred to B on Paretian grounds. Therefore, when we choose among overcompensation policies by the suggested procedure, we implicitly assume that the social impact of the amalgam of preference intensities relating each A to the *status quo* is more "favorable" than that of each B. We are implicitly making interpersonal comparisons of social effect (i.e., interpersonally comparable utilities weighted for social worth).

These interpersonal comparisons are like, but are not identical with, the comparisons implicit in the very use of the compensation principle to measure potential welfare. Since the compensation test used here is the Kaldor or at most the Kaldor-Scitovsky criterion, each chosen A is an overcompensation policy relative to the income distribution at the *status quo*, but it need not be an overcompensation policy at the new distribution brought about by first applying the comparable (rejected) policy B to the status quo. Policy A does not invariably increase potential welfare over the situation resulting from policy B. The selection of the former, then, does not result simply from the compensation principle. The interpersonal comparisons necessary are of the same type but are additional to, those entailed in the hypothetical compensation procedure.

The inability to implement all "production efficient" alterations of the economy, the need to select among them, leads to an important ambiguity for practical application. As we have seen, the procedure is justified in terms of its results over a substantial period of time. Clearly a temporal sequence of alterations is envisaged rather than a cluster at one point of time. Since the possibility that a policy can achieve overcompensation depends on the *status quo* commodity bundle and its distribution with which the policy's consequences are being compared, a given policy may be an overcompensation policy for some initial positions but not for others. Thus, the specific alternative made in the starting situation at an early time will determine which further alterations increase potential welfare. When faced today with the choice between two policies, A and B, both of which will increase potential welfare, our suggested procedure, in terms of which policy permits the greater overcompensation, is inadequate. It fails to indicate the linkage with future possibilities of improvement. If we form temporal sequences of alterations (to be referred to as "proper" sequences), such that only improvements that increase potential welfare are admissible successors in each sequence, then whole sequences or at least their final states should be compared, instead of simply their first states.

This modified procedure, however, opens Pandora's box. For it is conceivable that a sequence of this sort that begins with an alternative which does *not* increase potential welfare over the initial state may nevertheless be declared better than a "proper" sequence by the compensation principle itself (or by the relative overcompensation modification suggested here). Indeed, a sequence in which *more* than one item fails to increase potential welfare over its successor may "exceed" a "proper" sequence. For example, there are some initial states for which early, very drastic redistributions of income are needed to encourage production changes that substantially increase potential welfare in subsequent time periods. Thus, even if one is willing to use potential welfare as a basic criterion, the temporal connectedness of the impact and evaluation of different policies makes it inappropriate to be satisfied to select only among overcompensation policies. If one redefines the compensation procedure to refer only to last-item states, then it may be actually inconsistent with the procedure as Hicks seems to intend it.

Finally, a more informal note. The time sequence modification we have suggested is somewhat out of spirit with the major practical justification of the potential welfare approach. In a world where popular judgments about distribution are deemed controversial, the compensation principle is designed to provide a conservative rule-of-thumb which "plays it safe." A strategy in which something like 90 per cent of all the choice over time could conceivably be for individually non-overcompensation policies is hardly "safe" in this sense. Thus, considering the interpersonal comparisons which we have argued are embedded in overcompensation choices anyway, there is not a very much greater jump to the "riskiness" of judgments about absolute and relative distributions of income.

In sum, if we relax some of the rigor of our requirements for a useful welfare criterion the procedure suggested by Hicks does have some of the earmarks of a reasonable strategy. But, on this level, its principal interdiction against systematic interpersonal comparisons of well-being becomes much weaker, so that its difficulty of application, its *ad hoc* implicit interpersonal comparisons, its important ambiguities no longer can be offset by an epistemological justification claimed to be impeccable by its adherents. For economists who are willing to admit interpersonal comparisons explicitly anyway, these practical defects are doubly damaging, since the procedure therefore cannot even be defended by the argument that we ought to be satisfied with what we can measure well even if it diverges from what we should like to but can't measure. In the light of our arguments, potential welfare is not something that we can measure well.

Part 3

CARDINAL ANALYSIS

CHAPTER 6

The Independence of

"Irrelevant" Alternatives

6-1. Introduction

It will be remembered that Arrow's Condition 3, the "independence of irrelevant alternatives," is as follows:

"Let $R_1, \ldots, R_n$ and $R'_1, \ldots, R'_n$ be two sets of individual orderings and let $C(S)$ and $C'(S)$ be the corresponding social choice functions. If, for all individuals i and all x and y in a given environment S, xR_iy if and only if xR'_iy, the $C(S)$ and $C'(S)$ are the same."[1]

Of the five conditions offered by Arrow, this one has come in for by far the most criticism. Most efforts to resolve Arrow's paradox and construct (at least in principle) an "acceptable" Social Welfare Function have consequently begun by dropping or modifying this condition.

In this chapter I shall examine what really is involved in Condition 3 and attempt to evaluate its reasonableness as an acceptability condition. In following chapters I shall describe various attempts which have been made to formulate acceptable Social Welfare Functions without imposing Condition 3.

Let us begin by considering what, in the context of Condition 3, *is* an "irrelevant" alternative, and why it may be reasonable to ask that social orderings be independent of such alternatives. Arrow's own explanation is:

---

[1]Arrow, *Social Choice*, 27.

If we consider $C(S)$, the choice function derived from the social ordering R, to be the choice which society would actually make if confronted with a set of alternatives S, then, just as for a single individual, the choice made from any fixed environment S should be independent of the very existence of alternatives outside of S. . . . The choices made . . . from a given environment (should) depend only on the orderings of individuals among the alternatives in that environment. . . . The choice between x and y . . . (should be) . . . determined solely by the preferences of the members of the community as between x and y.[2]

He gives the following illustration. Suppose there is an election system in which voters rank all the candidates in order of preference. An election is held, and all the rankings are made. Then one of the candidates dies. "Surely the social choice should be made by taking each of the individual's preference lists, blotting out completely the dead candidate's name, and considering only the orderings of the remaining names in going through the procedure of determining the winner."[3]

Arrow's exposition appears to touch on not one but a number of different conceptions of "irrelevance." Under these circumstances, therefore, further analysis might conclude it advisable to reinterpret Condition 3 (by suitable modification) so that while "irrelevant" alternatives (in the more restricted sense) are still precluded from wielding influence on social comparisons, "acceptable" Social Welfare Functions can be constructed.

6-2. *Relevant and Irrelevant Alternatives*

The first conception of irrelevance is suggested chiefly by Arrow's election illustration. The ranking of the dead candidate is deemed to be irrelevant to ordering the remaining candidates. The irrelevance of the dead candidate's ranking suggests that *it makes no difference* to the ordering of the other candidates whether or not this candidate is included in the election.[4] It is hard to resist interpreting this as implying that the ordering of the remaining candidates would have been the same if the deceased candidate had not been a candidate as it was when he was a candidate. And this may be generalized to the following extreme position: Any ordering of n alternatives can be derived from a sequence of paired comparisons (between all x and y); the outcome of each of these comparisons will be invariant under (1) all specifications of sets of alternatives which exclude x and y,[5] and (2) all attitudes about the possible sets of alternatives excluding x and y. Thus, for any paired comparison, all alternatives not of

---

[2]*Ibid.*, 26, 28.

[3]*Ibid.*, 26.

[4]Indeed, "makes no difference" seems a wholly reasonable interpretation of the notion of "irrelevance."

[5]I.e., all conceivable alternatives, whether achievable or not, other than x and y.

the pair are deemed to be irrelevant. If we were to lay down as a condition on the construction of acceptable Social Welfare Functions that individual orderings be independent of irrelevant alternatives in this sense, then, we would in effect be limiting admissible individual orderings to those derivable from paired comparisons whose outcomes were independent of the existence and ordering of all alternatives outside each pair. This would be an unfortunate restriction.

It is important to understand first, however, that this restriction does not concern strategic considerations in voting. As we shall see in Chapter 11 below, in actual choosing situations, it may be advantageous for one or more individuals to misrepresent their true preferences in voting (i.e. express distorted preference scales) in order to guarantee, on the basis of knowledge about the potential distribution of voting strength in the group, that particularly distasteful alternatives will not be chosen by the group.[6] For example, if only alternatives x and y are being voted on, a certain individual will express a preference for x. Assume now an alternative z is introduced which our individual ranks below both x and y. If we further assume that he believes that y and z have the greatest voting strength backing them and that these strengths are fairly equally divided, then it is by no means unlikely that he will express a first choice preference for y. Thus, on the level of *actual* group choice the availability of an "irrelevant" alternative z can influence the *expressed* ordering of x and y — it can make a difference.[7] But Arrow's condition does not refer to preferences as expressed in voting; it refers to actual preferences. So the strategic effect of "irrelevant" alternatives on "relevant" ones in *voting* should not be adduced as an argument against Condition 3.

But besides this strategic influence on *action*, "irrelevant" alternatives, in the meaning currently discussed, have a fundamental influence on true preference orderings themselves. This influence *is* relevant to an evaluation of Condition 3. In a very real sense, the ability of each individual to formulate his "true" ordering of any pair of alternatives depends on other alternatives. For one thing, one's ability to evaluate alternative social states requires perception of differences and similarities, standards by which to compare them, and an ability to relate the different standards so as to obtain a single over-all feeling of relative desirability. This is by no means a simple achievement, since our analysis expects each individual to order total social states, each social state being a vector of innumerable dimensions, therefore differing from every other social state in innumerable possible ways. Any consideration of the realistic difficulties involved in this task must recognize the extent to which individuals develop the perception,

---

[6]This is true whether there is single- or multi-stage voting.

[7]See Chapter 11 for a fuller discussion of this type of phenomenon.

formulate the standards, and relate the multi-dimensional comparisons by drawing upon their total experience with all alternatives, be it direct or indirect.[8] A particular — changing — sub-set of "irrelevant" alternatives realistically influences every ordering of "relevant" alternatives.[9]

A modification of this interpretation distinguishes between alternatives outside of each x, y pair which are achievable and those which are not. The influence of the former on each x, y comparison is admitted as relevant while the influence of the latter is not. By this position, all unachievable alternatives are deemed "irrelevant." The justification for this is that a concrete choice situation necessitating the social ordering of the n achievable alternatives is, after all, a single situation. If in reality individuals behave differently in the presence of different sets of available alternatives, then building up an n-membered choice situation mosaic-like from pairwise comparisons is fallacious for the context of making a single choice from among more than two alternatives. Since only achievable alternatives belong in the choosing Gestalt, the inclusion of unachievable alternatives would purportedly blur the real distinction between individual motivation toward alternatives which are currently in contention and those which are not.

This modified approach, too, seems unrewardingly limited. Although it does meet the objection about strategic behavior, it does not meet the objection that "true" orderings of achievable alternatives are partly determined by experience with *all* alternatives, not just with those currently in contention. This "educative" factor in the formation of orderings is important. But there is also, even here, a neglected strategic factor which binds unachievable to achievable alternatives. In the real world, human decisions are time bound and have time consequences. We know from experience that our environment does change substantially, that what was unattainable yesterday is attainable today. And we know that it is our very decisions in the present which help to shape what the future will unfold. Our choices among achievable alternatives today are in this sense strategically formulated so as to make achievable in the future desirable sub-sets of alternatives which today are unachievable (but conceivable, however dimly). Our present ordering of achievable alternatives is therefore dependent on our attitudes toward unachievable alternatives and on the nature of the understood contingencies between the two sets.[10]

---

[8]Mention might be made here, and will be amplified in Chapter 13, of the actual practice of simplifying the necessary individual evaluations by delegating authority to "specialists" to make certain judgments *in behalf of* others.

[9]For further examination of the influence of experience on individual orderings, see Chapter 7, (Section 7.5), and the Appendix to Chapter 2: "Welfare Comparisons and Changes in Tastes."

[10]This problem would formally disappear, of course, if one conceived of every achievable alternative as specifying a whole time-shape of prospects into the future,

The alternative to excluding non-achievable alternatives as admissible influences on the formation of orderings among achievable alternatives is, of course, to admit the whole set of conceivable alternatives. This is the procedure followed in individual preference theory, where the individual's choice from the achievable set of commodity bundles contained within the half-space created by the budget hyper-plane is made by considering his whole preference map.[11] Moreover, the strong influence that strategic considerations have on the *expressing* of one's preferences for available alternatives can be made explicit, not by arbitrarily restricting the individual orderings but rather by specifying the game-theoretic structure of the particular *situations* in which strategy is important.

To summarize the foregoing, the "irrelevance" of certain alternatives has been deemed to reside in the admissibility of their affecting the very *formation* of an ordering of the achievable alternatives. If we examine, however, not Arrow's explanation of Condition 3 but Condition 3 itself, we shall find that irrelevance there does not concern influences on the formation of a particular ordering, but rather how we treat the ordering once it has been formed, howsoever that may have come about. But if this is true, then our strictures apparently apply to statements about irrelevant alternatives rather than to the particular conception embodied in Condition 3 itself. This suspicion will be borne out by discovering that Arrow's election illustration is itself irrelevant to Condition 3.

Condition 3 calls for a fixed environment *S*, the set of alternatives in contention (achievable). For such a fixed environment, it requires only that all changes in individual orderings of unachievable alternatives have no effect on the *social* ordering of achievable alternatives *so long as* (if and only if) these changes have no effect on the *individual* orderings of achiev-

---

thereby blurring not only the distinction between achievable and non-achievable alternatives insofar as *determining* orderings, but also in their symbolic *representation*. Seé Tjalling Koopmans, "Utility Analysis of Decisions Affecting Future Well-Being," *Econometrica*, Vol. 18, No. 2 (April, 1950), 175-177; Franco Modigliani, "The Measurement of Expectations," *Econometrica*, Vol. 20, No. 3 (July, 1952), 481-483; Albert G. Hart, *Anticipations, Uncertainty and Dynamic Planning* (Chicago: University of Chicago Press, 1940). Unquestionably every decision made today is a commitment to some shorter, or longer more or less uncertain future. However, we must beware of using an elegant notation to impound the future with the present too rigidly in a formal schema. It is too easy to use it in ways that imply that every choice represents a time commitment all the way to the planning horizon. Changes over the course of time in the composition of achievable and unachievable sets, in the contingencies between them, in the experience of individuals with their accumulating pasts, bring about frequent changes in commitments for the changing future. I am suggesting here that there is something to be said for retaining the methodological distinction between achievable and unachievable sets of alternatives, even though their significant covariance be recognized.

[11]Arrow, *op. cit.*, 12; Hildreth, "Alternative Conditions for Social Orderings," *Econometrica*, Vol. 21, No. 1 (January, 1953), 89-90.

able alternatives. In other words, it does not preclude that the appearance or disappearance of, or new attitudes toward, unachievable alternatives may induce changes in individual orderings of achievable alternatives. But, for such occurrences, the condition will have no content; it simply will not apply.

That Arrow's election system, from which we generalized the conceptions of irrelevance above, is itself irrelevant is easily seen by noting that it involves a change in environment S, a candidate who is "achievable" (i.e., in S) in one situation, is not achievable in the second situation.

Our analysis so far does have the following relevance to Condition 3.

(1) The environment S must be interpreted as the entire set of alternatives actually in contention. If the ordering of S is desired to be built up by having individuals *express* their preferences[12] in sequences of subsets of S (such as by paired comparisons or in triplets), the sequence of sub-set orderings will not in general represent the "true" ordering of this environment S, unless the individuals are aware, throughout the sequence, of the total set of alternatives to be ordered.

(2) Condition 3 will not apply to situations in which changes initially concerning alternatives outside S result in changed ordering of alternatives in S. Our analysis suggests that changes in the former set do typically affect ordering of the latter. This means that Condition 3 will not comprehensively insulate the set of individual orderings against the effects of "irrelevant" alternatives because its domain of application will be small. It remains to examine what kind of insulation will be forthcoming in order finally to locate the conception of "irrelevance" intended. To that task I now turn.

6-3. Preference Orderings and Preference Intensities

Condition 3 says that in passing from individual orderings to a social ordering of alternatives in S, only individual orderings in S are relevant. Two related emphases in this formulation deserve notice. One is that only the *orderings* of alternatives in S are admitted; the other is that only the orderings of alternatives *in S* are admitted. These are different things, but from a practical point of view arguments for violating either of them often involve the same kind of consideration.

Let us begin with the latter. Only orderings *in S* are admitted. What is here being considered irrelevant is, for given identical orderings in S, the orderings of alternatives outside of S. Symbolically, let

---

[12]In a revealed preference context.

$$R_1{}^k = R_1 \begin{Bmatrix} x_1 \\ x_2 \\ \cdot \\ \cdot \\ x_n \\ \cdot \\ \cdot \\ \cdot \\ x_N \end{Bmatrix} \quad \text{and} \quad R_2{}^k = R_2 \begin{Bmatrix} x_1 \\ x_2 \\ \cdot \\ \cdot \\ x_n \\ \cdot \\ \cdot \\ , \\ x_N \end{Bmatrix}$$

be two rankings for a certain individual 1 of the total set of social states

$$\overline{S} = x_1, x_2, \ldots, x_N,$$

where $x_1, \ldots, x_n$ are in S and $x_{n+1}, x_{n+2}, \ldots, x_N$ are outside of S. Condition 3 asserts that $R_1{}^k$ and $R_2{}^k$ should have the same effect in aggregating to a social ordering of $x_1, \ldots, x_n$ (for every k) if, and only if, the orderings they give to the n achievable states in S are the same, and even though their ordering of the remaining alternatives ($x_{n+1}, \ldots, x_N$) may be different. In other words, no two alternatives need have the same rank number in $R_1{}^k$ and $R_2{}^k$, yet if the ordering of the achievable alternatives ($x_1, \ldots, x_n$) are the same, $R_1{}^k$ and $R_2{}^k$ are to be treated as identical. Hildreth, in the article cited above, summarizes the issue by writing Arrow's Social Welfare Function (with modification to make his terminology comparable with mine)

$$R(S) = M\,(R^1(S), R^2(S), \ldots, R^m(S))$$

(where superscripts denote the individual concerned) in contrast to the more general

$$R(S) = M'\,(R^1(\overline{S}), R^2(\overline{S}), \ldots, R^m(\overline{S})).[13]$$

The more general method can be thought of as obtaining a social ordering of all alternatives, and from this, extracting the ordering of the achievable sub-set (S). The method implied by adherence to Arrow's Condition 3 is to obtain the ordering of S directly, by comparing only alternatives in S. The crux of the issue is not that the *individual* orderings of S may be different when derived from the two different methods! Indeed, Condition 3 itself precludes this; it applies only for situations in which each $R_1{}^k(S)$ *is* the same as $R_2{}^k(S)$ (interpreting $R_1{}^k(S)$ as the ordering obtained indirectly and $R_2{}^k(S)$ as the ordering obtained directly). The crux of the issue is the value question: Should $R_1{}^k$ and $R_2{}^k$ mean the same thing for the context of *social* choice even though they represent different individual rankings of the alternatives in $\overline{S}$: should $R_1(S)$ be the same as $R_2(S)$ when they refer to similar individual rankings of S but different rankings

---

[13]Hildreth, *op. cit.*, 84 and 89.

of $\bar{S}$? Does $R^k(\bar{S})$ tell anything relevant about individual values which is not told by $R^k(S)$?

Consider the S composed of two alternatives x_1 and x_2. $x_1P_1{}^kx_2$ and $x_1P_2{}^kx_2$ (i.e., x_1 is preferred to x_2 in R_1 and in R_2). But

$$R_1{}^k = x_1P_1{}^kx_3P_1{}^kx_4P_1{}^kx_5 \ldots x_NP_1{}^kx_2;$$

while

$$R_2{}^k = x_1P_2{}^kx_2P_2{}^kx_3P_2{}^kx_4 \ldots x_{N-1}P_2{}^kx_N$$

(in $R_2{}^k(\bar{S})$ there is no x_i in $\bar{S}$ such that x_1 is preferred to x_i while x_i is preferred to x_2). A number of economists[14] feel that in this example, $R(\bar{S})$ has relevant information for social choice not possessed by $R(S)$. The additional information concerns not preference order but preference intensity. Thus, in our example here, we are supposing that $R_1{}^k$ is such that x_1 is the individual's first choice while x_2 is his last choice. $R_2{}^k$ is such that x_1 and x_2 are the individual's first and second choices out of the same totality of social state alternatives. It is argued that we intuitively feel that, although the individual prefers x_1 to x_2 in both situations, he prefers x_1 to x_2 *more* in the first ($R_1{}^k$) than in the second — he has a greater preference intensity for x_1 over x_2 in the first. And this greater preference intensity warrants that the $x_1P^kx_2$ ordering in the first situation should be given greater weight in determining social choice than the same ordering in the second.

Hildreth, for example, argues as follows:

> Suppose that in Case I[15](individual) i barely prefers (alternative) X to Y, and j desperately prefers Y to X. In Case II let i desperately prefer X to Y and j barely prefer Y to X. By Arrow's Condition 3, the social ordering between X and Y must be the same in Case I as in Case II. Admittedly our facilities for distinguishing bare preferences from desperate preferences may often be questionable, but we have to decide whether or not this justifies us in excluding all variations in degrees of preference from consideration.[16]

What this kind of argument implies is that social choice be aggregated from individual ordering variables weighted by their respective preference intensities, the greater the intensity the greater the weight given to the particular individual preference.

Let us now return to the other possible interpretation of Condition 3. Only the *ordering* of alternatives in S is admitted. To contradict this

---

[14]E.g., Hildreth, *op. cit.;* Markowitz and Goodman, "Social Welfare Functions Based on Individual Rankings," *The American Journal of Sociology*, Vol. LVII, No. 3 (November, 1952), 257-262; W. E. Armstrong, "Utility and the Theory of Welfare," *Oxford Economic Papers* (October, 1951). I shall examine the constructive proposals of these authors in later chapters.

[15]Not to be confused with my illustration above.

[16]Hildreth, *op. cit.,* 90.

requirement is to assert that something other than the ordering alone be admitted into the formation of social choice. Here, too, the additional factor is preference intensity. This interpretation is indistinguishable from the first if our comparisons of preference intensities derive only from considerations about the complete ordering in $\overline{S}$. But it is conceivable that we may also be able to compare preference intensities by methods which need not involve this complete ordering. To be specific, we can compare an individual's preference intensities if we can generate his cardinal utility function.[17]

Assume that we possess a cardinal utility function for individual i specifying an index number for every social state alternative $U^i = U^i(x_r)$ and unique up to, say, monotone linear transformations.[18] We desire to compare i's preference intensity for x_1 over x_2 with that for x_3 over x_4. Preference intensity is defined in this context as the difference between utility index numbers. Consequently, let us obtain the numbers $U_1{}^i$, $U_2{}^i$, $U_3{}^i$ and $U_4{}^i$. Our comparison of preference intensities is simply

$$(U_1{}^i - U_2{}^i) \gtreqless (U_3{}^i - U_4{}^i).$$

Since our index is unique up to monotonic linear transformations, the comparison will be invariant for all choice of zero point and unit of measurement.[19] This procedure need not, but may, involve the total ordering of S (although as S becomes a larger and larger subset of $\overline{S}$, the differences in our two interpretations disappear for all practical purposes, at least as far as the ordering of $\overline{S}$ is concerned.)[20] What is minimally involved in the procedure is an implicit comparison between each alternative and a common reference or base alternative. Each utility index number is itself representation of a preference intensity — that for the given alternative over the zero alternative, e.g.,

$$U_r{}^i = U^i(x_r) - U^i(x_0) = U_r{}^i - 0.$$

---

[17]Indeed, particular formulations of the first interpretation may themselves reduce to the construction of cardinal utility indices. See, e.g., my discussion in Chapter 7 on the method of finite rankings proposed by Markowitz and Goodman.

[18]Thus, a zero point and a unit of measurement or scale are arbitrary.

[19]The property of the utility index as an interval scale referred to here is that utility differences are invariant under changes of scale. The *ratio* between utility levels, however, is not invariant under changes of scale. If we wish to preserve proportionality relations between utility levels, we require further restrictions on our utility index. We must be able to derive an absolute zero from the function itself. Only the unit of measurement may remain arbitrary. This is called a ratio scale. See Clyde Coombs, "Theory and Methods of Social Measurement," in L. Festinger, and D. Katz (eds.), *Research Methods in the Behavioral Sciences* (New York: Dryden Press, 1953), 471-535. See also S. S. Stevens, "Mathematics, Measurement and Psychophysics," in S. S. Stevens (ed.), *Handbook of Experimental Psychology* (New York: John Wiley & Sons, Inc., 1951).

[20]Of course, a cardinal utility scale does involve more than an ordinal scale. See below for further discussion.

In the actual measurement procedures devised to make empirical calculations, each $U_r{}^i$ may be derived from direct comparison with base alternatives or from chains of comparisons leading from a base alternative to the alternative in question by means of intermediate alternatives. In some procedures, no single base alternative is specified, but index numbers for particular alternatives are nonetheless derived by selected comparisons with other alternatives. So, a particular sub-set of alternatives in $\overline{S}$ may be arrayed over a numerical scale without necessitating the total ordering of all alternatives in $\overline{S}$.

Moreover, the formulation above directly indicates the relevance of cardinal utility to notions about "irrelevant alternatives." In every attempt to compare preference intensities by means of cardinal utility indices, the comparison depends on the existence of an invariant unit of measurement (for the given utility indicator). The existence of this unit of measurement typically implies that "irrelevant" alternatives have been brought into the comparison. In the simple case of the last paragraph,

$$(U_1{}^i - U_2{}^i) \gtreqless (U_3{}^i - U_4{}^i)$$

can be most generally taken to mean

$$(U_1{}^i - U_0{}^i) - (U_2{}^i - U_0{}^i) \gtreqless (U_3{}^i - U_0{}^i) - (U_4{}^i - U_0{}^i);$$

and x_0 is the "irrelevant" alternative which is very much relevant. If any of these intensities is taken to be equal to the unit of measurement (arbitrary, in the case of interval scales), say $(U_2{}^i - U_0{}^i)$ or $(U_3{}^i - U_4{}^i)$, then the above simplifies to a comparison of intensities with the unit intensity. In the general case, each $U_r{}^i$ is a multiple of the unit of measurement:

$$(U_r{}^i - U_0{}^i) = b_r(\overline{U}{}^i - U_0{}^i).$$

Letting $(\overline{U}{}^i - U_0{}^i)$ arbitrarily equal 1, the comparison above now becomes

$$(b_1 - b_2) \gtreqless (b_3 - b_4).$$

And here both x_0 and $\overline{X}$ are the "irrelevant" alternatives without which the comparison is not possible.[21]

It is worth reiterating that the notion of irrelevance of which the use of cardinal utility properties represents a violation, concerns how individual orderings, however found, are aggregated to form social choice. It does not concern how the individual orderings are themselves formed, since the operational introduction of alternatives analogous to x_0, $\overline{X}$, etc., is not currently deemed necessary for revealing simple orders in S or $\overline{S}$.[22]

---

[21]The logical requirements for cardinal utility will be dealt with more systematically in the following chapter.

[22]But see the contrary supposition suggested by a consideration of psychological scaling techniques in Chapter 7, Section 7.5.

6-4. *Cardinality and the Social Welfare Function*

Is it justified to violate Condition 3 for the purpose of weighting each paired comparison in the given ordering with its preference intensity? As indicated above, this is a question of value judgment. But the purely empirical question of whether or not individuals do differentiate preference intensities and, what is almost the same thing, whether their behavior is affected by these differentiations[23] is one which can help us decide on an answer to the value question.

I think it would be generally agreed, on the testimony of introspection and literature, and, as a matter of fact, on that of our daily behavior toward others, that persons can differentiate preference intensities. Whether this differentiation makes a difference is another question. One of the chief reasons for the triumph of ordinal preference theory in economics was its apparent ability to rationalize static economic choice behavior on simpler assumptions than the preceding formulations of cardinal utility theory.[24] Is there some type of economic behavior which can not be adequately explained on ordinal assumptions but can be by introducing cardinal properties of utility (preference intensities)? The current interest in the von Neumann-Morgenstern axiomatization of cardinal utility, and especially the exposition of its content as an empirical hypothesis by Friedman and Savage,[25] suggest that non-static consumer behavior, especially choice under uncertainty, may be far better explained by taking into account preference intensities than by working solely with preference orders. Of course, no definitive answer can as yet be given.

But the issue at stake must be clearly understood. The general acceptance of ordinal theory to rationalize consumer choice under static conditions has been accompanied by a general abandonment of cardinal theory. Cardinal theory is considered superfluous in this branch of positive economics. It has most frequently been deemed superfluous in welfare economics as well, I venture to suggest, largely because of its superfluity in positive economics. But this is not generally warranted. It would be warranted,

---

[23]The student of positive economics would perhaps prefer the following formulation: can we make consistently good predictions with a theory that postulates that individuals choose *as if they were* influenced by preference intensities as well as by preference orders?

[24]Yet even in ordinal theory there is room for the notion of preference intensity. Thus, consider the preference ordering of the three alternatives X, Y, Z. X is preferred to Y; Y is preferred to Z. Since we assume that the ordering is transitive, X is preferred to Z. We are justified from this in making the further inference that X is preferred to Z more than X is preferred to Y. Thus, we are comparing preference intensities. This is because Y is "between" X and Z. Under ordinal assumptions, "between-ness" enables us to derive a partial ordering of preference intensities. Of course, the information about preference order will not alone suffice to generate a complete ordering of intensities. Thus, we know nothing of the preference intensity of X over Y compared with that of Y over Z.

[25]See the citation for the articles referred to in Chapters 9 and 10.

of course; if the superfluity in positive economics were due to empirical refutation. In point of fact, however, only one kind of cardinal model has been convincingly refuted — that which assigns numerical measures to commodity bundles on the basis of numerical measures assigned to the separate commodities in these bundles.[26] Cardinal models in which numerical measures are derived directly for the bundle as a whole have not been critically tested. *Their* superfluity in positive economics stems only from the greater simplicity of ordinal theory in rationalizing static choice behavior. And, failing to be refuted, they *may* be superfluous in welfare economics as well if we insist that only those aspects of individual values (tastes) ought to count in determining social welfare which can be in principle deduced from actual market-type[27] choices by consumers. We need not insist on this, however. If we are convinced that individuals do experience different preference intensities and that differences in preference intensities are important to them, then we may well deem it worth while to relax our restriction for the purpose of including preference intensity as an admissible element of individual values. Cardinal properties of utility will in this event no longer be superfluous (or irrelevant) in welfare economics. And furthermore, if a cardinal theory like that of the von Neumann-Morgenstern hypothesis does justifiably point up certain kinds of choices for which our best "explanation" of these choices enables us to deduce cardinal utility indices, then we may introduce preference intensity as a determining variable of social choice without even having to relax our restriction.

Our determination to introduce preference intensity does not, of course, depend solely on whether it is an important experience for individuals. Preference intensity must be a concept which is amenable to analytic manipulation. Intensities must be homogeneous, so that they differ from one another only in magnitude. They must be in practice quantifiable, or at the very least, capable of being ordered consistently. If we wish to construct cardinal utility indices with our data on preference intensities, we require something more than consistent ordering, namely, that the intensities be reducible to a common unit. It is on these requirements that formulations of cardinal utility typically founder. They cannot be operationally defined so as to enable, even in principle, precise empirical comparisons of preference intensities. But recent treatments have made strong explicit attempts to resolve this difficulty. I shall discuss some of these proposed formulations (one is the von Neumann-Morgenstern cardinal utility) in following chapters.

---

[26]The basis for refutation being the implicit absence of commodity relatedness — substitutability and complementarity. See the discussion in Chapter 10, Section 1, on the Strong Independence Postulate.

[27]"Market-type" includes experimental situations in which simulated market choices are made.

Assuming that we can "measure" preference intensities with a tolerable degree of precision, is this the kind of factor which we *ought* to treat on a par with preference ordering in the context of social choice? My own opinion is that preference intensity is logically part of the very same description of individual values that includes preference order, and that if the experimental means exists to make it measurable, failure to use it constitutes an unjustifiable restriction on the validity of the schematization of social choice. I believe that my position is a representative one and, as I have argued above, that the hesitation of economic analysis in the thirties and forties to have truck with notions of cardinal utility is largely irrelevant for our purposes.

But the case is even stronger than these general remarks would indicate. The inclusion of preference intensities may well be *prescribed* by the incorporation of value judgments already accepted in the schema! Since the ordering of social states requires generalizing external relationships in consumption,[28] the consumer is being expected to express attitudes toward various different ethical principles and also toward the standards of living of the rest of the population. It is certainly reasonable to suppose that he feels more strongly about some of these external relations than about others.

On the other side of the coin, the assumption of consumer's (or citizen's) sovereignty suggests that while some of these relationships may rightly be viewed as "his business," others are pretty clearly "none of his business." Although it may not be strictly true that those attitudes concerning others' consumption which a person feels strongly about are those which consumer sovereignty would countenance, it would appear nonetheless to be a useful approximation. If we were to start from a particular social state and consider an individual's scale of preferences for alternatives giving him the same commodity bundle but differing in commodity assignments to others, I think we should expect that the intensity of his feeling about these alternatives would bear close relationship to the intensity of his preferences with respect to the basal state. Suppose that a particular change in the standard of living of one group of people means little to our individual, is it not reasonable to expect that he will be nearly indifferent between such a state and the original state? Where the change in others' standards is one about which he has strong opinions, he is likely to have strong preferences as well. So the inclusion of preference intensities into the model has a definite ethical aura. This aura appears to spell out some of the implications of the assumption of consumer sovereignty which are neglected by reliance on orderings alone.

An additional issue is of great importance. The individual cardinal utility indicators about which I have been speaking do not logically imply

---

[28]See Chapter 2.

interpersonal comparisons of utility. Thus, suppose for a two-person group, we construct cardinal utility indicators (assume even that each index is completely determined, nothing is arbitrary; it will make no difference to the following). Then the comparison between any two given states (x and y) will be associated with a number for each individual. Do these numbers tell us anything about the relative size of the prospective utility level changes for the two? No. They indicate the utility difference in two states for each individual *in terms of his own system of preferences*. However, they do not tell us how to translate the scale of one system into the scale of the other. Interpersonal comparisons of utility require that utility level changes for all members of a group of persons be expressible in terms of a common standard. This does necessitate an explicit relating of the entire preference system of every person with that of every other.[29] In the current state of epistemological chaos over interpersonal comparisons, it is an open question as to whether this final stage represents a question of fact or of value.

Individual cardinal utility indicators, then, are not sufficient to enable us to compare utility changes for different individuals. Indeed, they are not even necessary. It is conceivable to have social choice mechanisms in which only ordinal properties of individual utility systems are employed, and which, nonetheless, make interpersonal comparisons. Such a mechanism is given by majority rule voting together with the explicit social assumption that each person's preference order counts as much as every other's.[30] A modification of this, whereby majority rule is combined with differential assignments of multiple votes to different individuals, is another example.

Very similar to this last modification is a model of the market system in which ordinal preference theory gives a complete explanation of consumer behavior. In such a model, the direction given to productive effort through the influence of preference ordering, weighted by the initial (unequal) distribution of wealth, would represent the postulated social choice. A difference between this model and the differential voting mechanism above is that in this model the distribution of weights is an endogenous variable whereas it is exogenous in the latter. Moreover, although individual preference orders would apparently be uninfluenced by exogenous changes in the distribution of weights under the voting mechanism,[31] individual

---

[29]This will be discussed in Chapters 7 (Sections 7.4 and 7.5) and 8 (Section 8.4) below.

[30]Neglect of the explicit assumption leaves the rule open to the alternative interpretation that preference intensities *are* to be employed, but, in the absence of reliable means to measure them individually, only statistically, through reliance on the law of large numbers. Thus, it might be assumed in such a formulation that for any particular paired comparison preference intensities are rectangularly distributed (equal *a priori* probabilities of all preference intensities for a given preference order). Then majority rule gives a probability greater than one-half that the sum of the preference intensities supporting the chosen alternative exceeds that of the rejected alternative.

[31]Except for strategic considerations.

orderings may be a function of this distribution in the market system, in the sense that evaluation of two commodity bundles depends on the individual's income level.[32]

A set of individual cardinal utility functions is neither necessary nor sufficient for making interpersonal comparisons of utility. Yet its introduction is usually deemed at least a flirtation with such comparisons. So Hildreth says: "Condition 3 was undoubtedly motivated by Arrow's determination to exclude any possibility of interpersonal comparisons of utilities."[33] The methodological affinity at stake is very likely the convenience with which it is possible to express the relating of different individuals' preferences when they are represented by numerical (unique) functions. The relation is a system of equations — quantified, manipulable. And if the individual functions represent the fruit of experimental findings, their operationality tempts one to contemplate the epistemological nature of interpersonal comparisons.

This ease with which one can "fall" into interpersonal comparisons of utility should not be deemed a defect. Individual utility indices must stand or fall only on their success or failure in measuring the characteristics of individual preferences. It is the procedure set up to make interpersonal comparisons among these preferences which must be judged independently in case of unfortunate application. The distinction between the two kinds of procedures is important because all Social Welfare Functions, with the exception only of "imposed" functions and the "unanimity" functions stemming from the New Welfare Economics,[34] implicitly involve interpersonal comparisons of utility.[35] In all of them, comparisons are defined for situations in which some persons are better off and some worse off. Furthermore, even if the given social choice mechanism is not explicitly expressed in terms of a balancing of individuals' well-being, a formal

---

[32]Except for restrictions on individual preference maps like those of Gorman, cited in Chapter 4 (Section 4.1).

[33]Hildreth, *op. cit.*, 90.

[34]See Chapters 3 and 4.

[35]Cf. Hildreth, *op. cit.*, 90-91. Hildreth does not except "imposed" functions. Such exception seems warranted, though, because individual orderings under an "imposed" function are irrelevant to the determination of social choice, so calculations about who is better off and who worse off, and by how much, would also seem irrelevant. Almost the same is true of the "dictatorship" situation, but under dictatorship we have the logical option of saying that the social choice involves comparison of the welfare of the dictator with that of everyone else, as well as any incidental interpersonal comparisons of others made by the dictator in arriving at his own ordering. This last point, coincidentally, shows that when our individual orderings represent individual "values" instead of simply individual "tastes," they will have incorporated in them the habitual everyday interpersonal comparisons of utility which everyone makes. One's higher ranking of a state in which a friend is "rewarded" and an enemy "punished" translates into particular distributions of commodity bundles only by means of these comparisons. In this sense, social choice in even unanimity Social Welfare Functions depends to some extent on interpersonal comparisons of utility.

equivalence to this balancing can be constructed. Consequently, when one evaluates each Social Welfare Function, it is important to keep in mind the distinction between the procedures by which we describe individual preferences and those by which we relate the preferences of different individuals, for without it we cannot clearly locate the strengths and weaknesses of the particular schema.

So far, we have argued in favor of admitting preference intensity as a factor in social choice without considering how it might help or fail to help us resolve the problem of the present inquiry. As we shall observe in the following three chapters, the scaling of preference intensities for the purpose of constructing individual cardinal utility indices does not alone enable us to render group welfare judgments. But if we supplement such indices with a set of assumptions such that we (1) numerically relate the unit of measurement of different indices and (2) numerically weight the influence on social choice of the unit of measurement of different indices, then we will be able to render group welfare judgments. Our welfare function will be a function of weighted individual utilities.

So, after specifying the form of the welfare function

$$(e.g., \qquad W = \sum_{i=1}^{n} U^i \quad \text{or} \quad W = \prod_{i=1}^{n} U^i, \quad \text{etc.}),$$

we need, in addition to our individual indices, only a value judgment on interpersonal comparisons and evaluations of utility.

As we have seen in Chapters 3 and 4, we can render group welfare judgments even when we employ only ordinal utility indicators for individuals. Here too we will require additional assumptions: (1) a social ordering of relative welfare distributions, (2) a rule for judging welfare when the level of production criterion and the relative welfare distribution criterion give opposite verdicts. But this pair of assumptions involves no less than the substance of our problem itself. The use of ordinal indices solves the problem of securing an acceptable social ordering by assuming it away!

By contrast, the supplementary assumptions needed under cardinal indices do not beg the main question. A cardinal welfare analysis possesses at least this potential advantage over ordinal analysis. How great an actual advantage it possesses is another question. I have suggested that the problem of choosing appropriate Social Welfare Functions consists of the economist's selecting those value judgments which seem to him likely to secure pervasive agreement in the community. It seems intuitively plausible that the economist should be better able to generalize (empirically) about the community's beliefs concerning the relative capacities and social worth of different individuals, than about the community's agreed-on ranking of social states.[36] The final test of this assertion rests, of course, upon further empirical enquiry.

6-5. Summary: A Modified Condition on Irrelevant Alternatives

In summarizing, it seems appropriate to utilize the conclusions of the chapter to modify Arrow's Condition 3 in such a way as to retain a justifiable restriction on the independence of irrelevant alternatives. Our main conclusions are:

(1) In the limit, no social state alternative in $\overline{S}$ is irrelevant to the formation of an individual ordering in S.

(2) It is not reasonable to declare irrelevant the very possibility of considerations about preference intensity. Preference intensity is correlative with preference order in determining social choice, and each attempt at an operational definition should be evaluated on its own merits.

We may now suggest a modified condition on the independence of irrelevant alternatives. Let us introduce the notion of the welfare prospectus of an individual W_i. This is nothing but a matrix description of his preference ordering in $\overline{S}$ together with information about his preference intensities between alternatives in $\overline{S}$, i.e., $W_i = (R_i, I_i)$. In the general case we do not specify the form of I_i. In the specific case of individual cardinal utility indicators, each W_i is the numerical utility function.

Condition 3′. Let $W_1, \ldots, W_n$ and $W'_1, \ldots, W'_n$ be two sets of individual welfare prospectuses and let $C(S)$ and $C'(S)$ be the corresponding social choice functions. If, for all individuals i, and all x and y in a given environment S, xR_iy if and only if xR'_iy and $I_i(x,y) = I'_i(x,y)$ then $C(S)$ and $C'(S)$ are the same.

This general form has been presented for the purpose of covering both schemas in which preference intensities are derived from cardinal utility indicators and are therefore in numerical form, and schemas in which only incomplete non-numerical notions about preference intensities are employed (such as would be derivable in treatments where information is obtained from orderings alone). In the former case of cardinal indicators the condition can be simplified to the following form:

Condition 3″. Let $U^1, \ldots, U^n$ and $U^{1*}, \ldots, U^{n*}$ be two sets of individual cardinal utility functions and let $C(S)$ and $C'(S)$ be the corresponding social

---

[36]In Chapter 13 I shall argue, however, that he may well find it easier to generalize about the community's desired decision-making processes than about either its interpersonal comparisons or its social ordering, and that such consensus on decision-making processes may be sufficient to enable the economist to construct a useful Social Welfare Function.

choice functions. If, for all individuals i and all x and y in a given environment S,

$$U^i(x) = U^{i*}(x) \quad \text{and} \quad U^i(y) = U^{i*}(y),$$

then $C(S)$ and $C'(S)$ are the same.

In both modifications of Condition 3, irrelevance is not defined in terms of the formation of prospectuses or utility functions but in terms of their use thereafter. In both, irrelevance means that no alternative can influence a particular social choice except insofar as it can influence the content of welfare prospectuses or utility functions. Once *given* $R_i(x,y)$ and $I_i(x,y)$ for a particular comparison, the effect of the comparison on social choice is invariant (except, of course, in an action context where strategic considerations may be involved); it is independent of the achievability, the ranking and the preference intensities, of all other alternatives. In the case of cardinal utility functions, the condition is that once given $U^i(x)$ and $U^i(y)$, the effect on social choice is independent of all other alternatives.[37]

In the next three chapters I shall examine some attempts to construct acceptable Social Welfare Functions by dropping Arrow's Condition 3. One criterion by which these will be evaluated is the extent to which they fulfill our modified condition on irrelevant alternatives.

---

[37]This can be further simplified to state that once given $U^i(x)$, the alternative x will possess the same comparison strength no matter with which other alternative it is compared.

This might be compared with the analogous but not equivalent formulation by Hildreth: "The welfare value of any social state x is independent of the other states with which x is compared." "Measurable Utility and Social Welfare," *Cowles Commission Discussion Paper, Economics*, No. 2002 (December, 1950). The lack of equivalence is due to the fact that Hildreth's postulate may preclude the effect of other states in $\bar{S}$ on the *formation* of the welfare value of x.

CHAPTER 7

Preference Threshold and

Cardinal Utility

7-1. Introduction

With the contributions of Hicks and Allen in the 1930's the indifference curve approach to consumer demand came into general analytic usage. Under this approach ordinal properties of utility indices were deemed necessary and sufficient to rationalize all forms of consumer behavior then incorporated in economic theory. This supplanted the approach stemming from Jevons and Menger, under which analytic conclusions were based on cardinal properties of utility. The empirical implications of cardinal utility were deemed by many economists too controversial to stand at the base of demand theory. If less restrictive assumptions could "explain" all that was desired of a theory of consumer behavior, then such assumptions were preferable (by Occam's razor). A sizable literature was generated by the controversy over whether (1) the indifference curve approach did indeed eschew cardinal properties of utility, or (2) it could "explain" all that was desired.[1] The outcome of this controversy was that the indifference curve (or preference) approach did not involve cardinality[2]

---

[1] For example, R. G. D. Allen, "The Determinateness of the Utility Function," *Review of Economic Studies* (1935); J. M. Clark, "Realism and Relevance in the Theory of Demand," *Journal of Political Economy* (1946); Frank Knight, "Realism and Relevance in the Theory of Demand," *Journal of Political Economy* (1944); Oskar Lange, "On the Determinateness of the Utility Function," *Review of Economic Studies* (1934), to mention but a few of the journal articles.

[2] As employed in this paper, a cardinal index of utility is one for which at least a simple ordering of both preferences and preference intensities is defined, and intensities are relatable to a common unit. See Section 7.2 below for a fuller discussion.

and that the approach could "explain" the empirical content of the then-contemporary demand theory.

Two developments have recently reopened, if indeed it was ever closed, interest in the second issue. First, the von Neumann-Morgenstern *Theory of Games* derives a cardinal utility index by emphasizing the meaningfulness of certain consumer behavior in the face of risk.

Second (and more relevant to our purpose here), the "New Welfare Economics," formulated to derive *objective* (non-value saturated) conclusions on individual and community well-being from ordinal preference theory, has been revealed to possess serious shortcomings, shortcomings which currently prevent it from giving even approximately definitive counsel on any subject.[3] Some of the most important of these shortcomings depend on the lack of cardinal properties of the utility indices assumed for consumers. Cardinal utility indices would significantly strengthen the power and daring of welfare economics.

But does cardinality meaningfully exist? That is, are its implications consistent with observable consumer behavior, or (not quite identically) can cardinal utility indices be inferred from observable consumer behavior? Moreover, if we *can* construct cardinal indices of individual utility, and therefore measure preference intensities, will this enable us to construct an acceptable Social Welfare Function?

A model proposed by W. E. Armstrong[4] gives an affirmative answer to these questions. His conclusion and his introduction of rather novel ideas in economic analysis merit close scrutiny. This chapter will be chiefly concerned with his concept of "marginal preference" and its implications for welfare analysis.

7-2. Intransitivity of Indifference and Preference Threshold

Armstrong's important contribution concerns his use of the concept of "marginal preference" as an attempt to construct a powerful foundation for welfare economics. Most briefly, "marginal preference" arises out of an alleged intransitivity of indifference. Although preference theory has usually involved (either explicitly or by implication) transitivity of both

---

[3]See Chapters 3 and 4 above and also, as indicated there, e.g., Kenneth Arrow, *Social Choice and Individual Values;* I. M. D. Little, *A Critique of Welfare Economics;* Paul Samuelson, "The Evaluation of Real National Income," and *Foundations of Economic Analysis*, Chapter 8.

[4]"Utility and the Theory of Welfare," *Oxford Economic Papers* (October, 1951); "Comment on 'Marginal Preference and the Theory of Welfare'," *Oxford Economic Papers* (October, 1953); J. Rothenberg, "Marginal Preference and the Theory of Welfare," *Oxford Economic Papers* (October, 1953) and "Reconsideration of a Group Welfare Index," *Oxford Economic Papers* (October, 1953). The substance of this chapter is taken from these last two articles.

preference and indifference, a full treatment of the case where indifference is intransitive (but preference transitive) is given by Georgescu-Roegen in his 1936 article.[5] Armstrong's argument in support of intransitivity somewhat resembles Georgescu-Roegen's, but the implications which he draws are essentially different. The following is substantially his argument.

In preference theory, an individual is deemed capable of comparing any three commodity bundles or 'situations' A, B, C,[6] so as to determine between any two whether A is preferred to B, B preferred to A, or A indifferent to B. Moreover, his comparisons are deemed empirically constrained such that (1) if A is preferred to B, and B preferred to C, then A is preferred to C; (2) if A is indifferent to B and B is indifferent to C, then A is indifferent to C. (The "revealed preference" approach to demand theory initiated by Paul Samuelson has been shown in articles by Little, Houthakker, and Samuelson to be logically identical with preference theory of the Slutsky-Hicks-Allen type[7] and thus normally to involve transitivity of both preference and indifference. I shall examine an exceptional instance below.)

On empirical grounds, Armstrong rejects constraint Number 2. There are many instances, he claims, when an individual reports that he is indifferent between A and B; *and* between B and C, but *not* between A and C. The behavioral basis of his contention can perhaps be made clearer by extending this example: The individual reports that he is indifferent between A and B, B and C, C and D, D and E, E and F, but not between A and F. In general this means that any relation of preference between A and F can be broken down into a chain of successive indifferences (assuming throughout that the number of such alternatives as the individual can operationally compare, i.e.; 'real' alternatives, is significantly large throughout the entire range of choice). Moreover, if we neglect this empirical fact of intransitivity and insist on defining indifference as transitive in our system, we may get outright contradiction. Assume the individual prefers A to A^1. Now, introduce situations B, C, D, E, and F such that the individual is indifferent between A^1 and B, B and C, C and D, D and E, E and F. By direct comparison, he would prefer F to A^1 and F to A. With no such direct comparison, however, we would *infer* through

[5]"The Pure Theory of Choice," *Quarterly Journal of Economics*, Vol. L (August, 1936), 545-593.

[6]In this chapter I am using the notation A, B, C, . . . to refer to the alternatives of choice. This differs from the notation of previous chapters where alternatives were denoted by x, y, z, . . . or x_1, x_2, . . . etc. The justification for this change is that the analysis of the present chapter frequently calls for intricate manipulations of several identified alternatives. The argument would, I think, be more difficult to follow with either of the preceding notations.

[7]Paul A. Samuelson, "Consumption Theory in Terms of Revealed Preference," *Economica* (1948), 243-253; I. M. D. Little, "A Reformulation of the Theory of Consumer's Behavior," *Oxford Economic Papers*, No. 1 (1949), 90-99; H. S. Houthakker, "Revealed Preference and the Utility Function," *Economica* (May, 1950), 159-174.

transitivity of indifference that A^1 was indifferent with F and therefore that A was preferred to F.

Armstrong postulates that intransitivity arises because of the imperfection of human perception. In our original example, comparing A, B and C, A and B were declared to be indifferent, but they were, in fact, argues Armstrong, felt to be slightly different. The perception of difference involved here was not clear enough to warrant the individual preferring one to the other. C, however, indifferent to B yet also slightly different, was dissimilar enough from A so that a real preference could be perceived. Small, unperceived "preferences" cumulate into larger, perceivable preferences. In general, then, Armstrong would introduce into demand theory considerations about the intensity of preference, a concept not otherwise needed by ordinal preference theorists to deduce consumer behavior. His purpose in this is to derive a 'determinate' ('cardinal') utility function.

A first step in this direction is to redefine the distinction between preference and indifference. The intensity of preference, as an empirical fact, varies over a wide range. No assumption need be made at this point as to measurability of intensity, but a simple ordering is deemed possible. Some of these intensities are great enough to be called preferences, but some are great enough only to be distinguished from the smallest experienced intensity, that is, they are not great enough to be considered preference. In other words, there is a threshold in the perception of preference, such that intra-threshold intensities do exist but are not recognized as preference. On this scale of preference intensities one particular intensity is the greatest of those within the threshold; another is the smallest of those just outside the threshold — the smallest difference perceived as preference. Armstrong calls the first of these "marginal indifference," the second "marginal preference." If preference intensity is a continuous variable, then "marginal indifference" is identical with "marginal preference." Otherwise, they are distinct. To avoid confusion with some of the connotations of the term "marginal," it might be desirable to employ a different term. We may call a "marginal" (or threshold) preference a "bare" preference.[8]

The relation of preference and indifference can now be redefined. An individual prefers A to B if, and only if, he has at least a bare preference for A over B. An individual is indifferent between A and B if, and only if, he feels less than a bare preference between them. And the intransitivity of indifference (but not of preference) can be seen directly. A is indifferent to B; B indifferent to C. But in comparing A with C, the less-than-bare preference between A and B cumulates with that between B and C to give a total preference intensity which may well be greater than bare preference. Hence, A and C need not be indifferent.

---

[8]I am indebted to Professors Albert G. Hart and William Vickrey of Columbia University for their terminological suggestions.

How useful is this schema? Armstrong believes that it lays the foundation for a scientific welfare economics of far greater effectiveness than the "New Welfare Economics." His argument is really twofold. He believes, first, that the notion of intransitivity of indifference alone is sufficient for a more powerful analysis of group-welfare scales than is possible with traditional preference theory. Second, he believes that the concept of "bare preference" enables us to formulate a "determinate" (cardinal) index of group utility under which interpersonal comparisons are possible.

As for the first, how does Armstrong propose to obtain conclusions about group welfare not accessible to traditional ordinal preference theory? In the two-person group, individual 1 prefers situation A to B, while individual 2 prefers situation B to A. Now (1) introduce some situation C which 1 orders as follows: A preferred to C, C preferred to B; (2) introduce some situation D which 2 orders as follows: A indifferent to D, D indifferent to B, but B preferred to A (because of intransitivity).

(A) The situation A group-preferred to "a combination" of C for 1 and D for 2 (since 1 prefers A to C, and 2 is indifferent between A and D).

(B) The "combination" of C for 1 and D for 2 is group-preferred to B (since 1 prefers C to B, and 2 is indifferent between D and B).

Since group-preference is transitive, from (A) and (B) we infer

(C) A is group-preferred to B.

I believe this demonstration is faulty. The proof depends not only on the validity of indifference intransitivity, but also — and crucially — on the meaning of the concept of a "combination of C for 1 and D for 2." What does this concept mean? Steps (A) and (B) imply that the "situations" A and B can each be compared with a "situation" in which 1 experiences "situation" C and 2 experiences "situation" D. Is it possible for such a composite "situation" to exist? Under realistic circumstances I think not. For individual 1, A is preferred to C and C preferred to B, so C must be comparable with A and B. Similarly, A is indifferent to D and D indifferent to B for individual 2, so D must be comparable with A and B. It would appear to be possible for 1 to experience C at the same time as 2 was experiencing D only if C expressed a distribution of real income to 1 alone, and D expressed a distribution of real income to 2 alone. If C or D included commodities going to both individuals, then, in the general case of external relations in consumption, simultaneous occurrence of both C and D would be inconsistent. Yet C and D *must* refer to the real incomes of both 1 and 2, because both are deemed comparable with A and B, and A and B find their way into the preference scales of these individuals. So no meaning can be attributed to Armstrong's composite "situation."[9]

This can be seen as follows. First, my conclusion would appear to be

---

[9]It is interesting that Armstrong *can* infer that A is group-preferred to B by his method employing the concept of bare preference. This will be discussed below.

valid whenever there are external relations in consumption (the working assumption of the present work). It is not true only in the absence of all external relations. Thus, if individual 1 is affected by the consumption of individual 2, then a particular flow of goods to 1 will have different positions on his scale of preferences depending upon the corresponding real income of 2. Let A and B refer to commodity bundles going to both 1 and 2, C refer to a bundle going to 1 alone, and D refer to a bundle going to 2 alone. Then C cannot be uniquely ordered with A and B, since no real income for 2 is specified — C is not comparable with A and B for 1. Similarly, D cannot be uniquely introduced into a preference scale with A and $B - D$ is not comparable with A and B for 2.

Let A and B now refer to commodity bundles going only to one person, say, 1. Also let C and D refer to bundles going only to 1. All four alternatives are now comparable, but now the simultaneous occurrence of C and D is in general inconsistent.

Armstrong's proof is allowable only if C and D can refer to bundles going solely to 1 and 2 respectively, and yet be comparable with A and B. This is possible if there are no external relations in consumption. The preference ordering of each individual depends solely on goods going to himself. Thus, A and B refer to bundles going to both, but their ordering depends for each only on the goods going to himself. C now refers to a bundle to 1 alone, D to a bundle to 2 alone. The position of C on 1's preference scale is now uniquely fixed regardless of 2's income. The position of D is fixed uniquely for 2 regardless of 1's income. So the composite C-D situation has a meaning comparable to A and B, i.e., $(C$-$D)$ refers to an alternative of certain goods going to 1 and 2 — and is in general consistent.

But the assumption that there are no external relations in consumption cannot be accepted for application in welfare economics. So Armstrong's proof cannot be accepted.[10]

---

[10]Cf. Duesenberry, *Income, Saving and the Theory of Consumer Behavior* (Cambridge: Harvard University Press, 1949); also W. J. Baumol, *Welfare Economics and the Theory of the State* (Cambridge: Harvard University Press, 1952).

In his "Comment," Armstrong suggests that the combined situation can be interpreted in a manner which, although admitting the possibility of external relations in consumption, avoids this logical difficulty. C is defined to be a situation where 1 is to consume some commodity vector X and believes 2 will consume commodity vector Y. D is defined as a situation where 2 is to consume some commodity vector Y^1 and believes 1 will consume vector X^1. The combination of C for 1 and D for 2 simply refers to a situation where 1 is to consume X, and 2 is to consume Y^1, while 1 incorrectly *believes* that 2 is to consume Y and 2 incorrectly *believes* that 1 is to consume X^1 (where $X \neq X^1$ and $Y \neq Y^1$). So long as their beliefs are incorrect when C and D differ, there is no logical contradiction.

It is certainly true that external relations in consumption, and for that matter, all consumer behavior, depend on the consumers' beliefs about external circumstances. But this fact does not justify Armstrong's interpretation. What is the context within which we are observing the consumer? We are not, I submit, watching him making

In the second part of his argument Armstrong formulates a cardinal index of utility by introducing his Assumptions 5 and 6: Assumption 5 reads: "Any individual welfare variation, sufficient to give rise to prefer-

---

actual choices in the historically directed real world. The highly restrictive "selection" of situations C and D belies this notion. We are rather submitting him to an experimental procedure in which *we* must direct him to consider the situation C or D and the "combination." How shall we direct 1 to consider C? Must we not specify "C is a situation where you receive X and 2 *receives* Y"? How shall we direct him to consider the combination? Can we say: "The combination is a situation in which you receive X and you believe 2 receives Y, but in reality he receives Y^1 while mistakenly believing that you receive X^1"? If 1 responds at all to this, will it not be as though the situation were simply 1 receives X and 2 receives Y^1? This, however, is not what Armstrong means by the "combination." Furthermore, it is not permissible to direct 1 to the combination by telling him only: "You receive X and 2 receives Y." In such an instance, he would simply be responding to C, not to the "combination." Since the same argument holds for 2, one would be directing 2 to respond simply to D ("you get Y^1 and 1 gets X^1").

Armstrong's demonstration, then, would not appear to differ from the following. "1 prefers A to a certain situation C while 2 is indifferent between A and a different situation D. 1 finds B inferior to the situation C while 2 is indifferent between B and the different situation D." Individuals 1 and 2 are not comparing A and B to the *same* other situation, so the rules concerning transitivity of *group* preference, whereby A was judged group-preferred to B, do not apply. If Armstrong asserts that his "combination of C and D" is a unique situation he must show that it is operationally different from asking 1 to compare A and B with C and 2 to compare A and B with D. What my disagreement comes to, then, is that the interpretation of a "combined situation C for individual 1 and D for individual 2" which I believe Armstrong is advancing, does not appear to be capable of operational specification. I am not, of course, arguing that no operationally meaningful interpretation of such a combined situation is possible.

Armstrong's defense in the same article with respect to preferences based on the *fact* of other individuals' consumption (rather than merely on the *belief* about others' consumption) does not seem satisfactory either. He argues in his "Comment" (pp. 2-3):

> The fact that, on this view, it may be logically impossible to combine the situations C and D does not imply that it is logically impossible to have a combination of 'welfare of #1 corresponding to C' and 'welfare of #2 corresponding to D'. On the contrary, any combinations of individual welfares that are separately conceivable are logically possible . . . though it might be claimed that logical rigour needs an axiom to this effect. If this be granted, then by axiom (5) a group-welfare is conceivable that is lower than the group-welfare of A and higher than the group-welfare of B; and, therefore, the group-welfare of A is higher than the group-welfare of B.

What the introduction of C accomplishes is to indicate that for individual 1, who prefers A to B, a state is conceivable possessing, to use Armstrong's terminology, a level of 1's welfare lower than A but higher than B. Individual 2's ranking of D shows that a different state is conceivable for which the level of 2's welfare is perceived to be the same as for A and for B, even though the welfare level of B is higher than that of A. But this demonstration does not show a *single* hypothetical situation which, by the ordinal rules, is *group* preferred to B while being inferior to A. (Only the comparison of A and B with a single intermediate state carries with it group-preference implications in ordinal analysis.) Armstrong's demonstration can indicate that A is group-preferred to B only if it uses intermediate situations C and D to throw light on the relative preference intensities of 1 and 2 for A and B *and* then goes further to postulate some transformation by which 1's preference intensities are to be compared with 2's. Indeed, he does this but only by means of the concept of bare preference and not solely by introducing the intransitivity of indifference. In other words, his proof here is incomplete; it waits upon his later construction of a cardinal group-welfare index.

ence, causes a greater . . . variation of group welfare than any individual welfare variation, sufficient only to give rise to indifference."[11]

Assumption 6 reads: "If, in a group, there is a variation of the situation of one individual, within the limits of his indifference, then the variation of group welfare is trivial."[12]

From these assumptions, which Armstrong considers as reasonable, and therefore as acceptable, as any employed by ordinal preference theorists,[13] together with the concept of bare preference, Armstrong believes that a cardinal group-welfare index can be deduced logically. Bare preference becomes the unit by which all preference intensities are measured. But if preference intensities can be measured, then the alternatives of choice themselves can be scaled quantitatively.[14]

This last can easily be shown. Say that a certain individual orders four alternatives as follows: A, B, C, D (A preferred to B, B preferred to C, etc.). Here we have a simple order of alternatives. In addition, we have a *partial* order of preference intervals (intensities), i.e., we know that A is preferred to D more than A is preferred to B or to C, or than B is preferred to C or to D, etc., but we do not know whether A is preferred to B more than B is preferred to C or C preferred to D, etc. If we had a complete ordering of these intensities, we would know more about the placement of these alternatives on a figurative choice continuum. If, for example, we knew that A is preferred to B more than B is preferred to C, then we would know that the interval $\overline{AB} >$ interval $\overline{BC}$. Similarly, say $\overline{BC} < \overline{CD}$, and $\overline{AB} > \overline{CD}$.

Figure 11 represents one out of an infinite number of placements for which $A > B > C > D$ and $\overline{AB} > \overline{CD} > \overline{BC}$. Numbers could be given to the lateral positions of A, B, C, D, but no arithmetic operations could be performed on such numbers.

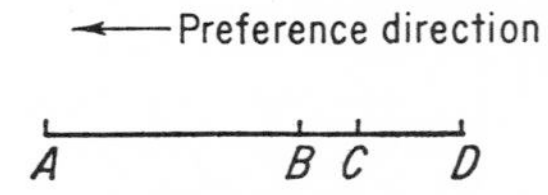

◄── Preference direction

A B C D

Figure 11

If now we had a common unit by which we could compare these intervals, then numbers could be applied to the positions A, B, C, D upon which arithmetic operations could be performed. Thus, arbitrarily taking $\overline{AB}$ as our unit, if it were operationally possible to determine that, say, $\overline{AB} =$ three times as large as $\overline{BC}$ and two times as large as $\overline{CD}$, then the interval $\overline{AB}$ could be given the number 1, $\overline{BC}$ the number $\frac{1}{3}$, $\overline{CD}$ the number $\frac{1}{2}$. And A, B, C, D could be given the numbers 0, 1, $1\frac{1}{3}$, $1\frac{5}{6}$, or 4, 5,

---

[11]"Utility and the Theory of Welfare," 264.

[12]*Ibid.,* 267.

[13]One such assumption, as quoted early in Armstrong's article, is: "If an individual prefers alternative A to alternative B, then his individual welfare is higher with A than with B." (p. 259)

[14]See the Appendix to this chapter, applying the concept of bare preference to ordinal preference theory.

$5\frac{1}{3}$, $5\frac{5}{6}$, or any linear transformation of these. These numbers could be added or subtracted, since the intervals remain invariant under such operations. (If, in addition, we knew that particular alternative X for which we could, with special justification, give the number zero, then the resulting scale — a ratio scale — would involve measurement on which all the operations of arithmetic could be performed.)[15]

Applying this to bare preference as the common unit, we can construct an interval scale of utility (where intervals between alternatives can be reduced to multiples of the common unit), and can quantitatively measure the intensity of any preference.

For the first, take some alternative A. Now choose some B, C, D, E, etc. such that B is barely preferred to A; C is barely preferred to B; D is barely preferred to C; etc. So $\overline{AE} = 4 \times \overline{AB}$ and if $\overline{AB}$, the bare preference interval, is given a number, say 1, then $\overline{AE} = 4 \times 1 = 4$, and E has the position $(4 + A)$. Again, it must be pointed out that the zero point and the number given to the common unit are arbitrary. For the second, we are given that some E is preferred to some A, and we desire to quantify the intensity of the preference. Now, choose some B, C, D, ... N for which B is barely preferred to A, C barely preferred to B, ... $(N - 1)$ barely preferred to N, and N indifferent with E. The intensity

$$\overline{AE} = N \times \overline{AB} = N \times \text{bare preference.}$$

7-3. Bare Preference and Interpersonal Comparisons of Utility

According to Armstrong, bare preference, as such a unit of measurement for individual and group welfare indices, follows logically from Assumptions 5 and 6.

> Since between two alternatives, A and B, A is preferred to B or B is preferred to A or A is indifferent with B, must hold for an individual, and since group-welfare rises with increase of individual welfare, there must be a minimum individual welfare-difference consistent with preference, for each and every member of the group, and this minimum individual welfare-difference must, for every individual, give rise to the same group-welfare relation. If we use the same number, e.g., unity, as a measure for this minimum for all individuals, a group-welfare function emerges having the simple characteristic that the same group-welfare variation results from any given individual welfare variation. In other words, group-welfare variation is a rising function of the sum of individual welfare variations.[16]

---

[15]Armstrong's article even proposes a solution to the problem of setting a zero point.
[16]*Ibid.*, 265.

This minimum discernible (or threshold) preference is what we have been referring to as "bare preference."

And to make explicit how interpersonal comparisons of utility are involved in his index, he argues that a bare preference

> . . . indicates the same welfare-difference, independently of the person exercising the preference. . . . A bare preference of any person has a greater effect on group-welfare than a bare indifference[17] (in the same direction) of the same or any other person by assumption 5. But a bare preference is adjacent, for any given person, to a bare indifference (in the sense that either is the boundary of the other). If, therefore, a bare preference of one person has a greater effect on group-welfare than a bare preference of another person, than the former's bare indifference cannot have a smaller effect. But this would contradict assumption 5. Therefore, a bare preference of one person must have the same effect on group-welfare as a bare preference of any other member of the group.
>
> If we assume that a variation of group-welfare is a function of individual welfare variation, it follows that a bare preference implies an individual welfare difference that is independent of the individual. *In other words, interpersonal comparisons of utility are logically implied by assumptions that economists do not seem to question.*[18]

This is quite a remarkable conclusion, all the more remarkable if it can, indeed, be deduced from Assumptions 5 and 6 and the definition of marginal preference. Moreover, if this conclusion does hold by logical implication, then effective criticism must be largely criticism of the seemingly innocuous Assumptions 5 and 6. *Does* cardinal utility follow deductively?

I shall try to indicate below that cardinal utility, and therefore interpersonal comparisons of utility, do not follow deductively. I shall do this by advancing an intuitive example in the present section. In the following section, I shall present a formal model of Armstrong's suggested group index, and through this demonstrate the general proof of my contention. Readers not interested in the more rigorous demonstration may omit Section IV.

For the first, assume a two-person group and an initial situation A. Now, from A generate a situation B which individual 2 barely prefers to A, but for which individual 1 has less than a bare preference (i.e., is indifferent between A and B). Assumption 5 tells us that B is socially preferred (i.e., has a higher group welfare) to A. But this conclusion follows also on strictly ordinal preference grounds, since no one *prefers* A to B, and at least one

---

[17]The maximum preference intensity compatible with indifference. In Armstrong's terminology, a "marginal" indifference. I have substituted "bare" for Armstrong's "marginal" throughout this quotation.

[18]*Ibid.*, 266, fn. 1. Italics mine.

person *prefers* B to A.[19] Similarly, from A generate C which 1 barely prefers to A, while 2 is indifferent between A and C. By Assumption 5, C is socially preferred to A, and this shows that a bare preference by individual 1 is "as good as" a bare preference by individual 2 in generating *social* preference. But again this conclusion follows from traditional ordinal preference theory. Does Assumption 5, then, take us any further than traditional theory? Does it, specifically, when combined with Assumption 6, take us as far as Armstrong claims?

Let us extend our example. From B generate D such that 2 barely prefers D to B and 1 is indifferent between D and B and also between D and A. From D generate E such that 2 barely prefers E to D and 1 is indifferent between E, D, B, and A. Now compare E with C. On ordinal preference grounds alone, 1 is indifferent between E and A. He prefers C to A. Allowing for intransitivity of indifference, either C is preferred to E or C is indifferent about E.[20] Individual 2 prefers E to D, D to B, B to A, so E to A (*preference* is transitive). He is indifferent between A and C. So either E is preferred to C or E is indifferent about C. As a result of these individual orderings, either C is socially preferred to E (1 prefers C to E, 2 is indifferent), E is socially preferred to C (2 prefers E to C, 1 is indifferent), or they are socially indifferent (both indifferent, or opposite choices).[21]

Now apply Armstrong's cardinal utility index to this comparison. The sum of the preference intensities of C to A is:

---

[19]The rules are that:
  (1) Where no one prefers A to B but at least one person prefers B to A, then B is socially preferred to A;
  (2) Where everyone is indifferent between A and B, A and B are socially indifferent;
  (3) Where at least one person prefers A to B and at least one prefers B to A, A and B are socially indifferent. (Majority rule, weighted voting, are exceptions.)
Although rule 3 is advanced by some economists, it will be remembered that we rejected it in our treatment of the New Welfare Economics in chapters 3 and 4 above. In our treatment, alternatives for which the preferences of different persons are contrary, are simply non-comparable. By this treatment, group-welfare comparisons enable only a partial ordering of alternatives.
  [20]E preferred to C is precluded. If E is preferred to C, then, since C is preferred to A, E preferred to A. But E is indifferent with A. So not E is preferred to C.
  [21]Note that we cannot employ the following analysis:
  (1) Comparing B to C, 1 prefers C to B, 2 prefers B to C, so B and C are socially indifferent;
  (2) Comparing E to B, 2 prefers E to B, 1 is indifferent between them, so E is socially preferred to B; and thus
  (3) E is preferred to C.
With intransitivity of indifference, (3) does not necessarily follow (1) and (2). And in fact, if rule 3 is not to be rejected, we know that a direct comparison between E and C shows, since 1 prefers C to E and 2 prefers E to C, that they are socially indifferent.
  This inconsistency illustrates Arrow's doubts about acceptable Social Welfare Functions with a vengeance.

$\overline{CA}_1 = 1$ (= bare preference, arbitrarily numbered 1) preference intensity of individual 1

$-1 < \overline{CA}_2 < 1$ (= nontransitive indifference between C and A) preference intensity of individual 2

$\overline{CA}_1 + \overline{CA}_2 = \overline{CA}_{1+2}$ where $0 < \overline{CA}_{1+2} < 2$

The sum of the preference intensities of E to A is:

$-1 < \overline{EA}_1 < 1$ (indifference)

$\overline{EA}_2 = \overline{ED}_2 + \overline{DB}_2 + \overline{BA}_2 = 1 + 1 + 1 = 3$ (sum of three bare preferences)

$\overline{EA}_1 + \overline{EA}_2 = \overline{EA}_{1+2}$ where $2 < \overline{EA}_{1+2} < 4$

Thus $\overline{EA}_{1+2} > \overline{CA}_{1+2}$, so E is socially preferred to C.

Now, do Assumptions 5 and 6, together with the concept of bare preference, tell us this much? They tell us that individual 2 cannot be indifferent between C and E; only a preference for E over C is consistent with his ordering. A and C are indifferent, but B is preferred to A. So by Assumption 5, B involves a greater individual welfare variation than C. Then, since D is barely preferred to B, and E to D, we know that the preference intensity of E to C is greater than marginal preference. So E is preferred to C. This individual preference then tells us that C cannot be socially preferred to E.

Can't they tell us more? Introduce L such that individual 1 is indifferent between L and C and also between L and A (thus A indifferent to L, L indifferent to C, and C preferred to A), and 2 barely prefers L to C. So, L is socially preferred to C. Now compare L with B. Since 1 is indifferent between A and B, he must either prefer L to B or be indifferent between them.[22] Individual 2 barely preferred B to A and was indifferent between C and A, so he is indifferent between B and L.

Continue by comparing E with L. For 1, E is indifferent with B and A; consequently, either L preferred to E or L is indifferent with E. For 2, E is barely preferred to D which, in turn, is barely preferred to B. Thus, by Assumption 5, D represents a larger welfare variation from B than does L,

---

[22]He cannot prefer B to L, since that would imply that he preferred B to A, which he does not. To see this, assume he prefers B to L. Now, he is indifferent between A and L and between L and C; however, since he prefers C to A, L must be actually preferred to A by less than bare preference, i.e., L must be "between" A and C. If he prefers B to L while C is only indifferent with L, then B must be farther from A in the preferred direction than C. Since C is preferred to A, so too B must be preferred to A.

and since E is barely preferred to D, the preference intensity of E over L is greater than bare preference.

If 1 were indifferent between E and L, then, E would be socially preferred to L, L socially preferred to C, so E would be socially preferred to C. The employment of Assumptions 5 and 6 along with the concept of bare preference would have rendered more information than ordinal preference analysis, and perhaps as much as a cardinal group utility index. But 1 is not in general indifferent between E and L. We cannot throw out the case where 1 prefers L to E. And with this case, we are back where we started in the comparison: 1 prefers L to E; 2 prefers E to L.

A further point must be made. Throughout this final extension of our example, we have proceeded as though bare preference and less-than-bare preferences were invariant distances in the preference continuum of the individual. We have inadvertently attributed cardinal properties to these concepts. It was these properties that enabled us to derive more information from Assumption 5 than out of strict preference theory. Thus, in our analysis above, "A and C are indifferent, but B is preferred to A. So by Assumption 5, B involves a greater individual welfare variation than C. Then, since D is barely preferred to B, and E to D, we know that the preference intensity of E to C is greater than bare preference, so E is preferred to C." Here we are adding numerically invariant magnitudes, a process which we cannot infer from Assumption 5.

All Assumption 5 does, in fact, is to suggest rules by which a cardinal unit of measurement, *already introduced into the description of individual preference*, may be specifically manipulated. It is not this assumption that leads to cardinality. It is rather the assumption that bare preference is an appropriate description of preference behavior. Without bare preference, Assumptions 5 and 6 tell us nothing which strict preference theory does not tell us. Without Assumptions 5 and 6, however, *bare* preference would nonetheless give rise to a cardinal index of utility.

All this concerns the appropriateness of bare preference in the behavior of a single individual. The reader will notice that even assuming such appropriateness in my example above did not suffice to secure as much information as was possible by Armstrong's numerical index. What was lacking was an additional assumption about the comparability of the bare preferences of different individuals. Assumption 5 does not guarantee such comparability. Bare preferences are not called on to affect group welfare directly, but rather *through the welfare of individuals*. Only an additional explicit assumption as to interpersonal comparability of welfare changes can lead to Armstrong's numerical index.

To summarize this section, then, a cardinal utility index allowing for interpersonal comparisons of utility does not follow logically from Assumptions 5 and 6. This will be proved for the general case in the next section.

7-4. A Model of a Group-Welfare Index

It will be remembered from the last section that the derivation of a group welfare index involves two steps: one, that a cardinal utility index can be constructed for each individual in the group, and two, that the individual cardinal indices can be combined to form a unique cardinal group index of utility. I have argued that if one accepts the concept of bare preference as employed by Armstrong, then individual cardinal utility indices can clearly be constructed. However, I claimed that combining these indices to form a unique cardinal group index requires making an assumption additional to Assumptions 5 and 6.

Let us concentrate now on this second step. In other words, in what follows I shall assume for the time being that preference intensities can be empirically measured in terms of bare preference units. Thus, given the preceding argument, I am assuming that unique[23] individual cardinal utility functions can be constructed. I shall drop this assumption at a later stage.

Let us assume then, that there exists a psycho-physical continuum of individual preference intensities which is subject to measurement.

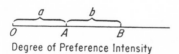

Degree of Preference Intensity

We may translate this into our previous terminology as follows: The preference intensity of situation A over situation 0 for some individual is a (a cardinal number); the preference intensity of B over A is $b;$ the preference intensity of B over 0 is $(a + b)$ which exceeds both a and b. The operation of addition can be performed on indices of preference intensity because measurement on the continuum is unique up to a linear transformation.

Definition 1. Individual welfare variation $\equiv$ the change in an individual's cardinal utility index when he moves from some situation A to some situation $B \equiv$ a function of the preference intensity of B over A[24]

$$V_{BA}{}^i = \Delta U_{BA}{}^i = U_B{}^i - U_A{}^i = V^i(P_{BA}{}^i) \qquad (i = 1, 2, \ldots, m)$$

where $U_B{}^i$ = individual i's utility index for situation B, and $P_{BA}{}^i = i$'s preference intensity index for B over A.

Assumption 1. Group welfare variation for any two situations A and B is an increasing function of the welfare variations of the individuals comprising the group:

---

[23]Unique at least up to a linear transformation. I have not dealt with Armstrong's interesting suggestion for further restricting the index by empirical specification of a zero point. As we shall see, no damage is done to our argument as a result of this neglect.

[24]The association of individual welfare with utility indices is, of course, the substance of our working assumption of consumer's sovereignty.

$$V_{BA} = \Delta U_{BA}$$
$$= f[(U_B{}^1 - U_A{}^1), \quad (U_B{}^2 - U_A{}^2), \ldots (U_B{}^m - U_A{}^m)]$$
$$= V(P_{BA}{}^1, P_{BA}{}^2, \ldots, P_{BA}{}^m).$$

$$A, B = A, B, \ldots L, \quad \text{and} \quad \frac{\partial V_{BA}}{\partial P_{BA}{}^i} > 0 \qquad (i = 1, 2, \ldots m)$$

Definition 2. Bare preference is a unique constant preference intensity just discernible by the individual as preference. (This would appear to be a reasonable interpretation of Armstrong's usage, especially in view of the philosophic justification he offers for his procedure.)

$P_0{}^i = k^i$ where $P_0{}^i$ is bare preference for individual i, k^i is a cardinal number, and $k^i \gtreqless k^j$ for all $i \neq j = 1, 2, \ldots m$.

Now let us introduce Armstrong's "Assumption (5)" as Assumption 2.

Assumption 2. "Any individual welfare variation sufficient to give rise to preference, causes a greater ... variation of group welfare than any individual welfare variation sufficient only to give rise to indifference."[25]

$$\frac{dV_{BA}}{dP_{BA}{}^i} \cdot \Delta P_{BA}{}^i < \frac{dV_{DC}}{dP_{DC}{}^j} \cdot \Delta P_{DC}{}^j$$

where $\Delta P_{BA}{}^i < k^i$, $\Delta P_{DC}{}^j \geq k^j$ for all i, j including $i = j$ and for all A, B, C, D, including $A = C$, $B = D$ where $i \neq j$.

From the assumption of a measurable preference intensity continuum, and from Definitions 1 and 2 and Assumptions 1 and 2, Armstrong infers:

(I) $$k^1 = k^2 = \ldots k^m \qquad \text{and}$$

(II) $$V_{BA} = V_{BA}{}^1 + V_{BA}{}^2 + \ldots + V_{BA}{}^m + b$$

for all A, B; b is a constant.

Are these inferences warranted? Let us examine the implications of Assumption 2 (Armstrong's Assumption 5).

From Assumption 1,

(1) $$dV = \frac{\partial V}{\partial P^1} dP^1 + \frac{\partial V}{\partial P^2} dP^2 + \ldots + \frac{\partial V}{\partial P^m} dP^m.$$

Assuming that the preferences of each individual are independent of the *tastes* of the other individuals (i.e., that $dP_{BA}{}^j/dP_{BA}{}^i = 0$), we substitute (1) into Assumption 2,[25a]

---

[25] In this connection see F. Y. Edgeworth's treatment of the *minimum sensibile* in his *Mathematical Psychics*, (London: C. Kegan Paul & Co., 1881), 7. I am indebted to Kenneth Arrow for calling my attention to this treatment.

[25a] Notice, we do not assume here that a person's preferences are independent of the *consumption* of the other individuals. Of course, individuals can deduce something about others' tastes from their consumption and indeed our analysis of tastes and values in Chapter 2 suggests that it is these estimates of others' tastes and not their consumption *per se* that frequently exerts the deciding influence. To the extent this is true our simplifying assumption is suspect.

(2) $$\frac{\partial V}{\partial P^i} dP^i < \frac{\partial V}{\partial P^j} dP^j \quad \text{where } dP^i < k^i, dP^j \geq k^j$$
$$(i \neq j = 1, 2, \ldots, m).$$

and $$\frac{\partial V}{\partial P^i} dP^i > \frac{\partial V}{\partial P^j} dP^j \quad \text{where } dP^i \geq k^i, dP^j < k^j$$
$$(i \neq j = 1, 2, \ldots, m).$$

if and only if (*assuming V is continuous*)

(3) $$\frac{\partial V}{\partial P^i} dP^i = \frac{\partial V}{\partial P^j} dP^j \quad \text{where } dP^i = k^i \text{ and } dP^j = k^j$$
$$i \neq j = 1, 2, \ldots, m.$$

This result means that if the group welfare variation index is subject to Armstrong's Assumption 5, then it must be such that an individual welfare variation arising out of bare preference for any one individual gives rise to the same group welfare variation as any other individual's welfare variation arising from his bare preference. This is, of course, substantially Armstrong's result.

For what kind of V functions will this hold?

Writing V_i for $\partial V/\partial P^i$; $i = 1, 2, \ldots, m$, we may rewrite (3) as

$$V_i dP^i = V_j dP^j \quad \text{for all } i \neq j = 1, 2, \ldots, m$$

or, since $dP^i = k^i$ and $dP^j = k^j$,

$$k^i V_i = k^j V_j \quad \text{for all } i \neq j = 1, 2, \ldots, m, \quad \text{so}$$

(4) $$V_i = a_{ji} V_j \quad \text{for all } i \neq j = 1, 2, \ldots, m;$$

where $a_{ji} = k^j/k^i = \text{constant}$.

This system of partial differential equations has, for a general solution:[26]

(5) $$V = f(w^1 P^1 + w^2 P^2 + \ldots + w^m P^m)$$

where the w's are constants and, since

$$\frac{\partial V}{\partial P^i} > 0, \qquad \frac{dV}{d(\sum\limits_{i=1}^{m} w^i P^i)} > 0.$$

Substituting (5) in condition (3), we obtain:

(6) $$w^i \frac{dV}{d(\sum\limits_{i=1}^{m} w^i P^i)} dP^i = w^j \frac{dV}{d(\sum\limits_{i=1}^{m} w^i P^i)} dP^j; \quad P^i = k^i; \ P^j = k^j$$

or

(7) $$w^i k^i = w^j k^j \quad \text{for all } i, j.$$

---

[26]Thus, let $w^1 P^1 + w^2 P^2 + \ldots + w^m P^m = S$. Then,

$$V_i = \frac{dV}{dS} \frac{\partial S}{\partial P^i} = w^i \frac{dV}{dB} \quad \text{for all } i.$$

Consequently,

$$V_i \div V_j = w^i \frac{dV}{dS} \div w^j \frac{dV}{dS} = \frac{w^i}{w^j} = \text{constant}.$$

Thus, since we may interpret each $w^i P^i$ as V^i, we have a group welfare index in which group welfare variations are calculated as a function of the sum of individual welfare variations, and such individual variations, as measured in bare preference units, are given equal weight in the group index for all individuals. Armstrong's case is the specific one where

$$f(\sum_{i=1}^{m} w^i P^i) = \sum_{i=1}^{m} w^i P^i, \quad \text{and} \quad k^i = k^j \quad \text{for all } i, j,$$

and therefore [from (7)], where $w^i = w^j$ for all i, j. His is obviously not the only solution possible, but the general solution does no violence to what seems essential in his position, namely, that the group welfare effect arising out of each individual's bare preference is the same, and therefore may serve as the effective unit of measurement for the group index.

It is my contention, however, that Armstrong's complete derivation, wherein he introduces Assumption 6, does not give rise to a V function that fits even special cases of (5). His V function is such that a determinate group welfare index can be constructed only with the aid of an additional set of assumptions — the explicit relating of the group welfare effect of different individuals' bare preference.

Armstrong introduces Assumption 6 because he feels that the index derived without it is ordinal and becomes cardinal only by its inclusion. "Assumption (6) implies . . . that group-welfare is determinate (a conclusion that is not warranted by (1), (2), (3), and (5) alone), for, since group-welfare can vary within the limits of indifference, we are now asserting that that variation is small as compared with other variations and is, in fact, small in an absolute sense."[27] Moreover, failure to incorporate (6) will occasionally lead to situations which violate the spirit (although not the letter) of Assumption 5. We may recollect that Assumption 6 (introduced into the present model as Assumption 3) asserts:

Assumption 3. "If, in a group, there is a variation of the situation of one individual, within the limits of his indifference, then the variation of group welfare is trivial."[28]

An example of the trouble which can arise when Assumption 6 is excluded is given forthwith. Assume we have a linear group welfare variation function V, for a one-hundred-member group. Moreover, assume the following:

(a) $\qquad w^i = 1$ for all $i = 1, 2, \ldots 100.$

(b) $\qquad k^i = 1$ for all $i = 1, 2, \ldots 100.$

(c) $\qquad P_{BA}{}^1 = 40; P_{BA}{}^j = -\frac{1}{2}$ for all $j = 2, \ldots, 100.$

$$V_{BA} = \sum_{i=1}^{100} w^i P_{BA}{}^i = 40 - 49\tfrac{1}{2} = -9\tfrac{1}{2}.$$

[27]"Utility and the Theory of Welfare," 267.
[28]*Ibid.*

The group index V would proclaim A group-preferred to B, yet no one prefers A other than with less-than-bare preference, while someone strongly-ly[29] prefers B to A. This kind of result appears to do violence to the purpose for which Assumption 6 was originally introduced. Moreover, for practical purposes, if only bare and more-than-bare preference intensities can be in fact measured for each individual, but not less-than-bare preferences,[30] then it is hazardous to use the group index to make even ordinal comparisons of different situations (as the example just presented shows: an inability to measure the less-than-bare preference intensities of the ninety-nine indifferent individuals makes it impossible to know whether the group prefers A or B). This is especially true when one is dealing with large groups. But it is of just such groups that welfare economics must speak.

Introduction of Assumption 6 resolves this difficulty. In the example above, the further restriction imposed by Assumption 6 enables us to assert that B is group-preferred to A, since if *all* less-than-bare preferences are trivial, then they cannot cumulate into substantial sums for moderate sized groups. Furthermore, inability to measure these trivial intensities results in no significant analytic loss.

But what are the mathematical implications of this assumption of triviality? By linear equation (5), an individual welfare variation can give rise to a trivial group welfare variation if, and only if, for this individual i, $w^i P^i$ is trivial when $P^i < k^i$. For the practical purposes envisaged, "triviality" would appear to be translatable as being less than some arbitrarily small number, or, in less technical language, being "of infinitesimal order." $w^i P^i$, then, must be less than some arbitrarily small number when $P^i < k^i$. But P^i is continuous so it may approach arbitrarily close to k^i. If w^i is the same for $P^i < k^i$ and for $P^i \geq k^i$, then $w^i P^i$, when $P^i < k^i$, approaches arbitrarily close to the value $w^i P_0{}^i$ (where $P_0{}^i = k^i$). In Armstrong's derivation $w^i P_0{}^i$ is the unit of measurement for each individual's welfare index, and, since the group index is only a function of the sum of these individual indices, it is the unit of measurement for the group index as well. Can the unit of measurement for a non-infinitesimal scale be continuous with, and only infinitesimally greater than, an infinitesimal? I should think not.

Can one resolve this dilemma by choosing a larger unit of measurement? Such a unit can be chosen at will so that, in any concrete analytic situation, all possible (or, to be less restrictive, all *probable*) combinations of individual less-than-bare preferences in the particular group at hand will cumulate to only a trivial group welfare variation. But this unit must then represent a

---

[29]Relatively speaking. In principle, by the way, the same difficulty is raised in non-linear V functions, i.e., where V is a non-linear function of S.

[30]A not unrealistic prospect, considering the currently available psycho-physical methods of scaling.

very much larger preference intensity than bare preference, depending on the size of the relevant groups. In such an event, what, then, is to be the function of the concept of bare preference upon which, presumably, Armstrong's whole presentation rests? Bare preference has at least a rough-and-ready reasonableness for serving as a cut-off point between those acknowledged preferences which "ought" significantly to influence group evaluations and those unrecognized vague discriminations which "ought" not bear significant weight in group evaluation. If it is not to be of even the same order of magnitude as the preference intensity chosen to represent the unit of measurement, then: (1) bare preference is superfluous in the formulation, and (2) the chosen unit is completely arbitrary and bears no externally persuasive justification for its use like that of bare preference.

If it be deemed desirable to salvage the concept of bare preference as providing the appropriate unit of measurement, then it would seem that this can be done (while retaining Assumption 6) only by adopting one or both of the following assumptions.

Assumption 4. Preference intensities are discontinuous at bare preference.

Assumption 5. The weight w^i, which expresses the influence of a preference intensity by some individual i on the group welfare variation, differs when the preference intensity is less than bare preference from when it is greater than or equal to bare preference.

When we accept either one or both of these assumptions, it can be shown[31] that Armstrong's index requires for its derivation a still further set of assumptions. Of the two presented here, Assumption 5 appears the more practicable, since on the basis of contemporary methods of psychological scaling, no convincing empirical evidence can be adduced to suggest the lack of continuity of preference intensities (or even, for that matter, to suggest the *presence* of continuity).

In contrast, differential weights for bare and less-than-bare preferences would seem to have the same kind of justification as the very determination to use bare preference as an experiential cut-off point. It might here be suggested that the assumption of transitive indifference in orthodox preference analysis is tantamount to setting the weights w^i equal to zero for all preference intensities less than bare preference when constructing a group scale, while setting finite values for the w^i's where intensities are equal to or greater than bare preference.

Indeed, at this point it seems that the requirements for a "determinate" group welfare index conflict somewhat with the emphasis that Armstrong places elsewhere on the intransitivity of indifference. Although it is not the less-than-bare preference intensities themselves which are here deemed

---

[31] I shall attempt to show this below.

trivial, their influence on group welfare *is* deemed trivial, which in effect comes close to the same thing. Apparently the chief difference in emphasis remaining, then, between Armstrong's formula and that of orthodox preference theory is that group welfare under the latter is treated as varying continuously while under the former it is considered as varying discontinuously by finite steps.[32]

Adoption of my Assumption 5 leads to a *discontinuous* non-linear group welfare variation function which unfortunately possesses difficulties that would not be encountered with continuous non-linear functions. For example, the operation of addition cannot be conveniently defined for the function. Consider the following arithmetic example:

(a) Define the group welfare variation function as the linear function $V = w^1 P^1 + w^2 P^2$.

$$w^1 = 1 \quad \text{if} \quad P^1 \geq k^1, \quad w^1 = \tfrac{1}{10} \quad \text{if} \quad P^1 < k^1;$$
$$w^2 = 1 \quad \text{if} \quad P^2 \geq k^2;$$
$$w^2 = \tfrac{1}{10} \quad \text{if} \quad P^2 < k^2.$$

(b) Assume $k^1 = k^2 = 2$.

(c) $P_{BA}{}^1 = P_{CB}{}^1 = 1; \quad P_{BA}{}^2 = P_{CB}{}^2 = 2; \quad (P_{CA}{}^1 = 2, P_{CA}{}^2 = 4).$
$V_{BA} = \tfrac{1}{10} \times 1 + 1 \times 2 = 2\tfrac{1}{10}$
$V_{CB} = \tfrac{1}{10} \times 1 + 1 \times 2 = 2\tfrac{1}{10}$

So $\qquad\qquad\qquad V_{BA} + V_{CB} = 4\tfrac{2}{10}.$
By direct computation of V_{CA},

$$V_{CA} = 1 \times 2 + 1 \times 4 = 6.$$

Since it seems reasonable to define $P_{BA}{}^i + P_{CB}{}^i \equiv P_{CA}{}^i$, one might also expect that

$$V_{BA}{}^i + V_{CB}{}^i = V_{CA}{}^i \quad \text{and} \quad V_{CA} = V_{BA} + V_{CB}.$$

But the discontinuity in the coefficients results in

$$V_{BA} + V_{CB} \neq V_{CA}.$$

The same difficulty applies to subtraction, multiplication and division.[33]
Now the important consequence of admitting my Assumption (5) into

---

[32]This characteristic of the schema employing bare preference makes it not unlike the modern physical concept of the quantum. It might be suggested that this interpretation of the group welfare function, including Armstrong's Assumption 6, is of the form described in Appendix 1 to this chapter as a variant of Type I (isolation of each welfare level rather than of each alternative of choice).

[33]The argument applies as well to the general case $V = f(\sum_{1}^{m} w^i P^i)$, except in the trivial instance where $dV = 0$.

Armstrong's axiom system is that it *lessens* the determinateness of the group index unless an additional set of assumptions is introduced.

From (2) above we obtain the following conditions that have to be satisfied:

$$\begin{aligned}\hat{w}^i \hat{P}^i &< w^j P_0{}^j \\ \hat{w}^j \hat{P}^j &< w^i P_0{}^i\end{aligned}\Big\} \quad \text{for all } i, j, \text{ including } i = j \qquad (8)$$

where $\hat{P}^i$ is any preference intensity less than bare preference, $\hat{w}^i$ the weight appropriate to any $\hat{P}^i$; $P_0{}^j = k^j$, and w^j is a weight appropriate to $P_0{}^j$.

Since in (S) $\hat{w}^i \neq w^i$ for all $i = 1, \ldots m$, the general solution here is *not*

$$w^i P_0{}^i = w^j P_0{}^j !$$

All we can say now is that the conditions assert that

$$\begin{aligned}w^i P_0{}^i &> \hat{w}^i \hat{P}^i < w^j P_0{}^j \quad \text{and} \\ w^i P_0{}^i &> \hat{w}^j \hat{P}^j < w^j P_0{}^j\end{aligned} \qquad (9)$$

It is reasonable that the coefficients W be determined such that

$$\begin{aligned}\hat{w}^i \hat{P}^i &\leq g^i \\ \hat{w}^j \hat{P}^j &\leq g^j\end{aligned} \qquad (10)$$

where g^i and g^j are constants specified only as being less than or equal to some other numbers, respectively. Substituting (10) into (9) and rearranging terms, we obtain

$$\begin{aligned}g^i &< w^i P_0{}^i > g^j \\ g^i &< w^j P_0{}^j > g^j\end{aligned} \qquad (11)$$

Consequently,

$$w^i P_0{}^i \gtreqless w^j P_0{}^j \quad \text{for all } i \neq j. \qquad (12)$$

$w^i P_0{}^i$ and $w^j P_0{}^j$ can diverge from one another only to the extent that g^i and g^j diverge from $w^i P_0{}^i$ and $w^j P_0{}^j$ respectively. In particular, in the case of a continuous group function,

$$\lim_{\hat{P}^i \to P_0{}^i} g = w^i P_0{}^i \quad \text{for all } i = 1, \ldots, m, \qquad (13)$$

and therefore at the limit $P^i = P_0{}^i$ and

$$P^j = P_0{}^j : w^i P_0{}^i = w^j P_0{}^j.$$

But the greatest divergence is possible where the g^i's are small. And this is exactly what is envisaged by Armstrong's Assumption 6. Now, given,

$$V = f\left(\sum_{i=1}^m w^i P^i + \sum_{i=1}^m \hat{w}^i \hat{P}^i\right) \qquad (14)$$

we may assert that we possess a determinate group welfare variation index, if and only if, for every V_{BA} and V_{DC}, we can decide either $V_{BA} > V_{DC}$, $V_{BA} < V_{DC}$, or $V_{BA} = V_{DC}$. Armstrong claims this is possible if we know only all the $P_{BA}{}^{i}$'s and $P_{DC}{}^{i}$'s,[34] and k^{i}'s — *and without having to know also the particular $w^{i}s!$* This follows because Armstrong's belief that bare preference for each individual has the same group welfare variation effect enables him to *deduce* all the w^{i}'s. Thus, for example, if $k^{1} = 6$ and $k^{2} = 3$, then $w^{2} = 2w^{1}$, since $w^{1}k^{1} = w^{2}k^{2}$. Armstrong need only arbitrarily specify a number for w^{1}, say 11, and he deduces that $w^{2} = 22$.

However, by (12) $w^{i}P_{0}{}^{i} \gtreqless w^{j}P_{0}{}^{j}$, so we cannot deduce the w^{i}'s from the k^{i}'s alone. But then, as is evident from inspection of (13), we cannot generally compare V_{BA} with V_{DC}.

Our conclusion is that the group welfare variation effects of individuals' welfare variations are similar only up to a linear transformation. So, without further information, no unique group index can be derived. A determinate group index can be derived, however, if we further specify the w^{i}'s. If Armstrong can do this by empirical procedures alone, well and good.[35] If he cannot, or does not,[36] then he apparently can derive a cardinal group welfare index (measuring invariant unit welfare variations) only by explicitly or implicitly assuming particular values for the w^{i}'s.[37] We may reiterate the conclusion of the last section. Armstrong cannot, then, deduce interpersonal comparisons of utility from his index.[38] Rather, he must assume interpersonal comparisons in order to deduce his index.

It is worth noting that the particular interpersonal comparisons implicitly assumed by Armstrong results in a unit change in each individual's utility index having the same influence on social welfare. We shall have occasion to expatiate on this particular set of assumptions in the next chapter. We may refer to it as the condition of interchangeability (the use of this term will be made clearer by the discussion later).

7-5. Bare Preference as an Hypothesis on Human Choice

The conclusion of the last section need not be fatally damaging to Armstrong's system. The assumptions of interpersonal comparability of utility (which will be discussed at greater length in the following chapter) may be

---

[34]These are to be calculated, according to Armstrong, by empirical observation.

[35]See Chapters 12 and 13 for a discussion of the problem of empirical specification.

[36]He does not appear to in his paper.

[37]A *cardinal* index of group welfare levels, whereby welfare *variations* can be compared, is derivable from a *determinate* group welfare variation index. We have discussed this in the preceding sections.

[38]And, of course, interpersonal comparisons of utility are not implied by the ordinal postulational system through Assumption (5).

arbitrary, but they need not be so unreasonable as to make the analysis worthless. Furthermore, Armstrong's Assumption 5 is in no especial need of being abandoned. We may well accept Assumption 5 within the context of the assumptions of ordinal preference theory,[39] and it seems eminently acceptable even under a set of assumptions by which a measurable unit of preference intensity could be calculated, thereby enabling derivation of a cardinal utility index. What is more, his point of departure, the intransitivity of indifference, is, on the basis of present observational evidence, neither verified nor refuted. Certainly empirical investigation is merited here.

However, closer examination does strongly suggest that we reject bare preference as an appropriate unit for measuring preference intensity. I question whether the concept of bare preference can support the edifice for which Armstrong intends it. I believe his use of the concept implicitly assumes a pattern of consumer behavior which we do not in fact see fulfilled.

Armstrong intends the concept of bare preference to support a formulation of cardinal utility. The logical dependence I have described above. The philosophic or psychological justification appears to me to be essentially contained in the following passage from Armstrong's "Comment."

> *Surely an individual is as well off as he thinks he is and that is all there is to it.* A bare preference is, therefore, an absolute standard for an individual of welfare-difference, and it matters not what analysis we make as to how such preference is supposed to arise from some combination of 'objects presented for discrimination' and 'discrimination between them'. . . . A bare preference can be used as standard both for welfare-difference and utility-difference . . . since the point of reference for a theory of choice or a theory of welfare is where indifference ends and preference begins. . . . If an individual's tastes change . . . a bare preference will continue to indicate the same welfare-difference. . . . And I cannot doubt that a bare preference has just the same significance to other persons as to me. I do not need to show that bare preferences are invariant in passing from mind to mind.[40]

The crux of the justification is apparently that a person is as well off as he thinks he is. Now, of course, modern psychology teaches us that this assertion is by no means as persuasive as it must once have been. Yet one may, at least provisionally, accept it and still ask how can one *measure* how well off a person thinks he is? Certainly in comparing two situations,

---

[39]Since perceptible welfare variations are assumed to be continuous, i.e., all positive preference intensities are discernible, and thus indifference is transitive, Assumption 5 asserts only that a positive or negative variation in group welfare can never come about solely as a result of some individual's shift giving rise to indifference, but can — although it need not! — come about as a result of some individual's shift giving rise to preference. This assertion is obviously a theorem deducible from the ordinal preference postulates. As such it is innocuous.

[40]Armstrong, *op. cit.*, 11-12. I have substituted "bare" for Armstrong's term "marginal."

A and *B*, an individual can tell under which he would be better off. But can he unambiguously say, for example, he is five bare preferences better off under *B* than under *A*?[41] What would such a declaration mean? I suggest that it would *not* mean a preference intensity five times as great as a certain constant observable intensity. It would not, indeed, mean a particular preference intensity at all!

A first problem is one of operationally defining bare preference between any two alternatives. Armstrong's discussion suggests a procedure whereby a single choice decision between the two stimuli would suffice to establish bare preference. Modern psychological experience in scaling suggests that such a procedure, because of necessarily operating close to the subjects' perceptual thresholds, would be subject to wide inconsistencies and ought to be supplemented by stochastic considerations, according to which bare preference is defined as preference expressed in a certain percentage of the total choosing situations.[42] But this would have the effect of making bare preference dependent on arbitrary labeling by the experimenter (the choice of the per cent of preference responses) rather than on a "flash of recognition" by the subject, and would consequently no longer fit Armstrong's justification: "An individual is as well off as he *thinks* he is."

Even if this philosophic difficulty were not involved, the use of a stochastic definition with techniques similar to those now in use in psychological scaling, would not generate an invariant bare preference for an individual. Say 75 per cent were chosen as the cut-off point. A certain individual prefers *A* to *B* 75 per cent of the time; and he prefers *C* to *D* 75 per cent of the time. Armstrong would seem to require, if he accepted this kind of definition of bare preference, that the preference intensity for *A* over *B* equaled the intensity for *C* over *D*. It is known, however, from work with the psychologist Thurstone's "Law of Comparative Judgment," that "differences" noticed equally often are not always equal. "Two pairs of stimuli having two unequal scale separations between the members of the pairs might still give equal proportions of judgments or two pairs having equal scale separations might give unequal proportions."[43] The inequality stems from differences in the individual's ability to evaluate his feelings about different alternatives. He is surer (i.e., in the technical terminology, has a smaller "discriminal dispersion") about some alternatives than about others.[44]

---

41 This appears to be the very core of Armstrong's claim.

42 "Situations" here is not to be confused with the term "situation" as used above, referring to an "object of choice" — a choice alternative.

43 J. P. Guilford, *Psychometric Methods* (New York: McGraw-Hill Book Company, Inc., 1936), 224.

44 This point rather interestingly suggests that ordinal choices may arise from basically cardinal evaluations rather than the reverse. Thus, a person hesitant about whether he prefers *A* to *B* may empirically be frequently found to be uncertain because he "doesn't

The same principle holds for non-stochastic definitions of bare preference as well. Any study of preference intensities, especially of intra-threshold intensities, must recognize the dependence of preference on the nature of perception. Bare preference depends crucially on perceptions of sameness and difference, comparisons not simply between quantities of a single commodity, but between complexes of many different commodities.[45] In order to be an appropriate unit of measurement, bare preference must either be nearly invariant or must vary in an orderly (highly predictable) fashion. But the perceptions on which bare preference depend are far from uniform for different people, or even for the same person. The level of discernment depends on individual constitution, motivation, the degree of learning of the individual, and even on the momentary state of the organism (for example, fatigue, elation, etc. will affect such perceptions). For a given individual, his level of perception will differ for complexes with different kinds of items,[46] since his motivation toward them and the degree of his knowledge about them will differ. Thus, to take an extreme example, if an individual barely prefers B to A and barely prefers C to A, then he may nevertheless prefer B to C, because the A–B and A–C comparisons are psychologically independent and do not determine a still-different comparison between B and C. Bare preference becomes a different thing for different comparisons, even comparisons taken at the same period of time.[47]

An example of the kind of evidence which makes us unsure that bare preference, however defined, measures some fixed thing, is the following account of a psychological experiment carried on in 1911 by E. K. Strong.

---

know exactly how he feels about A" or "doesn't know exactly how he feels about B," rather than that "he doesn't know how he feels about A versus B." He will thus be behaving as though he had a metric evaluative continuum onto which he arrayed the alternatives of choice and from which read off their preference order.

This point is not entirely consistent with the emphasis in this chapter below on the separate perceptual structuring of each choice situation.

[45]And actually, in accordance with our usage in this work, between various distributions of such complexes to the several members of the community.

[46]The fiction that every consumer consumes some of every commodity available must be dropped to achieve a degree of realism consistent with the discussion of bare preference.

[47]Notice that although my example is not consistent with the concept of a unique bare preference, it is consistent with traditional preference ordering. It may, of course, turn out that empirical studies emphasizing the diversity of choice will find even significant *ordering* inconsistencies, so that in some instances only partial orderings of preference can be accepted. (See Chapter 8 for a further discussion of intransitivity.) As is mentioned in Appendix 1, much of the problem about the specification of preference scales under intransitivity of indifference depends on whether finitude of levels of discretion (and welfare) is a more important phenomenon than fuzziness in different comparisons with a particular alternative.

Strong had asked 25 students to arrange 50 advertisements in piles at 'just noticeable intervals' in order of merit without specifying the number of piles. The number of piles ranged from 6 to 37. Each subject was then told to give a numerical value to each pile in a scale from 0 to 100. The distribution of the assigned scores approximated the normal form in spite of the fact that a sorting according to equal-appearing intervals had been the original aim.[48]

In addition to the problem of defining the bare preference between two alternatives so as to know what is being measured, there is the problem of knowing what is being measured when one scales two alternatives separated by more than bare preference. In Armstrong's treatment this boils down to finding a chain of intermediate alternatives, each one barely preferred to one predecessor and barely preferred to by one successor. Let us assume that we have experimentally constructed such a chain between B and A (A preferred to B). What does it tell us?

First, because of the variance of bare preference as a preference intensity over the relevant pairs of alternatives, the total preference intensity of a chain of n bare preferences will in general be different for each particular n-membered set. So in general, any notions about underlying preference intensities derived solely from comparisons between different bare preference chains may be mistaken. If, now, the individual and group welfare variation functions discussed in Section 7-4 above are to remain logically consistent in the face of this ambiguity, the preference intensity continuum must be redefined in terms of bare preference alone, so that "distances" will now represent only multiples of bare preference units and no longer refer to a more primary perceptual process. In this eventuality not much philosophic justification would seem to inhere in the welfare index.

But this leads to a further difficulty. Suppose we do redefine our continuum in terms of bare preference. Now, we may select a second chain between A and B. Because we can expect that, whether formally introduced into the system or not, the underlying preference intensity represented by bare preference will differ from alternative pair to pair, then we may also expect that the total preference intensity represented by one particular n-membered bare preference chain between A and B can be equaled by a second chain having a different number of links. Consequently, we obtain a different individual welfare variation value for the movement from B to A, depending on which of a large number of intermediate chains we choose — our individual index is indeterminate.

So far, we have assumed that at least the "real" preference intensity between A and B is unchanged for the different possible comparison paths. But even this is questionable in view of the importance of a frame of reference in each choice situation. It was noted above that the level of

---

[48]Quoted in Guilford, *op. cit.*, 258-259.

discernment in each situation (especially in view of the multiple dimensions of each choice alternative) depends upon motivation, relevant past experience, etc. Since our experimental procedure involves selection of particular sets of alternatives for presentation, it may be extremely difficult, if not unfeasible, to attempt to isolate the choosing behavior of the subjects from the special evaluative context established by the particular selection presented. The measurement procedures necessary to calculate bare preference chains will themselves affect how the subject perceives a given choice situation. So we might well expect to find, if we could measure the underlying preference intensity of each link in one bare preference chain between A and B, that the sum of these intensities differed from the analogous sum for a different chain between the same A and B.[49]

What, then, are we measuring when we bridge the preference distance between A and B with a chain of bare preferences? In terms of bare preference units, we may obtain different scale values for different chains, and if we possess an underlying psycho-physical preference intensity continuum, we do better to measure intensities without bare preference as intermediary. The attempt to make such measurements by stretching out a bare preference chain may give rise to different values on even this underlying scale for different chains.

The ambiguities pointed out refer to measurement at a *given* time. But the prospects are dimmer still, since an implication of the relationship

---

[49]As to the dependence of evaluative behavior on a context of relevant experience: "Scale values would seem to be altered owing to the mere presence of other stimuli. . . . The stimuli have one psychological value when seen alone or in one context and a different value when seen in another context." (Guilford, pp. 257-8) Certainly, as Armstrong clearly notes in his "Comment," this kind of consideration may in some cases lead to "inconsistent" behavior, i.e., intransitivity of *preference*.

The article by Kenneth O. May, "Intransitivity, Utility and the Aggregation of Preference Patterns," *Econometrica*, Vol. 22, No. 1 (January, 1954), 1-13, stresses the likelihood of preference intransitivity when the alternatives of choice have many — heterogeneous — dimensions. (See Appendix 2 for a discussion of this argument.) And the following, again from Guilford, may be suggestive: "The writer attempted to evaluate the degree of introversion or extroversion of the reaction to items of a typical questionnaire. Scale separations could be found between every item and every other one, but after the final average scale differences were obtained, the discrepancies between them and the experimentally determined scale separations were entirely too large. The reason is, of course, that the individual scale separations between pairs of items do not lie along the same linear continuum. The test items represented several different dimensions of personality." (p. 241)

Sketchy empirical evidence does not lead us to expect widespread actual intransitivity of preference. But the considerations presented here suggest that it may be foolhardy to expect unambiguous stable cardinal utility functions of the kind interpreted by Armstrong. "Near-intransitivity" of preference is far more damaging to assumptions about determinate preference intensities than to assumptions about determinate preference orders. Thus, Armstrong's formulation and ordinal preference theory do *not* stand or fall together on my criticism, as Armstrong would have us believe ("Comment").

between bare preference and perception is that bare preference can be expected to change frequently *over* time, more frequently than preference orderings (a given ordinal preference scale is compatible with many different bare preferences, but very likely not conversely). Can Armstrong's theory of bare preference effectively deal with changes over time?

One suggestion might be to treat future perceptions of preference the way future goods are treated in Hicksian comparative statics. On inspection, however, this scheme appears inapplicable. Present and future commodities can meaningfully be held within a single preference scale (e.g., there is a real sense in which present and future satisfactions are substitutable). But what can be the meaning of simultaneously contemplating a present perception of some two combinations (say *A* and *B*) and a future perception of the same two combinations? If the future perception can be conceived of in detail in the present, then it is part of the present perception. Changes over time in neither preference orderings (tastes) nor in perceptions of bare preference can be included within the preference frame of reference of a single point of time.

The situation is even more serious for changes in bare preference than for changes in tastes. The latter simply involve re-ordering alternatives, and the new and old preference scales are comparable. But changes in bare preference mean changes in the whole frame of reference of utility scales. The new scales are by no means obviously comparable with the old. So consistent temporal comparisons of utility change over time are most difficult.

The important consequence of these changes over time is linked to my doubt concerning the reality of a unique measure of smallest perceivable preference between vastly dissimilar multi-dimensional complexes at any *one* time. This is because changes in bare preference would not be necessarily uniform for different pairs of alternatives. At any one time the smallest perceivable preference between any one pair of alternatives might be *defined* as identical with that between any other pair. Then, if changes over time affected the comparison of every pair similarly, we might still be permitted to speak of "a" bare preference, albeit a changing one, since the original internal structure of preference comparisons would be unchanged. But if changes over time disrupt the original structure, and in largely unknown ways, then it is indeed questionable whether we can talk meaningfully about a concept which is assumed to have measurable characteristics yet at no time can be uniquely specified.

It might be objected that variations in bare preference are not necessarily fatal so long as these variations can be functionally explained. True, but it is not sufficient simply that changes in the unit of measurement be "explainable" by a less proximate set of variables. If these variables are themselves unpredictable, and especially if they give rise to frequent irregular fluctuations of, and within, bare preference, nothing is gained by the explanation, and we have a unit of measurement which is no unit at all. A more useful explanation, necessarily quantitative, does not appear to exist with the current level of psychological understanding.

I am thus suggesting here that when we construct a cardinal utility or welfare index for an individual on the basis of a bare preference unit of measurement; we do not really know what we are measuring, — whether or not we conceptualize an underlying preference intensity continuum! Certainly this assertion is relevant to the usefulness of Armstrong's system.[50]

If our individual indices are so significantly ambiguous, then our group index can be no less ambiguous; a group index would have to compare bare preferences for *different* individuals.[51] Moreover, the additional set of assumptions which must be incorporated into the postulational system to deduce Armstrong's conclusions is, considering the material of this section, a value judgment which by no means calls for indubitable assent.

Given the group of persons studied in Strong's experiment described above, for example, is it at all obvious that we should desire to give the same weight in the group index to the "bare preference" of the individual who distinguished the stimuli into thirty-seven intervals as to the bare preference of the individual who distinguished the same stimuli into only six intervals?[52]

7-6. Conclusion

We may summarize the conclusions of the present chapter as follows:

(1) Acceptance of non-transitivity of indifference neither logically nor empirically requires acceptance of the concept of bare preference. We can have the first without the second, although not conversely.

(2) Armstrong has not succeeded in proving, to my mind at any rate, that ordinary preference analysis, supplemented only by non-transitive indifference and Assumptions 5 and 6, itself implies a utility function with cardinal properties.

---

[50]In the same manner as in the earlier argument of this chapter, my argument in this section does not claim that Armstrong's index would be ambiguous with all logically possible specifications of measurement procedure, but that it does seem ambiguous with those currently available procedures which Armstrong's discussion and my own familiarity appear to make appropriate. I welcome a description of alternative procedures which, given modern findings in the field of psychological scaling, would render an unambiguous index based on "bare preference."

[51]Such comparisons would require not only that bare preference be meaningful for one individual, but also that "the" bare preference of individual A stood in some relatively constant relationship to "the" bare preference of individual B over time, so that they could at least be *defined* equal without such definition being uselessly arbitrary. Our consideration of bare preference for one individual suggests strongly that (1) we would have little knowledge about the original relationship, and (2) we would not be deluded into feeling that the relationship was very likely to remain undisturbed.

[52]See the next chapter for an elaboration of this consideration.

(3) The concept of bare preference, as developed so far, does not appear to lend itself to a useful formulation of cardinal utility either for individuals or for groups. It certainly does not at this time provide the key to interpersonal comparisons of utility. We gain little toward the construction of an acceptable social welfare function by employing it.

APPENDIX 1:

The Application of Bare Preference to Ordinal Preference Theory

Modifying traditional preference theory with Armstrong's considerations is not easy. Two general courses suggest themselves. We can translate bare preference and the various degrees of intra-threshold preference into a band of fuzziness, or penumbra, 1) around each indifferent curve, or 2) around each alternative of choice. With either course, the implication is that an individual's levels of welfare discrimination are decreased sharply to some finite number (in the realistic case of a saturation area. Cf. J. M. Clark, *op. cit.*, 349-350). But these reductions lead to difficulties.

Under the first course, it might be expected that a possible interpretation would be one in which the indifference curves are viewed as step functions, the step interval being equal to an assumed constant bare preference. This interpretation, however, leads to a contradiction, since it will not necessarily be true that a combination at one welfare level is at least barely preferred to any combination in the next lowest welfare level. A preference intensity less than bare preference can give rise to a welfare change of bare preference. To see this, consider the following diagram.

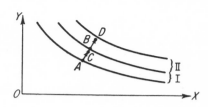

For graphical purposes we may simplify our alternatives of choice into two-dimensional vectors, i.e., combinations of commodities X and Y. Our curves do not here specify particular preference levels but rather each pair of curves expresses the boundaries of all combinations of A and B which are perceived as giving the same satisfaction. All combinations within the area I are equally satisfactory. Similarly for area II, each combination is deemed barely preferable to any combination in I.

If we could assume that the dimensions of our commodity space were homogeneous, we could take distances in the preference direction, i.e., as measured along gradient vectors, as representing preference intensities.

Since this is not usually appropriate, we shall measure intensities, somewhat more awkwardly, as distances along Engel curves.[1]

For this, we must assume a continuum of continuous indifference curves within areas I and II. The difference between any two such indifference curves within the same perception band (as given content by the non-transitivity of indifference which we are temporarily assuming throughout area II) represents less-than-bare preference intensity. Measuring such distances is, of course, tolerably proximate only if we confine ourselves to sufficiently small areas. But since our discussion need concern only a few adjoining perception levels (out of a much larger totality) this condition is met both for less-than- and greater-than-bare intensities involved.

An alternative B, just within the lower boundary of area II must be barely preferred to alternative A, just within the lower boundary of area I (and with B on the Engel curve through A for simplicity). So bare preference must be a preference intensity at least as great as but no greater than preference distance $\overline{AB}$. If it were greater, A and B would be indifferent; if it were less, some C within area I would be barely preferred to A, which is a contradiction.

Let preference distance $\overline{CD}$ equal $\overline{AB}$ (where C is in area I, D in area II, and both are on A's Engel curve). D is barely preferred to C. But B is also barely preferred to C, because they are in adjoining perceptible preference levels, by definition. And $\overline{CB}$ is less than $\overline{CD}$. Hence, in this interpretation, a preference intensity less than bare preference can give rise to a welfare change of bare preference, if bare preference implies the existence of less-than-bare preferences.

A variant of this, whereby we assume that the upper boundary of area I is separated from the lower boundary of area II by a preference distance equal to bare preference, might avoid this contradiction. But it could not explain how B could be *just* barely preferred to A, unless no preference intensities *within* area I were admitted. In other words, step-function indifference curves can express constant preference distances only when less-than-bare preferences do not exist, when indifference is transitive. But with transitivity of indifference the preference distance between indifference levels can no longer be interpreted as *bare preference*.

If we wish to retain the concept of bare preference, the dilemma above can presumably be reconciled either if bare preference is not held to be a constant preference distance (which the realism of finite fuzzy levels of discrimination makes additionally attractive; also see the last section of this chapter for a more searching critique of its "constancy"), or we must adopt the second major course of approach mentioned above, treating every *alternative* rather than every welfare level as having its area of intra-

---

[1] I am indebted to William Vickrey for this point.

threshold preference. A suggested illustration of this is given in the diagram. All alternatives within a given circle are indifferent with the focus alternative (the center of the circle); but indifference is not transitive. Thus A is indifferent with C, C is indifferent with B, but A is not indifferent with B. Note too, that the contradiction above does not apply here. The area of less-than-bare preference might approximate the more familiar tubular shape convex to the origin only if one could specify preference directions, but this would necessitate each alternative being completely indifferent (absence of even less-than-bare preference) with a set of sufficiently many other alternatives. The more tubular the shape, however, the closer we would be approximating the step-function interpretation, and progressively less would be gained by treating each alternative rather than each welfare level as a focus.

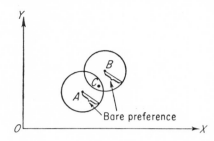

This second general interpretation of bare preference seems closer to Armstrong's emphasis on non-transitivity of indifference (and to the revealed preference approach), but its full implications, other than a possibly significant range of indeterminacy in predicting consumer behavior, are not clear at this writing.

One last point should be made. With significant non-transitivity of indifference, the Hicks-Allen indifference approach seems translatable into the first but not the second major interpretation type, whereas Samuelson's revealed preference approach seems translatable into the second but not the first. Only if indifference classes are large, do the two interpretations become very similar. Under strong non-transitivity of indifference, with or without constancy of bare preference, indifference curve and revealed preference analysis do *not* appear to be logically equivalent.

APPENDIX 2:

A Model of Preference Intransitivity

In his article, "Transitivity, Utility and Aggregation in Preference Patterns," Kenneth O. May advances a model of individual choice which claims to throw light on how intransitivity of preference arises. In brief, it is the heterogeneity of the various criteria for judging between alternatives which leads to intransitive choice. Each alternative of choice is a composite of many elements (or dimensions), and the desirability of an alternative to an individual will differ with changes in any one element or in any group of elements. Any two alternatives are apt to differ in more than one element, and in many such pairs the relative desirability of the two will be different with respect to different comparable elements. For example, suppose alternative X consists of three suits, two pairs of shoes, a six-room apartment and an 1800 calorie daily diet, and alternative Y consists of two suits, five pairs of shoes, a four-room apartment and a 2000 calorie diet. Then, in terms of two of the criteria, suits and housing, X is better than Y, but in terms of the other two criteria, shoes and food, Y is better than X.

Although there is no obvious way for an individual to reduce all these criteria, and in the general case of social state alternatives the incomparably greater multiplicity of criteria, to a single dimension, the individual does nevertheless, we assume, render over-all judgments about alternatives like X and Y. He in some way (it is tautologous to say that he does it by maximizing the satisfaction to be derived from alternative commodity bundles) balances the "partial" and contradictory judgments of the several criteria. He "aggregates" these partial preferences. The pattern of such "aggregation" is referred to by May as the "preference aggregating function." It is obvious that, from a formal point of view, the Social Welfare Function itself is a "preference aggregating function" when each of the several preference elements (or criteria) is the preference scale of some individual. Indeed, May explicitly relates his results to Arrow's formulation of the intransitivity of social choice which results from conflicting individual valuation patterns.

Finally, the effect of having to choose between any two alternatives on the basis of such conflicting criteria is that the over-all preferences are apt to be intransitive when any three alternatives, related to one another like X and Y above, are being compared. The individual may well prefer X to Y and Y to some Z, but prefer Z to X. May refers to this as a "circular" (or cyclical) preference pattern.

Let us examine the formal presentation. Consider any single pair of alternatives x and y such as we have been considering throughout. X is the vector $(x_1^1, x_2^1, \ldots, x_n^1; \ x_1^2, x_2^2, \ldots, x_n^2; \ldots; \ x_1^m, x_2^m, \ldots, x_n^m)$, expressing amounts of commodities 1 to n going to individuals 1 to m, y is the vector $(y_1^1, \ldots, y_n^1; \ \ldots; \ y_1^m, \ldots, y_n^m)$. Now consider the relationship between each x_j^r and the desirability of the alternative x for some given individual. Clearly, as x_i^r takes different values, the desirability of x to the individual changes. Another way of putting this is that if alternatives x and y differed only with respect to the single element x_i^r, then the individual's choice between them would depend on his ordering of x_i^r and y_i^r (thus, if our individual were individual r, his ordering of x and y would depend on which gave him more of commodity i). Typically, however, alternatives presented for choice will differ in more than one element. Then the choice between x and y will be a function of the set of orderings $(x_i{}^r \gtrless y_i{}^r)$. To generalize, the ordering of any set of alternatives $x, y, \ldots, w$ is a function of the set of orderings $(x_i{}^r \gtrless y_i{}^r, \ldots, x_i{}^r \gtrless w_i{}^r, y_i{}^r \gtrless z_i{}^r, \ldots, y_i{}^r \gtrless w_i{}^r, \ldots)$.[1] This is May's "preference aggregating function."

May now imposes five conditions on this function. They are essentially Arrow's acceptability conditions for a Social Welfare Function. Taking advantage of the formal similarity between the preference aggregating function and Arrow's Social Welfare Function, he derives Arrow's General Possibility Theorem for his function. Since he has not *defined* the preference aggregating function as transitive, the Possibility Theorem implies that the aggregate ordering (i.e., simply the individual's ordering of alternatives $x, y, \ldots, w$) which fulfills Arrow's conditions is not transitive; it has at least one circularly ordered sub-set (where, e.g., xPy, yPz, $\ldots$, tPw, but wPx).

May concludes from this that wherever choices among alternatives depend on more than one criterion, where the several criteria are not reducible to one another and where they give conflicting evaluations about the various alternatives, these over-all choices will not be transitive. The theorem is meant to have a far wider application than our notation expresses, since May would apply it even to the derivation of each separate component ordering $x_i{}^r$, $y_i{}^r$, $\ldots$, $w_i{}^r$. He asserts: "Even an individual commodity is really a vector of its specifications and other attributes such as its price."[2]

It is clear that although May's and Arrow's models are formally similar, they differ in an important respect. Arrow introduces his Acceptability Conditions as explicit value judgments. Hence one can agree that no Social Welfare Function as defined exists only if he is also willing to insist that these conditions be imposed on it. He is not *required* to insist that they be. The theorem has no empirical content whatever. It cannot be empirically refuted. But May's model is explicitly an attempt to explain certain behavior; it is an hypothesis about the real world. The conditions he introduces are not to be accepted or rejected at someone's discretion. They are intended as descriptions of individual choosing behavior, and the "resulting" intransitivity of choice is intended as a refutable prediction about such behavior.

With this in mind, it is by no means evident that the theorem is valid over the domain suggested by May. Two qualifications must be made for the model. First, as Duncan Black, Arrow, and others have shown,[3] the

---

[1] These orderings need not themselves be transitive, but May assumes them to be so for the purpose of analytically isolating the source of intransitivity.

[2] May, *op. cit.*, 22.

[3] See the bibliography and the greatly amplified discussion of this in Chapter 11.

Acceptability Conditions will be consistent — a transitive aggregate ordering will exist — if the ordering of every component $x_i{}^r$ is, in Black's terminology, "single-peaked." The constraint means that the several orderings (criteria) must have certain common ways of "lining up" the alternatives even though they may rank them differently. It is not unlikely that the several criteria *for a single individual* will in point of fact possess this characteristic. I expect that the discussion in Chapter 11 will clarify the point.

Second, whether or not the first qualification does justifiably apply to May's postulate system, it does suggest that the derivable theorems will differ with different restrictions placed on the component orderings and on the function itself. The theorems will differ with respect to the transitivity of the aggregative choices. Moreover, given the contrast in character of the system from that of Arrow, it is not proper for May's system, although it was proper for Arrow's system, that his conditions be as *weak* as possible to enable him to derive non-transitivity. Rather, his conditions ought to be as *strong* as he feels will be empirically verified, i.e., his hypothesis should be as fruitful, as non-empty, as possible. This requirement is not one of convenience or aesthetics alone, since the lesson of our first qualification suggests that further specification might well reverse May's conclusions.

To be concrete, a few formal similarities do not warrant an assertion not more deeply supported that the same weak postulates fruitfully apply to an individual's choices among commodity bundles as to his choices among single commodities. Again, although the postulates do not intuitively appear to conflict appreciably with current knowledge about choice behavior, they do not imply any of the integrative regularities studied by psychologists, e.g., considerations about motivational factors and configurational aspects of perception. A richer theory would seem to be formulable on the basis of present accumulated evidence. May's failure to show that such a *richer* theory would lead to intransitivity, and his emphasis on the *weakness* of his postulates and the ease with which they can be reinterpreted to apply to different kinds of choice situations, hint at a misunderstanding about the character of his demonstration. One last word to justify my strictures. The usefulness of an empirical hypothesis explaining the source of intransitive individual choices and, incidentally, providing a predictive content to direct future investigations in the field, is undeniable. The usefulness of a "normative" postulate system within which intransitivity is a derivable property, is dubious. It is for this reason, and because of the context of earlier portions of May's paper, that I have interpreted the character of his demonstration in a way which apparently contradicts his own understanding of it.

CHAPTER 8

Finite Rankings and

Preference Intensity

8-1. A Model of Social Choice

It will be remembered from Chapter 6, concerning the modification of Arrow's condition on irrelevant alternatives, that there are two distinct avenues by which preference intensities may be introduced into the Social Welfare Function.[1] An example of one of them, construction of cardinal individual utility indices, has been discussed in the last chapter. In this chapter I should like to illustrate briefly the second approach, that made through individual orderings alone. The particular model dealt with is that of Leo A. Goodman and Harry Markowitz, presented in "Social Welfare Functions Based on Individual Rankings."[2]

The point of departure for this model is the kind of circumstance envisaged in Chapter 6. In two different situations, a given individual prefers alternative x to y. But in the first situation he prefers y to every other possible alternative (excepting only x), while in the second situation he prefers every alternative to y. It is claimed to be intuitively obvious that the individual has a greater preference intensity for x over y in the second situation when y is his last choice than in the first when y is his second choice. In this example, the number of alternatives which are ordered intermediately between any two given alternatives, or more simply, the rank numbers of the given alternatives, presumably throw light on

---

[1] We shall see what is in effect a third avenue, group choice, in Chapter 13.
[2] *The American Journal of Sociology*, Vol. LVII, No. 3 (November, 1952), 257-262.

the preference intensity between the two. Since the same is true for every individual, the rank numbers received by any alternative from the various individuals will tell something about the position at which it is placed in the respective individual orderings, and their position will suggest something about both preference order and preference intensity. So a social ordering of the sets of rank numbers received by all alternatives would represent a social ordering of alternatives which considered both individuals' preference orders and their preference intensities.

The model itself is as follows. First, let us "assume that each individual has only a finite number of indifference levels or 'levels of discretion'. . . . A change from one level to the next represents the minimum difference which is discernible to an individual."[3] No comparison of the number of discretion levels, or of the minimum difference between levels, for the several individuals is postulated.

Now we state the various resolutions and conditions which Goodman and Markowitz wish to impose on "acceptable" Social Welfare Functions. The resolutions essentially parallel, and modify, Arrow's Conditions 2 and 3.

Let us write $l_{i^0 j^0}$ for the discretion level at which individual i^0 ranks alternative j^0 (the lower the level, the more desirable the alternative), where $j = 1, \ldots, N$, $i = 1, \ldots, M$, and $1_i = 1, 2, \ldots, L_i$ with $L_{i'} L_{i''}$ for every i', i''. "Given the matrix l_{ij}, a Social Welfare Function will rank [every candidate] 1 and 2."[4]

Resolution 1. "A Social Welfare Function shall not be rejected as unreasonable on the sole grounds that candidate j^0 falls in the social ordering, when, for some [individual] $i = i^0$, $l_{i^0 j^0}$ increases — the other l_{ij}'s remaining the same."

This resolution parallels Arrow's Condition 2 (positive association of individual and social values), but, contrary to Goodman's and Markowitz's belief, does contradict Arrow's requirements in some cases. Arrow's Condition 2 is included in this resolution but not conversely. Thus, if the increase in $l_{i^0 j^0}$ is accompanied by an ordering change, such that j^0 falls in i^0's ordering,[5] then we have Arrow's situation, and a change in the social ordering is permitted. But $l_{i^0 j^0}$ can rise without an ordering change. And the present model would permit a corresponding change in the social ordering. Such a change, however, would violate Arrow's Condition 3, since the ordering of S would have been unchanged.

Resolution 2 introduces an important modification of the above. In actual empirical practice it is not the discretion levels of alternatives which can be measured but only their rankings. These rankings throw light on the underlying discretion levels. The matrix of rankings $A = (a_{ij})$ of the N

---

[3]*Ibid.*, 259.
[4]*Ibid.*, 259.
[5]This can of course be accomplished without changing the other l_{ij}'s.

alternatives by the M individuals, where a_{ij} is the rank number of the j'th alternative by the i'th individual, is consequently considered a "state of information" about, or approximation to, the matrix (l_{ij}).[6]

Resolution 2. "A social welfare function shall not be rejected on the sole grounds that it changes the ordering of j_1 and j_2 as the state of information changes."[7]

What is envisaged here is that the social ordering will be a function of A.

Resolution 3. "For a given state of information, the welfare function should order the 'candidates' independently of their availability."

This is a modified condition on the independence of irrelevant alternatives. As we shall see, it is somewhat narrower than the modification suggested in Chapter 6.

The following formal conditions are now imposed. I quote for brevity:

"For any given state of information (. . . matrix $A = (a_{ij})$ of orderings) the social welfare function gives a simple ordering of alternatives, independently of their availability . . . [It] is defined for all states of information. . . [The social] ordering satisfies the following conditions:

"*Condition 1* (Pareto optimality). — If nobody prefers j_2 to j_1 and somebody prefers j_1 to j_2 then j_1 is socially preferred to j_2, i.e., if $a_{ij2} \geq a_{ij1}$ for all i and $a_{ij2} > a_{ij1}$ for some i, then $(a_{ij2}) > (a_{ij1})$.[8]

"*Condition 2* (symmetry). — The social ordering is unchanged if the rows of A are interchanged.

"*Condition 3.* — Suppose voter i has exhibited L_j levels of discretion. The social ordering among candidates 1 and 2 remains unchanged if we replace a_{i1} and a_{i2} by $a_{i1} + C$ and $a_{i2} + C$, respectively. The constant C must be an integer such that $1 \leq a_{ij} + C \leq \max(L_i)$ for all j."[9]

It can be mathematically shown that only one Social Welfare Function fulfills these conditions. It prescribes:[10]

j_1 is socially preferred to j_2, if and only if,

$$\sum_{i=1}^{M} a_{ij1} < \sum_{i=1}^{M} a_{ij2};$$

j_2 is socially preferred to j_1, if and only if,

$$\sum_{i=1}^{M} a_{ij2} < \sum_{i=1}^{M} a_{ij1};$$

j_1 and j_2 are socially indifferent, if and only if,

$$\sum_{i=1}^{M} a_{ij1} = \sum_{i=1}^{M} a_{ij2}.$$

---

[6]In this chapter I shall be employing the term "rank" to mean what may perhaps be better conveyed by "class number." If, for example, the individual prefers three items to all the others, and is indifferent between these top three, then by my usage here he will give "rank" 1 to each of the three, and "rank" 2 to whatever item is next preferred.

[7]Goodman and Markowitz, *loc. cit.*

[8]The sign ">" is interpreted here in its numerical sense of "greater than." In the present context it carries the opposite preference denotation: "inferior to," since rank numbers are inversely related to order of preference.

[9]Goodman and Markowitz, *op. cit.*, 260.

[10]For a given state of information.

The welfare index is the summation of rank numbers. That alternative with the lowest total of the ranks assigned by individuals is socially ordered best; the alternative with the next lowest total is second; etc. In this way, a complete ordering of alternatives is obtained.

8-2. Individual Cardinal Utility Indices

Let us examine this model more closely.[11] It is crucially important to every model of the type being considered in this chapter that Pareto optimality is introduced only as a sufficient condition for welfare optimization, but not as a necessary condition. If we are comparing two alternatives in which we can make a unanimity judgment (in the Paretian sense employed in Chapter 3), then Condition 1 determines the content of that judgment. But if we are comparing two "heterogeneous" alternatives, Condition 1 does not forbid a welfare judgment; it does not make unanimity choice necessary for formulating a social choice. This distinction is the avenue by which interpersonal comparisons of utility, overtly expunged from the New Welfare Economics, are readmitted into social choice in this particular model. Thus, Goodman and Markowitz say, "If we require only Condition 1, any monotonic ordering function defines a social welfare function, and these are the only acceptable ones."[12]

Let us see what kind of interpersonal comparisons of utility are involved when one employs rank summation as a group welfare index. First, the rank summation alone for any alternative, an integer, suffices to determine its position in the social ordering. Consider Table 3.

TABLE 3

Rank Numbers Ascribed to Four Alternatives
by Three Individuals

Individual	Alternatives			
	x	y	z	w
1	5	5	1	1
2	5	6	8	7
3	5	4	6	6
Rank Summation	15	15	15	14

[11]In what follows it is important to note that we shall be evaluating the model from the point of view of this book and not from that of Markowitz and Goodman themselves. Markowitz and Goodman intended, primarily, to persuade the reader that preference intensities ought to "count" in social preferences, and that differences in rank numbers furnish a reasonable rough-and-ready approximation to these intensities. Further, their purpose is to demonstrate that if preference intensities are admitted into the social choice mechanism, even in the form of approximations based on rank differences, then a Social Welfare Function can be formulated which fulfills all but Arrow's Condition 3. It is clear from Chapter 6 above that, notwithstanding the criticisms we shall make in the rest of this chapter, we are in substantial agreement with Goodman and Markowitz about the adequacy of the model to realize *their* intentions.

[12]*Loc. cit.*

Alternatives x, y, and z are socially indifferent, and w is preferred to all. The comparison between x and y discloses that a given (numerical) rank difference for one individual is treated by this procedure as exactly offsetting the same rank difference for any other individual. The comparison between x and z discloses that a given rank difference for one individual exactly offsets the equivalent numerical result of addition on the rank differences of any sub-set of individuals in the group. The comparison between x and w, in the context of the previous comparisons, discloses that the indifference among x, y, and z is the result of a numerical offsetting of rank differences and not simply of a definitional equality in comparisons between heterogeneous alternatives.

If now, the rank summation index pretends to give rise to group choice solely on the basis of the properties of individual preferences, this "offsetting" must presumably be an offsetting of the weighted preferences of different individuals. In this model the differential weighting is not meant to reflect the relative importance of different persons; it is meant to reflect, rather, differential properties of the preferences themselves with all persons treated interchangeably (Condition 2), i.e., it reflects preference intensities. We may therefore interpret these weighted preferences as determining the coordinates for points on indices of individual satisfaction (or utility).

In other words, then, when we declare x socially indifferent to y, we are asserting that the loss in satisfaction of individual 2 in going from x to y is exactly equal to the gain in satisfaction of individual 3 in going from x to y. Losses and gains in satisfaction for all individuals are measured by rank differences, and a given number stands for the same satisfaction no matter to which individual it is applied. A corollary to this is that alternatives separated by the same number of ranks represent the same difference in satisfaction in the entire range of a single individual's ordering and in comparing one individual with another.

These properties of ranking sums can be rationalized, if and only if, each individual's ranking of alternatives is interpreted as a completely determined cardinal utility index with the utility difference between any two adjacent ranks serving as the invariant unit of measurement. Are we justified in making this interpretation? What are the elements of this model by which we may obtain cardinal measurement of utility?

It is evident that the crucial assumption is that which postulates a finite number of levels of discretion for each individual such that " . . . a change from one level to the next represents the minimum difference which is discernible to an individual."[13] This assumption is very similar to that which is implied by the concept of bare preference. And the individual utility index which is logically derivable is essentially the same as that which we considered in the last chapter.

---

[13]Goodman and Markowitz, *op. cit.*, 259.

One important difference between the two schemata is that the notion of "discretion level" emphasizes a band of fuzziness around each indifference curve, whereas bare preference may be interpreted either in this fashion or alternatively as fuzziness around each commodity bundle (Appendix 1: Chapter 7). As we noted above, the two interpretations have an important operational distinction. Construction of an index under the second makes that index dependent on the base commodity bundle chosen; similar construction under the first makes the index dependent on a base satisfaction level. Subject to all the qualifications discussed above, we possess psychological scaling devices which may enable us to array different commodity bundle alternatives along a scale at differential distances corresponding to preference intensities between alternatives. The scale intervals are derived from preference comparisons between specific alternatives; they are only intervals separating specific alternatives. But we possess no device for assigning alternatives to operationally pre-discovered indifference intervals, intervals which are independent of the particular set of alternatives being compared. Figure 12 will indicate the difference.

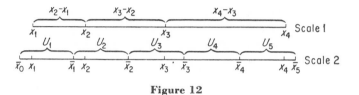

Figure 12

In Scale 1, the distances between the set of alternatives being compared (x_1, x_2, x_3, x_4) refer only to the preference intensities among these four alternatives as experimentally derived. They have no reference to anything outside this experimental procedure (except, of course, that intermediate alternative chains are experimentally admissible). In contrast, the placement of x_1, x_2, x_3, x_4 in Scale 2 depends not only on comparisons between pairs of them (admitting intermediate chains which, crucially, are chosen depending entirely on the specific comparison pair), but also on comparisons between the relevant alternatives and a set of alternatives which are completely independent of the set to be scaled. Thus, the placement of x_1 and x_2 is determined by a procedure of the following kind. x_1 is placed uniquely without regard to x_2, by being scaled in relation to the particular fixed alternatives $\bar{x}_0$ and $\bar{x}_1$; x_2 is placed uniquely, and independently of x_1, by being scaled with respect to the particular fixed alternatives $\bar{x}_1$ and $\bar{x}_2$.

The crucial characteristic of this procedure is the "landmark" function played by $\bar{x}_0$, $\bar{x}_1$, and $\bar{x}_2$. How are these "landmark" alternatives chosen? They are chosen not arbitrarily, but to reflect specific levels of satisfaction for the individual. In other words, we require some operational procedure by which each preference level can be identified with a particular commodity bundle. How is this to be done?

One possibility suggested by the treatment of Goodman and Markowitz is as follows. Suppose we know how many discretion levels a given individual possesses. Let it be the number n. Then we ask the individual to rank a larger and larger number of alternatives until he has assigned n different rank numbers. (In general we shall have offered him more than n alternatives to rank, since some will be indifferent with one another.)[14]

Now, if we further assume that less-than-bare preferences refer to trivial differences in individual satisfaction (like Armstrong's Assumption 6 for group-satisfaction), or, in effect, that they refer to zero differences,[15] we may choose any of the commodity bundles with a given rank number as representing a particular discretion level. We thus obtain our set of landmark bundles $\bar{x}_0, \ldots, \bar{x}_n$.

It is immediately apparent that this procedure assumes away the real problem, namely, how *do* we get to know how many discretion levels a given individual possesses? Further, even if we should manage to discover the number, it is by no means guaranteed that we shall be able experimentally to offer enough alternatives to cover every discretion level.

The first consideration is of critical importance. Can we conceive of a procedure which will even in principle reveal the number of discretion levels which a given individual possesses? We may try by asking him to rank a larger and larger sub-set of the alternatives in $\bar{S}$. But we cannot stop short of requiring him to rank the entire set $\bar{S}$; say, for example, that we reach a certain subset S_1 in $\bar{S}$, and that, as we now add more alternatives, the individual ranks these as indifferent with alternatives in S_1, and no matter how many new alternatives we add short of the set $\bar{S}$, no new rank numbers are forthcoming. Can we then assert that the individual possesses no more discretion intervals than the number of separate ranks in S_1? No, because some other alternative, which is in $\bar{S}$ but not in the set of alternatives presented, may disclose an additional discretion level. We can never stop short of ranking all alternatives in $\bar{S}$. And even this may not suffice. It is not inconceivable that the individual should possess more discretion levels than can be revealed from a ranking of $\bar{S}$. Operationally, this means that some new alternatives *becoming conceivable in the future* (through technological change, for example) *could* reveal more discretion levels than does the present composition of $\bar{S}$. But if this is true, then in principle we shall not be satisfied to draw conclusions from any *finite* set of alternatives. (And

---

[14]If we have offered him $n + r$ alternatives, then the number of alternatives which are indifferent to one or more other alternatives is greater than or equal to r and less than or equal to $2 r$. In the limiting case where no rank position has more than two alternatives, there will be $2 r$; where all the duplications are in one rank position there will be r.

[15]I.e., that indifference is transitive. See the Appendix to the last chapter.

this objection can be made even stronger, for what meaning can be ascribed to the presentation for comparison of alternatives which are not yet even conceivable?)[16]

If the number of an individual's discretion levels is in principle discoverable, the appropriate psychological model by which this can be accomplished in practice does not apparently exist at the present time. I do not, of course, hazard that it can never exist.

8-3. Marginal Utility and Discretion Levels

For the purpose of further examining the Goodman-Markowitz model let us, however, assume that we can somehow discover the number of each person's discretion levels. Our model now requires that we possess enough alternatives to "cover" each level, i.e., that we have discovered an $\bar{x}_i$ for every U_i. (Notice that the second objection made above depends on the discretion levels being more numerous than what is revealed by ordering $\bar{S}$. Let us waive this objection too.) So the rank numbers reflect the underlying satisfaction levels; they represent a uniquely determined numerical index of utility.

The restrictions placed on these indices to derive the summation of ranks rule are Conditions 2 and 3. Let us examine Condition 3 first.

Assume in a two-person group (individuals A and B) we have the rankings of two alternatives x and y as shown in Table 4.

TABLE 4
Rank Numbers of Two Alternatives in a Two-Person Group

	Situation 1		Situation 2		Situation 3	
	x	y	x	y	x	y
A	3	12	5	14	3	12
B	21	13	21	13	23	15
Total of Ranks	24	25	26	27	26	27

Given these rankings we know that in situation 1 the difference in satisfaction for A between x and y is equal to the increase of satisfaction which would result if he were to change from an alternative in his twelfth discretion level to one in his third discretion level. The difference in satisfaction for B between x and y is equal (in the opposite direction, he prefers y to x) to the increase of satisfaction he would realize if he were to move from an alternative in his twenty-first discretion level to one in his thirteenth discretion level. Say now that our rule for social choice[17] results in x

---

[16]We do not deal here with a converging series to help us.

[17]Not necessarily the summation of ranks rule. We are currently examining what it means to derive this rule from the conditions on individual utility indices.

being socially preferred to y. This means that if we may proceed with our assumption that the social choice is a function of individual utilities, then the rule implicitly asserts that the social welfare effect of the utility difference between A's third and twelfth discretion levels is greater than that between B's thirteenth and twenty-first discretion levels.

Now assume that A experiences a change in tastes for x and y such that both are ranked two discretion levels lower (situation 2).[18] Since the utility significance of every level of discretion does not depend on any particular set of alternatives being ranked or on the preferences toward alternatives in that set, we may say that if A were given x he would be worse off by the loss involved in going from the satisfaction of discretion level 3 to discretion level 5, whereas if he were given y he would be worse off by the loss of satisfaction involved in going from his twelfth to fourteenth discretion level. Condition 3 says that, under these circumstances, x must still be socially preferred to y.

For the symmetry of this condition to be fulfilled, it would appear that the condition implies that the utility difference between A's third and twelfth discretion levels is equal to that between his fifth and fourteenth discretion levels. If the second were permitted to be less than the first, then it is conceivable that the social welfare effect of B's preference intensity for y over x might exceed A's revised preference intensity for x over y, thereby violating Condition 2. But it cannot be permitted to be more than the first either. Consider situation 3, in which B has experienced the same kind of change in tastes that we described in situation 2. If the utility difference between x and y for A in situation 2 can be greater than that in situation 1, then by the same reasoning it is conceivable that the utility difference for B can be greater in situation 3 than in situation 1. But if B's preference intensity for y over x is greater in situation 3 than in 1, it is conceivable that it may have a greater social welfare effect in situation 3 than A's preference for x over y (which is defined as the same as in situation 1), and therefore that y will be socially chosen — thereby violating Condition 2. So A's and B's respective preference intensities cannot be different in situations 2 and 3 than in situation 1 if Condition 2 is to be fulfilled. But to require this equality has unfortunate implications.

What we mean by asserting that A's preference intensity for x over y is the same in situation 2 as in situation 1 (or more generally, the same in each pair of situations where a_x, a_y and $a_x + C$, $a_y + C$ are the respective rankings of x and y, for all $1 \leq a + C \leq$ max.l) is that a change from one

---

[18]We must interpret the mathematics of Condition 2 into a change in tastes and not simply the introduction of new alternatives into the ordering without a change in tastes (in the terminology of Goodman and Markowitz, a change in the state of information) because we have postulated that all discretion levels are "covered" by ranked alternatives. In this circumstance, the introduction of new alternatives will not change any existing ranking.

discretion level to the next brings about the same change in utility no matter in what part of the ranking the change occurs. A one-rank change represents a constant change in utility throughout the scale and can therefore be taken as a unit of measurement of utility. Condition 2 does nothing less than translate changes in discretion levels into changes in utility.

Clearly, however, nothing in our construction of individual utility indices *requires* that adjoining discretion levels represent the same difference in utility — that discretion levels be "equally spaced" over the utility scale. They are separated only by "the minimum difference discernible to an individual."[19] We met essentially this same argument when discussing the concept of bare preference. The assumption of a constant bare preference in all comparisons was questioned by us, and on broadly similar grounds the assumption of "equally spaced" discretion intervals must also be questioned. In view of the evidence adduced in the former discussion, the burden of proof would seem to fall on anyone assuming an "equal spacing of discretion levels."[20] No validation has yet been given.[21]

---

[19]Goodman and Markowitz, *loc. cit.*

[20]I am of course abstracting from the problem of deriving the discretion intervals in the first place. This is a somewhat artificial procedure because the empirical properties of discretion intervals depend foremost on the kind of derivation, if any, which is possible.

[21]Instead of attempting to deduce "equal spacing" from our construction of utility indices, we may, of course, attempt to *impose* "equal spacing" upon our indices by designing our experimental procedure so as to *ask* for rankings in which every rank is separated from another by the same satisfaction difference. Such a procedure would dispense with the concept of "discretion level" altogether, since only accidentally would equal satisfaction differences be expressible in terms of minimum discernible satisfaction differences. Moreover, it would make for greater demands on the informants than the request for a conventional ranking — very likely, therefore, we should not treat it as a ranking procedure at all. In any case, it is significantly different from the procedure of Goodman and Markowitz under consideration here. However, if it could be successfully utilized it *would* give rise to individual utility indices with constant marginal utility.

The procedure strongly resembles certain techniques in psychological scaling such as rating scales, etc. In fact, it should probably be considered a form of the "method of equal appearing intervals," a scaling technique employed by Thurstone and others. See Thurstone, "The Measurement of Opinion," *Journal of Abnormal and Social Psychology*, Vol. 22 (1928), 415-430; L. L. Thurstone, and E. J. Chave, *The Measurement of Attitude* (Chicago: University of Chicago Press, 1929); J. P. Guilford, *Psychometric Methods* (New York: McGraw-Hill Book Company, Inc., 1936), Chapter V, 143-165; S. Stevens (ed.) *Handbook of Experimental Psychology* (New York: John Wiley & Sons, Inc., 1951). These techniques have been used in attitude scaling but not in problems of choice. Two difficulties may stand in the way of satisfactory early applications to choice behavior. The first is the consistency of the resulting scales; the second is their reliability.

In the method of equal appearing intervals, attitude specimens are scaled on an interval scale only after securing the (independent) responses of many informants. The scale positions adopted represent statistical averages of the several responses. What is important from our standpoint is that the average is a better measure than the response of a single individual, not because the individual holds a particular degree of the given attitude (since this is irrelevant to the scaling purpose) but because the task is a crude one, and so a knowledge of response dispersion is indispensible to predictions about the consistency of future responses to the same scale. Since the purpose of applying the "equal appearing intervals" technique to preferences would presumably be the derivation

8-4. Interchangeability:
Interpersonal Comparisons of Utility

It might be wise at this point to state the properties of our indices as so far traced. Neglecting all the methodological difficulties posed above, we can construct for each individual a unique cardinal utility index. This index is the individual's ranking of the alternatives in $\bar{S}$. The rank number given to a particular commodity bundle by the individual is a numerical representation of the absolute level of utility which it has for him. Moreover, equal numerical differences between rank numbers represent equal utility differences for the individual. We know also that the social ordering is a function of these individual rankings, but we have as yet said nothing about how to compare rank numbers in the ranking of one individual with rank numbers taken from different individual's ranking. In other words, the steps so far analyzed refer only to the measurability of each individual's utility; they do not make assumptions about interpersonal comparisons of utility.

Interpersonal comparisons of utility are introduced by means of Condition 2. We now turn to that condition. Goodman and Markowitz refer to it as a symmetry condition. "The social ordering is unchanged if the rows of [the state of information] A are interchanged." More simply, this means that if we are considering two rankings R_1 and R_2 of alternatives in $\bar{S}$, and two individuals A and B, then the social ordering is the same whichever way the rankings are distributed between the individuals. It makes no difference whether A has R_1 and B has R_2, or A has R_2 and B has R_1. Let us examine the implications of this. Consider Table 5.

TABLE 5
Rank Numbers of Two Alternatives
by Two Individuals

	Situation 1		Situation 2	
	x	y	x	y
A	3	13	21	12
B	$\dfrac{21}{24}$	$\dfrac{12}{25}$	$\dfrac{3}{24}$	$\dfrac{13}{25}$

of *individual* utility indices, the source of the analogous response dispersion is problematic. (The solution of this problem for the bare preference technique would be the suggested stochastic definition of bare preference.)

The second problem concerns itself with discovering what the scale does in fact measure. It would appear to be a most difficult feat to determine whether or not, once a scale had been constructed, the scale did really measure what was desired. The difficulty stems from an apparent absence of choice behavior with which predictions based on the scale could be confronted for verification. We remember that ordinary static consumer choice can be rationalized on ordinal considerations alone. As we shall see in the chapter immediately following, however, the requisite behavior may be choice in risk situations. Cardinal utility indices constructed by modified "equal appearing interval" techniques and by the expected utility hypothesis, to be described below, might conceivably be employed reciprocally as observational evidence.

In situation 1 we are given that x is socially preferred to y.[22] So in situation 2, which is derived from situation 1 simply by A giving x and y the same ranking as B in situation 1, and B giving x and y A's ranking in situation 1, Condition 2 requires that x be socially preferred to y. We may treat situation 2 as though the x and y referred to different alternatives from the x and y in situation 1 (with tastes unchanged).[23] We may then interpret Condition 2 as asserting that given the individual rankings of two alternatives and a resulting social choice between the two, we impose a restriction on the social choice between two other alternatives derived in a certain way from the original alternatives.

In Table 3, call x,y in situation 2 x',y' to differentiate them from x,y in situation 1. Now, x' is derived from x in such a way that A would lose eighteen units of *his* satisfaction in changing from x to x'; and B would gain eighteen units of *his* satisfaction in making the change. Similarly, y' is derived from y in such a way that A would gain one unit of *his* satisfaction and B would lose one unit of *his* satisfaction in making the change. Condition 2 therefore requires that if x is socially preferred to y, then a situation such that with respect to x, A is made worse off by eighteen units of *his* satisfaction while B is made better off by eighteen units of *his* satisfaction, which is socially preferred to a situation such that with respect to y, A is made better off by one unit of *his* satisfaction while B is made worse off by one unit of *his* satisfaction. We may go further. See Table 6.

TABLE 6

Rank Numbers of Three Alternatives by Two Individuals

	Situation 1			Situation 2		
	x	y	z	x'	y'	z'
A	3	13	11	21	13	11
B	21	13	11	3	13	11
Ranks	24	26	22	24	26	22

Clearly we may conceive of two alternatives such that the interchanging of rank numbers will affect only one of the alternatives. Now, x is assumed

---

[22]Not because of rank summation; we have not yet introduced that final criterion into our derivation.

[23]Thus, we are not really *transforming* Mr. A into Mr. B, i.e., giving him B's entire discriminating apparatus, but we simply are putting into the context of his own utility index the *rank numbers* which were originally expressed within the context of B's utility index. In other words, since we distinguish between the utility scale and the distribution of different alternatives to different parts of that scale, A is putting into the interval of his scale, numbered twenty-one, the alternative which B put into *his* twenty-first interval in situation 1, while B is putting into his third interval the alternative which A put into *his* third interval in situation 1.

to be socially preferred to y. For x' to be socially preferred to y' means saying that a loss by A of eighteen units of *his* satisfaction, combined with a gain by B of eighteen units of *his* satisfaction, is still socially preferred to y. But since in situation 1 we may choose y arbitrarily "close" to x and introduce z which is socially preferred to x (so that by Condition 2 z' must be socially preferred to x') also arbitrarily "close" to x,[24] then x' can be constrained to remain "between" z' and y' only if it bears the *same* social welfare value as does x (since z' and y' bear the same social welfare values as z and y, respectively). Thus, the social welfare effect of A's loss of eighteen units of *his* satisfaction must exactly balance the social welfare effect of B's gain of eighteen units of *his* satisfaction; or, more generally, a unit change in A's satisfaction has the same social welfare effect as a unit change in B's satisfaction. In the terminology of the last chapter, this means that $w^i P_0{}^i = w^j P_0{}^j$, for all i, j (the social welfare effect of a bare preference is the same for all individuals). And furthermore, since the cardinal utility indices represented by rankings are such that the unit change of satisfaction for any individual is given the number *one* in his utility index (i.e., that $P_0{}^i = P_0{}^j = P_0{}^k = \ldots = 1$), then $w^i = w^j$, and the social welfare index for any alternative is a function of the sum of individual rank numbers ascribed to that alternative

$$U_x = f(\sum_{i=1}^{n} R_y{}^i).$$

Condition 2, then, has the following function in this model:

(1) To restrict all individual utility scales to equivalence except for additive constant (*interpersonal comparisons of utility*),

(2) to weight each individual's utility unit equally as an influence on social choice (*interpersonal evaluations of utility*).

In the next chapter we shall meet a condition fulfilling the same function. For future reference, therefore, let us call it the condition of *interchangeability*.

Properties 1 and 2 above are derivable only on the assumption that we possess cardinal utility indices for the individuals in our group. If only ordinal indices are admitted, i.e., indices unique up to any monotone transformation, then the properties of interchangeability must be derived through the compensation analysis discussed in Chapters 3 and 4 above, but these are properties of the compensation principle itself. Thus, individual A prefers x to y, and B prefers y to x. Now calculate whether compensation could be paid to make both better off if we were to go from x to y. Assume that it could. So y with compensation is better than x. Interchangeability

---

[24]This means simply that we must be able to fulfill Condition 2 with *all* y, z such that z is socially preferred to x and x socially preferred to y.

now requires that if we interchange the preferences of A and B we shall obtain the same social choice. When B prefers x to y and A prefers y to x, we must again have the possibility of compensation so that y with compensation will be preferred to x. But in our indifference map context, this is guaranteed by the very nature of the compensation principle. So, in the context of *ordinal* utility, interchangeability takes us no further than our previous unanimity analysis. The conclusion follows because apparently all that we can mean by "interchanging" preferences is that we are comparing two alternatives such that A is now willing *to pay* exactly the amount of compensation for moving from the "transmuted" x to the "transmuted" y that B was willing *to pay* before interchange (previously A required to be paid to make the change, since he preferred x to y); B now requires to *be paid* the same amount of compensation for moving from the "transmuted" x to the "transmuted" y that A previously required (whereas previously B was willing to pay). Obviously the positive and negative compensations are identical in amount with the situation before interchange, and since the compensation principle does not require to know who is paired with what compensation, the social choice, if compensation is actually paid, will be identical before and after interchange.

Suppose, therefore, that we possess a set of individual *cardinal* utility indices. Does interchangeability impose reasonable restrictions on such a model which would be generally accepted? My feeling is that property 2 may well do so; deeper examination of property 1, however, discloses a probably unwarranted degree of arbitrariness.

Property 2 is clearly a social value judgment. But it is in accord with a widely held belief in the equal treatment of equals before the law in a political democracy.[25] Property 1 is more complicated. It means that all individuals should have utility *scales* which, although they may differ from one another insofar as the total number of discretion levels is concerned (i.e., they may differ by an additive constant), must have in common that a unit movement along one individual's scale represents exactly the same amount of *satisfaction* as a unit movement along any other individual's scale. If it is in principle possible to conceive of different persons' satisfaction being empirically measured in common terms (i.e., if the question of the comparability of utility has empirical content), then property 1 is the following descriptive statement of fact; the different scales *are* in fact or can be *made* in fact equivalent.

---

[25]As I noted in Chapter 6 above, though, other beliefs are conceivable even within a democratic context. For example, the satisfaction unit of the poor should be more highly weighted than that of the rich. Of course this is not quite a differential weighting of specific individuals, since the higher weight applies only so long as a particular person *is* poor. In the Social Welfare Function, where *all* distributions of real income are admissible variables, this example would not involve differential weights to different individuals.

If it is not in principle possible to specify an empirical content to interpersonal comparisons of utility, then property 1 is a social value judgment. Which is the more appropriate treatment is, of course, the open question *par excellence*, in welfare economics. I do not hope to settle it, but I do believe it is possible to throw some empirical light on the question, and in any case, to suggest that either as a social value judgment or as a statement of fact, Property 1 is not especially reasonable.

In Section 8.3 above, I argued that the evidence about perception of preference adduced in the preceding chapter strongly suggested that when one considered a single individual, the assumption of constant satisfaction difference for unit index changes was hazardous. Any appreciable inequality of spacing for bare preference judgments at different parts of the individual's scale, would violate property 1.

When one considers more than one individual, there is yet a further complication. First, there are intuitive grounds for believing that different individuals may possess different total discretion levels, second, that different individuals may possess different total capacities, and, third and most important, that the two factors are not identical. That they are distinct can, I think, be suggested by the hypothetical case of a man with a capacity for "great joy" and "great suffering," but whose perception of satisfaction changes between the extremes is poor, so that he has but few discretion levels.[26] In the same tenor, one can conceive of a highly discriminating person, trained to make fine distinctions in his states of being, but who is not "passionate." In the first case, moving from one discretion level to the next represents a relatively large part of the individual's total satisfaction range. In the second, such a movement represents a very small part of that individual's total satisfaction range. *If* different persons' satisfactions are comparable as matters of fact, and *if* this comparison differs in substance from a comparison between their respective discretion levels, the discretion level unit of the first may well reflect a greater satisfaction change than that of the second. Property 1 will not be fulfilled. This consideration is certainly not on its face ridiculous. If interpersonal comparisons are allowed an empirical content it is even a plausible objection and would require empirical refutation to be escaped.

But suppose interpersonal comparisons are not allowable as matters of

---

[26]Certainly, the distinction is tenable only if we can in principle measure individual satisfaction (states of the organism) at least in part independently of the subject's perception of his satisfaction (i.e., of his preference intensity). For if we cannot, then our knowledge about his intensity is derivable only as a function of his own discretion levels. If we can, however, then interpersonal comparisons of utility are in principle matters of fact. When we say that a person is "capable of great joy" we do implicitly make such a comparison. But, of course, the crucial question in this is: can such comparisons be verified? Cf. Lionel Robbins, "Robertson on Utility and All That," *Econnomica* (May, 1953).

fact. Now, continuing the foregoing consideration, I submit that we habitually employ different empirical criteria in our daily affairs to judge an individual's perceptiveness than we employ to judge his total capacity to "feel." For the first, our criteria refer to fineness of discrimination in choosing; for the second, we are interested in behavior attendant on choice, such as expressive actions, release of tension, willingness to sacrifice, etc. Thus, even if we cannot *verify* the distinction, our daily usage makes it reasonable to suppose that we may well insist that such a distinction *ought* to count, that we *ought* not to judge a person's capacity to feel solely on the basis of his perceptiveness, and vice versa. If this is so, then, by the analysis of the last paragraph, we may well find it undesirable to judge that equal interval jumps represent equal preference intensity jumps for different individuals. Thus, if in particular we should, e.g., make the value judgment that everyone ought to be treated as possessing the same capacity for satisfaction, we may nonetheless judge this to be compatible with the empirical possibility that different individuals have a different number of discretion levels. We should thereby be showing a willingness to violate property 1.

To summarize, we have reason to believe on empirical grounds that equal discretion interval jumps do not represent equal satisfaction jumps for a given person throughout his utility scale. This alone makes suspect property 1. If in addition it is empirically demonstrable or only unverifiably believed because of this and other considerations that the measure of satisfaction for an individual is to some extent independent of his own perception of it, then property 1 may be properly viewed as unreasonably arbitrary. I am arguing that we have grounds for this view.

8-5. Rankings and Preference Intensities

Suppose we attempt to meet some of our foregoing objections and make the model more realistic. Specifically, let us drop the assumption that we know the number of discretion levels possessed by the different individuals and therefore also the assumption that our alternatives "cover" all levels. This is exactly the procedure of Goodman and Markowitz. Their formulation runs in terms of rankings alone, without an *explicit* relating of these rankings to the underlying discretion levels. Indeed, our parallel derivation of the summation of ranks criterion does some violence to the authors' intentions towards Resolution 2, where changes in social orderings as a result of changes in the state of information are deemed admissible. When all discretion levels are "covered," a change in the state of information means a change of tastes for one or more individuals. On this interpretation the resolution is trivial. But if all discretion levels are not covered by the ranked alternatives, then the introduction of additional alternatives may cause one or more individuals to give original alternatives new rank numbers even though their tastes remain unchanged, and therefore the social ordering may change without there having been a change in tastes. This can be seen from Table 7 following.

TABLE 7

	Alternative			
	w	x	y	z
Discretion level	3	7	9	12
Rank, situation 1	1	–	2	3
Rank, situation 2	1	2	3	4

A certain individual ranks alternatives w, y, and z 1, 2, and 3 respectively. Since we do not know whether or not these cover all the discretion levels, we can only be sure that the underlying discretion level numbers are a particular monotone transformation of this ranking, say, 3, 9, 12. Now introduce x (with discretion level 7). With no change in attitude toward w, y, and z whatever, the rank numbers of y and z will nonetheless change, since x *displaces* y from the second rank, and this displacement causes further displacements down the line. The introduction of x represents a change in the state of information. We apparently know more about the underlying discretion levels. Indeed, as the number of introduced alternatives increases, our rank numbers more and more closely approximate the underlying discretion levels.

Assume now that our alternatives w, x, y, z do cover all discretion levels. Then their rank numbers (1, 2, 3, 4) are identical with their discretion levels. Now introduce some alternative t. Can this affect the given rank numbers? No. By hypothesis, t must be indifferent with one (and only one) of the given alternatives; it must therefore have the *same* rank number as one of the given alternatives. It does not *displace* any of the given alternatives. Consequently, the given rank numbers are undisturbed. It is for this reason that a change in the given rank numbers must refer to a change in tastes on the part of the individual concerned.

The use of rank numbers as an approximate way to include preference intensities in the choice mechanism has two great advantages. (1) It is extraordinarily simple; (2) There is an undeniable intuitive connection between the comparison of rank differences and preference intensities, e.g., the preference difference between one individual's first and second choices reasonably *ought* to count less in social choice than the difference between another individual's first and last choices. This procedure could probably gain widespread approval as a better device for capturing the flavor of consumer sovereignty than the compensation principle (in either actual or potential welfare form). But the question of exactly how good a method it is must come to terms with at least the following two difficulties.

The issues raised in our discussion of Table 7 suggest a first difficulty of this approach: it violates in spirit our modified condition of the independence of irrelevant alternatives (Chapter 5). In that condition it was envisaged that, given the calculation of preference intensities (or utility levels), the social ordering of any pair of alternatives was independent of whatever other alternatives were being ordered. In the present model, however, the relevant preference intensities (rank differences) can never be calculated *except* by reference to whatever other alternatives are being ranked. So long as all discretion levels are not covered, as the ranking subset changes the rank difference between any two alternatives may change, and therefore, the social choice may change.

Placing this violation in perspective, what is involved is that our modified condition does not integrate the state of experimental ignorance into the choice mechanism itself, whereas this model does introduce it as a function of the set of ranked alternatives itself. We envisaged that preference intensities could be calculated uniquely, the calculation depending, it is true, on the total set $\overline{S}$ of alternatives as background (consequently, they might change as $\overline{S}$ changed, an admission of experimental ignorance), but once they were calculated for a given $\overline{S}$, they would be invariant over the availability of any alternative. This would be true of ranking indices too but only if every ranking were of all alternatives in $\overline{S}$. Once we employ rankings of sub-sets of $\overline{S}$, however, which seems clearly an intention of our greater realism in dropping the tie between ranks and discretion levels, then *for given* $\overline{S}$ we may obtain different "calculated preference intensities" depending upon which particular subset of $\overline{S}$ we rank, i.e., our intensities depend upon the availability of "irrelevant" alternatives. My quarrel is not that one approach involves ignorance, the other not. Clearly, both involve ignorance. But rankings of subsets of $\overline{S}$ compound the ignorance by excluding what we know about the remainder of $\overline{S}$, and even the ranking of all $\overline{S}$ does not tell us how good our state of information then is. The information is too limited; remember, we can never be certain that a finite set of alternatives, however large, exhausts all possible information about preference intensities. Other psychological investigation is necessary. And rankings freeze a too-mechanical relationship between the state of information and preference intensities onto the model to utilize such supplementary information.

Even more substantial than this criticism, however, is the objection that when we employ the summation of ranks criterion we do not know what we are precisely measuring. So long as our ranking sub-sets do not cover all discretion levels (especially when we do not know how many levels are involved), we cannot use rank differences to measure preference intensities. For illustration, let us refer to Table 7. On the basis of the state of information in situation 1, we would induce that the preference intensity between w and y was equal to that between y and z. In situation 2, we would induce that the w-y intensity was greater than the y-z intensity. The crucial point is that despite the fact that situation 2 supposedly represents more information than situation 1, we cannot be satisfied that 2 gives the better answer. If the discretion levels were as listed in Table 7, 2 *would* give the better answer. However, the underlying discretion level of z could just as well have been 35, and for such an eventuality the ranking in 1 would give the better answer. Unless we know the underlying discretion levels, we just do not know which situation to trust.

It may be objected that if situations 1 and 2 differed significantly in the amount of information conveyed, we should then be willing to trust the state of "better" information. Thus, suppose situation 1 ranks three alternatives while situation 2 ranks one hundred. Should we not then place greater faith in the second? Possibly. But there are two factors that should strictly qualify even this modest affirmation: (1) our ignorance as to even the approximate number of discretion levels involved, and (2) the lack of "convergence" in the series. Every time a new discretion level is discovered, it increases the rank number given to all alternatives inferior to it, and therefore it changes by one unit the measured "rank difference" between all pairs of alternatives in which one alternative is situated above and the other below the new discretion level, while leaving the measured rank difference between all other alternative pairs unchanged. The number and identity of alternative pairs which will be affected depends not at all on how many discretion levels have been already discovered, or how large is our sample of alternatives. It will depend only on which particular hitherto unknown discretion level has been revealed by a new alternative, and this is a random variable rectangularly distributed (i.e., we have no a priori information on where it may fall). Thus, the situation differs from that usually treated in statistical sampling theory, where the trustworthiness of sample estimates is reasonably held to be a function of sample size. The latter is "convergent." For example, if a population average is being estimated from sample averages (say the percentage of heads in the tossing of a coin) then a particular "run" of heads or tails will have far greater effect on the sample estimate if the sample is small than if it is large. Thus, in the present case we just have no dependable statistical decision rule to tell us when or to what extent there is improvement in the degree of "information" conveyed by different "states of information."[27]

If we frequently cannot draw clear inferences about preference intensities from rank numbers, then the summation of ranks criterion must be

---

[27]It is no answer that we would know which set of rank numbers to use if we independently knew more about the underlying discretion levels; for then we would not need rank numbers at all, but only the approximate discretion level numbers themselves.

interpreted with the greatest of caution. In this model we are even bereft of the subterfuge (which we discussed above for bare preference) of *defining* underlying preference intensities in terms of rank differences. Since rankings change with changes in information, while tastes remain unchanged, such a definition would be difficult to interpret. So the criterion in the realistic case of ranking any particular sub-set of alternatives whatever, despite its advantages, does not seem to fulfill satisfactorily our stipulated requirements for a formulation of social choice as a function of individual tastes.

CHAPTER 9

Expected Utility and Measurability:

I. The Expected Utility Hypothesis

9-1. Introduction

We have argued above that an (operationally justifiable) cardinal analysis is potentially more powerful than an ordinal analysis in meeting the problems of the present enquiry. Yet the two cardinal models which we have discussed so far are unsatisfactory in several respects. First, an admittedly far-from-systematic empirical confrontation casts serious doubt on whether the scales really measure preference intensities. Second, insofar as we maintain as a tacit working assumption that the consumer tastes which are "to count" are those revealed through consumers' consistent[1] market-type choices,[2]

---

[1] It would not do to state the qualification as calling for "rational" choice behavior. This would make the assumption tautologous since rational choice is usually defined as choice in accordance with an underlying set of goals (or values). The distinction, by the way, indicates that rational choice need not be consistent choice since the choice may be in accordance with an inconsistent set of goals. But this possibility does not make consistency the wrong qualification since, when we are in the presence of inconsistent choice, we cannot discover whether it results from irrationality or from rationality with contradictory goals. It might finally be pointed out that although all goal types are potentially conflicting in that "disproportionate" attention by the individual to any one makes it more difficult psychologically to achieve the others, outright explicit contradiction between goals might for observers be deemed itself irrational.

[2] This is similar to, but not quite the same as the assumption that the tastes which are to count under consumer's sovereignty are those revealed under procedures of "freedom of choice." The difference arises from the possibility that tastes may be revealed by choices in experimental situations — "simulated choices."

This similar formulation, by the way, helps to indicate the important distinction between "consumer's sovereignty" and "freedom of choice." In the latter, there is a valuational element attached to the *process* of choosing as distinct from the *content* of choice. (Cf. Bergson, "Socialist Economics," in the *Survey of Contemporary Eco-*

then these models are simply irrelevant for our purposes. What such choice behavior reveals (under static assumptions) is sufficient to narrow down the pattern of choice to a family of utility functions among which only preference order is invariant; nothing whatever is revealed about preference intensity.

Given this background, the expected utility model which we shall discuss in this chapter is important in three respects. First, it provides a promising empirical hypothesis on the basis of which cardinal utility indices may be constructed. Second, it is a model in which market-type choices themselves reveal enough information to enable us to narrow down the pattern of choice to utility functions among which preference intensities as well as preference orderings are invariant;[3] choice itself in this model implies cardinal utility. The expected utility hypothesis is one in which the notion of preference intensity belongs as a coordinate dimension of individual preference systems (along with preference order) even if we should insist upon restricting the admissible elements of tastes in the welfare function to what is revealable by choice. Third, as a result of the property just noted, the model enables us to appraise the very concept of "preference intensity" itself. We can reciprocally compare predictions derived from a scale constructed by means of the expected utility hypothesis and from one constructed by means of, say, some appropriate version of the "equal appearing intervals" technique. A high degree of mutual predictive consistency would much more warrant the notion of "preference intensity" as a behaviorally significant entity than would a low degree of predictive consistency. If "preference intensity" is to be a useful concept in the analysis of individual ends, one would, I think, expect that an individual's differential weighting of different preferences could in some way influence choices, at least in, say, situations where preference orders alone did not suffice to determine these choices. Although the lack of correspondence between any two techniques pretending to measure preference intensity would be no definitive refutation of preference intensity as an empirically important, in principle measurable, concept, it would question our present ability to make a fruitful definition of such a concept.[3a] A positive finding

---

nomics, 423). Consequently, it is possible to have consumer's sovereignty without freedom of choice. For example, tastes may be revealed by, say, governmental action *on behalf of* the consumers; the social choices are made *for,* but not *by,* the individuals concerned.

[3]This interpretation differs from that of some stringently operational approaches, such as D. Ellsberg, "Classic and Current Notions of 'Measurable Utility'," *Economic Journal,* Vol. LXIV, No. 255 (September, 1954), 528-556; Friedman and Savage, "The Expected Utility Hypothesis and the Measureability of Utility," *The Journal of Political Economy,* Vol. LX, (December, 1952), 463-474. The justification for the present interpretation is given in point three below and its discussion.

[3a]An analogy of the issue involved from physical science can be seen with regard to the concept "weight." We call "weight" both what is measured by a beam balance and by

would, in contrast, considering the unique characteristics of expected utility, strongly support a justification of cardinal analysis in welfare economics.

In this chapter I shall describe the expected utility model and attempt to evaluate it on the basis of some available evidence. We shall be especially interested in the respect in which cardinal utility properties are inferrable from consumer choices, in the realism of the formulation, in its scope, and in the manner by which it lends itself to incorporation in a model of social choice.

9-2. Expected Utility and Ordinal Analysis

As is well known, the axiom system of expected utility applies to choices involving risk.[4]

Ordinal theory, of the Pareto-Hicks-Allen-Slutsky type, refers to situations in which the individual is hypothetically asked to order every pair of commodity bundle alternatives A and B, or every triplet A, B, and C. Would he prefer receiving A to receiving B, or vice versa, or be indifferent between them? The question appears to involve a single choosing instance, but actually is employed in theory as signifying flows of A, B, or C over time. The preference for A over B, for example, is taken to mean that the individual would prefer receiving flows of the bundle A over time to flows of B. The choice commitment extends to the future but is valid only so long as the future is certain, so long as the particular future flow can be specified (which is definitional), so long as present preferences remain unchanged.[5] In short, the passage of time is formal only: there is really only one long present in terms of opportunity, evaluation and outcome. It is for this reason the theory is termed static.

---

a spring scale. This is because we have obtained closely similar sets of outcomes from the two techniques. Indeed, the very concept of "weight" is an important one only *because* similarities of this sort have enabled us to generalize it as an abstract relationship with implications extending beyond those of either — in fact, beyond both — techniques. The significance of the concept is that it gives coherence to a whole set of otherwise isolated phenomena.

[4]Von Neumann and Morgenstern, *The Theory of Games and Economic Behavior* (Princeton, N. J.: Princeton University Press, 1947); W. S. Vickrey, "Measuring Marginal Utility by Reaction to Risk," *Econometrica*, Vol. XIII (1945), 319-333; Jacob Marschak, "Rational Behavior, Uncertain Prospects and Measurable Utility," *Econometrica*, Vol. XVIII (April, 1950), 111-141 and, "Why Should Statisticians and Businessmen Maximize Moral Expectation?" *Proceedings of the 2nd Berkeley Symposium on Mathematical Statistics and Probability* (1951), 493-506; Friedman and Savage, "The Utility Analysis of Choice Involving Risk," *Journal of Political Economy*, Vol. LVI (August, 1948), 279-304 and, "The Expected-Utility Hypothesis and the Measurability of Utility," *Journal of Political Economy*, Vol. LX (December, 1952), 463-474; Mosteller and Nogee, "An Experimental Measurement of Utility," *Journal of Political Economy*, Vol. LIX (October, 1951), 371-404.

[5]These present preferences, it should be noted, refer to future commodities as well as to present commodities.

The von Neumann-Morgenstern (Bernoulli) theory is also static in that current evaluations are projected forward for the choices among future commodity flows. But it is non-static in that it unfreezes one of the most important characteristics of the real future — its uncertainty. The choice situation can be schematized as follows: Does the individual prefer a particular opportunity of obtaining *either* commodity bundle A *or* commodity bundle B, or a particular opportunity of obtaining *either* commodity bundle C *or* commodity bundle D? The choice here is not between receiving different commodity bundles but between different *prospects* of receiving commodity bundles. Each alternative, then, involves two elements: the commodity bundles which are the possible future outcomes of the situation, and the relative strengths of the possibility of obtaining the different outcomes (the probabilities of obtaining the different bundle flows). If either element changes, the prospect changes.

The von Neumann-Morgenstern hypothesis is as follows: When faced with choice among alternatives which are risk prospects, the individual will choose as though he were maximizing his expected utility, i.e., he will choose that alternative for which the mathematical expectation of utility is greatest. This hypothesis was first formulated, for the most part, by Daniel Bernoulli in 1738.[6]

The hypothesis was first formulated as a solution to the St. Petersburg Paradox, namely, to explain how persons could refuse to pay more than any specified amount of money to play a gamble, the mathematical expectation of whose money payoff is infinitely great. The gamble is as follows. The "banker," individual A, tosses a coin until it comes up heads. He pays to the "player," individual B, an amount of money which depends solely on the number of tosses it takes before the coin comes up heads. If heads comes up on the n'th toss, A's payment to B equals 2^{n-1} dollars. What is the highest price B should be willing to pay for the opportunity to play this gamble? The mathematical expectation of money payoff to B is infinitely great:

(1) $$E(M) = \tfrac{1}{2}2^0 + (\tfrac{1}{2})^2 2^1 + (\tfrac{1}{2})^3 2^2 + \ldots + (\tfrac{1}{2})^n 2^{n-1} + \ldots = \infty.$$

We do not find individuals willing to pay anything like fantastically high prices for the opportunity to play. George L. Leclerc[7] found in the eighteenth century that the actual payoff (i.e., from "banker" to "player") in 2048 tabulated games averaged $4.91 per game, and it can be shown in

---

[6]*Specimen Theoriae Novae de Mensura Sortis.* English translation by Louise Sommer, "Exposition of a New Theory on the Measurement of Risk," *Econometrica*, Vol. 22, No. 1 (January, 1954), 23-36.

[7]Cited in Harold T. Davis, *The Theory of Econometrics* (Bloomington, Indiana: The Principia Press, 1941), 55-6.

general that in any sequence of 2^k games the average payoff will be only slightly greater than $k/2$ dollars.[8]

The Bernoulli solution asserted that persons are motivated in such risk situations to maximize not the mathematical expectation of the money payoff itself, but the mathematical expectation of the money's *worth to them* — it's "moral expectation." Bernoulli formulated the relation between money income and utility as

$$(2) \qquad\qquad U = a \log \frac{I}{I_0}$$

where a is a constant, I is current money income and I_0 is minimum subsistence income. Thus, the marginal utility of money income diminishes as income increases:

$$(3) \qquad\qquad \frac{du}{dI} = \frac{a}{I}.$$

Consequently, the moral expectation of a given money income prospect will be less than the utility of the mathematical expectation of the prospect; the individual will offer an amount of money less than its mathematical expectation of money payoff for the privilege of playing. Given the specific probability values associated with the game (i.e., $\frac{1}{2}$ for heads, $\frac{1}{2}$ for tails) and the particular type of utility function chosen by Bernoulli, the money worth of the St. Petersburg game to a player will be *finite*, the amount depending upon the exact parameters chosen. Thus, his model is a solution to the Paradox.[9]

Von Neumann and Morgenstern's important contribution is not, then, in being first to suggest that individuals choose so as to maximize moral expectation (expected utility). Rather, their contribution is to present a set of postulates which is necessary and sufficient to derive the hypothesis. (They both imply and are implied by the hypothesis.) These postulates and the hypothesis are logically equivalent. The importance of the alternative formulation is that it suggests a large number of implications of the hypothesis by which it may be subject to empirical verification.[10]

---

[8]Davis, *loc. cit.*

[9]The qualifying terminology of the previous sentence emphasizes that it is the specifics of the model and not simply the two assumptions that moral expectation is crucial and that the marginal utility of income falls with income, that solves the Paradox.

Indeed, Menger has shown that, if we make a slight modification of the game to allow for continuous probabilities, *and* if the utility function is unbounded, then it is possible to specify probability and payoff distributions such that the gamble has infinite utility, and hence infinitely great money value. ("Das Unsicherleitsmoment in der Wertlehre," *Zeitschrift für Nationalökonomie*, Vol. 5 (1934), 459-485.) I am grateful to Kenneth Arrow for calling my attention to this work.

[10]Friedman and Savage, "The Expected-Utility Hypothesis and the Measurability of Utility," 466. We shall have occasion below to refer to an axiomatization of expected utility based on subjective, rather than as here, objective, probability.

It must be noted at this time, and it will become evident in the subsequent discussion, that the system presented here is not meant to *define* the real world so that cardinal utility is meaningful. Rather, it is truly an hypothesis about the real world; it is capable of being empirically refuted. Indeed, one debate in the literature stemmed from a criticism of expected utility on the ground that exceptions were *conceivable!*[11] Thus, its usefulness must be evaluated like that of an empirical hypothesis in any scientific discipline, in terms of its "coherence . . . with the rest of economic theory,"[12] and of the relative and absolute frequency of correct and incorrect predictions obtained by employing it.

9-3. Moral Expectation and Cardinal Utility

Let us now examine the relationship between risk situations and cardinal utility. Consider a situation where our given individual prefers alternative C to alternative A and A to B.[13] If the individual is simply asked to choose from among these alternatives in a non-risk context, we can deduce from his choices only a preference ordering. We know nothing about the preference intensities between the three.

It is different if he is asked to choose in a risk situation. Suppose one alternative is the certainty of receiving outcome A; the other is a prospect of getting either outcome B or C, but not both (B and C are mutually exclusive), with probabilities $1 - a$ and a respectively. Our assumption now is that the individual is capable of including risk prospects in his ordering of alternatives. (Another way of putting this is that the individual can find a "certainty equivalent" — an outcome obtainable with certainty with which the risk prospect is indifferent.)[14] Say a is $\frac{1}{2}$; the choice is then between A or a fifty-fifty chance of B or C. We turn to the analysis of von Neumann and Morgenstern.

> We expect the individual under consideration to possess a clear intuition whether he prefers the event A to the 50–50 combination of B or C, or conversely. It is clear that if he prefers A to B and also to C, then he will prefer it to the above combination as well; similarly, if he prefers B as well as C to A, then he will prefer the combination too. But if he should prefer A to, say, B, but at the same time C to A, then any assertion about his preference to A against the combination contains

---

[11]William J. Baumol, "The Neumann-Morgenstern Utility Index — an Ordinalist View," *Journal of Political Economy*, Vol. LIX (February, 1951), 61-66. The criticism was translated into the perspective of the present work by Friedman and Savage, "The Expected-Utility Hypothesis . . . ."

[12]Friedman and Savage, *op. cit.*, 466.

[13]These alternatives refer to the non-risk commodity bundles of previous chapters.

[14]We are making the traditional assumption here that indifference, like preference, is transitive.

fundamentally new information. Specifically: if he now prefers A to the 50–50 combination of B and C, this provides a plausible base for the numerical estimate that his preference of A over B is in excess of his preference of C over A.

If this standpoint is accepted, then there is a criterion with which to compare the preference of C over A with the preference of A over B. . . . Let a be a real number between 0 and 1, such that A is exactly equally desirable with the combined event consisting of a chance of probability $1 - a$ for B and the remaining chance of probability a for C, then we suggest the use of a as a numerical estimate for the ratio of the preference of A over B to that of C over B.[15]

In what respect does the choice of A or the combination provide information about preference intensities?[16]

Let us examine first what information is self-evident in the fifty-fifty chance. It is essential here to emphasize that the nature of the choice situation itself, risky or otherwise, does not *self-evidently* justify our treating A, B, and C as though they had a cardinal utility significance, i.e., riskiness *per se* does not impose the further restrictions on our ordinal utility functions. It is only a particular empirical uniformity in the *content* of the choices made in such risky situations that justifies accepting the additional restrictions. Say the individual finds the combination indifferent with A. By implication of the analysis in the quoted passage, this means that we believe that the preference intensity between A and B equals the intensity between C and A. Thus:

(4) $U(C) - U(A) = U(A) - U(B), \qquad 2U(A) = U(B) + U(C)$

(5) $U(A) = \tfrac{1}{2}U(B) + \tfrac{1}{2}U(C).$

Moreover, indifference between A and the combination implies that they have the same utility, i.e.,

(6) $U(A) = U(C,B;\ a)$

where $(C,B;\ a)$ is a notation for the risky alternative where C has a probability of occurring of a and B of $1 - a$. Combining (5) and (6), we obtain

(7) $U(C,B;\ a) = \tfrac{1}{2}U(B) + \tfrac{1}{2}U(C),$

and, in general

(8) $U(C,B;\ a) = aU(C) + (1 - a)U(B).$

This indicates that the assertion comparing preference intensities is equivalent to the assertion that the individual acts in choosing situations as if he evaluated risk situations on the basis of their mathematical expectation

---

[15]*The Theory of Games and Economic Behavior,* 18.

[16]Which is the kind of information, we know, that is sufficient for a cardinal index of utility. See Chapter 6 on bare preference.

of utility and then chooses from among alternatives that alternative possessing the greatest mathematical expectation; he maximizes "expected utility."

But what do these assertions entail? This much can be accepted as "self-evident": Since the individual's preference ordering is CAB, the desirability of the combination will be equal to that of B for $a = 0$ and to that of C for $a = 1$. Moreover, it would appear to be highly reasonable that for intermediate values of a the combination is more desirable than B, since the outcome of the combination can be no worse than B, and there is a probability of a that it will be more desirable. Similarly, there is a strong presumption that the combination is less desirable than C, since no possible outcome is better than C, and there is a $1 - a$ chance that the outcome will be worse. And finally, we might expect that as a increases from zero toward one, the desirability will increase from that of B toward that of C.

Yet these expectations concerning intermediate values of a are not so highly "self-evident" after all. First, an individual's preferences may be such that there are some alternatives C for which *all* probability mixtures of C and B are preferable to the certainty of A (where C is infinitely desirable) or some B for which the certainty of A is preferable to all probability mixtures of C and B (where B is infinitely undesirable). We shall discuss in a later section circumstances under which preferences like these may exist. Second, with the introduction of risk, a new element enters. The individual may well possess attitudes toward "gambling" *per se.* If, for example, the individual is exhilarated by gambling, he may actually prefer the combination to C; if he has a strong aversion to gambling, he may prefer the certainty of B to the gamble. But the expected utility assertion requires that the desirability of the combination $(0 < a < 1)$ be less than C and more than B. Thus, another non-obvious assumption entailed in the hypothesis, in other words, another potential source of fruitfulness in the hypothesis,[17] is the restriction that no such attitudes toward gambling remove the desirability of the combination from between B and C.

The unique characteristic of the expected utility hypothesis is the additional restriction further locating the desirability of the combination between B and C. This placement is solely a function of a. The preference intensity of the combination over B is a times the preference intensity of C over B.[18] Thus, the relative pulls of the desirability of B and C are weighted by the probabilities of their occurrence in the combination. Here again is an arbitrary procedure. Attitudes toward uncertain situations may conceivably be influenced by the dispersion of the utility risk and by still

---

[17]Friedman and Savage, "The Expected-Utility Hypothesis," 464-465.

[18]

$$\frac{aU(C) + (1 - a)U(B) - U(B)}{U(C) - U(B)} = \frac{a[U(C) - U(B)]}{U(C) - U(B)} = a.$$

higher moments of the probability distribution of utility as well as by the mathematical expectation.[19] They may be influenced by other aspects of the distribution as well, or by those same attitudes toward gambling *per se* already mentioned. The restriction that the desirability of any combined situation is determined by this simple probability weighting of outcomes does indeed make for a refutable, hence, not empirically empty, hypothesis.

Moreover, identifying the desirability of the combined alternative with the result of a numerical calculation gives us Equation (5) above (p. 206), and thus Equation (4) when $a = \frac{1}{2}$. If A is found indifferent to the combination, we obtain (2) and from this, we obtain (1). So it is the hypothesis that choices among risk situations will reveal the empirical regularity posited here, maximization of expected utility, that provides the basis for a cardinal utility index. When it is asserted that choices under risk *reveal* cardinal utility properties, this means only that the necessary postulates of a particular hypothesized rationalization of such choice behavior imply these properties.

We shall now indicate in some detail how choices under risk imply a cardinal utility index, indicating, indeed, that the very existence of the index implies empirical regularities of choice. Assume the individual has a complete ordering of all alternatives, whether sure outcomes or probability mixtures. Given such an ordering, the correspondence can be seen by rephrasing the expected utility hypothesis in the following highly suggestive form:

> "For a given individual . . . a set of numbers exists . . . with the two properties: (1) it is one of the sets expressing the individual's actual preferences among sure outcomes (i.e., it is one of his ordinal utility indices); (2) numbers are assigned to sure outcomes in such a way that, if moral expectations of *prospects* were computed on the basis of these numbers, one prospect would have a higher moral expectation than another if, and only if, the person actually preferred the former to the

---

[19]It is these characteristics of the frequency distribution of *utility*, not of *money income*, which are excluded by the expected utility hypothesis. If utility is a function of money income, then it is consistent with the expected utility hypothesis for higher moments of the frequency distribution of *money income* to be arguments of the utility function. The presence or absence of higher moment terms in the utility function determines the form of the relationship between utility and money income. Thus, if the variance of money income is an argument of the utility function, this implies that utility is a second degree function of money income. Conversely, if we are told that the utility function is of second degree, then this implies that the variance of income is an argument of the function. Other characteristics of the frequency distribution of money income become relevant variables for maximization with utility functions of appropriate degree. It is only if utility is a linear function of money income that all terms other than the mathematical expectation (first moment) of money income disappear.

Having made this distinction, we must hasten to admit that it is probably not amenable to empirical test within the context of the expected utility approach, since use of this apparatus implies that observations of choices will be taken to specify the form of the utility function, not to verify whether respondents are really maximizing some expected utility or not.

latter, and two prospects would have the same moral expectation if, and only if, the person were indifferent between them."[20]

This statement suggests a method for calculating the individual's numerical utility function.[21] Consider any two alternatives, B and C, which the individual orders CB. Arbitrarily assign C the utility number 1 and B the utility number 0. Now, select a third alternative A which our subject orders CAB. We can select A by one of two methods. (1) We stipulate the prospect of obtaining C with some given probability a and B with probability $(1 - a)$ and seek that sure outcome for which the individual is indifferent between the prospect and the sure outcome. (2) We stipulate a particular A and experimentally vary the probability a in prospect $(C, B; a_1)$.[22] Then from the hypothesis, there exists a number $U(A)$ such that, for some $0 < a_1 < 1$:

(9a) $$U(C) > U(A) > U(B)$$

(9b) $$U(A) = a_1 U(C) + (1 - a_1) U(B)$$

Mathematically, it is trivial that there does exist a number $U(A)$ which satisfies Equations (9a) and (9b). It is clear from our earlier discussion about what was self-evident in the hypothesis that if either attitudes toward gambling, *per se*, or an infinitely desirable or undesirable outcome between B and C, make the individual prefer $(C,B; a)$ to A or A to $(C,B; a)$ for all a $(0 < a < 1)$, then his behavior conforms to these conditions:

(10a) $$U(C) > U(A) > U(B)$$

(10b) $$U(A) \lesseqgtr aU(C) + (1 - a)U(B) \quad \text{(for all } a, 0 < a < 1)$$

Here there is no number $U(A)$ which fulfills Equation (9a) and either inequality of Equation (9b). Thus, if the individual's behavior violates the hypothesis or its implications, the result is that it is not possible to calculate a utility function for him; he does not "possess a utility function." We shall meet this phenomenon again. It is crucial for understanding the sense in which choice behavior reveals cardinal utility.

Having scaled C, B, and A, we may scale other alternatives by essentially the same device. Thus, select D such that CDB and, for some a_2, D is indifferent with $(C,B; a_2)$. Then, calculate $U(D)$ such that (1) $U(C) = 1 > U(D) > U(B) = 0$, and (2) $U(D) = a_2 (1) + (1 - a_2)(0)$. Here again a number $U(D)$ can be found to satisfy these conditions (and again, such a number cannot be found if the second calculation is an inequality

[20]D. Ellsberg, "Classic and Current Notions of 'Measurable Utility'," *Economic Journal*, Vol. LXIV, No. 255 (September, 1954), 539.

[21]The emphasis of the method bears heavily on Ellsberg's treatment, *op. cit.*

[22]The second method has greater facility than the first. Social state alternatives are not "homogeneous" in the sense of being obviously arrayable in a sequence to facilitate choice of A. Probability numbers, however, are. They can be varied continuously with monotonic effect on the desirability of risk prospects.

for all $0 < a_2 < 1$). But a new complication enters. If CDA, then we may find $U(D)$ by discovering an a, (a_3), such that D is indifferent to $(C,A;\ a_3)$, and thus, the hypothesis requires that $U(D) = a_3 U(C) + (1 - a_3) U(A)$. $U(D)$ must be the same whether calculated with respect to $(C,B;\ a_2)$ or $(C,A;\ a_3)$. If D is such that CAD, then we experimentally discover a_4 such that $U(A) = a_4 U(C) + (1 - a_4) U(D)$, and we may again calculate $U(D)$.

The requirement that $U(D)$ be invariant for the method of calculation is by no means trivial. It hinges on a special configuration of preferences since it affects not only the relatively simple ordering of sure prospects but also the more complicated ordering of uncertain prospects, *e.g.*, that the individual is indifferent between $(C,B;\ a_2)$, and $(C,A;\ a_3)$. Indeed, the utility number of D is a reflection of the simple ordering of C, B, A, D, $(C,B;\ a_2)$, $(C,A;\ a_3)$, $(C,B;\ a_1)$, and, indeed of all other prospects which can be constructed out of sure prospects. As we scale more and more sure outcomes, we create preference implications for an increasingly rich profusion of uncertain prospects. If, despite the number of ways in which a given prospect A_i can be scaled, it is assigned a utility number such that (1) A_i is preferred to every B_i if, and only if, $U(A_i) > U(B_i)$, and (2) a probability mixture involving A_i is preferred to any other probability mixture if, and only if, the mathematical expectation of utility of the former exceeds the mathematical expectation of the latter; then the individual "possesses a utility function". The necessary and sufficient condition for this (where the number of all alternatives is infinite) is that, for any initial arbitrary assignment of utility numbers to two alternatives (which sets the origin and unit of measurement), each sure outcome receives the same number, no matter what sub-set of alternatives is employed to scale it. Possession of a utility function *means* then, in the present context, that the individual's total structure of preferences among sure *and* uncertain prospects is consistent with the expected utility hypothesis. If his preferences, and therefore his choosing behavior (since this is completely determined by the former) are incompatible with the expected utility hypothesis, then he simply does not possess a utility function. Some alternatives cannot be scaled at all, or some receive different scale values when different sub-sets of alternatives are employed to scale them. In general numbers cannot be assigned to all alternatives so that their mathematical expectations will be consistent with preferences.

Finally, the index derived from this procedure is unique, one and only one number is assigned to each alternative, only insofar as a particular zero point and scale are specified. If, instead of assigning the numbers 0 and 1 to B and C respectively, we had assigned 62 and 114, then a different alternative would have ended up with zero, and the referential unit preference difference $U(C) - U(B)$, i.e., the scale of the index, would have equaled 52 instead of 1. The utility numbers assigned to the other alternatives would similarly change; we would have a new index. But the new index (V) would be related to the old (U) as follows.

(11) $$V(A_i) = m + nU(A_i) \text{ for all } A_i$$

All utility indices which are derived from the same preference ordering of sure and uncertain prospects are linear functions of one another. These are the only ones. No one index is better than any other; all preserve the same relations of preference difference between the same alternatives.

We must notice that it is the preference *ordering* of alternatives alone that suffices for the derivation of the utility index. No preference intensities are postulated; none are explicitly involved in the calculating procedure. This fact has led a number of strict operationalists[23] to assert that although mathematical manipulation of utility numbers may lead to implications about utility differences,[24] these utility differences are not to be interpreted as the same preference intensities we have examined in earlier chapters in connection with cardinal utility functions derived from choices among sure outcomes only. They argue that whereas the latter has been thought to be relevant to welfare economics, especially in Jevonsian-Marshallian tradition, the former has no such relevance. Briefly, the argument is as follows. The von Neumann-Morgenstern cardinal utility index is derived from operations which explicitly concern only preference order and not preference intensity. The domain of the function differs appreciably from that of the traditional utility function since risky prospects are included in the former. There is some evidence that application of the von Neumann-Morgenstern approach to behavior which is relevant to it (such as gambling and buying insurance) results in an implication about preference differences, namely, a range of rising "marginal utility of income," which is at variance with what is presumed to be the comparable pattern of preference intensities derived under the older approach from behavior relevant to *it*, universally decreasing marginal utility of income.[25] Since the preference differences of this approach are operationally different from those of the traditional approach, and since they may differ on an overlapping domain, the two should be considered different concepts. Furthermore, the older concept of preference intensity could reasonably believed be relevant to welfare economics because it presumably formed the content of introspectively verified ex-

---

[23]Notably Ellsberg, *op. cit.*, but also Friedman and Savage, "The Expected Utility Hypothesis."

[24]Indeed, we have just indicated that all appropriate indices for a given total ordering of alternatives preserve the same relation, $\lessgtr$, between the comparison of any two utility differences, i.e., for continuous functions, all have the same sign of the second derivative at any point.

[25]M. Friedman, and L. J. Savage, "The Utility Analysis of Choice Under Risk," *The Journal of Political Economy*, Vol. LVI (1948), 279-304; also H. Markowitz, "The Utility of Wealth," *The Journal of Political Economy*, Vol. LX, No. 2 (April, 1952).

periences of well-being; but the von Neumann-Morgenstern preference difference is simply a mathematical by-product of regularities in choices under special circumstances (risk). It seems, so it is argued, that it should therefore have no particularly persuasive role to play in defining the substance of the general welfare.

This book does not accept this position. As we have already argued, the mere fact that two concepts are operationally distinct does not mean that it is not useful to ascribe to them both a common burden. Coalescence of this kind will be acceptable if there is a tolerably close correspondence between the two concepts in the sub-domain which they have in common and if this sub-domain is a significant part of the total domain. It will be useful as well if the complementarity they render one another in the sub-domains they do not share is coherent with the corpus of accepted theory. In connection with the first point, the possibility that applying the von Neumann-Morgenstern approach to gambling and insurance will imply increasing marginal utility of income does not necessarily contradict the older approach. The universality of diminishing marginal utility under the old approach was never tested. Indeed, rationalizations of the existence of the increasing range under the von Neumann-Morgenstern approach may have as much relevance for the older approach as for the newer, thereby suggesting that if a non-risky utility function can be constructed, it too may contain a range of increasing marginal utility.[26]

---

[26]In the version presented by Friedman and Savage there is a range of absolute money income levels for which marginal utility is increasing. In the Markowitz version, there is a range of positive and a range of negative deviations from the individual's "customary" level of income, (taken as the origin of measurement), for which marginal utility is increasing. The point of "customary income" is a point of inflection between a convex (upward) section to the left and a concave section to the right. A rationalization of the first is that there are two distinct "styles" of life achievable over the total range of income, and there is an intermediate range between the two where, as income increases, more and more elements of the "higher style" infuse the "lower style." This intermediate range ends where all the *minimally* necessary elements for the "higher style" are present, and further increases in income enable only elaborations of the basic pattern. Marginal utility declines wherever income increases enable only elaborations of either basic style; but it increases where higher income makes it possible for a "low style" consumer to partake *somewhat* of the glamor, prestige, etc. of "high style" living. This continues to be true until he possesses all the minimal ingredients necessary for full participation in the "high style". Thus, the intermediate range between the two styles will show increasing marginal utility.

In Markowitz' version the interpretive key seems to lie in the concept of "customary income (or wealth)". Invariably to form an inflection point suggests that it represents a boundary to the style of life. "Customary income" may be interpreted as a level of income to which the individual has had the opportunity to make a full optimal adjustment. He has achieved complete identification with his current style of life. Assume that each individual, regardless of his absolute income (or wealth) level, perceives a higher style and a lower style than this as well. Any increase of income will enable him to partake at least partially of the higher style since, at the customary income level, all the minimal elements necessary for the intermediate style have been satisfied. Therefore, no extra income need be spent in that direction. However, moderate de-

Do the two types of preference intensity really involve very different experiences for the individual? As we have seen earlier, psychologists find little difficulty in operating on the assumption that orderly discriminations of the form, "My preference for *A* over *B* is greater than my preference for *C* over *D*," are well within the capacity of individuals.[27] Consider placing some sub-set of simple alternatives before a subject. Calculate a cardinal utility index by some psychometric scaling device (such as the method of equal-appearing intervals.[28] Assume that the subject possesses a von Neumann-Morgenstern utility function, and calculate this function for the same alternatives. In the latter, the individual chooses as though he were maximizing expected utility among alternatives (including risky prospects) or, what is logically equivalent, chooses as though he were comparing weighted preference intensities.[29] The ordinal scale for sure prospects must

---

creases in income will not require him to assume a lower style, since he may continue to partake of many of the elements of his current style while having to sacrifice some elements. For increases, our argument in the Friedman-Savage case suggests that marginal utility will increase as he approaches fuller participation in the higher style, up to the level at which all minimum necessary elements are present, and then it will decline as further income increases lead only to elaborations of the higher style. For decreases, utility will fall slowly for small changes since the consumer can remain at his current style while giving up some few elements of his erstwhile full participation. As the decrease gets larger, utility falls faster because he must discard more and more of the insignia of the higher style and approaches the lower style. Once income has fallen so much that he is pushed into the lower style, the worst has happened, and utility then falls much more slowly for further decreases. Thus, there is an asymmetry between increases and decreases from customary income.

Granted that these rationalizations, especially the second, are neither perfect nor unique for their respective hypotheses, they are clearly as appropriate, or inappropriate, for a riskless utility function as for one defined in the context of risk. This suggests that empirical findings compatible with a range of increasing marginal utility defined in terms of the latter type of utility function would by no means necessarily contradict the shape of any function of the former type which could be calculated from corresponding observable behavior.

[27]Although it is true enough that they do not deal with alternatives of choice as multi-dimensionally complex as we do. But for that matter, with such complexity, even our assumption of simple ordering is heroic.

[28]L. L. Thurstone, "Attitudes Can Be Measured," *American Journal of Sociology*, Vol. 33 (1928), 529-554; L. L. Thurstone, and E. J. Chave, *The Measurement of Attitude*, (Chicago: University of Chicago Press, 1929); L. L. Thurstone, "A Law of Comparative Judgment," *Psychological Review*, Vol. 34 (1927), 273-280; Clyde H. Coombs, "Theory and Methods of Social Measurement," *Research Methods in the Behavioral Sciences*, 520-523; J. P. Guilford, *Fundamental Statistics in Psychology and Education* (New York: McGraw-Hill Book Co., Inc., 1950), Chapter 19, especially pages 556-559. Helen Peak, "Problems of Objective Observation," L. Festinger, and Daniel Katz, *Research Methods in the Behavioral Sciences* (New York: The Dryden Press, 1953), 255-260. See the last four items for a larger bibliography on the subject.

[29]Thus,

$$aU(B) + (1 - a)U(C) > aU(D) + (1 - a)U(E)$$

implies

$$a[U(B) - U(D)] > (1 - a)[U(E) - U(C)],$$

and, if $a = \frac{1}{2}$,

$$U(B) - U(D) > U(E) - U(C).$$

be the same under both procedures. Under these circumstances it is difficult to believe that the hypothetical preference intensities which are weighted linearly to form expected utilities are not essentially the same as those computed from psychometric riskless contexts.

Suppose first that the individual does actually choose by forming mathematical expectations of utility and selecting that alternative which gives the highest expected utility. Since we have assumed that the subject can distinguish, compare, and order preference intensities for sure prospects, what other kind of experience of differential desirability must one postulate exists in the process of formulating expected utilities? Admittedly, neither the former psychometric procedures nor the expected utility approach may succeed in measuring these intensities accurately or, indeed, with the same degree of inaccuracy. But for normative purposes what is important is the epistemological question of whether the evaluative experiences under the two types of procedure refer essentially to the same internal projections of relative desirability — relative well-being. It surely seems overly dogmatic to assert that the two are necessarily different. I believe it far more reasonable to assume that, if the individual actually does respond to uncertain prospects in terms of expected utility, he does so by referring to the one and only set of evaluations he possesses about differential desirability of the alternatives.

The case is somewhat different if it is argued that expected utility calculations are only fictitious, that the individual actually goes through a complicated process which just happens to result in an ordering of all alternatives (including risky prospects) such that it is possible to find numbers with the property that preference always conforms to the relative size of linear probability-weighted combinations of these numbers. This might be an effective argument against our position *if* we were not ready to argue that individuals can order riskless preference intensities. For all it does is say that the behavioral regularities which are consistent with expected utility maximization do not necessitate that we postulate the existence of riskless preference intensities. The latter is not a necessary condition for the former, since the content of the former is, most strictly speaking, only a regularity about preference ordering. If we do anyway postulate the existence of these intensities, however, the case is quite different. Then the hypothesis that it is these intensities, linearly weighted by probabilities, which determine choice, is much the simplest that can be made. Any more complicated hypothesis for the same phenomena must probably eschew the notion of linear probability combinations as well as of relative desirability to avoid being simply a circumlocution of a literal expected utility hypothesis. An hypothesis of such proliferating complexity which merely duplicates the predictive power of a literal expected utility hypothesis is not likely to be persuasive. Thus, if we are ready to accept the independent meaningfulness of orderly discriminations about preference intensity, it seems natural to interpret expected utility maximization. literally and therefore to identify the probability-weighted first differences implied by the expected utility formula as indicators of real evaluations of differential desirability, the individual's unique evaluations of that sort.

A last epistemological point. It has frequently been noted that for an individual to pay attention solely to the mean value of the probability distribution of utility is not especially self-evident.[30] If we calculated a cardinal utility function within a riskless context and applied it to make predictions about an individual's preferences between risky prospects, it would not be amiss to suggest that variables like the variance or skewness of the probability distribution of *utility* outcomes be included in the predictor formula along with mean value. It would, however, be very definitely amiss to suggest that a predictor formula using von Neumann-Morgenstern utility numbers include *anything* other than mean. The reason for this is, of course, that the very existence of the von Neumann-Morgenstern utility function for the individual logically *implies* that his preferences are consistent with the hypothetical process of taking these very utility numbers and selecting alternatives solely in terms of their expected utility value, the mean value of the probability distribution of utility outcomes.[31]

This difference in applicability between the two concepts would warrant belief in their essential dissimilarity if it implied that "psychometric utilities" were "pure" whereas von Neumann-Morgenstern utilities were compounds of "pure" and probability elements. It can be shown, however, that no such inference can be made. The relationship between von Neumann-Morgenstern utilities and parameters of the probability distribution of outcomes has been pointed out in footnote 31. Consider the calculation by which we assign a utility number to some alternative A. Alternative A is found to be indifferent to $(B,C; a_1)$, where we already know the utility numbers for B and C. If the variance, say, of "raw" outcomes B and C matters to the individual, this will be reflected in the utility numbers given

---

[30]*e.g.* Maurice Allais, "Le Comportement de l'Homme Rationnel Devant le Risque," *Econometrica*, Vol. 21 (1953), 503-546; Allais, "La Psychologie de l'Homme Rationnel Devant le Risque," *Journal of Social Statistics*, Vol. 94 (1953), 47-73; W. J. Baumol, "The Von Neumann-Morgenstern Utility Index — An Ordinalist View," *Journal of Political Economy*, Vol. 59 (1951), 61-66.

[31]It must be pointed out that we are speaking of the distribution of *utility* outcomes, not of money income or commodity or social state outcomes. The distinction, admittedly difficult to test empirically, has sometimes been overlooked. Actually, expected utility maximization can logically take into consideration variance and other features of the probability distribution of "raw" outcomes, features which are important for determining the shape of the resulting utility function. Thus, if only the mean of the "raw" distribution is important for the individual, his utility function will be linear; if variance is important as well his utility function will be a second degree curve; and so forth. See footnote 19 above.

to A,B, and C. But the calculation $U(A) = a_1U(B) + (1 - a_1)U(C)$ will express this only in the value of a_1 which equates the two, since the utility values of B and C have already been given. Logically speaking, this is tantamount simply to the statement that the equating value of a_1 determines the behavior of the slope of the utility function between B and C (A is located between these). The dependence of $U(A)$ on variance does not mean then that the particular variance of *utility outcomes* in $(B,C; a_1)$ has any effect; that a prospect $(D,E; a_2)$ with the same expected utility but different variance of utility outcomes might not be indifferent with either A or $(B,C; a_1)$. We have already indicated that, for a von Neumann-Morgenstern utility function to exist, the assignment to any alternative must be the same no matter with what sub-set of alternatives it has been compared. Thus, it must equate with all prospects of equal expected utility despite the fact that they have vastly differing variances of utility outcome. The preface intensities implied by the von-Neumann-Morgenstern utility function *are* "pure" intensities.

What the expected utility procedure does do that differs from "introspective"[32] procedure is to impose the condition that only mean values of utility outcomes be considered. Thus, if the particular individual happens to choose prospects only on the basis of expected utility, he will possess a von Neumann-Morgenstern utility function, and this function will imply the same "pure" preference intensities as those revealed "introspectively." If, however, he chooses by considering not only the probability mean of "pure" utility outcomes but also their dispersion or skewness, etc., then this can be described by the appropriate non-linear function of "pure" utilities (derived "introspectively"), but the individual will *not possess* a von Neumann-Morgenstern utility function. In such a situation, there is only one set of preference intensities ("introspectively" derived), not two sets which differ in content. Considering both cases, therefore, there is no good reason for assuming that the two concepts can be simultaneously meaningful, and yet refer to substantially different evaluative experiences for the individual.

In sum: we argue that the Von Neumann-Morgenstern type of cardinal utility function implies information about preference intensities which should be accorded the same normative relevance as was the comparable information implied by the traditional riskless cardinal utility function. Our argument is really the assertion of an empirical hypothesis: that we should expect to find a high degree of correspondence between utility indices

---

[32]"Introspective" is enclosed in quotes to emphasize that a number of psychometric procedures for scaling utilities in riskless contexts involve overt choosing behavior by the subject. For example see, Clyde Coombs, and J. E. Milholland, "Testing the 'Rationality' of an Individual's Decision Making under Uncertainty," *Psychometrica* (1954); P. Suppes, and Muriel Winet, "An Axiomatization of Utility Based on the Notion of Utility Differences," *Management Science* (1955), 259-270.

formulated by the two different approaches. The empirical testing is of course yet to be done.

9-4. *Axioms for Expected Utility*

We may now present the modern axiomatization of the expected utility hypothesis. Besides the statement of von Neumann and Morgenstern in *The Theory of Games*,[33] there have been a number of very similar formulations. One that should be mentioned because it precedes *The Theory of Games* is that made by Frank Ramsey in 1926.[34] Others have been, for the most part, reworkings of the postulates in *The Theory of Games* with the most significant difference being, in most cases, a spelling out of the so-called "Strong Independence Assumption." The particular treatment presented here is an amalgam of the essentially similar treatments of von Neumann-Morgenstern, Marschak,[35] Armen Alchian,[36] Friedman and Savage.[37], and Savage,[38] leaning most heavily on the next to last named, because of its simplicity.

Consider for a given individual the possible "events" or outcomes, commodity bundles, money incomes, etc., $x_1, x_2, \ldots, x_n$. The alternatives of choice for the individual, or "prospects," are various frequency distributions of these possible outcomes, i.e., every particular prospect f specifies a probability f_i for each x_i. Thus,

$$f = (f_1, f_2, \ldots, f_n),$$

and the sum of the f_i's equals 1. Similarly

$$g = (g_1, g_2, \ldots, g_n) \quad \text{and} \quad \sum_i^n g_i = 1.$$

Introduce now the non-negative numbers a, where $0 \leq a \leq 1$. Now,

$$af + (1 - a)g = [af_1 + (1 - a)g_1, af_2 + (1 - a)g_2, \ldots, af_n + (1 - a)g_n].$$

Interpreting the a's as probabilities, $af + (1 - a)g$ is a "mixture" of f and g; it is a new probability distribution of the outcomes $x_1, \ldots, x_n$, such that the probability attached to each x_i is $af_i + (1 - a)g_i$. Multiplication and addition are defined for ordinary vectoral operations. If f and g are distributions such the x_r and x_s are sure prospects in the respective distributions, then the mixture is a probability distribution for which

---

[33]Second Edition, Appendix.

[34]*The Foundations of Mathematics and Other Logical Essays*, (New York: The Humanities Press, 1950), pp. 166-190.

[35]Jacob Marschak, "Rational Behavior, Uncertain Prospects, and Measurable Utility," and "Why Should Statisticians and Businessmen Maximize Moral Expectation?"

[36]"The Meaning of Utility Measurement," *American Economic Review*, Vol. XLIII (March, 1953), 36.

[37]"The Expected Utility Hypothesis," 468.

[38]*The Foundations of Statistics*.

x_r and x_s are mutually exclusive possible outcomes with respective probabilities a and $1 - a$.

The terminology $af + (1 - a)g$ for a chance of distribution f with
probability a and a chance of distribution g with probability $(1 - a)$
implies that the ordinary combinational rule for joint probabilities applies
to joint gambles at different degrees of remove from the sure outcomes of
the system; there is nothing to distinguish the probability elements of
gambles of very dissimilar structure.

The set of all conceivable prospects F is the universe of discourse of the
following postulates. For every f,g in F, the "mixture" $af + (1 - a)g$ is
also in F; the mixture space is convex. In the postulates the relations $>$, $\leq$,
$=$, referred to prospects signify, respectively, "is preferred to," "is not
preferred to," "is indifferent to."

Postulate 1. "Preference of the person in uncertain situations to which
probability applies are governed solely by the probabilities attached to each
possible outcome."[39]

Corollary 1. The prospect $af + (1 - a)h$ has the same value to the
individual no matter what the process is for determining the outcome.[40]

Postulate 2 — Complete ordering. The individual has a complete ordering
of alternatives (prospects), and this ordering is transitive.

---

[39]Friedman and Savage, "The Expected-Utility Hypothesis," 467.

[40]Alchian, "The Meaning of Utility Measurement," *American Economic Review*,
Vol. XLIII, No. 1 (March, 1953), 36. Thus, for example, it must make no difference to
the individual whether the outcome of the prospect of getting income X_1 with three-
eighths probability, and X_2, with five-eighths probability, is obtained by drawing from a
single urn containing three black balls and five white, or by tossing a coin (fifty-fifty
chance) to see whether to draw from one urn containing one black and one white ball,
or another urn containing one black and three white balls.

Thus, in general, the prospect $af + (1 - a)h$ is equivalent to the prospect g, i.e.,

$$g = [af_1 + (1 - a)h_1 = g_1, \quad af_2 + (1 - a)h_2 = g_2, \ldots, af_n + (1 - a)h_n = g_n].$$

The postulate asserts that any mixture whose elements similarly equal $[g_1, g_2, \ldots, g_n]$ is
indifferent to $af + (1 - a)h$.

This assertion is not made as a separate postulate in von Neumann-Morgenstern,
Marschak, or Friedman-Savage; it, rather, underlies the other postulates, since its burden
is that any prospect is equivalent to another prospect with the same probability combination of outcomes. We have chosen to present it separately because we intend evaluating it at some length.

Samuelson explicitly introduces this condition as part of the postulate on complete
ordering: "All situations can be completely ordered and in terms of their associated
prizes alone." "Probability, Utility, and the Independence Axiom," *Econometrica*, Vol.
20, No. 4 (October, 1952), 672. An "associated prize" is the simple prospect, like

$$\tfrac{3}{8}X_1 + \tfrac{5}{8}X_2,$$

which is derivable from any compound multiple stage gamble, like,

$$\tfrac{1}{2}(\tfrac{1}{2}X_1 + \tfrac{1}{2}X_2) + \tfrac{1}{2}(\tfrac{1}{4}X_1 + \tfrac{3}{4}X_2).$$

The desirability of presenting it as a separate axiom is to keep distinct the implications
of complete ordering for any kind of alternatives whatever from a condition about
the value, or rather, lack of value, of "game participation."

"For all f, g, h (not necessarily distinct) in F:

(1) $f \leq g$, or $g \leq f$. (Either gamble f is not preferred to gamble g, or g is not preferred to f.) (Connexity).

(2) If $f \leq g$ and $g \leq h$, then $f \leq h$." (Transitivity).

Postulate 3 — Continuity. The preference relation is continuous. "If $f \leq g$ and $g \leq h$, then there is some value of a, $0 < a < 1$, for which $g = af + (1 - a)h$."[41]

Postulate 4 — Strong independence. "For $0 < a < 1$, $af + (1 - a)h \leq ag + (1 - a)h$, if and only if, $f \leq g$."[42]

---

[41]Marschak, "Rational Behavior," 117.
We can demonstrate that this postulate involves continuity of the preference relation roughly as follows. Since a takes all values between 0 and 1 (actually $0 < a < 1$), the gamble $af + (1 - a)h$ is, abstracting from inherent likes or dislikes about risk itself, not preferred to h. Also, f is not preferred to the gamble. Moreover, assuming for the moment that the individual is not indifferent among f, g, and h (since in this case the postulate is trivial), the gamble can be made to approach h in desirability by decreasing a. Since a is a continuous variable, the gamble could be made indifferent to any alternative (r_k) more desirable than f and less desirable than h, and thus to some alternative r_j indifferent to g, but only if the individual were able to discriminate differences in the gamble brought about by arbitrarily small variations in the weights a and $(1 - a)$!
In the axiom system presented in "The Expected Utility Hypothesis," 468, Friedman and Savage render the continuity postulate as: "If $af + (1 - a)h \leq g$ for all a such that $0 \leq a < 1$, then $f \leq g$." (p. 467). This does not appear to be equivalent to our Postulate 3, but it does similarly suffice to establish continuity. That it does so is not so intuitively evident as with Postulate 3. A rough demonstration follows.
The Friedman and Savage postulate says in effect that since a and the expression $af + (1 - a)h$ can vary continuously, the preference relation must be sensitive to differences arising from continuous differentials. Thus, assume f to be very slightly preferred to g. Then, combine this f in a risk situation with some h such that when the probability of obtaining f is zero, the gamble is not preferred to the certainty of g. Clearly the certainty of h is not preferred to the certainty of g. Now, increase the probability of obtaining f in the gamble. a may take all values greater than zero and less than 1. For every such value a_k, the gamble will be indifferent with some alternative r_k obtainable with certainty. By the condition of Postulate 2, each r_k must not be preferred to the certainty of g. Now, every r_k must be preferred to h, and f must be preferred to every r_k (since $f > g \geq h$). But we may increase a arbitrarily close to 1 so that the gamble becomes almost indistinguishable from the certainty of $g - r_k$ apparently approaches f in desirability very closely. In these circumstances, r_k can remain $< g$ only if there is some a_m such that $r_m \leq g$ and all a greater than a_m but less than 1 give rise to r_k's which the individual deems indifferent with r_m. In other words, there is a discontinuity in the perception of differences in situations, a discontinuity in the preference relation itself. We of course have met the same thing in our discussion of bare preference. But in this situation the postulate would be falsified, for although the gamble is never preferred to g, we can not justifiably deduce $f \leq g$. Consequently, only if we have a continuous preference relation is the postulate fulfilled, i.e., that $f \leq g$ if the gamble is never preferred to g.
[42]"The Expected-Utility Hypothesis," 468. Marschak's formulation is similar. If $f = g$ and $0 < a < 1$ and if $f' = ah + (1 - a)f$, and $g' = ah + (1 - a)g$, then $f' = g'$. This is obviously the special case of Postulate 3 where $f = g$. Marschak refers to this postulate as "the rule of substitution between indifferent prospects." ("Why Should Statisticians and Businessmen Maximize Moral Expectation?", p. 500).

Formally speaking, given these four postulates, we can deduce the expected utility hypothesis as the following theorem.[43] "Theorem. There are numbers $c_1, \ldots, c_n$ such that $f \leq g$ if and only if

$$\Sigma f_i c_i \leq \Sigma g_i c_i.$$

Moreover, any two such sequences of numbers c_i and c'_i are connected by an equation

$$c'_i = s + t c_i$$

for some s, t, with $t > 0$."[44]

In this theorem the numbers c_i may be taken as the index of utility;

$$\sum_i^n f_i c_i$$

is the mathematical expectation of utility of the uncertain prospect f. We may paraphrase this theorem as asserting that an individual's preferences between any two prospects depend on the mathematical expectation of utility of each prospect. Moreover, the utility index numbers which can be applied to the components of each prospect, such that this correspondence with preference holds, are unique up to a linear transformation. Employing our preference terminology:

$$fPg, \text{ if and only if, } \Sigma f_i c_i > \Sigma g_i c_i \text{ [45]}$$
$$gPf, \text{ if and only if, } \Sigma g_i c_i > \Sigma f_i c_i$$
$$gIf, \text{ if and only if, } \Sigma g_i c_i = \Sigma f_i c_i.$$

---

[43]For the proof of this derivation for an analogous set of axioms see, *The Theory of Games*, 2nd ed., 617-628; Marschak, "Rational Behavior, Uncertain Prospects and Measurable Utility," 115-134; Savage, *The Foundations of Statistics*, 73-76.

[44]Friedman and Savage, "The Expected-Utility Hypothesis," 468.

[45]Preference here, it will be remembered, means $g \leq f$ and not $f \leq g$. If not $f \leq g$, then not

$$\Sigma f_i c_i \leq \Sigma g_i c_i,$$

i.e., if $f > g$, then

$$\Sigma f_i c_i > \Sigma g_i c_i.$$

Similarly, indifference means $g \leq f$ and $f \leq g$, therefore

$$\Sigma g_i c_i \leq \Sigma f_i c_i \quad \text{and} \quad \Sigma f_i c_i \leq \Sigma g_i c_i,$$

hence

$$\Sigma g_i c_i = \Sigma f_i c_i.$$

CHAPTER 10

Expected Utility and Measurability:
II Evaluation

10-1. Evaluation of the Axiom System

Since the expected utility theory is empirically refutable, the controlled experiment, in which predictions made by employing the hypothesis are confronted by experience, would appear an ideally appropriate mode of evaluating the theory. Up to the present time, however, direct empirical verification has not yielded anything like conclusive evidence for or against the theory. Some of the experiential phenomena which lend support to the theory are discussed in articles by Vickrey, and Friedman and Savage.[1] In addition, a formal experimental confrontation has been performed by Mosteller and Nogee.[2] This experiment did not contradict the hypothesis, but neither did it offer strong support. On the one hand, the expected utility hypothesis did not in fact significantly exceed the predictive performance of an alternative hypothesis that choices are rationalized by maximization of the *mathematical* expectation of a gamble (rather than of the *moral* expectation). On the other hand, the experimental situation may have been structurally incapable of distinguishing even in principle between the performance of the two hypotheses.[3]

---

[1] Vickrey, "Measuring Marginal Utility by Reactions to Risk"; Friedman and Savage, "The Utility Analysis of Choices Involving Risk."

[2] "An Experimental Measurement of Utility."

[3] In the experiment, a number of subjects were confronted with a sequence of different (and repeated) gambles, any of which they were free to play or not at a variety of specified odds. The size of money bets, and the range of possible total gambling accumu-

A set of experiments undertaken by the psychologist Ward Edwards presents some evidence against the expected utility hypothesis.[4] In these experiments subjects chose among risky prospects in such a way as strongly to suggest that they have "general preferences or dislikes for risk-taking, and specific preferences among probabilities."[5] These preferences could not be subsumed under expected utility maximization; the concrete choices were inconsistent with calculation of a von Neumann-Morgenstern utility function.[6]

---

lations, were so small relative to the annual incomes of the subjects that no real test of the hypothesis may have been involved. With the stakes on each play extremely small, the smallest planning unit where the player's utility was involved might well have been the outcome of the entire experiment. If this were so, maximization of moral expectation would lead to a strategy *within* the experiment aimed at maximizing the total accumulated money reward to be approximately gained from the experiment as a whole. But this goal is rationally met by playing every gamble whose mathematical expectation of money reward is positive, i.e., the goal is met by choosing so as to maximize the *mathematical* expectation of each gamble. In other words, the two different motivations would lead to indistinguishable behavior within the experimental situation.

I am indebted to Professor William Vickrey for this point.

A qualification of the foregoing would seem in order. The smallness of the single bet was judged in this criticism in relation to each individual's annual income. Yet this may underestimate its importance to the individual in the actual context of the experiment. The experiment was carried on in ten (?) weekly sessions. Each concrete play situation was therefore part of a single weekly session. It is conceivable that the repetitiveness of the gambling situation in the weekly schedule of the subjects might have led some individuals to incorporate their decisions in any one session within the frame of reference of weekly commitments, rather than to view the total experiment as part of one's annual strategy. The influence of one session's accumulation on weekly income is not insignificant; and the far fewer number of possible bets in any one session in comparison with the single bet makes a mathematical expectation strategy for each session less obviously desirable than if the whole experiment were being borne in mind.

The force of this qualification is not known. But its importance is to suggest that we analyze more deeply the time dimension of choosing behavior, certainly the relationship between choices made with respect to different time interval contexts. Much of the content of current economic theory, e.g., the theory of the firm, founders on an inability to give operational content to this relationship.

Over and above this basic reservation concerning the results of the Mosteller experiment, there are reportedly others. For example, it has been reported to the author by Professor A. G. Hart that there were indications during the experiment that the subjects did not grasp the notion of objective probability. Their misunderstanding apparently was concentrated on long odds. Of course, this difficulty may not be exclusively a structural defect of the particular experimental situation; it may well be an experimental conclusion about the hypothesis itself, since the hypothesis claims that individuals *do* choose on the basis of objective probabilities. See the discussion to follow in this section for more on this.

[4]Ward Edwards, "Experiments on Economic Decision-Making in Gambling Situations," *Econometrica*, Vol. 21 (1953), 349-350 (Abstract); "Probability Preferences Among Bets with Differing Expected Values," *American Journal of Psychology*, Vol. 67 (1954), 56-67; "The Reliability of Probability Preferences," *American Journal of Psychology*, Vol. 67 (1954), 68-95.

[5]Ward Edwards, "The Theory of Decision-Making," *Psychological Bulletin*, Vol. 51, No. 4 (1954), 396.

[6]General pro or con attitudes toward risk taking *per se*, and preferences among

However, an experiment undertaken by Davidson, Suppes, and Siegel[7] lends support to a related but importantly dissimilar hypothesis, namely that when individuals are faced with a set of risky alternatives, *all of which consist of the same probability mix of different pairs of sure outcomes,* they choose as if they were maximizing expected utility. This statement is implied by the expected utility hypothesis, but not conversely. Out of nineteen subjects, the experimenters were able to construct utility functions for fifteen.

In this experiment the subject is offered only pairs of alternatives for which the actual single outcome depends on the same chance event.[8] We shall argue below that it is possible to test whether choice behavior reflects attitudes toward risk (or gambling, suspense or participation, etc.) or, more

---

probabilities are incompatible with the expected utility hypothesis. If an individual possesses a von Neumann-Morgenstern utility function, then, once utility numbers have been assigned, any two prospects with equal expected utilities are indifferent no matter how dissimilar the probability weights in the two prospects are (even in the extreme case where one of the prospects is sure). However, what looks like probability preferences (including a probability of 1) in a smallish sequence of choices need not be inconsistent with expected utility maximization. In a major experiment Edwards shows that, when faced with pairs of choices between prospects having the same expected value of money outcome, subjects chose systematically in favor of some probability mixes and against others. This pattern of apparent probability preferences is repeated in other experiments where the expected values of money outcomes differed within each pair in such a way as to encourage exactly opposite choices if choices were governed by expected outcomes rather than by probability preferences. In the second context, and even in the first, systematic choices may be perfectly consistent with the expected utility hypothesis. Where the individual possesses a von Neumann-Morgenstern utility function, the pattern of choice, refusing a risky prospect in favor of a sure one, preferring one probability mixture to another, simply reveals the shape of the utility function. For certain small sub-sets of paired alternatives, such choices may give the appearance of having been motivated by preferences about probabilities. Such an appearance would disappear as the sub-set of alternative pairs increases exhaustively. The strength of Edwards' conclusion against the expected utility hypothesis is that he attempted, but was unable, to construct reasonable utility indices consistent with the choices made by his subjects. Those constructed required far too many points of inflection to be credible in the given experimental situation. (The experimental situation involved such small gains and losses that a utility function linear with income is probably the most reasonable to expect over that small range, i.e. a function with *no* inflection points!) This certainly makes it likely that the observed probability preferences are not simply experimental artifacts consistent with expected utility maximization.

[7]Donald Davidson, and Patrick Suppes, in collaboration with Sidney Siegel, *Decision Making: An Experimental Approach* (Stanford, Calif.: Stanford University Press, 1957), Chapter 2.

[8]The chance event used for a given subject, by the way, is that for which *that* subject's personal, or subjective, probability equals the subjective probability of its complement, i.e. E^* is chosen such that $P(E^*) = P(\text{not-}E^*)$. It is theoretically possible, and, indeed, the actual experimental practice here bears it out, that E will differ for each subject. This subject-specific probability differs from the one envisaged in Von Neumann and Morgenstern's treatment and the one actually employed in Mosteller's and Nogee's experiments. It is not in itself incompatible with the expected utility hypothesis. We shall consider the difference between the latter's so-called "objective" probability concept and "subjective" or "personal" probability further below.

generally, what we refer to below as probability-utility relatedness; that such attitudes are likely to be relevant where subjects are asked to choose among prospects which differ substantially as to probability mix; and that where they have an effect they tend to make behavior incompatible with the expected utility hypothesis. Thus, in effect, the expected utility hypothesis implies that choices are never affected by such attitudes. The scope of the expected utility hypothesis therefore includes situations where one should expect probability-utility relatedness, if such a phenomenon is at all important, and the hypothesis asserts that such relatedness will never "count." The Davidson, Suppes, and Siegel experiment carefully excludes most[9] situations where relatedness should arise. Their utility functions are consistent with an hypothesis of much smaller scope than the expected utility hypothesis. Its scope approaches that of the latter only insofar as the latter is not falsified in that part of its domain which is not included in the domain of the former. Then behavior which is consistent with the narrower will also be consistent with the wider hypothesis.[10]

The small volume and inconclusive character of direct evidence on expected utility is not fatal since our knowledge of a logically equivalent set of axioms enables us to evaluate the hypothesis to some extent by examining the axioms. It has sometimes been urged that testing axioms is not a satisfactory way to evaluate an empirical hypothesis.[11] Since hypothetical systems are formulated to solve particular predictive problems, the adequacy of the system can be reckoned in terms of how close the *implications* of the axioms come to solving the given problems. That is, the acceptability of any given degree of predictive (or explanatory) power is based on the ultimate predictive requirements that gave rise to the formulation in the first place. But if one tests the axioms of the system, by what criterion can one judge their acceptability? All axioms are to some extent unrealistic. How can we decide which forms and degrees of unreality are unacceptable, which acceptable? Presumably, only by reference to their effect on the implica-

---

[9]Most, but not all. We argue below that some relatedness patterns may be specific to particular outcomes, in which case they may occasionally arise even in choices subject to the same chance event.

[10]The relative narrowness of the Davidson-Suppes-Siegel model does not necessarily disqualify it for our purposes. Quite the contrary. If the "contaminating" effects of attitudes toward risk, etc. are substantial, the basic von Neumann-Morgenstern model cannot be used to derive utility functions. Our purpose here, as should always be remembered, is not to discover powerful descriptive hypotheses, but to estimate individual utility functions for normative ends. Therefore, we should eagerly turn to the narrower hypothesis if the wider performed badly in just that part of its domain which the narrower eschewed. But our choice between them does depend on how well the broader performs since, if it is well supported, it is the much more flexible of the two for large-scale computation.

[11]Milton Friedman, "The Methodology of Positive Economics," *Essays in Positive Economics* (Chicago: University of Chicago Press, 1953), 3-43.

tions, the predictions, of the model. We are thereby forced back to the predictive adequacy of the model as a whole; we cannot self-containedly evaluate axioms.

There is some force in this argument for our purposes.[12] We do not fall seriously under its strictures, however. We are not intending to make a definitive evaluation of the expected utility hypothesis. Rather, from casual observation we believe that there is a range of actual behavior which violates the hypothesis. Examination of the axioms should help to suggest in what areas and for what reasons the hypothesis is likely to be violated. It should help to suggest, when conjoined with more adequate direct evidence, where and how to improve the theory.

There is an additional function which may be served by examining the axioms of the system, although, for reasons to be stated, we shall only slightly avail ourselves of it. Savage[13] has modified the expected utility hypothesis so as to include it in a system of subjective, rather than as presented here, objective, probability evaluations. Although the axiomization of personal probability is itself representation of an essentially descriptive, positive, set of operations, Savage attaches it to the expected utility postulates so as to render more effectively the system as a whole normative. The system is intended to characterize the process of rational choice under uncertainty (or risk). The postulates state how individuals *ought* to choose under conditions of uncertainty (or risk). Because the system is normative it makes little sense to "test" it by comparing its implications with actual practice. Large-scale divergence between the two would only indicate that individuals are behaving irrationally; they are making errors; they *ought* to behave differently. The appropriateness of the normative system depends rather on its persuasiveness, on the willingness

---

[12]As a general methodological rule, an extreme form of this argument, namely, that theories should never be tested by axioms but only by implications, has real dangers. For one thing, logically speaking, every axiom is an implication of its system. It is not always obvious which implications merit special attention. Secondly, and more important, the approach appears to neglect a critical aspect of the scientific enterprise. If scientific truth were a question of once-for-all substantiation, such that each theory is either good or bad and, if good, retained in unchanged form forever, if bad totally cast aside, then reference to its predictive power alone might be warranted. But the scientific process is one of constantly improving on what one has. At every stage of enquiry each hypothesis is understood to have predictive (or explanatory) faults. It is the evaluation of the axioms which gives investigators some of their best clues as to how to improve on existing inadequacies since the alternative direct testing of implications cannot easily do this for us. Each direct confirmation of implications of the model as a whole tests, indeed, the model as a whole. It cannot localize the culpable portion. Although it is true, then, that axioms cannot be evaluated without some reference to the over-all predictive machine of which they form a part, so too the testing of implications is blind unless informed with regard to the reasonableness of the underlying axioms.

[13]L. J. Savage, *The Foundations of Statistics* (New York: John Wiley & Sons, Inc., 1954).

of others besides its author to agree that it truly characterizes rationality. Since the hypothesis is logically equivalent to its postulates the persuasiveness of the system can be most easily "tested" by examining the general acceptability of the postulates as characterizing the substance of rationality.

It might be thought that the interpretation of the expected utility maximization as a normative system would be an improvement for purposes of welfare economics, since behavior that conflicts with it does not nullify it; only an agreement on values can do that. This is not true. In our present situation we have turned to the expected utility hypothesis for the purpose of discovering the individual's structure of preference intensities between pairs of alternatives. If the individual chooses behaviors consistent with the positive hypothesis, we can assign numbers which enable us to infer these intensities. If it is not consistent, we cannot assign numbers with this property. But suppose we have re-axiomatized the system (for personal, instead of objective, probability) to make it normative. Then, if behavior is in conflict with the system, we still cannot assign such numbers. It does not matter that we may now say that it is not the fault of the system but only of the subject (who is "wrong"). We are still prevented from learning about the subject's preference intensities, which is, rather than allocation of praise or blame, our purpose.

The normative system does have something to commend it in this context. If the postulates really were highly persuasive, then an individual who chose "erroneously" might be persuaded, after his "error" had been pointed out to him, to change his choice in accordance with the postulates, thereby revealing the structure of his preference intensities. In principle this does not distort the "measurement situation." In practice it does. First, it almost surely requires an actively experimental context rather than one which consists predominantly of observations. Second, a slight burden would be entailed only if small self-contained acts of contradiction could be isolated and reformed. But this is not often possible. It would probably require a type of temporal sequencing in presentation of the stimuli which is both interruptable at any point and yet not destructive of the unity — the all-at-onceness — of the individual's preference system. This is very difficult to achieve. The subject's choices are not easily isolable; if examination of the individual's complete set of choices showed inconsistencies, the interrelatedness of choice would make it almost impossible to localize the trouble. Possibly the most practicable method would be to subject the individual to deep exposure of the postulates and their implications either before the first total presentation or afterwards if inconsistencies were discovered in his choices. Then the individual should be retested. This is an onerous procedure. It is hard to say to what extent the resulting choices would reflect the individual's "true" preferences (whatever that may mean) and to what extent his suggestibility.

A last possibility must be provided for. It is clearly possible that an individual whose behavior does not fit a normative expected utility system may not be persuaded that he is wrong. A utility function cannot be assigned to him. Moreover, if enough such persons can be found, their "intransigence" becomes a test of the system itself. The potential advantage rendered us by the normativeness of the system depends, therefore, on how generally accepted are the postulates.[14]

We intend, given our argument above, to evaluate the axiom system of expected utility maximization. It is wise, before doing so, to remind the reader of the over-all orientation within which we are interested in the system. In effect, this will pose the broad features of the kind of direct test of the hypothesis which unlike the two we cited above, meets the specialized interests of the present work.

Our point of departure is the attempt to array social state alternatives on a numerical scale. The hypothesis to be tested is that a particular scale of social states, calculated by means of the expected utility technique, is consistent with the choices of the given individual. This test situation differs from the Mosteller experiment, and from the type of situation usually thought of in connection with expected utility, in that these latter concern utility functions of money income level. They typically focus on the behavior of marginal utility of income over the range of the scale. Since social state alternatives are not obviously arrayable as varying over a single dimension,[15] there is no place in our test for notions of marginal utility. Our test must focus rather on the ability to predict choices within one set of alternatives on the basis of pre-observed choices within a different set of alternatives. We have seen in Section 9-3 above how such predictions can be made.

Let us turn now to appraise the axiom system.

(1) I shall discuss Axiom 1 in some detail under the next section.

(2) Axiom 2 is the same assumption as is made in ordinal preference theory. There is a complete (connected) ordering of alternatives, and this ordering is transitive; both preference and indifference are transitive (indifference must be transitive because if $f \leq g$ and $g \leq h$, then $f \leq h$, and if also $h \leq g$ and $g \leq f$, then $h \leq f$. Thus, if $f = g$ and $g = h$, then $f = h$). Although we have discussed the adequacy of this assumption to some extent in earlier chapters, some further comments may be in order.

(2A) Complete ordering of alternatives is an idealization of human

---

[14]A word of warning should be given against a possible misinterpretation of our argument. Although the substitution of personal (subjective) probability for objective probability was the only detail presented in describing Savage's system, it is to Savage's normative interpretation of it alone that we have addressed ourselves. We shall consider the effect of the probability replacement separately in a later section, when we treat the empirical applicability of the expected utility hypothesis.

[15]But see Chapter 11.

behavior. It is not seriously to be considered a true picture. What is debatable, however, is how serious is the discrepancy from the idealized conception. What is really at issue is the question of whether the deviation is of such nature that some alternative assumption about evaluating alternatives would better fit experience. Thus, we find the assumption being implicitly and explicitly belabored by economists who nonetheless are satisfied to employ it as the best working approximation. Samuelson, for example, says in a somewhat jocular vein:

> The individual ought to be given a couple of years to brood over his answers . . . . It is anything but a casual thing to have and know one's complete ordering or set of indifference curves; and if you ask a casual question, you must expect to get a casual answer.[16]

However, this assumption, together with the constancy of tastes, has been subject to criticism of a less tolerant nature. I refer to considerations about the dependence of the very perception of an evaluation on the individual's past experience, his motivation, etc. Some of these considerations were raised in the Appendix to Chapter 2. They need not be repeated here, but it should be noted that they involve knowledge of an empirical regularity which can be formulated for inclusion in the postulate system. One such formulation is the model by Georgescu-Roegen.[17] In this model he attempts to explain what in substance we have referred to above as "corrective changes" in orderings as a function of that particular sub-set (of the set of all alternatives objectively relevant to the given environment) which has been experienced by the individual. The complete ordering of alternatives which reflects an elaboration of the basic predispositional pattern of some individual is thus explicitly made an extreme "value," but not the only value which is admissible, of a particular empirical functional relationship.

Another considerable criticism emphasizes the attentional-motivational relationship in behavior. Even abstracting from the preceding "ignorance" factor, for most individuals a complete ordering of alternatives is irrelevant. An individual's behavior is highly organized around a few key, for him conventional, evaluations. His motivation pattern literally concentrates his attention away from all but these alternatives. The rest are simply not pertinent to the particular substantial commitment made by the individual in becoming his present self. They may truly be considered not comparable with the set that has relevance to him. It is only when the structure of his personality is challenged that new clusters of alternatives become meaningful for him to consider. Unfortunately for the possibilities of prediction, the

---

[16]"Probability, Utility, and The Independence Axiom," *Econometrica*, Vol. 20, No. 4 (October, 1952), 678.

[17]"The Theory of Choice and the Constancy of Economic Laws," *Quarterly Journal of Economics*, Vol. 64 (1950), 125-138.

opening of such new "horizons" are usually accompanied by substantial revisions of existing orderings; tastes change. Thus, the very selectivity of the evaluative function is an important characteristic of an individual's tastes. The assumption of complete ordering is suspect on this count, therefore, not because it represents a kind of central tendency with too large a random dispersion, but because it systematically distorts aspects of human valuation and choice.

To summarize, complete ordering of alternatives is an idealization of choice behavior. One can raise questions as to how close and unbiased an approximation it in fact is. No one has yet deeply assessed such questions. In the absence of close examination, the assumption has proved mathematically convenient for the theory of choice. The desideratum is of course a better assumption. I would hazard the guess that better assumptions may perhaps be found if it is discovered that complete ordering represents significant systematic distortion, but not if its only shortcoming is that it simply is not a very close first approximation. To put this into perspective, it should be acknowledged that this assumption has received probably the least criticism of all the elements of ordinal and cardinal utility theory.

(2B) Transitivity of both preference and indifference, also, is an element of both ordinal and cardinal utility theory. Moreover, it fulfills a crucial function in both theories. Although it is not strictly true that transitivity is the only refutable empirical content of ordinal theory, it certainly comprises a large portion of that content.[18] As far as cardinal utility theory is concerned, whether via moral expectation or other models, transitivity is a necessary condition for numerical utility.[19]

---

[18]Much of the literature on the content of ordinal preference theory is devoted to discussion of the "revealed preference" approach. For example, see Paul A. Samuelson, "A Note on the Pure Theory of Consumer's Behavior," *Economica*, New Series, Vol. V, No. 17 (February, 1938), 61-71, 353-4; "Empirical Implications of Utility Analysis," *Econometrica*, Vol. 6 (1938), 344-356; *Foundations of Economic Analysis*, Chapters V and VI, especially 107-116 and 146-163; "Consumption Theory in Terms of Revealed Preference," *Economica*, New Series, Vol. XV, No. 59 (August, 1948), 243-253; "Consumption Theorems in Terms of Overcompensation Rather than Indifference Comparisons," *Economica*, New Series, Vol. XX, No. 77 (February, 1953), 1-9; I. M. D. Little, "A Reformulation of the Theory of Consumer's Behavior," *Oxford Economic Papers*, New Series No. 1 (January, 1949); Harvey Wagner, "The Case for 'Revealed Preference'," *The Review of Economic Studies*, Vol. XXVI, No. 3 (1959), 178-189; "An Eclectic Approach to the Pure Theory of Consumer Behavior," *Econometrica*, Vol. 24, No. 4, (October, 1956), 451-466.

[19]Kenneth O. May, "Transitivity, Utility and Aggregation in Preference Patterns," *Econometrica*, Vol. XXII, No. 1 (January, 1954), 1-14.

May's proof, sketchily, is that transitivity of indifference is necessary and sufficient for the existence of indifference classes since transitive indifference is an equivalence relation, and if the set of indifference classes possesses certain technical properties which almost every set with economic relevance will possess then it will be possible to map the set of indifference classes ". . . onto a subset of the real numbers so as to preserve order . . . ." pp. 10-11. The necessary properties are that the set be finite, or if infinite, that it be

In contrast, it seems intuitively obvious that the existence of a cardinal utility function normally implies transitivity of both indifference and preference.[20] If AIB, if and only if, $U(A) = U(B)$, and BIC, if and only if, $U(B) = U(C)$, then, the U's being numbers, AIB and BIC implies AIC. Similarly, if APB, if and only if, $U(A) > U(B)$ and BPC, if and only if, $U(B) > U(C)$, then, for the same reason, APB and BPC implies APC.[21]

The empirical facts about transitivity are very sketchy. Almost no factual investigation has been undertaken and little analytic attention has been devoted to it.[22] Some attempts to rectify this neglect may be cited.[23] These report the results of experiments undertaken to evaluate the validity of the assumption of preference transitivity. Some possibly significant departures from transitivity are reported. In May's paper, similar findings by M. M. Flood are cited.[23a] None of these findings can claim to be anything but suggestive. Their proper function would seem not to be to express any

---

denumerable or else non-denumerable but continuous and separable (so that it " . . . can be partitioned into a finite or denumerable number of disjoint ordered sets . . . ."), pp. 10-13. The conditions relate to ordinal utility. A necessary condition for cardinal utility is, of course, that alternatives be subject to complete ordering.

[20]It should be clear from our discussion of bare preference that intransitivity of indifference does not imply intransitivity of preference, nor does transitivity of preference imply transitivity of indifference. For a discussion of the close connection between the "integrability conditions" and transitivity of preference, see H. S. Houthakker, "Revealed Preference and the Utility Function," *Economica*, New Series, Vol. XVII, No. 66 (May, 1950), 159-174; Samuelson, "The Problem of Integrability in Utility Theory," *Economica*, New Series, Vol. XVII, No. 68 (May, 1950), 355-385; N. Georgescu-Roegen, "The Pure Theory of Consumer's Behavior." For the question of intransitivity of indifference within a utility function see the stochastic utility theory in R. Duncan Luce, "A Probabilistic Theory of Utility," *Econometrica*, Vol. 20 No. 2 (April, 1958), 193-224.

[21]The qualification "normally" in the last two paragraphs reflects the fact that we may define classes as utility differences less than threshold (bare) preference. Consider the argument made in Chapter 7. Introducing bare preference (and assuming it to be an invariant preference intensity) AIB, if and only if, $U(A) = U(B) + \hat{V}$ where $\hat{V}$ can take the positive or negative value of any utility difference between two alternatives separated by less than bare preference (including zero preference intensity). If, specifically, $U(A) = U(B) + \hat{V}_1$, and $U(B) = U(C) + \hat{V}_2$, then $U(A) = U(C) + \hat{V}_1 + \hat{V}_2$. But $\hat{V}_1 + \hat{V}_2$ may exceed $\hat{V}$ so, A need not be indifferent with C. Nevertheless, we can derive (in principle) a numerical scaling of alternatives where the utility difference between any two alternatives equals some multiple of the utility difference between alternatives separated by bare preference (i.e., $U(A) - U(B) = m\hat{V}_0$). Utility differences are functions of bare preference units.

[22]The following articles are among the exceptions: W. E. Armstrong, "The Determinateness of the Utility Function," *Economic Journal* (1939); "Uncertainty and the Utility Function," *Economic Journal* (1948).

[23]Kenneth O. May, "Transitivity, Utility and Aggregation," A. G. Papandreou, "Experimental Test of an Axiom in the Theory of Choice" (December, 1952); A. M. Rose, "A Study of Irrational Judgments," *The Journal of Political Economy*, Vol. LXV, No. 3 (August, 1957); see also a critique of these studies: Harvey Wagner, "A Note in Testing the Transitivity Axiom," *Southern Economic Journal*, Vol. 22, No. 4 (1956), 493-4.

[23a] "A Preference Experiment," P-256, P-258, P-263 (November, 1951–January, 1952), The Rand Corporation, Santa Monica, Calif.

formal assertion about the extent and characteristics of preference intransitivity in actual choice, but rather to make apparent that the postulate of transitive ordering is not a closed question; it might well repay study.

In addition, it will be recalled that in Appendix 2 to Chapter 7 we discussed an argument whose major implication was that pervasive intransitivity of preference and indifference exists in the preference systems of most individuals. Although we could not accept that conclusion on the basis of the argument presented, we could not definitely reject it either.

We may therefore summarize the question of transitivity as follows. There is not now conclusive reason to believe that the assumption of transitivity of preference in individual choice is deeply suspect. There are, however, grounds for being willing to make deep empirical investigation into the validity of the assumption.

(3) Axiom 3 involves an assumption that the preference relation is continuous. One facet of this assumption is closely connected to the question of the transitivity of indifference. If indifference is transitive, then every preference intensity, no matter how small, gives rise to perceivable preferences; there is a zero threshold in the perception of preference. No less-than-bare preference, in our previous terminology, is greater than zero. This seems to be exactly what is implied by continuity of the preference function. Since we have gone into the matter at some length in Chapter 7, it seems appropriate simply to summarize our views. Continuity is an idealization. Here too, there are suspicions that serious deviations from continuity may sometimes exist, but the *evidence* is largely sketchy, introspective and intuitive. Some evidence is available about non-zero thresholds in psycho-physical phenomena.[24] But to my knowledge no critical confrontation of the elements in the *economist's* problem with experience has been undertaken. We therefore have little sense of the extent to which discontinuity may be present in choosing behavior. Again, what evidence we do possess suggests that we treat the question as an open one. It is deserving of further study.

There is another aspect to Axiom 3 which we have not treated. In addition to stipulating that all points on the utility continuum between two given points are "feasible," it stipulates that some points outside these points, for example, points of infinitely great or little utility, are not "feasible." In other words, the utility function is bounded from above and below. The Axiom asserts: for $f \le g \le h$ there exists some a, $0 < a > 1$, such that $g = af + (1 - a)h$. If, e.g., $f = -\infty$ or $h = \infty$, there exists *no a*

---

[24]See, e.g., Andrews, *Methods of Psychology*, Chapter 5, 125-134; S. S. Stevens, "Mathematics, Measurement and Psychophysics," *Handbook of Experimental Psychology* (ed. S. S. Stevens)(New York: John Wiley & Sons, Inc., 1951), 33-36, 48-49; Charles E. Osgood, *Method and Theory in Experimental Psychology* (New York: Oxford University Press, 1953), 72-77.

between zero and 1 for which the equation holds. For this reason, Axiom 3 is sometimes referred to as the Archimedean postulate, after the comparable postulate of Archimedes for geometry.[25]

Possibly this requirement of boundedness seems entirely unexceptionable. It is, however, equivalent, as far as this postulate goes, to another which may be more seriously questioned, namely, that utility not be lexicographic. If we are comparing three prospects, f, g, and h, h need not have an infinitely great utility to violate Axiom 3. It is violated if h is incomparably greater than g, and this can come about without h having infinitely great utility if the utility function is lexicographic. A function is lexicographic if it is multi-dimensional (a vector), $U = (U_1, U_2, U_3 \ldots, U_n)$, and if any prospect g is preferred to any prospect f if and only if, whenever $U_{fi} > U_{gi}$ there is some j, $j < i$ such that $U_{fj} < U_{gj}$. This means that preference between prospects is determined by the relative size of the *first* utility element in which the two prospects differ. If, e.g., g and f have the same first two elements and g exceeds f in their respective third element, then g is preferred to f no matter how all subsequent elements compare. No amount of excess by g over h in any or all subsequent elements can affect preference. "Later" excess simply cannot *substitute* for "earlier" deficiency. If the sequence of elements stands for different commodity categories, then the ordering of the sequence is made according to which commodities are prime requisites, or prerequisites, or incomparably more important than others. There will be as many dimensions as there are categories of sequentially incomparable importance to the individual. The key to the dimensionality of the utility function is that no amount of increase in any or all *subsequent* categories can compensate for a deficiency in an earlier (more important) category; there is no substitutability across categories.[26]

It has recently been strongly argued that the utility function of individuals is lexicographic.[27] Underlying an individual's preferences are his

---

[25]Archimedes' axiom is: "Further, of unequal lines, unequal surfaces, and unequal solids, the greater exceeds the less by such a magnitude as, when added to itself, can be made to exceed any assigned magnitude among those which are comparable with [it and with] one another." Archimedes, *On the Sphere and Cylinder*, in *The Works of Archimedes* (ed. T. L. Heath)(New York: Dover Publications), 4. A translation from algebra is: "If h and k are rational numbers > 1, then . . . there is a positive integer n such that $h^n > k$. In the additive notation, if h and k are > 0 there exists an integer n such that $nh > k$." John S. Chipman, "The Foundations of Utility," *Econometrica* Vol. 28, (April, 1960), 215.

[26]This presentation owes much to Chipman, "The Foundations of Utility."

[27]N. Georgescu-Roegen, "Choice, Expectations, and Measurability," *Quarterly Journal of Economics*, Vol. 58 (1954), 503-534. The formal properties of lexicographic utility have been presented in Melvin Hausner, "Multidimensional Utilities," *Decision Processes* (eds. R. M. Thrall, C. H. Coombs, and R. L. Davis)(New York: John Wiley & Sons, Inc., 1954), Chapter XII; Gerard Debreu, "Representation of a Preference Ordering by a Numerical Function," *Decision Processes*, Chapter XI; R. M. Thrall, "Applications of Multidimensional Utility Theory," *Decision Processes*, Chapter XIII; John S. Chipman, "Foundations of Utility."

wants, and these are hierarchical. Individuals do not seek to satisfy less important wants until more important wants are satisfied. A desperately thirsty man in the midst of the desert is very unlikely to be willing to exchange his last water for any conceivable number of pieces of fine damask. An alternative, deficient in this prime necessity, will be considered inferior to one which contains it no matter what other elements are contained in the former. There is no substitutability across utility categories so long as the minimal necessary water is absent.[28] Within each category there will, of course, be substitutability, and many want complexes and their associated satisfier commodities may typically be subsumed within a given category. All alternatives which differ in the commodities relevant to the given category but not to an anterior category will be "comparable," i.e., commodity changes within the category can change preferences between any two such alternatives. Alternatives which differ in commodities relevant to different categories will be "incomparable;" no changes in the commodity structure of the inferior which maintains the differential in the anterior category will be able to substitute for its inferiority. Thus, only certain particular pairs or triplets of alternatives will be incomparable. But, for these, Postulate 3 will be violated. Thus, if f consists of being executed at dawn, g of receiving three safety pins and h of receiving five safety pins, there may well be for some individuals no probability mix given by a for which g is indifferent to $\infty f + (1 - \infty)h$.[29]

It seems likely that there are some, possibly very many, individuals for which some triplets of alternatives violate Axiom 3. Surely, since our set of social states includes some particularly fearsome consequences to certain individuals, one would expect that lexicographic types of priority would be sometimes involved (in connection, e.g., with illness, death, minimal food and drink requirements etc.). The critical question is how pervasive are these priority considerations? One may accept the notion that wants are hierarchical without, at the same time, expecting that *complete* non-substitutability will exist between categories or that non-substitutability will apply to more than a few types of alternative. If we assume that an unpleasant "premature" death is strongly repulsive to most people and that its presence in an alternative renders the alternative *incomparably* inferior to alternatives omitting this element, then we should expect never to observe

---

[28]The first utility category here would not be simply "water;" it would be "amount of water *less than x ounces*." Beyond the minimum necessary amount, water — via thirst — would cease to be the primary desideratum: alternatives containing more than X would be compared in terms of the desirability of their respective second elements (in which function water above X oz. *might* be, but need not be, an argument.)

[29]Hausner, *op. cit.*, 185. Cf. Chipman, "The Foundations of Utility." Chipman argues for lexicographic utility also. He adverts to much the same type of example. Thus, he asks rhetorically, "Is there some number of trinkets that will induce a starving coolie to part with one bowl of rice?" *Op. cit.*, 221.

those people choosing risky prospects containing this alternative as an element over risky or sure prospects in which it is not an element. Consider the case of an individual deciding whether to cross a city street. Alternative g is the sure prospect of remaining on the same side of the street, h the sure prospect of safely crossing over to where he wants to go, f the sure prospect of getting killed by a car while crossing. Obviously, $f < g < h$. If f is incomparably worse than g, the individual will not cross the street, since the marginal probability of obtaining f is generally known to be non-zero. By such reasoning therefore, we ought to see very few people crossing city streets, traveling in airplanes, smoking cigarettes, swimming and, indeed, performing most of the activities which people do perform. That actual observation differs so much from this expectation probably indicates that some substitutability among elements, and thus comparability of alternatives, exists over a wide domain for most people.[30] But the possible unscalability of some alternatives ought always to be kept in mind.[31]

(4) Axiom 4 is sometimes called the Strong Independence Assumption, and sometimes the "Sure-Thing Principle." It has provoked a lively debate in the literature, and seems to be the focus of most of the criticism leveled against the expected utility hypothesis.

It is informative to examine the significance of its title. We discover that this axiom is designed to perform an analogous function to that of "independent utilities" in older formulations of cardinal utility. Since it was largely because of the postulate of "independent utilities" that previous formulations were deemed unsatisfactory, the strategic importance of the Strong Independence Assumption to our present axiom system, and of assertions by critics of the hypothesis that it is vulnerable to older criticisms of "independence" is understandable.

The function of independence in the derivation of older, cardinal utility functions can roughly be seen as follows.[32] We are interested in assigning a utility number to every alternative of choice. Each alternative represents a bundle of various commodities. We desire that the number given to any alternative be a function of the component commodities, so that if we are

---

[30]In fairness, this interpretation may be oversimple. An implication of lexicographic utility is that small changes in the probability of obtaining a "non-comparable" outcome does not change preferences. Then, if we analyze crossing a city street within the broader context of the individual's life, we may find him "unavoidably" already subject to a noninsignificant probability of violent death from all sorts of "background sources." As a result the slight increase in this probability from crossing a street has almost no effect on his choices. This approach, indeed, is compatible with much behavior labeled "living dangerously." The upshot is that casual observation of choosing behavior is probably inadequate to settle the issue at hand.

[31]It is instructive to see the remarks on this subject by von Neumann and Morgenstern themselves: *The Theory of Games and Economic Behavior*, 630-632.

[32]For a full analysis of independent utilities and cardinal utility see Samuelson, *Foundations of Economic Analysis*, Chapter 7, 173-183; also Kenneth Arrow, "The Work of Ragnar Frisch, Econometrician," *Econometrica*, Vol. 28, No. 2 (April, 1960), 176-178.

given any combination of commodities, we will possess a procedure by which a knowledge of the components alone enables us to assign a number to the group.

To give "extensive" significance to our concept of utility requires further, that if each component can itself be considered a commodity bundle with a utility number, then the utility number of a large bundle must be a function of the sum of the utility numbers of the components. Given these requirements, our utility index is given by:

$$U(X) = f[U(X_1) + U(X_2) + \ldots, + U(X_n)]$$

where X_i is the amount of commodity i in the group. Our utility function is a function of a sum of the utility function for each commodity.[33] In order that $U(X)$ be unique, each $U(X_i)$ must itself be a function (i.e., single-valued). This means that for any given quantity of commodity i, say X_i, there must be one and only one value of $U(X_i)$. But X_i will typically be consumed as part of a commodity bundle, i.e., $(X_1, \ldots, X_i, \ldots, X_n)$, or $(Y_1, \ldots, X_i, \ldots, Y_n)$, or, $\ldots$, or $(W_1, \ldots, X_i, \ldots, W_n)$. So what we seek is a single value of

$$\left. \frac{\partial U}{\partial X_i} \right| x_1, \ldots, x_n$$

for every value of X_i, from which we may derive $U(X)$ by integration. The marginal utility of X_i must be the same whatever the composition of the remainder of the commodity bundle, or else we have no determinate $U(X_i)$ function. This constancy requires that the individual's satisfaction from consuming each commodity i be unaffected by — be independent of — his contemporaneous consumption of all other commodities. The necessary assumption of "independent utilities" is therefore an assumption that there are no complementary or substitutive relationships (in the Pareto sense[34]) among commodities.[35]

---

[33]Most simply, let $U(X) = U(X_1) + \ldots, + U(X_n)$.

[34]That is, in terms of the effects on marginal utilities or marginal rates of substitution. In the Hicksian sense (the sign of compensated cross-derivatives), all commodities are substitutes in the additive utility model. I am indebted to Kenneth Arrow for this point.

[35]Another kind of formulation is possible. Let us assume that the utility of only one commodity is independent. For each value of this commodity (o), say X_o, we have a single value of $U(X_o)$. Assign arbitrary values to the function $U(X_o)$. Now we may assign non-arbitrary numbers to every other alternative of choice by simply finding that quantity of commodity o which the individual finds indifferent with the alternative in question. The ability to scale a large part of the total number of alternatives by this procedure depends on the rapidity with which the individual is satiated with commodity o in comparison with other alternatives. It should also be noted that the utility of a particular combination of commodities can never be discovered from that of its components. For our purposes in this procedure, however, the important point here is that independence of the utility of at least one commodity is necessary to construct the numerical scale on which the other alternatives will be placed by the indifference relation since relative valuations of different commodity combinations must not depend on relatedness properties between the former combinations and the "numeraire." Cf. Irving Fisher, "A Statistical Measure for Measuring 'Marginal Utility' and Testing

To summarize, when we have two elements of choice (commodities or commodity bundles), and we know the utility value of each for some individual, the assumption of independence enables us to calculate the utility value of the combined elements from that of the separate elements since it imposes the requirement that there be no commodity relatedness effects on the satisfaction of the individual between the two elements.

This is similar to the function of the Strong Independence Assumption in our present axiom system. "For $0 < a < 1$, $af + (1 - a)h \leq ag + (1 - a)h$, if and only if $f \leq g$." Our expected utility hypothesis asserts that we calculate the utility value of the prospects $af + (1 - a)h$ and $ag + (1 - a)h$ from the utilities of their component prospects f, g, and h. Only these component utilities and the probability weights are to be decisive; there are to be no commodity relatedness effects when the elements of f and g respectively are "combined" with those of h. But this is exactly what is implied by the Strong Independence Assumption. This can be seen because if the "combined" prospects permitted such effects then the combined prospect $af + (1 - a)h$ might involve important complementary consumption patterns, thereby enhancing its desirability, whereas the prospect $ag + (1 - a)h$ might involve important substitutive consumption patterns, thereby lessening its desirability. The consequence of this could well be $af + (1 - a)h > ag + (1 - a)h$ even if $f \leq g$. Since the postulate is meant to hold for all combined prospects, and this implies for all prospects whatever,[36] the suggested violation of the Strong Independence Assumption could clearly be constructed.

The assumption prohibits such effects. The crux of the debate in the literature[37] considers what is implied by this prohibition. Consider the meaning of $af + (1 - a)h$. Prospect f can occur with probability a *and*

---

the Justice of a Progressive Income Tax," *Economic Essays Contributed in Honor of John Bates Clark* (New York, 1927), 157-193; Ragnar Frisch, *New Methods of Measuring Marginal Utility* (Tubingen, 1932); Paul Samuelson, *Foundations*, 174-183; Kenneth Arrow, "The Work of Ragnar Frisch," *Econometrica*, *loc. cit.*

[36] By definition every combined prospect $af + (1 - a)h$ is a new prospect whose elements are

$$[af_i + (1 - a)h_i]x_i$$

where $af_i + (1 - a)h_i$ is the probability $(0 \leq af_i + (1 - a)h_i \leq 1)$ of outcome x_i occurring, i.e., it is the prospect $r = (r_1, \ldots, r_n)$ where $r_i = af_i + (1 - a)h_i$. Thus, since every set of probabilities $r_i(0 \leq r_i \leq 1)$ can be expressed as the result of an arithmetic combination of some a and $(1 - a)(0 \leq a \leq 1)$ with pairs of f_i and h_i $(0 \leq f_i, h_i \leq 1)$, every prospect can be expressed as a combined prospect.

[37] The most extended treatment of the controversy is to be found in the following articles and notes in the October 1952 (Vol. 20, No. 4) issue of *Econometrica*, 661-680: H. Wold, "Ordinal Preferences or Cardinal Utility"; additional notes by G. L. S. Shackle, L. J. Savage, and H. Wold; Allan S. Manne, "The Strong Independence Assumption — Gasoline Blends and Probability Mixtures" (with Note by A. Charnes); P. A. Samuelson, "Probability, Utility and the Independence Axiom"; E. Malinvaud, "Note on von Neumann-Morgenstern's Strong Independence Axiom."

prospect h can occur with probability $(1 - a)$. This signifies that in any one "play" of the gamble either f *or* h can occur, *but not both!* They are mutually exclusive. Consequently, in no "play" are the elements of *both* prospects "obtained" at the same time. But the relatedness of commodities with which the "independent utilities" assumption was concerned involved commodities consumed as part of the same consumption pattern — commodities consumed in the same consumption planning period. The absence of this contemporaneity in the combined prospects of our present axiom system (and abstracting also from intertemporal transfers via storage) makes criticism of the "independent utilities" assumption on the ground that many goods have important complementary and substitutive relationships with one another irrelevant. When the Strong Independence Assumption asserts that a combined prospect is independent of the effects of commodity relatedness it is not proscribing such relatedness within the commodity bundles involved.

What, then, is involved? The following is Samuelson's succinct justification (with appropriate terminological revisions):

> Suppose you admit that (g) is at least as good as (f). Now imagine two alternative compound lottery tickets that will give you with probability $(1 - a)$ the same lottery ticket (h). Then if on the first draw (h) turns up, there is nothing to choose between the two. However, with probability a, the second compound ticket gives as a prize (f) whereas the first gives as a prize (g). Then *no matter whether (h) is or is not drawn*, the first lottery ticket must be at least as good as the second. A similar argument can be made for the concepts of 'definitely not as good as' and 'indifferent to' . . . .[38]

Actually, this explanation does not completely cover the axiom unless an additional assumption is made, namely, that every two combined prospects $af + (1 - a)h$ and $ag + (1 - a)h$ for which the axiom is to hold, must refer to the same gamble reflected by the probabilities a and $1 - a$. The two prospects must represent alternative sets of consequences for the individual, depending on the occurrence or non-occurrence of some random event E. Then a is really the probability of E occurring. If, after choosing the first prospect, E does occur, then the individual would obtain f as a consequence. If, under the same circumstances he had chosen the second prospect, g would be the consequence. If E does not occur, then the consequence h would come about, no matter which prospect he had chosen.

Only in this kind of situation are there only two possible alternative consequence choices. If E occurs, there is the choice between f and g; if E

---

[38]"Utility, Preference, and Probability," 7; hectographed abstract of paper given before the conference on *Les Fondements et Applications de la Theorie du Risque en Econometrie* (March 15, 1952), cited in Manne, "The Strong Independence Assumption," *Econometrica* (October, 1952), 667.

does not occur, the (trivial) choice between h and h.[39] There are, however, other kinds of situations which would seem to fit the entities of the axiom. The a, $1 - a$ gamble of one prospect may not be the same a, $1 - a$ gamble of the second, even though the probabilities are the same. For the first prospect, whether f or h is the consequence depends on the occurrence of E; whereas for the second, whether g or h is the consequence depends on the occurrence of some event F. Thus, E may be the appearance of a head on coin number 1, F the appearance of a head on coin number 2. Both appearances have the same probability, but the outcomes are independent. In this situation we have four alternative consequence choices instead of two.

Consider the following table for a comparison between the two kinds of situations.

TABLE 8

Possible Two-Coin Outcomes

Consequence of Choosing Particular Prospect	EF	$\overline{E}F$	$E\overline{F}$	$\overline{E}\,\overline{F}$
$\frac{1}{2}f + \frac{1}{2}h$: Number 1	f	h	f	h
$\frac{1}{2}g + \frac{1}{2}h$: Number 2	g	h	h	g
Choice from consequence	$f \leq g$	$h = h$	$f > h$	$g > h$

Samuelson's "sure-thing" description of the axiom is presented in the first two columns of Table 8. Since no possible consequence could make the outcome of number 1 preferred to the outcome of number 2, it seems quite reasonable to assume that the individual will not prefer number 1 to 2.

But when the gambles are independent, all four columns represent possible consequences. And in the third column there is a possible consequence for which the outcome of number 1 would be preferred to the outcome of number 2. Now, the individual may, even though faced by such a possibility, still not prefer number 1 to 2 (it is likely that he will not), but his choice is no longer based on a "sure-thing." In other words, the Strong Independence Assumption may, without additional specification, be empirically justified, but it is not quite so intuitively plausible as Samuelson's demonstration would make it seem.

If the greater plausibility be desired, some such condition, as is suggested here for making the gambles dependent, would be called for. This, unfortunately, might lessen the empirical fruitfulness of the hypothesis by considerably restricting the experimental procedures for constructing actual utility indices. Since there is reason to believe that these procedures, even

---

[39]Friedman and Savage, in their exposition of the Independence Axiom, do spell out this type of situation. But they, too, appear to believe it equivalent to the axiom. "The Expected-Utility Hypothesis," 469.

without additional restriction, may not be capable of dealing with as large a sub-set of alternatives facing an individual as desired, further constraint may make effective implementation of the hypothesis unfeasible.[40]

If Postulate 4 is valid, then it plays a most crucial role in the derivation of the expected utility hypothesis. Every $af + (1 - a)h$ has been defined simply as a prospect, the elements of which have probabilities derived from a combination of the corresponding probabilities of the two other prospects. Postulate 4 in the presence of the essentially weak Postulates 1 to 3, adds to this definition, however, that the two terms can be interpreted as a component pair and that arithmetic operations on each component are meaningful. It is this that enables us to reinterpret the combination as equivalent in utility to the probability-weighted sum of two prospects, i.e., as having a utility value equal to the expected utility of its components.[41]

The clearing away of the difficulties of principle involved in the debate cited above, leaves an apparently plausible assumption. It is to be expected, however, that it will be by no means easy to meet the empirical criteria suggested above by Samuelson. We have already commented on the analytic lacuna concerning time interval contexts in decision making. In addition, we must now look into the relationship between the independence assumption and "gaming and suspense" elements.

Postulate 4 asserts: for a,

$$0 < a < 1, af + (1 - a)h \leq ag + (1 - a)h,$$

if and only if, $f \leq g$. Preferences among sure prospects are asserted to carry over into risky prospects. This may be quite reasonable if the attractiveness of consequences is independent of the context by which they may be obtained — the probability of obtaining them. If, however, their attractiveness is affected by whether they are certain or only probable, then Postulate 4 can be violated. Suppose an individual prefers g to f when these refer to sets of sure outcomes. Now he is offered the choice between $af + (1 - a)h$ and $ag + (1 - a)h$. Although there is no question of relatedness here between the exclusive outcomes of each prospect (e.g., f and h), there may be a relatedness between any of the separate outcomes and the probability mixture in which it is imbedded (e.g., f and a). The attractiveness of some outcomes may be enhanced by being placed in a risky

---

[40]See Appendix 1 on the debate over this interpretation of the Strong Independence Assumption. The upshot of the controversy seems to be that the foregoing interpretation is valid so long as we carefully specify the time dimension of the entities of the theory.

[41]This is, of course, only a rough informal statement. It is not in any way intended as a proof. For the latter, a much more complicated problem, see von Neumann and Morgenstern, 618-628; Jacob Marschak, "Rational Behavior, Uncertain Prospects and Measurable Utility," *Econometrica*, Vol. 18, No. 2 (April, 1950), 115-134; Savage, *The Foundations of Statistics*, 73-76.

context, that of others diminished. Thus, in our hypothetical example, f may become relatively more attractive, and g relatively less attractive when embedded in risky prospects. If this is so, the individual may prefer $af + (1 - a)h$ to $ag + (1 - a)h$ despite $f < g$.[42]

It should be pointed out that this type of risk-outcome relatedness is not equivalent to like or dislike of gambling. Though we can indicate the way in which the former violates expected utility postulates, the nature of the latter violation cannot be represented in terms of the von Neumann-Morgenstern system since we cannot define "love of gambling" in these constructs. We have already seen that if an individual refuses (accepts) a fair bet instead of its actuarial outcome, this tells us something about differences between pairs of assigned utility numbers (i.e., the shape of the utility function of outcomes), not that he dislikes (likes) gambling. No pattern of choices consistent with expected utility maximization tells us anything about attitudes toward gambling, and choices inconsistent with the hypothesis simply indicate that the individual does not possess a von Neumann-Morgenstern utility function. It is true that an individual will fail to possess such a utility function in both the case of specific patterns of relatedness as cited above and that of more general attitudes toward gambling, *per se*. But the analysis of the two cases by alternative technical apparatus will differ.

Attitudes toward gambling *per se* can only be defined if we possess a cardinal utility function for the individual which is not derived by using the expected utility hypothesis — what we have referred to above, for simplicity, as an "introspective" utility function. If we do, the individual's behavior, whether or not consistent with expected utility maximization, can be described in terms of probability combinations of "introspective" utility outcomes. We have argued above that consistency or inconsistency of the behavior with von Neumann-Morgenstern utility will be indicated by the ability or inability to rationalize it as maximizing the expected value of introspective utility. In this context we can define attitudes toward risk in terms of choices between bets which are fair in terms of *utility* outcomes and their expected utility sure outcome equivalents. If the individual prefers g to $af + (1 - a)h$ for all combinations of $a(0<a<1)$, f, g, h such that

$$\overline{U}(g) = a\overline{U}(f) + (1 - a)\overline{U}(h)^{43}$$

then we say he has a general aversion to risk; if the reverse is true, then he has a general attraction for risk. The earlier case of differential relatedness

---

[42]This is suggested by a formulation in Alchian, *op. cit.*, 37, which differs by speaking of the effect of the like or dislike of gambling *per se* on the evaluation of risky versus non-risky prospects. We here emphasize *the differential* relatedness of riskiness with *different* outcomes. See the text discussion of this immediately below.

[43]$\overline{U}$ indicates an introspective indicator, as opposed to U which indicates a von Neumann-Morgenstern indicator.

referred to above assumed that he would reject the gamble for some f,h combinations but accept it for others.[44]

If the individual has attitudes toward risk as defined here, his behavior will violate Postulate 4. Select one prospect $af + (1 - a)h$ such that $\overline{U}(g) = a\overline{U}(f) + (1 - a)\overline{U}(h)$. We shall call it g'. Then assume $g > g'$. Therefore, by Postulate 4 we expect that

$$bg + (1 - b)k > bg' + (1 - b)k,$$

where $0 < b < 1$. But if the preference for g over g' stemmed from the fact that g was a sure prospect while g' was a risky one, it is probable that when g becomes imbedded in a risky prospect its attractive force relative to g' will diminish. It is therefore quite possible that

$$bg + (1 - b)k \leq bg' + (1 - b)k.$$

We can force a violation as follows. By varying f, select instead of g' a mixed prospect

$$g'' \equiv af'' + (1 - a)h$$

for which $g = g''$ and

$$\overline{U}(g) < a\overline{U}(f'') + (1 - a)\overline{U}(h).$$

Now Postulate 4 requires that $bg + (1 - b)k = bg'' + (1 - b)k$.[45] But here the diminished attractiveness of g relative to g'', when the former is embedded in a risky prospect, makes unavoidable

$$bg + (1 - b)k < bg'' + (1 - b)k.$$

We may generalize attitudes toward risk by attempting to isolate explicit variables to which these attitudes are attached. It has frequently

---

[44]Where specific risk-outcome relatedness patterns are unimportant but general attitudes toward risk are important, a "risk-free" utility function can be approximated by the experimental procedure of Davidson, Suppes and Siegel in *Decision Making* (chap. 2), where only alternatives with the same probability mix are ever offered the subject. There are no comparisons between a sure and a risky prospect. Differences in variance due to different probability mixes are excluded. Finally, since each prospect contains only two component outcomes and the uniform probability mix is $(x, y; 1/2)$, skewness and other differences that might count here are excluded as well.

[45]$g = g''$ implies $g \leq g''$ and $g \geq g''$, so Postulate 4 requires both

$$bg + (1 - b)k \leq bg'' + (1 - b)k \quad \text{and} \quad bg + (1 - b)k \geq bg'' + (1 - b)k,$$

requires therefore

$$bg + (1 - b)k = bg'' + (1 - b)k.$$

been held[46] that having attitudes toward risk implies that the individual's preferences are influenced by characteristics of the probability distribution of utility outcomes other than its first moment (mean), such as the second (variance) or higher moments, range, skewness, etc. If any of these does influence choice we can show that such choices violate Postulate 4. Assume the individual is aversive to large variance; he likes to be relatively secure about the approximate character of the outcome. Let $g_1 \equiv a_1 f_1 + (1 - a_1)h_1$, $g_2 \equiv a_2 f_2 + (1 - a_2)h_2$, such that:

(1) $$\text{variance } \overline{U}(g_1) > \text{variance } \overline{U}(g_2)^{47}$$

(2) $$g_1 = g_2.$$

Since high variance is aversive to the individual, g_1 must have a higher expected utility than g_2 in order to be considered as good, i.e.:

(3) $$a_1\overline{U}(f_1) + (1 - a_1)\overline{U}(h_1) > a_2\overline{U}(f_2) + (1 - a_2)\overline{U}(h_2).$$

Now embed g_1 and g_2 as elements of two risk prospects, d_1 and d_2, respectively:

$$d_1 \equiv bg_1 + (1 - b)k \quad \text{and} \quad d_2 \equiv bg_2 + (1 - b)k.$$

We know that the individual's indifference between g_1 and g_2 is in part related not to the attractiveness of the separate component outcomes but to the particular combination in which these outcomes appear — there *is* a relatedness relevant to choice between the component utility outcomes of each prospect. But the combinational relationship between g_1 and g_2 no longer holds in d_1 and d_2. The prospect in which g_1 is embedded (d_1) will often (but not always) have a higher utility variance than the prospect in which g_2 is embedded (depending on the choice of b and k); but neither the ratio nor difference of variances between g_1 and g_2 will be preserved, except

---

[46]E.g., see G. Tintner, "A Contribution to the Nonstatic Theory of Choice," *Quarterly Journal of Economics*, Vol. 56 (1942), 274-306. A. G. Hart, "Risk, Uncertainty and the Unprofitability of Compounding Probabilities," *Studies in Mathematical Economics and Econometrics* (eds. O. Lange, F. McIntyre, and T. O. Yntema) (Chicago: University of Chicago Press, 1942), 110-118. N. Georgescu-Roegen, "Choices, Expectations and Measureability," *Quarterly Journal of Economics*, Vol. 59 (1954), 503-534. M. Allais, "Le Comportement de l'homme rationnel devant le risque: critique des postulats et axiomes de l'école amèricaine," *Econometrica*, Vol. 21 (1953), 503-546. M. Allais, "L'Extension des théories de l'equilibre economique général et du rendement social au cas du risque," *Econometrica*, Vol. 21 (1953), 269-290. M. Allais, "La Psychologie de l'homme rationnel devant le risque: la théorie et l'expériénce," *Journal of Sociological Statistics*, Vol. 94 (Paris, 1953), 47-73.

[47]Where

$$\text{variance } \overline{U}(g_1) \equiv [\overline{U}(f_1) - \{a_1\overline{U}(f_1) + (1 - a_1)\overline{U}(h_1)\}]^2 \\ + [U(h_1) - \{a_1\overline{U}(f_1) + (1 - a_1)\overline{U}(h_1)\}]^2$$

and variance $\overline{U}(g_2)$ is similarly defined.

by very special selection of b and k, or for a highly insensitive relationship between variance and preference. Let us suppose that the variance difference between d_1 and d_2 is less than that between g_1 and g_2.[48] Then variance differential will add less to the attractiveness of d_2 over d_1 than it did for g_2 over g_1. The greater desirability of g_1 than g_2 in terms of mean utility will carry relatively greater weight in the over-all evaluation between d_1 and d_2. This decline in the attractiveness of g_2 relative to g_1 results in the individual preferring d_1 to d_2 despite the requirement of Postulate 4 that they be indifferent. We could show a similar type of violation where higher moments of the probability distribution of utility outcomes, or skewness, or range, etc., were determinants of the individual's preferences.

It might be thought that the sort of preference behavior we have been describing violates Postulate 1 as well as Postulate 4. This is not so. The individual's preferences here *are* governed "solely by the probabilities attached to each possible outcome," since, once we know the form of the dependence of preferences on variance, etc., the probability distribution is the only additional information we need to know to determine preferences uniquely.

We have indicated that there are two forms of dependence within risky prospects that violate Postulate 4, relatedness not between exclusive outcomes but between outcomes and the probability mixtures in which they are embedded. The first stems from how the attractiveness of particular outcomes is affected by the probability mixture in which the outcomes are embedded. The second stems from the way more general attitudes toward risk affect the evaluation of prospects as a whole, not of the separate components of these prospects. How widespread are preferences such as these likely to be? The author knows of no reliable empirical investigation of this phenomenon. Indeed, such investigations are not likely to be soon forthcoming. We have argued that these particular types of violation of Postulate 4 (and of expected utility maximization), especially the second, could not be identified by procedures using the paraphenalia of the expected utility hypothesis. Many forms of behavior inconsistent with the hypothesis would show the same overt sort of violation. We must have recourse to "introspective utility" as a benchmark in order to test for the pervasiveness of this type of behavior. All we can do here is to consider how reasonable it may be to take more of the probability distribution of utility into account than simply its expected value.

---

[48]Such as in the following example: $g_1 = (10, 40; \frac{1}{2})$, $g_2 \equiv (33, 35; \frac{1}{2})$ where outcomes refer to utilities. So Var $g_1 = 144$, Var $g_2 = 1$, and: Var g_1 − Var $g_2 = 143$, Var g_1/Var $g_2 = 144$. Now $d_1 \equiv (g_1, 26; \frac{1}{2})$, $d_2 \equiv (g_2, 26; \frac{1}{2})$. So Var $d_1 = 88$, Var $d_2 = 23$, and: Var d_1 − Var $d_2 = 65$, Var d_1/Var $d_2 = 3.8$. Here both the absolute difference and ratio decrease. Another example shows that Var d_1 could be less than Var d_2 despite the fact that Var g_1 exceeds Var g_2. For the same g_1 and g_2 as above, let d'_1 be $(g_1, 8; 12/13)$ and d'_2 $(g_2, 8; 12/13)$. Then Var d'_1 is 57.1 and Var d'_2 is 90.6.

What seems crucial is that when one chooses a mixed (risky) prospect, one *cannot* expect to receive a stream of the component outcomes of the prospect combined in proportions equal to the probability weights. One receives only one of the component outcomes. Whatever mixing is done is done in the mind of the chooser as a way of comprehending the prospect. So, the actual consequence of the gamble *cannot* be its moral expectation, unless the single component which occurs happens to have the same value as the moral expectation. In this context (always assuming the existence of introspective cardinal utility), it is by no means obvious that moral expectation is the only information worth considering. The utility dispersion of the prospect, its range, skewness, and kurtosis all help the individual get a closer feel of what single thing will probably happen, of what will be the probable cost to him of being wrong. In the light of findings like those of the psychologist Ward Edwards, who discovered that individuals behave asymmetrically between chances of winning and chances of losing (they do not like chances of losing),[49] two prospects with identical positive expected utility, in one of which the individual has a chance to fall substantially below his present level while in the other only chances of rising above his present level exist, are not very obviously indifferent. We should expect that different individuals will choose differently.

Let us consider what might lead to different choices in such situations. First, we should expect that different personality types will choose differently.[50] They differ systematically in how they respond to the uncertain future. There are plungers as well as timid souls. They differ not so much in how much they appreciate different rewards, but in the strong drift of their beliefs about whether things will "go their way" or not, for given probabilities.[51]

Second, the relation between the individual's present style of life and his past experiences may lead to a violation through attitudes toward risk, whether of a general kind or specialized toward particular outcomes. We have had occasion to refer to Markowitz's hypothesis on the shape of the von Neumann-Morgenstern utility function. The key to this formulation rested on individuals responding to the magnitude of possible displacements from a *status quo* ratherthan to the absolute level of possible outcomes. It seems intuitively reasonable to suppose that individuals whose present

[49]Ward Edwards, "Probability-Preferences in Gambling," *American Journal of Psychology*, Vol. LXVI (1953), 349-364.

[50]For an interesting analogous examination of the personality assumptions that underlie the minimax strategy in the theory of games, see Daniel Ellsberg, "The Theory of the Reluctant Duelist," *American Economic Review*, Vol. XLVI, No. 5 (December, 1956), 909-923.

[51]It may sometimes be possible to systematize such "distortions" of "probabilities" as an orderly "personal" or "subjective" instead of "objective" probability. Since a von Neumann-Morgenstern utility can be defined and calculated on a subjective probability ordering, such "distortions" would not violate expected utility maximization.

situation represents the continuation of a strongly stable tendency would be more likely to pay attention to the degree of displacement from the present than would individuals who have experienced widely dispersed outcomes in their recent past. Among these former there is a real possibility for violation of Postulate 4.

If any such person has special attachment for his present situation, this alone will not violate Postulate 4. It may mean simply that moderately and highly favorable outcomes are felt to add only slightly to well-being, and moderate and heavy losses detract substantially from well-being; and this is consistent with a von Neumann-Morgenstern utility function which is sharply concave (from the origin) throughout most of its domain. The possibility of violation stems rather from the fact that if the individual's utility function is calculated by observing his behavior when induced to incur significant variations in his actual situation (namely, at different levels of wealth), then choices made after he has fluctuated substantially from his original *status quo* will not be consistent with the von Neumann-Morgenstern utility function which fit his choices at that *status quo*. In effect, his tastes will have changed, either because he has changed to a new stable *status quo* from which the size of displacements are important, or because he has experienced more variation in situation than heretofore. This makes the absolute level of possible outcomes more important and the size of displacements from a *status quo* less important in evaluating uncertain prospects. The very act of measuring utility changes the object of measurement. Thus, since the variance, range, etc., of prospects selected in sub-set comparisons influence the course of changes in the individual's actual situation, they affect his preferences, and thus, in effect, fall under our analysis of risk-utility relatedness.

A third kind of source for risk-utility relatedness refers to specialized effects toward particular outcomes. Consider two prospects, f and g, assigning positive probability to the same outcomes. Suppose very extreme positive and negative outcomes are among these. Suppose also that f assigns very low probabilities and g quite high probabilities to these extremes. We now invoke a distinction between short-run and long-run utility. Short-run utility is essentially one-period utility, the well-being attainable from a consumption bundle in a given time period without recourse to how instrumental it is for attaining well-being in subsequent time periods or in influencing the whole pattern of well-being over time. Long-run utility, in contrast, refers to the multi-period pattern of well-being. One of its central concerns is the degree to which each period's well-being can serve as an instrumentality for the well-being of subsequent periods.[52]

---

[52]We may explore this a bit further. It may be remembered from the Appendix to Chapter 2 that we defined tastes for purposes of making welfare comparisons as basic personality orientation. The long-run utility function represents a crucial aspect —

It is the author's empirical conjecture that when an individual chooses a risky prospect in which it is highly improbable that an extreme outcome will occur, he rarely takes relatively inexpensive steps to prepare for the "linkage of risks"[53] which its occurrence would occasion, i.e., if very bad, then the downward spiralling of future opportunities which would occur as well; if very good, then the widening horizons which would become available: it never rains but it pours. Such steps would help to offset the bad or take fuller advantage of the good. He does much more frequently take these steps when the probability of such an extreme outcome is high. We suggest that, at the base of behavior like this, is the fact that the individual does not take the improbable "seriously"; the individual integrates it only into his short-run utility, not into his long-run utility. It is only when the probability of an outcome is significantly non-zero that he evaluates it as though he might really have to live with it. It is only then that he attempts to consider its intertemporal implications, its implications for the whole time-shape of his style of life. To the extent that this conjecture is true, individuals' evaluations of particular outcomes will differ depending on the particular probability with which they are associated in the prospects under consideration. This represents very clear relatedness between risk and utility.

How extensive are all these relations between risk and utility elements? The author has no idea. The purpose of our exploration must be solely to suggest that this family of considerations which may lead to violation of

---

perhaps *the* crucial aspect — of this orientation. It represents the individual's valuation of his general style of life, of the general kind of person he finds himself and would like to be. It is in decisions concerning large commitments of his time, energy, and interest that his basic personality orientation is most in evidence.

This kind of consideration suggests how to make symbolic sense of the following apparent absurdity: "I dislike beer, because if I didn't dislike it I would drink it, and if I drank it I might get to like it, and I dislike it." I interpret this for our purposes as: "I refrain from selecting a certain commodity bundle because, if I were to select it, then I should gradually adjust myself to it, and, under its influence, would go on to select certain other commodity bundles, and I *don't* want to become (notice: not "I *wouldn't* want to become") the kind of person who selects that kind of commodity bundle." The individual's long-run valuations, which, of course, may themselves change gradually with further experience, are rejecting a particular time profile of real income, even though its first item might well be preferred to the alternate first item of any other possible time profile. The individual refuses to trust the maintenance of his present long-run goals to the revised orientation resulting from a particular probable sequence of experiences.

The opposite kind of situation is possible as well. The individual may commit himself to a particular probable sequence of experiences *in the hope that* he will at its termination be in a better position to make long-run commitments than at present. This is an especially likely pattern if the individual is aware of limited perspective due to immaturity or ignorance of specific contingencies, or recent trans-valuating experiences, etc. I am indebted to Prof. A. G. Hart for suggestions about this kind of analysis.

[53]Albert G. Hart, "Anticipations, Uncertainty and Dynamic Planning," especially pp. 60-74.

Postulate 4 is not overly inaccessible or eccentric. If the grounds seem at all reasonable as well, we might expect that their occurrence may not be of trivial magnitude.

Here is a numerical example of this type of violation due to Allais,[54] and discussed by Savage.[55]

Situation 1

$$f \equiv (\$500,000; \quad 1)$$
$$h \equiv (\$2,500,000, \quad \$500,000, \quad 0; \quad 0.1, \quad 0.89, \quad 0.01)$$

Situation 2

$$g \equiv (\$500,000, \quad 0; \quad 0.11, \quad 0.89)$$
$$k \equiv (\$2,500,000, \quad 0; \quad 0.1, \quad 0.9)$$

I cite Savage's explanation of the preferences:

> Many people prefer . . . [*f* to *h*] . . . because, speaking qualitatively, they do not find the chance of winning a very large fortune in place of receiving a large fortune outright adequate compensation for even a small risk of being left in the status quo. Many of the same people prefer . . . [*k* to *g*] . . . , because, speaking qualitatively, the chance of winning is nearly the same in both gambles, so the one with the much larger prize seems preferable.[56]

The pair of choices $f > h$ and $k > g$ violates Postulate 4, as can be seen if they are placed in expected utility notation.[57] Possibly an even more direct way to see the violation is as follows. Looking at $f > h$ as a refusal to exchange f for h, this preference means that the individual refuses to accept a decrease of 0.11 in the probability of obtaining \$500,000 in exchange for an increase of 0.01 in the probability of obtaining no reward and an increase of 0.1 in the probability of obtaining \$2,500,000. Similarly, $k > g$ implies

---

[54]M. Allais, "Le Comportement de l'Homme Rationnel Devant le Risque: Critique des Postulats et Axioms de l'Ecole Amèricaine," *Econometrica*, Vol. 21, No. 4 (October, 1953), 503-546.

[55]L. J. Savage, *The Foundations of Statistics* (New York: John Wiley & Sons, Inc., 1954), 101-2.

[56]*Ibid.*

[57]

(1) $U(\$500,000) > 0.1\ U(\$2,500,000) + 0.89\ U(\$500,000) + 0.01\ U(0)$

(2) $0.1\ U(\$2,500,000) + 0.9\ U(0) > 0.11\ U(\$500,000) + 0.89\ U(0)$

From (1) we obtain:

(3) $0.11\ U(\$500,000) > 0.1\ U(\$2,500,000)$

From (2) we obtain:

(4) $0.11\ U(\$500,000) < 0.1\ U(\$2,500,000),$

clearly a contradiction.

that the same individual now wants to make exactly this same trade that he repudiates in the first choice!

This behavior certainly appears inconsistent. Such appearance would seem to lend credence to the belief that expected utility maximization is not likely to be often violated. But such a view begs the question. We generated an appearance of outright contradictions by adding and subtracting separate components of each prospect, an operation which implicitly assumes that no relatedness exists between the utility of outcomes and the probability mix in which they appear in a given prospect. But in the context of the full prospects, the loss of 0.11 probability weight for $500,000 in $f > h$ is just not the same as the same loss in $k > g$, since, among other things, although in both it increases the dispersion of outcomes, in the former, it transforms a sure prospect into a risky one. It is not at all unreasonable for an individual to have an aversion to gambling such that the first loss of 0.11 from certainty is a greater loss, dollar for dollar, than any subsequent loss of 0.11. The preferences $f > h$ and $k > g$ are consistent with such an aversion.

Another type of violation of Postulate 4 may now be mentioned briefly. There are two urns. Let h be the sure outcome of drawing a white ball from either urn, f the sure outcome of drawing a black ball from the first urn and g the sure outcome of drawing a black ball from the second urn. Drawing a black ball instead of a white earns the subject $100. The subject has just seen 300 balls placed into the otherwise empty first urn, of which 200 were black and 100 were white. The second urn was already filled but the subject has just seen three balls drawn from it and replaced, of which two were black and one was white. If the subject is allowed to draw from only one of the urns, will any such subject have preferences about from which urn to choose, or will every subject be indifferent between them?

Assume that the subject assigns the number 2/3 to the probability of drawing a black ball from either urn (and thus 1/3 to the probability of drawing a white one). Then $\frac{2}{3}f + \frac{1}{3}h$ is the prospect of drawing from the first urn, $\frac{2}{3}g + \frac{1}{3}h$ the prospect of drawing from the second. Since $f = g$, Postulate 4 requires that every subject be indifferent between the two. But it is not intuitively obvious that every subject *will* be indifferent. Although the probabilities of drawing black balls are equal for the two urns, the subject's degree of confidence in this probability assignment differs (we could have filled urn number 1 with *300,000* balls in the indicated ratio instead of 300) in the two cases. There is more uncertainty in the second. So plungers may prefer to choose from the second because, although the odds are 2:1 in both urns, the greater uncertainty in the second provides more leeway for luck to operate in their favor. Timid souls are likely to prefer the first urn for the opposite reason. Only intermediate subjects are likely to be consistently indifferent between the two. We should expect

Postulate 4 to be not uncommonly violated in this sort of choosing situation.[58]

The violation represented by this example contains two elements. One element is that even apart from the over-all prospect context a given probability number may not be responded to unambiguously. The degree of confidence in the assignment of given probability numbers may make a difference for the subject's response. The second element is that, at least in our interpretation of the numerical example, differences in the degree of confidence in probability assignments affect choice by widening or narrowing the degree of uncertainty in the choosing situation and thereby make relevant to these situations the kind of attitudes toward risk (uncertainty) which we discussed at length above. The second element is particular to Postulate 4, but the first concerns Postulate 1 as well. We earlier noted that Postulate 1 underlay other postulates in the system. It does so in this sense of a given type of behavior violating more than one postulate simultaneously. It is more convenient to deal with the first element under our discussion of Postulate 1 below. Therefore, since we have already discussed the second, we shall say little more about this type of violation at the present time. This does not mean that it has no importance independent of its two component elements. This particular combination of elements *is* important for our purposes, because as such a *combination*, it provides an operational variable for empirically testing the extent to which expected utility maximization is satisfied. Although its two elements can be analytically distinguished, it is likely that they would prove difficult to separate empirically. It has not yet been as rigorously so employed, however, to the best of the author's knowledge.

Let us summarize our discussion of Postulate 4. When an individual selects a risky prospect, he does not generally *obtain* the mean utility outcome (e.g., by a stochastic process of frequent "drawings"). So the maximization of moral expectation is not *a priori* a unique prescription for rational behavior. It is not unreasonable, hence not irrational, for individuals to have preferences which can be explained in terms of types of relatedness between the probabilities and utilities of any prospect. In the terminology of "introspective utility" this can often be described as the individual having attitudes toward risk; he is influenced by characteristics of the probability distribution of utility outcomes other than its mean. We cannot jump from this negative statement to the positive one that Postulate 4 will in fact be violated frequently. As we observed earlier, all we can do here is suggest that it is not simply human "error" that leads to violations. We have, in effect, hypothesized that there are circumstances where viola-

---

[58]This type of violation was suggested by Daniel Ellsberg in a lecture given at the University of Chicago in 1959, and at the Econometric Society meeting in St. Louis, December, 1960.

tions are to be expected as the rule instead of the exception. The delineation of such circumstances, and the empirical confrontation of the implications of the alternative hypotheses have yet to be performed.

10.2. Postulate 1 and the Scope of Applicability: Some Reformulations of Welfare Analysis

Postulate 1 and corollary assert, we remember, that "preferences of the person in uncertain situations to which [numerical] probability applies are governed solely by the probabilities attached to each possible outcome," and that "the prospect $af + (1 - a)h$ has the same value to the individual no matter what the process is for determining the outcome."

There are two major considerations under which this postulate is likely to be violated. The first, as we have suggested above, is that probability numbers do not exhaust the individual's structuring of uncertainty (or risk). The individual does not simply assign probability numbers to possible outcomes; he is capable as well of making judgments about the confidence with which he assigns these numbers. Now, it must be obvious that questions about degree of confidence in probability are trivial if the individual is faced with prospects for which assignment of *objective* probabilities is proper. For these objective probabilities are virtually unanimous probabilities, and they can be virtually unanimous only if the features of the prospect situation make one set of probability assignments clearly more fitting than all others.

We shall argue below, with Savage, Edwards and others,[59] that the scope of applicability of the expected utility hypothesis would be exceptionally narrow if it were restricted solely to situations in which it was obvious to everyone concerned, subject and observer alike, what the uniquely appropriate probability was for every possible outcome. To rectify this, investigators like Ramsey, Savage, and Davidson, Suppes and Siegel, have axiomatized "subjective" or "personal" probability, the structure of probability assignments made by individual subjects themselves, for all situations in which they can at least order outcomes in terms of a relation like "no more likely than." Expected utility maximization can be formulated in terms of "personal" probability as well as of objective probability. We shall deal with this further below. At this point we simply assume that the decision has been made to extend the scope of the hypothesis in terms of personal probability. This means that there will be many situations in which the judgment about probability assignments is by no means a trivial thing. For such situations, differences in the degree of confidence placed

---

[59]Savage, *The Foundations of Statistics*; F. P. Ramsey, "Truth and Probability" in *Foundations of Mathematics and Other Logical Essays* (New York: Harcourt, Brace & Company, 1931).

in the assignments decided upon for any given set of numerical probabilities, may be substantial (as in our example of the two urns with 300 versus 3 ball samples from which to assign probabilities). If substantial differences do exist, individuals (perhaps those with attitudes toward risk *per se*, those for whom, e.g., variance of the probability distribution of introspective utility outcomes is an important consideration) will sometimes be induced to make different judgments about the desirability of alternative prospects. Degree of confidence will thus share with probability in determining, and thus (for the observer) in rationalizing and predicting, preferences.

It is not clear how serious a violation of expected utility maximization is involved here. We *can* expect that very substantial differences will be encountered in the degree of confidence toward particular probability assignments. What is less clear is the extent to which these will make a difference in preferences. This question is linked up with the pervasiveness of the kinds of attitudes toward risk which we discussed in the last section. The two questions are not, of course, equivalent, since risk-utility relatedness often refers to situations in which notably dissimilar probability mixes are involved. But the extent of these attitudes provides an upper limit to the importance of the present variable.

The second type of influence that could lead to violations of Postulate 1 is the connection between the number of stages in a prospect and the existence of suspense and gambling elements. It is clear that every probability distribution of outcomes is equivalent to a simple prospect, to some combinations of simple prospects, to some combinations of combinations of simple prospects, etc. Thus:

(1) $(f_1, f_2, \ldots, f_n) \equiv$
$$[ag_1 + (1 - a)h_1, ag_2 + (1 - a)h_2, \ldots, ag_n + (1 - a)h_n]$$
where $f_i = ag_i + (1 - a)h_i \quad i = 1, \ldots, n$

and

(2) $(g_1, g_2, \ldots, g_n) \equiv$
$$[bd_1 + (1 - b)k_1, bd_2 + (1 - b)k_2, \ldots, bd_n + (1 - b)k_n]$$
where $g_i = bd_i + (1 - b)k_i \quad i = 1, \ldots, n$

and

(3) $(h_1, h_2, \ldots, h_n) \equiv$
$$[cl_1 + (1 - c)r_1, cl_2 + (1 - c)r_2, \ldots, cl_n + (1 - c)r_n]$$
where $h_i = cl_i + (1 - c)r_i \quad i = 1, \ldots, n$

and further,

(4) $(d_1, d_2, \ldots, d_n) \equiv$
$$[es_1 + (1 - e)t_1, es_2 + (1 - e)t_2, \ldots, es_n + (1 - e)t_n]$$
where $d_i = es_i + (1 - e)t_i$
etc.

By this postulate and corollary we require that the individual be indifferent between all such alternatives reducible to the same probability distribution. This means that, if we interpret the compound prospects as multistage gambles, it should make no difference to the individual how many stages a particular gamble has.

It is evident that his indifference will not hold so long as the individual has attitudes, positive or negative, toward suspense or gambling. Multistage gambles do not necessarily involve more of such elements than do single-stage gambles, but there is a presumption that they generally will.[66] Consequently, we should expect occasions on which gambles with more stages will be preferred to gambles with the same reduced probability distribution but with fewer stages, and vice versa.

Samuelson suggests that the frequency with which we can expect Postulate 1 and the corollary to be violated depends on whether we are dealing with "ultimate" consumer ends or only instrumental ends. Thus, we should expect more frequent violation when observing consumers engaged in playing games of chance than when observing the decisions of a statistical quality control expert.[61] In the first case, suspense elements are part of the vector of ends served by any experience; in the second case, suspense is completely irrelevant to the purposes of quality control, so it may be easily suppressed in comparing alternatives.

These two sources of possible violation of Postulate 1 both refer to behavior which falls within the domain of the postulate, namely, choices by a "person in uncertain situations to which [numerical] probability applies." It is instructive to consider not only the pervasiveness of behavior which refutes the postulate, and thus the expected utility hypothesis, but also the range of behavior which is included in its scope. Such enquiry enables us to make an over-all evaluation of the scope of applicability of the hypothesis. It is to this that we now turn.

A tautologous but suggestive notion is that the hypothesis is applicable to all choice behavior which fulfills its axioms. It is inapplicable to all behavior which does not fulfill its axioms. The size of this latter group testifies to the power, or lack of power, of the hypothesis. But it is useful to distinguish between phenomena which are outside the scope of the hypothesis and phenomena which refute it. If we schematize every hypothesis as

---

[60]If only the final outcome of any gamble is reported to the "player" it makes no difference how many stages the gamble went through. Again, if each of the several stages of the multi-stage gamble takes only a brief time and the stages succeed one another with very little pause, then a single-stage gamble whose "play" is prolonged may well have more suspense. Duration of time, full reporting of the "play," and, usually, participation are necessary to evoke these elements. The upshot is that a multi-stage gamble would seem to be easier than a single-stage gamble to structure as an exciting game.

[61]"Probability, Utility and the Independence Axiom," 677.

asserting: "If A, then B," then the former are phenomena which can be recognized as not falling within the class A, the latter are phenomena which fall within A, but not within B. Referring back to our hypothesis, the class A would be all situations in which an individual is to choose among alternatives to which numerical probabilities can be applied. The class B is all choices consistent with maximization of expected utility. Our evaluation of Postulates 1 through 4 has been designed to estimate the extent of refuting behavior. Our task in this section is to estimate the extent of behavior which is within the scope of the hypothesis as defined by Postulate 1, i.e., all behavior falling within class A.

We have cited the content of class A, as given in Postulate 1, as choices by a "person in uncertain situations to which [numerical] probability applies." We may remember our previous citation from *The Theory of Games:* "[The expected-utility hypothesis is] vitally dependent upon the numerical concept of probability."[62] In other words, we are dealing with choices by an individual faced by a set of alternatives each of which specifies a number of mutually exclusive, exhaustive outcomes and their respective numerical probabilities.

How inclusive is this class of choices? We are dealing with a sub-set of choices among uncertain prospects. How inclusive are choices among uncertain prospects? I quote an extreme opinion on this.

> Upon reflection it will be seen to be the practically universal problem of choice. Can the reader think of many cases in which he *knows* when making a choice, the outcome of that choice with absolute certainty? In other words, are there many choices — or actions — in life in which the *consequences* can be predicted with absolute certainty? Even the act of purchasing a loaf of bread has an element of uncertainty in its consequences; even the act of paying one's taxes has an element of uncertainty in the consequences involved; even the decision to sit down has an element of uncertainty in the consequence. But to leave the trivial, consider the choice of occupation, purchase of an automobile, house, durable goods, business investment, marriage, having children, insurance, gambling, etc., ad infinitum. Clearly choices among uncertain prospects constitute an extremely large and important class of choices.[63]

Suppose we should agree with Alchian's estimate. Does it follow that the sub-set of these choices to which the hypothesis is applicable is also "an extremely large and important class of choices?" I submit that the crucial issue hinges around the range of choices to which *numerical* probability applies.

Let us treat "numerical probability" at this point in the way von Neumann and Morgenstern seemed originally to introduce it, as the limit of relative frequency "objective" probability.

---

[62]P. 19.
[63]Alchian, "The Meaning of Utility Measurement," 34.

Consider how many of the choice areas cited by Alchian are apt to have relatively precise numerical probability values observable in this sense. Is it really likely that a consumer could typically specify the alternative of buying a particular automobile as a precise set of outcomes to which he was able to attach precise relative probability weights? Could he, when faced with marriage, or buying a house, or having children? How would he find out the objective probabilities (or even, for that matter, the set of possible outcomes)?

The ability to elaborate a set of exhaustive possible outcomes and to affix to these, as von Neumann and Morgenstern would like, relative frequency probabilities, would seem to be restricted to areas where actuarial experience is appropriate and highly developed, such as in insurance or in *some* games of chance.[64]

Another area where outcome sets and objective probabilities can often be handled within the requisite degree of precision is that of experiment. Under experimental conditions outcomes and their true odds can sometimes be specified. We have noted this possibility in the Mosteller-Nogee experiment which combined both a game of chance in which odds were naturally relevant, and the experimental communication to the subjects of the true odds for all alternatives.

If we insist on employing objective utility we are restricted to a very narrow domain of choosing situations from which to construct our utility functions. We shall not be able to scale more than a very small percentage of the relevant alternatives. The solution suggested for this difficulty is to employ a different notion of probability in formulating choice among risky prospects. The probability to be assigned to any constituent outcome of a risky prospect is what *the subject thinks it is*. Providing the subject holds orderly beliefs about probability assignments, their use by investigators is advantageous. Individuals do apparently attribute probability weights to outcomes where decisive actuarial evidence is lacking. Gambling on the outcomes of sports contests is a case in point. Individuals in these situations respond to publicly communicated odds. It is not totally unreasonable to believe that they are able to formulate "odds" in other situations where past experience is not qualitatively more ambiguous despite the fact that no public communication about such odds takes place. So use of this "personal" (subjective) probability can extend the domain of measurability when used in the context of the expected utility hypothesis. How wide an extension is possible will be suggested below.

---

[64]Many gambling situations superficially appear to involve "objective" numerical probabilities but in fact do not. Thus, "odds" in horse racing or boxing do not represent direct empirical information about the limit of relative frequences, but only such fragmentary subjective information as seeps through what is only a degree of consensus in the opinions of a group of individuals.

But there is a second, hardly less important, advantage in the use of subjective probability. Both casual and formal observations of choosing behavior strongly suggests that even where the experiential basis for objective probability exists, individuals' subjective probability assignments differ, sometimes appreciably, from the objective values. In the experiment of Davidson, Suppes and Siegel cited earlier,[65] the seven subjects for whom the subjective probability of a given chance event were calculated showed substantial divergence from the objective probability of the event. Most individuals estimated below the objective 0.25. They differed among one another and — what is even more striking — in their probability estimate of the same chance event in three different choosing situations, they differed in their own three estimates about as much as they differed among one another.

Other studies suggest what might be the source of some of the divergence. There is some suggestion in Mosteller and Nogee,[66] Ward Edwards[67] and Davidson, Suppes and Siegel,[68] that the pattern of betting is affected by the size of one's cumulated winnings and losings and/or of the actual pattern of winning and losing outcome-probability mixtures. Davidson, Suppes and Siegel report, for example, what they learned from a pilot study they ran:

> It was necessary to control the effects of cumulative and immediate reinforcement. Winning or losing several times in a row made subjects sanguine or pessimistic and tended to produce altered responses to the same offers. Increases and decreases in the size of the stake [i.e., cumulated winnings] also had distorting effects.[69]

It is of course possible to try to interpret these changes as due to changes in the attractiveness of outcomes, but, whereas changes in wealth position may reasonably be thought to be so related, the pattern of successes and failures in outcomes is far less amenable to such an interpretation.

When there is a divergence between the objective and subjective probabilities assignable to any prospect, it is of course the subjective that we must use. Only the latter expresses the subject's own sense of the uncertainty of the situation. Thus, subjective probability is doubly important for our purposes: it corrects our characterization of the subject's estimate of the situation where objective probabilities can be calculated; it gives us the only characterization of the subject's estimate in situations where objective probabilities can not be calculated.

----

[65]*Decision Making*, Chapter 2, especially pp. 66-68.
[66]Mosteller and Nogee, *op. cit.*
[67]See the bibliography cited above.
[68]Davidson, Suppes and Siegel, *op. cit.*, 53-55.
[69]*Ibid*, 53.

The use of subjective probability substantially complicates the calculation of individual utility functions. If it were not necessary to turn from objective to subjective probability, the probabilities assigned to risky prospects by any group of subjects could easily be computed, and they would be the same for all the subjects. But subjective probabilities may differ for all. They have in any case to be separately discovered for each individual. To do so requires a procedure at least as cumbersome as calculation of the utility function, and in some respects a procedure that is less flexible, since if objective probability is known to estimate individual assignments accurately, a utility function can be inferred by observation only, although discovery of a subjective probability function is more likely to require an experimental procedure.[70]

The derivation of subjective probabilities can be accomplished relatively simply in principle. Two main approaches not very dissimilar may be mentioned. According to one approach, subjective probability is given no independent axiomatization from that of utility and both are empirically derived simultaneously. This is essentially the method of Ramsey[71] and Davidson, Suppes and Siegel.[72] In the empirical procedure of the latter, the particular subject is offered a choice between $f \equiv [x,y; P(S)]$ and $g \equiv [y,x; P(S)]$, where x and y are sure prospects and $P(S)$ is the probability of chance event S occurring. Because of the symmetry of f and g, a preference of one for the other, *assuming the expected utility hypothesis to be true*, implies that $P(S) \neq P(\overline{S})$ ($\overline{S}$ = not-S). Only $f = g$ implies $P(S) = (\overline{S})$. Thus, when the experimentor has succeeded in finding a chance event S^* such that $f = g$, he has succeeded also in finding a chance event to which the subjective probability weight of 0.5 can be assigned. Making use only of this event S^* a utility function is obtained linkwise by varying x, y, z, w to elicit indifference between prospect pairs like $[x,y; P(S^*)]$ and $[z,w; P(S^*)]$, where utility numbers have already been assigned to three of the four sure outcomes.[73] Once a utility function has been derived the subjective probability function, $P(S)$, is derived *by assuming the expected utility hypothesis true* and finding, for each chance event S, some x, y, z, w

---

[70]The distinction is between observation of a subject without the latter's direct awareness or his direct participation in the observation as against observation which includes either or both of these elements. This distinction applies to inanimate phenomena as well. Thus, observation of a single electron partakes of experimental elements because it involves a stream of electrons (photons) from the observer's illumination of the electron actually interacting with the observed electron. It is presumably this interaction, by the way, which prevents determinate predictions from being made about velocity and position of individual electrons.

[71]"Truth and Probability."

[72]*Decision Making.*

[73]Thus, $1/2U(x) + 1/2U(y) = 1/2U(z) + 1/2U(w)$,
or $U(x) + U(y) = U(z) + U(w)$.

such that $[x,y;\ P(S)] = [z,w;\ P(S)]$, and solving for the only unknown $P(S)$.[74]

The second approach is represented notably by Savage.[75] Here subjective probability (Savage prefers the name, personal probability) is axiomatized independently of utility except that the subsequent axiomatization of utility depends on the prior axiomatization of probability, and the two are based on the same way of looking at choice behavior under uncertainty. The axiom system for probability is based on the inference that the influence of any outcome on the desirability of the prospect in which it is embedded is a monotonic function of the probability weight attached to it. Thus if $f < g$, where $f \equiv [x,y;\ P(S_1)]$, $g \equiv [x,y;\ P(S_2)]$, and $x > y$, then the preference of g for f must indicate that the individual feels he is more likely to obtain the preferred outcome x if that depends on occurrence of S_2 than if it depends on S_1. From this we infer that S_2 is more probable than S_1. The procedure envisaged by Savage is that all situations S_i (each S_i is really a sub-set of the set of all sure outcomes) can similarly be compared. The main requirements for a subjective numerical probability are: (1) that there be a complete ordering of states S_i in terms of a relation "not more probable than" defined in terms of these preferences; (2) that there exists a partition of the set of states S such that, if $S_1 < S_2$ (S_1 is less probable than S_2), then the union of S_1 with *each* element of the partition[76] is still less probable than S_2.[77] This second requirement has much the same force as assuming that the set of states S can be partitioned into an arbitrarily large number of equivalent sub-sets,[78] unions of fewer or more such sub-sets defining equal probability increments.

As with the expected utility hypothesis the critical question is: How widely are the requirements for a numerical personal probability fulfilled? Again as with the expected utility hypothesis, the answer depends on the results of empirical tests. These tests have not, to the author's knowledge,

---

[74]Let $P(S) = a$, then $P(\bar{S}) = 1 - a$. So:
$$aU(x) + (1 - a)U(y) = aU(z) + (1 - a)U(w),$$
and
$$a = \frac{U(w) - U(y)}{[U(x) - U(z)] + [U(w) - U(y)]}$$
which is soluble because all utility numbers have already been derived.

In a somewhat similar vein, see G. C. Archibald, "Utility, Risk and Linearity," *The Journal of Political Economy*, Vol. LXVII, No. 5 (October, 1959), 437-450. Archibald does not discuss subjective probability, but does emphasize the manipulation of probabilities as a way of performing empirical tests of the expected utility hypothesis since a central implication of the hypothesis is that, although the utility of a prospect may or may not be linear in money income, it *is* linear in probability.

[75]*The Foundations of Utility*, Chapters 2 through 4.

[76]I.e., the larger domain of possible outcomes S_1 *or* each separate element of the partition.

[77]Savage, *op. cit.*, Chapter 3.

[78]*Ibid.*, 33, 38-9.

been made. In the light of this dearth we may remind ourselves of the data from the Davidson-Suppes-Siegel experiment. Only two states were ordered probabilistically, the first being the chance event with 0.5 probability. As for the second, the same event was given a probability number in each of three different choice situations, i.e., the same probability mix with three different pairs of alternatives. The results showed that a different range of probabilities could be inferred for each individual to the same chance event in each of the three situations, and moreover, that these differences for each individual's responses were about as great as the differences among the responses of the several individuals tested. For two of the seven the intra-individual differences were so great that the probability ranges in the three situations had no numbers in common (i.e., zero intersection)! This is not overly encouraging, considering how favorable were the characteristics of the experimental situation: the alternatives dealt with involved different amounts of a homogeneous commodity, money winnings; the uncertainty of the situation consisted only in the relatively well-structured, homogeneous context of tosses of special dice; the number of plays was great; and the stakes involved in each play were small enough to prevent a sense of irreversible outcomes.

Consider how much less orderly individual probability estimates may be where outcomes are multi-dimensional, where uncertainty stems from the working of several random and quasi-random processes, where the situation has such elements of novelty that the question of which past experience is most relevant is highly ambiguous, where only one play or at most a few replications can be expected, and where the stakes in any one play are so great that some or all outcomes will be irreversible. Yet such relatively "unique" choices[79] are likely to be encountered if the scope of the von Neumann-Morgenstern hypothesis is to be expanded significantly. In particular, they will be encountered in the problem which is the central concern of the present work, namely, the ordering of social states. The suggestion is not that individuals cannot make such choices — they obviously can and do — but that the probability estimates involved in a group of such choices will be too disorderly and imprecise to guarantee the existence of a (numerical) probability measure; they will very likely generate only a partial likelihood ordering of outcomes at most.[80]

---

[79]For example, decisions about marriage, buying a house, making a large, lumpy business investment, choosing a profession.

[80]A much more radical objection is sometimes made. It is claimed that where events are unique, both in respect to a relevant past and to a repetitive future, additive numerical probability is not even *in principle* appropriate. For an elaboration of this argument, see G. L. S. Shackle, *Expectation in Economics* (London: Macmillan Company, 1949), last chapter. As a constructive adjunct to his criticism, Shackle has presented an apparatus for dealing with choices under uncertainty, an apparatus which does not depend on any sort of additive numerical probability. See Appendix 2 to this chapter

The final point to be noted in this regard is that even if a subjective probability measure can be derived for a subject, the wide diversity in the confidence with which different probability assignments will have been made makes likely the kind of violation of Postulates 1 and 4 which we discussed above. On *a priori* grounds, then, we believe that the scope of applicability of the expected utility hypothesis may well fall short of what would be required for the purpose of the present enquiry.[81]

---

for a description of this alternative calculus. Shackle's objection to the relative frequency objective probability approach has merit, but it is far less convincing against subjective probability, given the latter's great flexibility.

For a defense of the use of the probability calculus in dealing with "unique" decisions see R. S. Weckstein, "The Use of the Theory of Probability in Economics," *Review of Economic Studies*, Vol. XX (3), No. 53 (1952-3), 191-198. He is essentially defending another form of non-relative frequency probability: "degree of confirmation." Here, as with the personal probability notion, probability measures can be applied to single instances. "Instance confirmation (Rudolf Carnap, *Logical Foundations of Probability*) is the degree of confirmation [a purely logical relation between sentences] on the basis of the given evidence, of the hypothesis that the individual case of concern to the individual is predicted by the law. . . . [It is] an estimate of statistical probability . . . a rational evaluation of available [limited] information." (pp. 194-5).

Weckstein essentially argues that the uniqueness of decisions with regard to paucity of relevant past experience and significance of consequences is illusory. There always exists some relevant past experience, although it is not always employed efficiently. More efficient marshalling of this experience, especially through a linkwise structuring to bear clearly on the present, would remove the aura of uniqueness. Moreover, individuals only very rarely are truly interested in a single play. Where it appears so, a larger context can usually be found within which the "unique" event is only one of a sequence.

The argument may be adequate as a rebuttal to the objection that probability is in principle inappropriate, although even here it may beg the question by the sanguineness of its assurance that larger relevant contexts can always be found. But it must not be taken as an assertion that a numerical non-relative frequency measure can be empirically derived. Granted that the past is never totally irrelevant to any present decision, the real question is how unambiguously the past states its case. It may not take much ambiguity to prevent an individual from revealing a complete probability ordering of outcomes or from attributing a partition of the total set of outcomes with the requisite properties. Furthermore, a class of future decisions similar to ones under consideration may be found; but these can hardly be deemed replications of the latter since their "crucialness" means that whatever happens is likely to change the subject's initial situation irrevocably, drastically changing his subsequent opportunities and altering his relative evaluations as well. The upshot of all this is, again, that the question of the empirical usefulness of subjective probability in the context of expected utility waits upon the results of much more empirical investigation than we have yet had.

[81]One particular procedure for extending the scope might be worth examining were it not for at least one important defect. Briefly, one could derive a utility scale for money incomes within the scope of the hypothesis by varying money bets and associated probabilities. One could then ask the individual to declare the money value of each uncertain prospect, thereby presumably obtaining a utility value for each such prospect (on a scale arbitrary as to scale and zero point). One difficulty is that the utility scale for money income is independent of a particular starting income (but see the contrary view expressed in Markowitz, "The Utility of Wealth," *Journal of Political Economy*, Vol. LX, No. 2 (April, 1952), 151-158), whereas the evaluations of uncertain prospects in terms of money are not. If money income changes, these evaluations will change,

In addition to this direct difficulty, the limitation of scope of the expected utility hypothesis has a relevance for our problem of more indirect nature. It is apparent that many of the kinds of uncertain choices for which we believe the expected utility hypothesis might be poorly adapted are choices which we would expect individuals to have to consider in comparing social states: taking a particular job, buying a particular house, etc. We have heretofore proceeded as though the component entities of social state alternatives were unproblematic, that a social state represented an unambiguous *state of affairs*. Our argument now makes plain that this procedure in effect assumes away time. It is somewhat more suggestive now to regard each social state as representing not so much specific "things" going to different persons as rather specific activities engaged in by these persons: living in this house, working at this job, etc. It represents particular commitments by individuals, commitments of varying strengths, to the future. Each commitment has consequences for the individual and for others. Its desirability unquestionably is determined partly with reference to these consequences. The desirability of a social state, in turn, is realistically to be interpreted at least in part as an appraisal of future consequences. The question of *what* future is, unfortunately, insoluble in general terms, since each individual has different planning horizons for different kinds of commitments (depending on his values and his ability to predict). This complicates our ability to specify the temporal dimensions of our alternatives.

But perhaps more seriously for our purposes, each social state should be considered an uncertain prospect, since the individual will probably never normally predict for each state a unique set of outcomes with certainty. Yet these prospects contain as components some of the very uncertain situations which our analysis above argues are probably inappropriate for the expected utility hypothesis. Such social state uncertain prospects can probably not be numerically scaled by the expected utility hypothesis. We should like to be able to deal with means and ends interchangeably, specifying criteria of choice either in terms of the "ultimate" outcomes or of the proximate outcomes which are the means for bringing them about. If we interpret the nearby social state outcomes as means, we now find that

---

but even in Markowitz's model where utility scales have meaning only for *deviations* of money income from the current money income level, the utility index change will bear no necessary relationship to the changes in "money equivalents."

In addition to this, a warning is necessary. Each prospect outcome must specify an entire budgetary allocation for the individual. Otherwise, what the individual is willing to pay for a particular outcome will differ, depending on what remaining commodities the individual conceives of consuming in addition to the possible prospect outcomes. This is, of course, a necessary condition for the Strong Independence Assumption to be satisfied.

they should be considered risky prospects of obtaining more remote (ultimate?) outcomes. And the limitation of scope of our theory for handling risky prospects breaks the unique connection between the two: it leaves us with no obvious isomorphic linkage between criteria for proximate and ulterior outcomes.

This may be taken a step further. The purpose of welfare economics itself is to inform public policy. Our interest in the ordering of social states derived from the general belief that such an ordering could be projected back into a uniquely determined ordering of public policies. But the predictions of economic theory which connect policy with outcome are scarcely single-valued. Based on current analytic knowledge, and quite likely that of the foreseeable future, each public policy is a risky prospect of social state outcomes. Although occasionally theory can prescribe the probability mixture with precision (indeed, with objective probabilities) this is generally far from being the case. The resulting motley of probability assignments is not likely to fulfill the conditions for a numerical probability measure. Even if the problem (of the next section) of formulating *social* preferences is solved, therefore, the convenient solution to choice among risky prospects provided by the expected utility hypothesis is not likely to be available. A possible type of approach to follow, suggested by the example of Savage,[82] is to define the whole problem originally in terms of choices among policies. But the details of such an approach are not clear since it seems to leave in the dark the central question of what *ought* to make for the relative desirability of different policies.

We may summarize this section as follows. The numerical scaling of public policies seems somewhat dubious when it is realized (1) that the scaling of social states on which it depends is itself dubious, since it involves a scaling of uncertain prospects, the components of which prospects are not obviously rationalizable by the expected utility procedure; and (2) that the procedure by which we obtain a scaling of policies from a scaling of social states is necessarily crude so long as the probability predictions of economic theory are crude.

Our pessimism stems largely from reinterpreting social states and public policies as uncertain prospects to obtain greater realism. It may well be, however, that on this level of "realism" no *general* formulation of social choice in the near future can yield a tolerably useful solution for welfare analysis. When faced with a barrier like this, it is not unreasonable to make compromises. We must retreat either from our desire for realism or for an abstract *general* formulation of social choice. Probably we should do some of both.

---

[82]*The Foundations of Statistics.*

10-3. *Expected Utility and the Social Welfare Function*

In the last two sections we have emphasized doubts about the ability of the expected utility hypothesis to generate cardinal utility indices adequate to our purposes. In the present section we shall waive these doubts in the interest of examining how such individual indices could be employed to construct an acceptable Social Welfare Function.

We must first assume that the "utility" which we interpret the members of the group as individually maximizing is the content of the "welfare" which we are interested in ordering for the group. We have argued at some length in Chapter 9, in contrast to much of the literature, that the preference intensities implied by a von Neumann-Morgenstern utility function are intrinsically the same as those revealable through non-risky psychometric procedures (so-called "introspective utility"). We argued that whereas the justification for introducing cardinal utility into normative economics is not at all the same as for introducing it into positive economics (e.g., superfluity in rendering operational implications does not disqualify it from the former but it does from the latter), nonetheless it does depend importantly on the empirical significance of the notion of preference intensity. Such significance would seem to require strong correspondence between preference intensity as an introspective reportable phenomenon and as a determinant of choice in situations where preference order (among sure outcomes) alone does not suffice to determine choice. We do not now possess evidence on the presence or absence of such correspondence, but the point at issue for us is that its presence equally justifies both notions; its absence is negative justification for both. If our argument be accepted, then the welfare relevance of von Neumann-Morgenstern utility, like that of introspective utility, is introduced into the system by little more than the assumption of consumer's sovereignty.[83]

Some critics have argued, not that von Neumann-Morgenstern utility differs from introspective utility, but that it is too arbitrary a measure.

> This theorem does not, as far as I can see, give any special ethical significance to the particular utility scale found. For instead of using the utility scale found by von Neumann and Morgenstern, we could use the square of that scale; then behavior is described by saying that the individual seeks to maximize the expected value of the square root of his utility. This is not to deny the usefulness of the von Neumann-Morgenstern theorem; what it does say is that among the many different ways of assigning a utility indicator to the preferences among alternative probability distributions, there is one method (more precisely, a whole set of methods which are linear transforms of each other) which has the property of stating the laws of rational behavior in a particularly convenient way.

---

[83]It should be clear from our earlier discussions that the criterion of welfare, *no matter how it is given content*, is always introduced as a value judgment for a given welfare analysis; it is never empirically induced.

This is a very useful matter from the point of view of developing the descriptive economic theory of behavior in the presence of random events, but it has nothing to do with welfare considerations, particularly if we are interested primarily in making a social choice among alternative policies in which no random elements enter. To say otherwise would be to assert that the distribution of the social income is to be governed by the tastes of individuals for gambling.[84]

Moreover, more generally, "If we accept the view that *any* index obtained from a valid index by a monotone transformation is also valid, those results . . . [referring] to the shape of the . . . marginal utility curve, lose all their meaning,"[85] and only an ordinal significance remains.

The second position is not correct. The intention to employ a von Neumann-Morgenstern utility in welfare analysis stems from the fact that one infers from it a unique ordering of preference intensities which is consistent with his actual choices. This ordering is deemed to possess welfare significance since it provides information by which we may weight the relative importance of different individuals' preferences in a Social Welfare Function. It is true that any linear function of a particular utility is also a utility; it also preserves this unique ordering of preference intensities. Since it is to obtain this ordering that we resort to the expected utility hypothesis, our purpose is accomplished with any member of the family of linear functions of a utility indicator. Thus, despite the fact that our choice of any one member is arbitrary, the function is not arbitrary in the sense of having no welfare relevance. Finally, it is not true that any monotonic transformation of a member of this select family is also "valid"; a monotone transformation which fails to preserve this particular ordering of preference intensities is *not* as acceptable as one which does since the pattern of preference intensities implied by such a transformation is either not interpretable (if only an ordering of sure outcomes is at stake) or, if interpretable, can be made consistent with behavior only by hypotheses more complicated than the expected utility hypothesis.[86] In the context of positive theory, simplicity is a reason for accepting one hypothesis over another as a better explanation of reality. The preference intensities revealed by the von Neumann-Morgenstern indicators will be considered more accurate than any others (this, of course, assumes that behavior is consistent with expected utility maximization).

Much the same can be said about the first position. If preference inten-

---

[84]Arrow, Kenneth J., *Social Choice and Individual Values* (New York: John Wiley and Sons, Inc., 1951), 10.

[85]Baumol, "The Von Neumann-Morgenstern Utility Index — An Ordinalist View," *The Journal of Political Economy*, Vol. LIX, No. 1 (February, 1951), 61-66, especially p. 65.

[86]As for example, the notion that the sun rotates around the earth can be sustained by a theory that specifies orbits with shamefully many epicycles.

sity is assumed to possess welfare relevance (whether or not it possesses relevance for a positive theory of static choice), then that indicator, or family of indicators, will be deemed most relevant which most accurately describes the individual's preference intensity. We may admittedly speak of a selection between empirical hypothesis on grounds of "convenience;" but a hypothesis so chosen has traditionally been accorded the distinction of being better than others — truer than others. If the von Neumann-Morgenstern hypothesis is accorded this distinction over a substantial domain of applicability, then preference intensities implied by it can with some justification be considered more accurate than others. Normative theory always avails itself of what is currently known in positive theory, notwithstanding that no such knowledge can ever be certified as final. The last part of the first quote, concerning the importance of the risk context of the theory, is really an argument that von Neumann-Morgenstern and introspective utilities are different entities. Our position on this was given in Chapter 9.

Although controversial, let us assume that our first step has been taken. We have a preference ordering of outcomes and an ordering of preference intensities for each individual (i.e., we have a family of utility indicators). We now make a second value judgment and express social welfare as a function of these orderings. It is natural to take advantage of the cardinality of our indices by specifying a simple function like addition or multiplication. Summation is the usual form specified in the welfare tradition.[87] We remember, however, that each individual utility index is unique only up to linear transformation. This means that for each individual we are not able to specify *the* "true" index but only the "true" family of indices. We are

---

[87] A suggestion for a Social Welfare Function as the product of individual welfares is found in John J. Nash, "The Bargaining Problem," *Econometrica*, Vol. 18, No. 2 (April, 1950). Bergson suggests that assuming the Social Welfare Function to be a summation of individual utilities implies the assumption that there is no social value in the interrelationships of different households' (individuals') utilities. A given total utility for one household has the same social value no matter what the living standards of other households. Or, conversely, no household feels "its total utility affected by general changes in living standards of other households." ("Socialist Economics," p. 419). This would certainly be a dubious assumption to have to make. Admittedly, it is not the same as the assumption of fact that the pattern of tastes for any household is independent of the consumption of others. But even so, it is questionable whether it is implied in a schema in which the individual utility functions relate to values instead of tastes. Each household's evaluations of different social states would presumably have considered total distribution of welfare as well as simply the particular items of consumption of different individuals. Its utility function would already reflect the effects of these considerations and consequently, as long as consumer sovereignty is assumed, the social welfare would correspondingly already reflect these considerations.

A Social Welfare Function as a *product* of individual indices would by its very form have a different marginal effect on social welfare for each different distribution of welfare (i.e., for each point on a multi-dimensional utility possibility locus) — even when individual utilities reflected *tastes* in the narrow sense, not values.

consequently unable to obtain a unique sum of individual utility values for any alternative; nor can we even obtain a family of sums for each alternative which will bear some invariant relationship to the similar family of sums for any other alternative. Our Social Welfare Function will remain essentially undefined unless we impose further restrictions on the individual utility indices.

The additional restrictions are, of course, those assuming interpersonal comparisons and evaluations of utility.

A number of specific models of acceptable social welfare functions have been presented, making use of individual von Neumann-Morgenstern utilities. We shall briefly mention three: those of Hildreth, Harsanyi and Strotz.[88] In all three, the use of cardinal individual utility functions enables the authors to show that acceptable social welfare functions exist which fulfill Arrow's conditions, so long as Condition 3 is modified to allow preference intensities to count.

Hildreth's postulate system does not raise new issues for us. His assumptions on interpersonal utility reduce, on inspection, to Interchangeability. It is instructive to examine this reduction because Hildreth's formulation of these assumptions has an intuitively more persuasive impact than the formulation of Chapter 8. The equivalence of the two sets throws light in the ethical aura possessed by the Interchangeability condition. We shall consider this proof in Appendix 3 of this chapter.

Strotz's system also employs an assumption quite similar to Interchangeability, which he refers to as Isomorphism. Although this is sufficient to generate an acceptable welfare function, Strotz adduces additional assumptions to specialize the welfare function. He postulates unusual, very strong linkages between individual and social preferences. First, if two alternatives x and y are *socially* indifferent, and it makes no difference if a chance event (S) is used to make an actual selection between them, then any alternative f which all individuals rate equal to the risk prospect $[x,y; P(S)]$, where $P(S)$ can take all values $0 \leq P(S) \leq 1$, is to be considered socially indifferent to x and y. This is *not* a unanimity judgment, it must be pointed out, since no individual need actually be indifferent between x and

[88]Clifford Hildreth, "Alternative Conditions for Social Orderings," *Econometrica*, Vol. 21, No. 1 (January, 1953), 81-91; John C. Harsanyi, "Cardinal Welfare, Individualistic Ethics and Interpersonal Comparisons of Utility," *The Journal of Political Economy*, Vol. LXIII, No. 4 (August, 1955), 309-321; Robert Strotz, "How Income Ought to be Distributed: A Paradox in Distributive Ethics," *The Journal of Political Economy*, LXVI, No. 3 (June, 1958), 189-205. See also William Vickrey, "Utility, Strategy, and Social Decision Rules," *The Quarterly Journal of Economics*, Vol. LXXIV, No. 4 (November, 1960), 507-535, for a more informal discussion than these of the problems involved in fashioning social welfare functions from von Neumann-Morgenstern utility functions. The discussion is especially interesting for examining the technical implications of using functions of different forms and admitting alternatives of different types into the choice functions.

f or y and f in order for f to be the "certainty equivalent" to $[x,y; P(S)]$ for him. Second, if x is deemed socially preferred to y, and, by a version of the sure-thing principle, the risky prospect $[x,d; P(S)]$ is deemed socially preferred to $[y,d; P(S)]$, then any sure alternative z which all individuals find indifferent to $[x,d; P(S)]$ is to be deemed socially preferred to any sure alternative w which all individuals find indifferent to $[y,d; P(S)]$, where $P(S)$ can take all values, $0 \leq P(S) \leq 1$. Again, no actual unanimity determines the social choice between z and w. In both cases the structure of individual utility functions is not so much determining the *content* of social preferences as determining which other social preferences are to be considered relevant for any given social choice decision. These are cases where Arrow's fears come true; individual propensities for making individual gambles determine social preferences. The unconvincing arbitrariness of the linkages in this particular model stems from the fact that the individual utility functions, which determine not only the arguments of the social welfare function, but also, by these linkages, as we have seen, the *form* of the Social Welfare Function itself, are assumed to depend solely on the income of the given individual; no distributive considerations, no well-being externalities at all are allowed.[89]

Strotz's model is in a sense a halfway house between Hildreth and Harsanyi. The unconvincing linkages between individual and social preferences have the effect of attributing some of the properties of von Neumann-Morgenstern utility to social preferences. Harsanyi's model goes all the way. He postulates that both individual *and* social preferences satisfy the postulates for von Neumann-Morgenstern utility. These assumptions plus a unanimity linkage between concrete individual and social preferences enable him to deduce the same stronger linkages as in Strotz's system. Here the linkages are somewhat more persuasive, *given the assumption about social preferences*, since individual preferences here take into consideration consumption externalities. It is, of course, rather the assumption about social preferences which is the main issue. The strength of this assumption enables him to derive acceptable Social Welfare Functions which are weighted sums of the individual utilities. The weights, which make the individual utilities comparable, involve our usual value judgments about interpersonal comparability and interpersonal evaluations.[90]

---

[89] For a detailed evaluation of Strotz's model, see Franklin M. Fisher and Jerome Rothenberg, "How Income Ought to be Distributed: Paradox Lost," *The Journal of Political Economy*, Vol. LXIX, No. 2 (April, 1961); and "How Income Ought to be Distributed: Paradox Enow, "*The Journal of Political Economy*, Vol. LXIX, No. 4 (August, 1961).

[90] However, Harsanyi argues that interpersonal comparisons of utility are matters of fact, somewhat in the manner of Little in *A Critique of Welfare Economics*, 316-321.

Why should we be willing to assume that social preferences fulfill the conditions for von Neumann-Morgenstern utility? Harsanyi argues that these are the conditions for rational choice under uncertainty. We have already noted the contention that expected utility maximization should be treated as a normative system, stipulating the rules for rational choice under uncertainty. We know that this can never be true by assertion, that at most the axiom system is designed to *persuade* us to agree with it. Our subsequent examination of the types of behavior that would violate the several postulates should make clear that there are several types of behavior inconsistent with the postulates which are not obviously unreasonable in the given circumstances. Furthermore, the von Neumann-Morgenstern postulates apply to individual preferences. They do not refer directly to social preferences. The author has not formed a definite opinion as to its persuasiveness in the context of social choice, but it is not at all established that the postulates are equally reasonable there. The kinds of consideration we wish to enter into social choice (e.g., various compromises for the sake of vastly dissimilar evaluating orientations), and the way we wish elements to be considered there (e.g., in terms of impersonality, time horizons) often differ from the content and form of individual choice. Even if we should be persuaded of the rationality of expected utility maximization for individual preferences, therefore, this of itself would not constitute a definitive argument in its favor for social preferences. The burden of persuasion is on the advocate.

Harsanyi does present additional argument, an indirect justification in the form of an ingenious alternative model which implies the same kind of welfare function. He argues that each individual has a Social Welfare Function "based not on the utility function (subjective preferences) of *one* particular individual only (namely, the individual whose value judgments are expressed in this welfare function), but rather on the utility functions (subjective preferences) of *all* individuals, representing a kind of 'fair compromise' among them!"[91] The individual's Social Welfare Function is based on preferences that "express what this individual prefers . . . on the basis of impersonal social considerations alone"[92] ("ethical preferences"). "An individual's preferences satisfy this requirement of impersonality if they indicate what social situation he would choose if he did not know what his personal position would be in the new situation chosen (and in any of its alternatives) but rather had an equal *chance* of obtaining any of the social positions existing in this situation, from the highest to the lowest . . . . He ought to judge the utility of another individual's position not in terms of his

---

[91]Harsanyi, *op. cit.*, 315.
[92]*Ibid.*

own attitudes and tastes but rather in terms of the attitudes and tastes of the individual actually holding this position."[93]

By this interpretation, every choice situation placed before a Social Welfare Function represents a choice among risky prospects. Assuming that individual preferences must satisfy the conditions of expected utility maximization if they are rational, Harsanyi infers that rational choice by a Social Welfare Function must consist of a choice that maximizes the expected value of utility, i.e., that the welfare function is the weighted sum of the utility functions of all individuals.[94] Thus, by the identification of the Social Welfare Function with a special type of *individual* choice criterion, he succeeds in ascribing the persuasive impact of von Neumann-Morgenstern utility for individual preferences to "social" preferences.

The weakness in this demonstration seems to the author to lie in Harsanyi's insistence that being put into some social position in the chosen alternative means that the evaluator is "put into the place of any individual member of the society, with regard not only to his objective social (and economic) conditions, but also to his subjective attitudes and tastes."[95] It is this complete transfer of personalities that makes it appropriate to express the desirability of each outcome for the evaluator in terms of *some other individual's* utility function instead of his own. But such a complete transfer of personalities belies the persuasive intent of the procedure. If it is impersonal for the evaluator to choose from alternatives where he does not know where *he* would be placed, on the basis of *his* highest expected utility, then this would suggest that it is the mean (unweighted, since all social positions have equal probabilities by assumption) of *his* utilities at each position that constitutes the "social" choice criterion. This is not equivalent to the result of Harsanyi's main model. To insist on complete transfer destroys the intuitive sense that the impersonality of the procedure consists in the uncertainty of the *evaluator's* payoff. For why should he *become* some other concrete individual in order to experience one position or another? No one individual is uniquely suited to any one social niche.[96] The need to *become* other individuals is gratuitous and destructive of the sense of the procedure. If the evaluator must *become* others, then the procedure is purely and simply one in which the choice criterion is the average of everybody's utility payoff in some particular social state. There is no uncertainty about anybody's position — certainly not the evaluator's. But

---

[93]*Ibid.*, 316.
[94]*Ibid.*, 316.
[95]*Ibid.*, 316.
[96]Since no one concrete individual belongs in any unique social position, the evaluator would have to *become* each and every concrete individual in each and every possible social niche. Each alternative would represent one possible allocation of the evaluator as all other individuals to the available niches.

if there is no uncertainty, then the evaluator's choice has nothing to do with maximization of *his* expected utility. So the assumption of von Neumann-Morgenstern rationality does not suffice to determine his choice. In the absence of uncertainty elements, the assertion that maximizing the simple average of everyone's utility is the uniquely appropriate choice criterion is a separate and additional assumption. The alternative model, then, no longer bears on the original model; it is no longer a justification for the assertion that rationality in social choice necessitates satisfying the von Neumann-Morgenstern postulates.[97,98]

10-4. SUMMARY

The structure of a Social Welfare Function employing the utility indices derived from the Bernoulli hypothesis is much the same as for the cardinal indices discussed in previous chapters. Attempts to fuse expected utility maximization in whole or part to the structure of social preferences as well as simply to individual preferences seem less successful. The usefulness of the expected utility hypothesis in welfare economics depends partly, then, on the usefulness of cardinal utility analysis for individuals in general; it depends, in other words, on the tractability of interpersonal utility assumptions.

Within this context, however, we have noted the, as of now, unique contribution of the Bernoulli theorem in making utility measurement revealable from choice. The potential deepening of the justification for cardinal analysis in welfare economics stems from this property of the model. We have not attempted in the present work to test the correspondence of this notion of preference intensity with that from introspective sources since this would seem to wait on more definitive evaluation of the expected utility model itself. But we have indicated the direction in which such a test of correspondence would proceed.

As to the appraisal of the model itself, we have not presented a critical confrontation with observation. Instead, we have tried, for the most part, to illuminate the kinds of behavior which would refute the hypothesis. Our

---

[97]Harsanyi actually speaks in terms of satisfying Marschak's postulates, but these are essentially the same.

[98]Vickrey, *loc. cit.*, pp. 523-525, reformulates the second version of Harsanyi's argument for the normative relevance of the von Neumann-Morgenstern postulates in a way that avoids this criticism. The critical emendation is to assume that every member of the population, including the evaluator, has the same tastes. Then the desirability of any possible outcome (a social niche) to the evaluator can be equally measured by the evaluator's own utility function or by the utility function of the observed inhabitant of the particular niche involved. Of course, the remedy is quite drastic, the assumption of identical tastes being itself capable of simplifying away most of the normative problems to which the present book is devoted.

discussion here concentrated largely on the existence of positive attitudes toward characteristics of the probability distribution of utility outcomes other than the mean. In addition we were led, by way of a discussion of uncertain choice situations to which the present theory may be poorly applicable, to reinterpret the alternatives of choice with which our enquiry is fundamentally concerned. This reinterpretation, in the light of the aforementioned limitation of scope of the expected utility theory, raised doubts that cardinal scaling of these alternatives is empirically feasible. It is an open question how serious are the possible refutations and the more fundamental doubts. Our discussion suggests that the question is an urgent one.

APPENDIX 1:

Debate on the Strong Independence Assumption

Critics of the Strong Independence Assumption agree that in the case of a single event either f or h can occur but not both. However, they argue that what is envisaged in the assumption, especially given the use of probabilities a and $1 - a$ in the limit of relative frequency sense,[1] is a repetition of the gamble a large number of times. If this is so, then the consumer can expect $af + (1 - a)h$ to mean a steady *flow of both f and h* in the proportions a and $1 - a$ respectively, over the duration of the repeated plays. Since, even in static ordinal (nonstochastic) theory, related commodities are not literally consumed simultaneously, and significant time may often pass between their consumption, it is argued that, in this analogue to the static situation of continued unchanging flows, there may well be a similarly adequate temporal proximity in consumption of the two commodities (or commodity bundles) to make the same relatedness apply in the two situations.[2]

This argument is defective[3] because it juxtaposes two assertedly similar situations which are not in principle comparable. The nonstochastic case of repeated flows does not involve mutually exclusive events, since ordinal

---

[1]"Probability has often been visualized as a subjective concept more or less in the nature of an estimation. Since we propose to use it in constructing an individual, numerical estimation of utility, the *above view* of probability would not serve our purpose. The simplest procedure is, therefore, to insist upon the alternative, perfectly well-founded interpretation of probability as frequency in long runs. This gives directly the necessary numerical foothold." (von Neumann and Morgenstern, *The Theory of Games*, p. 19) It should be pointed out that the frequency interpretation is not the only interpretation possible for this derivation. The authors go on to suggest that in the event the frequency interpretation is not accepted, preference and probability can be axiomatized together.

[2]Cf. Manne, *op. cit.*, 667.

[3]My evaluation is based on Samuelson, "Probability, Utility and the Independence Axiom," 673-677.

theory clearly envisages orderings of alternative time profiles of consumption, and commodity bundles to be consumed at one time point on each profile will certainly influence the ordering of commodity bundles to be consumed at other points. Ordinary commodity relatedness surely applies here.

In contrast, the stochastic situation comparable to this is not the choice of a single gamble. It is, rather, the choice of a time profile of specific gamble commitments which will be made with all contingent relationships detailed. In Samuelson's terms it is the advance specification of a strategy which will "cover all possible actual outcomes of chance and decision problems."[4] Each strategy will result in a probability for every possible time profile outcome. Thus, in the comparable stochastic case to which the Independence Assumption applies, different time profiles will be mutually exclusive, and although *within each*, commodity relatedness applies, *between any two* no such relatedness is relevant.

The moral of the foregoing is that "the independence axiom must always be applied to a definite set of entities . . . . The independence axiom then has implications and restrictions upon choices among such entities; but strictly speaking, it need not impose restrictions upon some different (and perhaps simpler) set of entities."[5] The fruitfulness of the expected utility theory lies in "finding a significant range of human behavior that can to a satisfactory degree of approximation be accounted for by the Bernoulli concepts as applied to a finite, specifiable, and convenient set of entities."[6]

APPENDIX 2:

A Non-Probabilistic Model of Uncertainty

G. L. S. Shackle has advanced[1] what seems to be an empirical generalization of choosing behavior under uncertainty which dispenses with the notion of probability. The formulation of risk estimates in this schema are not adequate for the expected utility axiomatization. I am presenting it, therefore, not as a substitute calculus for use in the Bernoulli hypothesis, nor even as an alternative model of the Social Welfare Function, but solely to throw light on those aspects of choice under uncertainty which assertedly seem inappropriately treated in the expected utility approach.

---

[4]*Ibid.*, 676.

[5]Samuelson, *loc. cit.* Examples of kinds of entities which might be dealt with by expected utility theory are: "(1) single-event money prizes, (2) single-event vectors of goods, (3) single-event money prizes *cum* gaining and suspense feelings, (4) stationary plateaus of money or of goods-vectors, and (5) alternative time profiles of goods, with or without associated suspense sensations, etc." (p. 676).

[6]*Ibid.*, 677.

[1]*Expectation in Economics.*

Shackle argues that individuals, when forced to choose in situations where precise numerical probabilities are not in practice discoverable, do not make estimates of these probabilities, but rather gauge their "potential surprise" at the various possible outcomes. The "potential surprise" affixed to an outcome measures only the degree of surprise that an individual expects he would feel if the outcome were to occur. Potential surprise can vary from zero, where the individual would be not at all surprised, to infinity, where the individual would feel the outcome to be impossible; but these numbers can be treated only as ordinal indicators.

Potential surprise is non-additive, so that the measure for any one outcome is independent of how many other possible outcomes are envisioned, and independent of the potential surprise of these other possible outcomes. A sure prospect, or certainty of some A, would translate into zero surprise for outcome A and infinite surprise for all other outcomes. Complete uncertainty, where the individual has no information about the likelihood of different outcomes occurring, would translate into *zero* surprise for an innumerable number (n) of outcomes (in comparison with classical probability where the probability of each outcome is very *small* — $1/n$). A feature of the nonadditivity of potential surprise is that if we have a given potential surprise distribution, and then we introduce the possibility that an additional outcome might occur, the introduction of this new possible outcome need not (but might) change the potential surprise of a single other outcome! In the probability calculus, the introduction of the new outcome would necessarily change some or all previously assigned probabilities since the sum must always equal unity.

Another aspect of non-additivity is the way in which an individual responds to his potential surprise distribution. In the probability calculus, the individual is thought to be able to "sum up" an entire probability distribution, to *combine* in his mind mutually exclusive events, so that he holds them simultaneously in his mind. Shackle believes that individuals do not perform this feat. Rather, the individual obtains a particular stimulation, positive or negative, in considering each possible outcome with its associated potential surprise. Of all the outcomes, one will afford the greatest stimulation of possible gains; another (with its associated potential surprise) will afford the greatest stimulation of possible losses. These are the "focus gain" and "focus loss," respectively. Every alternative action has a potential surprise distribution, hence a focus gain and loss.[2] The individual evaluates each action solely in terms of this selected pair of possible outcomes. He chooses among alternative actions by ordering these

---

[2]To make these comparable, the individual presumably compares each focus outcome to that outcome which, if associated with zero potential surprise, would afford the same stimulation. These are the *standardized* focus-gain and *standardized* focus-loss, respectively.

standardized focus pairs (in terms of a "gambler indifference map"). Summating each action into *two* outcomes instead of one indicates that people behave asymmetrically with respect to gains and losses.

Shackle's theory is an empirical hypothesis about individual choosing behavior when faced with uncertainty. It is capable of empirical specification like the Bernoulli hypothesis. A suggested procedure for making such specification and for testing its consequences has been given by Arrow.[3] The theory has not been tested, but it does possess some consequences which appear unsatisfactory. For one thing, "there is no law of large numbers, . . . [so] no amount of repetition in independent trials would lead to a reduction of risks . . . . [It] does not lead, even in the limit [where there is justification for the probability calculus], to the probability theory."[4] Other difficulties, of a rather technical nature, have been pointed out.[5]

APPENDIX 3:

A Proof on Interchangeability

We shall prove here that the restrictions in Hildreth's model are equivalent to the Interchangeability condition. (See pp. 182, 190 ff.)

This can be proved as follows. We may remember that Interchangeability involves restricting each individual utility index and its weighting in the Social Welfare Function, so that a unit change in every individual's utility results in the same change in social welfare. Now Hildreth's comparable restrictions are:

(1) there are at least two social states (say $\bar{x}$, $\bar{y}$) which are similarly ordered by every individual;

(2) "the social ordering is independent of the way in which (utility) indices are assigned to individuals." (Hildreth, p. 86.)

What do we mean by "assigning" or reassigning utility indices to the several individuals in the population? A utility index is a scaling instrument like, say, a thermometer. Just as a certain heated body will register one number of degrees on a Fahrenheit scale and a different number of degrees on a centigrade scale, so we will suppose that we, the economists, possess indices of different calibrations such that a given preference intensity for some individual registers a different index number on one

---

[3] "Alternative Approaches to the Theory of Choice in Risk-Taking Situations," *Econometrica*, Vol. 19, No. 4 (October, 1951), 419-420, 432-434.

[4] *Ibid.*, 419-420.

[5] *Ibid.*, 433; J. de V. Graaff, and W. J. Baumol, "Three Notes on 'Expectations in Economics', II," *Economica*, New Series, Vol. 16 (November, 1949), 338-342..

index than on another. Suppose, furthermore that we possess as many "utility thermometers" (each containing, figuratively, a different expansive "substance") as there are individuals in the population. An assignment of indices simply means to measure the preferences of the population for the various alternatives by distributing these "utility thermometers" among the population in a particular way. Hildreth's second restriction, then, requires that the social ordering between any two alternatives must be the same no matter what particular distribution of these "thermometers" is decided upon. Superficially, this certainly appears a reasonable requirement.

Let us examine the relationship between these various utility indicators. Hildreth, by assuming the meaningfulness of reassignments (or interchanges) of indicators to different individuals, is tacitly assuming that interpersonal comparisons of utility are matters of fact, or, more simply, that the utilities of different persons are comparable. To see this, assume that they are not. Then the utility indicators of different individuals will be measuring different *kinds* of things. For instance, one may be measuring temperature and another measuring the number of apples. Now, what meaning can there be to counting apples with a gadget that measures temperature? And vice versa? To bring the matter home, assume that one indicator counts apples and the other counts peaches. Can we interchange these indicators? Not if one gadget can only count apples and the other only peaches. We can interchange them if both can count fruit, or round objects, or even just "things." But then what each was really counting before the interchange was not apples, or peaches, but fruit, or round objects, or "things." Both indicators were before and after the interchange counting comparable entities. The same is true of utility indicators.

Now, assume we have three indicators: one that measures "true" utility for any individual (U^0) and two others ($\overline{U}$, and $\underline{U}$ respectively). $\overline{U}$ and $\underline{U}$ have different scales and zero points from U^0, and let us assume for simplicity that any one scale is a linear transform of any other. Thus, $\overline{U} = p_1 U^0 + p_2(p_1, p_2$ are constants), $\underline{U} = q_1 U^0 + q_2(q_1, q_2$ are constants). Then,
$$\overline{U} = p_1(\underline{U} - q_2) \div q_1 + p_2 = p_1 \underline{U} \div q_1 + (p_2 - p_1 q_2 + q_1) = r\underline{U} + t.$$
We can express any two linear functions of some "true" indicator as a linear function of each other. When we interchange utility indicators, therefore, we shall be substituting linear transforms.

Our problem is to discover the necessary relationship between all such indicators such that our Social Welfare Function is the unique sum of weighted individual utilities, and orderings derived from this Social Welfare Function are invariant under all interchanges of indicators to members of the group.

$$(1) \qquad\qquad U(x) = \Sigma\, w^i U^i(x)$$

where $U(x)$ is the social utility value, $U^i(x)$ is the utility function of individual i, w^i is the weight attached to the utility of individual i.

The social ordering between alternatives x and y will be determined by $V_{xy} \gtreqless 0$ where

(2) $\qquad V_{xy} \equiv U(x) - U(y) = \Sigma\, w^i[U^i(x) - U^i(y)] \equiv \Sigma\, w^i y_{xy}{}^i.$

Consider this ordering explicitly as a function of the utility differences in individuals 1's and 2's utility indicators, $\overline{V}_{xy}$ and $\underline{V}_{xy}$ respectively.

(3) $\qquad V_{xy} = w^1 \overline{V}_{xy}{}^1 + w^2 \underline{V}_{xy}{}^2 + \sum_{i=3}^{m} w^i V_{xy}{}^i,$

where, e.g., $\overline{V}^1 = \overline{U}^1(x) - \overline{U}^1(y)$, or

(4) $\qquad w^1 \overline{V}_{xy}{}^1 + w^2 \underline{V}_{xy}{}^2 = k$

where

$$k = V_{xy} - \sum_{3}^{m} w^i V_{xy}{}^i, \quad \text{and} \quad \overline{V} = r\underline{V}$$

Now we shall interchange indicators, so that $\overline{V}$ will apply to individual 2 and $\underline{V}$ will apply to individual 1. It is very important whether we interpret Hildreth's condition as asserting that the weights w^1 and w^2 are to be interchanged as well. Since in his treatment the only possible source of unequal weight on social welfare stems from the utility indicators, we may proceed either as though equal weights have already been assumed (Property 1 of Interchangeability), or that the weights are assigned not to the different individuals but to the different utility indicators. Let us therefore rewrite Equation 4 to emphasize this attachment:

(4a) $\qquad \overline{w}\overline{V}_{xy}{}^1 + \underline{w}\underline{V}_{xy}{}^2 = k.$

When we interchange indicators the social ordering must be unchanged. Since this must hold for *all* x, y and all pairs of individuals, the following must hold:

(5) $\qquad \underline{w}\underline{V}_{xy}{}^1 + \overline{w}\overline{V}_{xy}{}^2 = k.$

To see this assume instead

(5a) $\qquad \underline{w}\underline{V}_{xy}{}^1 + \overline{w}\overline{V}_{xy}{}^2 \overset{\cdot}{>} k.$

Now, since $\sum_{3}^{m} w^i V_{xy}{}^i$ is unchanged by the interchange, Equation 5a implies that $V_{xy}{}^* > V_{xy}$ (where $V_{xy}{}^*$ is the social utility change as calculated by interchanged indicators). Therefore, if $V_{xy} = 0$ (x and y are indifferent), $V_{xy}{}^* > 0$ (x is preferred to y) violates the condition; similarly, since the condition is to hold for all x, y, we can choose x, y such that V_{xy} will be less than, but arbitrarily close to, 0. Then $V_{xy}* > V_{xy}$ would again violate the condition.

The same argument holds for $\underline{w}\underline{V}_{xy}{}^1 + \overline{w}\overline{V}_{xy}{}^2 < 0$.

From Equations 4a and 5 we obtain

(6) $$\overline{w}\overline{V}_{xy}{}^1 - \overline{w}\overline{V}_{xy}{}^2 = \underline{w}\underline{V}_{xy}{}^1 - \underline{w}\underline{V}_{xy}{}^2.$$

Since $\overline{V} = r\underline{V}$ we obtain

$$r\overline{w}\underline{V}_{xy}{}^1 - r\overline{w}\underline{V}_{xy}{}^2 = \underline{w}\underline{V}_{xy}{}^1 - \underline{w}\underline{V}_{xy}{}^2$$

(7) $$\underline{V}_{xy}{}^1(r\overline{w} - \underline{w}) = \underline{V}_{xy}{}^2(r\overline{w} - \underline{w})$$

for all x, y, and all 1, 2.

Hildreth goes a little further under the implicit assumption that $\overline{w} = \underline{w}$ for all 1, 2. By his first restriction cited, everyone orders $\bar{x}$ and $\bar{y}$ similarly, so that $U^i(\bar{x}) - U^i(\bar{y}) \equiv V_{xy}{}^i$ can be defined as the common unit of measurement for everyone's utility scale. Each scale is unique as far as the zero point, since we may arbitrarily set $\overline{U}(\bar{x}) = a$ and $U(\bar{y}) = b$.

Equation 7 has two possible solutions. First, $\underline{V}_{xy}{}^1 = \underline{V}_{xy}{}^2$ for all x, y and all 1, 2. This means that all individuals have identical tastes — a trivial solution. Second, $r\overline{w} - \underline{w} = 0$, or $r\overline{w} = \underline{w}$. But by Equation 4, $\overline{V} = r\underline{V} = \underline{V}(\underline{w} \div \overline{w})$, so $\overline{w}\overline{V} = \underline{w}\underline{V}$ for all i. This means that a unit change in every individual's utility indicator represents the same change in group welfare. It is, of course, Armstrong's condition, and it combines the two properties of the Interchangeability condition (since if $\overline{w} = \underline{w}$ for all i, then $r = 1$). This concludes our proof that Hildreth's second restriction is a sufficient condition, in the presence of cardinal utility, for the fulfillment of interchangeability.

To show that it is a necessary condition is equivalent to showing that if we have Interchangeability we must have fulfillment of Hildreth's restriction (i.e., that Interchangeability is a sufficient condition for Hildreth's restriction). Thus, we have $\overline{w}\overline{V}^1 = \underline{w}\underline{V}^2$, $r = 1$, and $\overline{w} = \underline{w}$. Now interchange indicators. We have

(8) $$\begin{cases} \overline{w}\overline{V}_{xy}{}^1 + \underline{w}\underline{V}_{xy}{}^2 = k \quad \text{and} \\ \underline{w}\underline{V}_{xy}{}^1 + \overline{w}\overline{V}_{xy}{}^2 = k \end{cases}$$

since $\underline{w}\underline{V}_{xy}{}^1 = \overline{w}\overline{V}_{xy}{}^1$ (because $\underline{V} = \overline{V}$) and $\underline{w}\underline{V}_{xy}{}^2 = \overline{w}\overline{V}_{xy}{}^2$. But Equation 8 satisfies Hildreth's restriction. So this and Interchangeability are necessary and sufficient for one another; they are logically equivalent.

Part IV

A MIXED MODEL

CHAPTER 11

Single-Peakedness and Consensus

11-1. Single Peakedness and an Acceptable Social Welfare Function

Let us reconsider the so-called "Paradox of Voting" presented in Chapter 2. Three alternatives A, B, and C are ordered by three individuals as follows: for number 1, ABC; for number 2, BCA; for number 3, CAB. By majority vote A is preferred to B, and also B is preferred to C. Transitivity for social choice would require that A be preferred to C. But in fact by majority vote C is preferred to A.

This paradox was advanced as an example of the difficulty which Arrow's Possibility Theorem generalizes. It is conceivable that if we discover the source of intransitivity in this situation we may in turn generalize for the Possibility Theorem itself.

It has been suggested that the difficulty stems from an inadequate analysis of the voting situation presented, and a consequently unreasonable identification of social choice. To elaborate:

> We are not 'forced' to say that A is preferred to C [when A is preferred to B and B preferred to C] unless we first postulate a 'community' preference that is different from the preferences of the people in it. We are no more 'forced' to say that the 'community' prefers A to C than we are 'forced' to say it prefers C to A, or B to C. Two people prefer A to B; two (a different pair) prefer B to C; and two (still a third pair) prefer C to A; conversely two people would vote against A as the *most* desirable alternative, another pair would vote against B as the *most* desirable alternative, and a third pair would vote against C as the *most* desirable alternative. In this situation one can only say

that the majority is not agreed on the most desirable alternative; nor is any one choice more rational than the others. There is no 'community' preference.[1]

The criticism emphasizes that the composition of the voting majorities in the paradox situation is not the same. Though it is not unreasonable to ask that the choices made by a given majority be transitive, it *is* unreasonable to expect transitivity of the separate choices made by different majorities. Only if the same two individuals preferred A to B and B to C should we expect that *they* also would prefer A to C. But this requirement could be met quite easily; we should simply require that each individual's ordering be transitive.

The criticism appears ill-founded. First, when we consider majority rule as a possible Social Welfare Function we do not by any means suggest that the social choices in such a situation be the choices made by an unchanging majority group in the population. In a real sense such a proposal would amount to disenfranchising perhaps a substantial segment of the electorate. Majority rule as a Social Welfare Function identifies every choice supported by a majority of the electorate as the social choice, regardless of the composition of the majority. This is significant because in communities which actually make decisions through majority voting, the composition of the majority generally differs from one issue to the next.[2]

Furthermore, it can be shown that the source of the paradox does not even reside in the differing composition of the majority. Thus, let us make a simple modification in the ordering of individual number 3. Instead of CAB, let us assume that his ordering is CBA. Now it is still true that a majority opposes each alternative as the most desirable alternative. Yet a majority prefer B to C and also C to A, and the required transitive choice C over A is now borne out by a direct comparison between the two! A transitive social choice is forthcoming even though the composition of the majority changes for different pairs of alternatives (there is one majority for BC, another for CA and BA) in this situation as well as in the one presented above.

Is the success of the modified ordering for individual number 2 in giving us transitive social choices accidental, or can it be generalized? Important contributions by Duncan Black which developed formal resemblances in the content of political science and economics prove that our modification can be generalized.[3]

---

[1]Robert A. Dahl, and Charles E. Lindblom, *Politics, Economics and Welfare* (New York: Harper & Brothers, Publishers, 1953), 423.

[2]Despite the fact that in many such communities the majority on many issues over certain time intervals is apt to contain a common core.

[3]"On the Rationale of Group Decision-Making," *Journal of Political Economy*, Vol. LVI, No. 1 (February, 1948), 23-34; "The Decisions of a Committee Using a Special

Briefly, the generalization involves imposing a restriction called "single-peakedness" on all admissible individual orderings. Consider the following sets of individual orderings of four alternatives w, x, y, z.

Individual	Set 1	Set 2
Number 1	$w \, x \, y \, z$	$w \, x \, y \, z$
Number 2	$x \, y \, w \, z$	$w \, z \, x \, y$
Number 3	$y \, z \, x \, w$	$w \, y \, x \, z$

Figure 13(a) is a graphic representation of Set 1 orderings and figure 13(b) a graphic representation of Set 2 orderings. The relative heights of

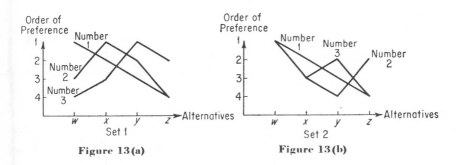

Figure 13(a)   **Figure 13(b)**

the function at different alternative abscissas represent only preference order — the higher the function, the higher the ranking of the given alternative in the preference order. Set 1 is a set of individual orderings all of which fulfill the condition of single-peakedness. The orderings of Set 2 do not. The crucial difference is that set 1 is such that there is at least one arrangement of the alternatives along the horizontal dimension of the figure such that plotting the individual preference orders *for such an arrangement* gives rise to curves *all of which* have a single peak and rise throughout toward this peak from both directions without reverse movement. (Actually, of course, for every one there will be a second possible arrangement for which this will be true when the orderings are single-peaked. The second is always the exact opposite of the first. Thus, for Set 1, the arrangement $z \, y \, x \, w$ would suffice as well.) For Set 2 there is no arrangement of alternatives for which this will be true. Inspection of Figure 13 by the reader will verify this.

If all individual orderings are single-peaked, the method of majority rule

Majority," *Econometrica*, Vol. 16, No. 3 (July, 1948), 245-261; "The Elasticity of Committee Decisions with an Altering Size of Majority," *Econometrica* (July, 1948), 262-270. Also see the description in Arrow, *Social Choice and Individual Values*, 75-80. For an extended treatment of this and other materials, see D. Black, *The Theory of Committees and Elections* (Cambridge: Cambridge University Press, 1958).

will give rise to a connex and transitive social ordering of alternatives for which Arrow's Conditions 2 through 5 apply.[4]

Let us first examine how choices are made under majority rule when individual preferences are single-peaked. The procedure envisaged by Black is a series of votes on the various alternatives, whereby each pair of alternatives is put to a vote.[5] For any set of m alternatives, this will require $m(m-1)/2$ separate votes.[6] The chosen alternative is that one which receives a majority vote when placed against every other alternative. The alternative second in the social ordering is that which can obtain a majority vote against all but the chosen alternative. Third in the social ordering is that alternative which can obtain a majority against all but the first two alternatives, etc.

Now consider Figure 14.

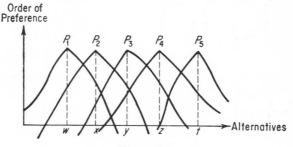

Figure 14

Each of the curves represents an individual ordering of the five alternatives. There are five individuals. Place w against each other alternative. It is evident that it will not be chosen. Against, e.g., x, it will receive only the vote of the individual (number 1) who has his peak there. The other individuals all will vote for x since their respective peaks are "closer" to x than to w; under single-peakedness the greater the "distance" of alternatives from the alternative most preferred, the lower in the preference ordering that alternative will be. Similarly, while x will defeat w and *may* be able to defeat both z and t,[7] it will be defeated by y. Alternative y, however, will defeat w by at least 3 to 2 (and by 4 to 1 if individual number 2 prefers y to x); it will defeat x by 3 to 2; for exactly the same reasons y will defeat

---

[4]Assuming also that the number of individuals is odd.

[5]The following leans heavily on Black, "On the Rationale of Group Decision-Making."

[6]Each alternative is placed against every other alternative. The necessary number of votes is the number of combinations of m things taken two at a time.

[7]Whether it can or not depends on the individual orderings of alternatives in second, third, fourth, etc., places. In this example we are concentrating on the individuals' first choices only. Indeed, that we may do this and obtain the same social ordering as when entire orderings are considered on every vote is an important property of this method. Some of its implications will be explored later.

both z and t. Alternative y can win a majority over every other alternative. By the same kind of calculation we see that neither z nor t can win a majority over every other alternative. Indeed, it is not even necessary to perform these calculations since we already know that y can win universal majority and consequently, whenever *any* other alternative is placed against it, that alternative will lose. For a given set of individual orderings, there is never more than one alternative that can obtain a majority over every other.

It is worth emphasizing the consideration that enabled our voting to render a determinate verdict. By the assumption of single-peakedness, all individuals arrange the alternatives in the same pattern and their preferences bear a similarity of structure. We may therefore introduce the concept of "betweenness."[8] Consider the preference scales of three individuals: $x\,y\,z\,w$, $z\,y\,x\,w$, $y\,z\,w\,x$. We shall attempt to give them a diagrammatic interpretation by means of an array of the three alternatives in a single spatial dimension. Consider the first scale. Define the owner of the scale as being "located" at that point on the array which corresponds to his most preferred alternative. Then the relative position of alternatives on either side of this "location" is determined by the owner's preference order for those alternatives, such that the greater the distance of a given alternative from the "location" — *in terms of the number of alternatives between it and the most favored alternative* — the lower it stands on the preference scale.

For any two alternatives in the same direction from the most preferred alternative, the more preferred alternative will be nearer to the "location" than will the less preferred; the former will be "between" the most preferred alternative and the latter.[9] Now, from the ordering $x\,y\,z\,w$ we can construct all of the following arrays, among others, by following these rules:

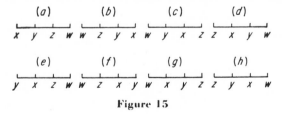

Figure 15

<hr />

[8] Cf. Arrow, *Social Choice*, 77.

[9] We emphasize that distance is measured only in terms of the number of intervening alternatives to point up the fact that the spatial scale is not a true metric. Although a given ordering can be "located" completely on a spatial array, a given "location" on a particular array does not, in general, enable us to infer backwards the original ordering. All we can infer is a lattice, a partial ordering for the alternatives on each side of the "location" consistent with the original complete ordering. Alternatives on one side cannot be compared to alternatives on the other. For a full discussion of the logic of the spatial array and the assumption necessary to convert it into a true metric, see the author's, *The Theory of Economic and Political Decision Making as a Single System*, forthcoming.

(Since we are interested only in relative positions and not left-right orientation, we can ignore inversions (b), (d), (f), and (h) as superfluous.) From $x\,y\,z\,w$ we *cannot* construct the following arrays (neglecting, among others, simple inversions):

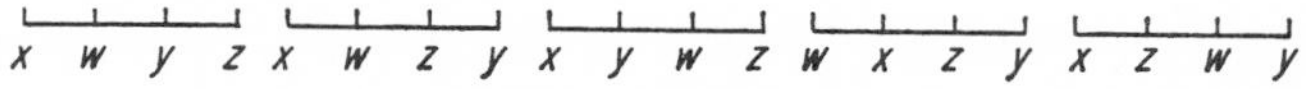

$$x\ w\ y\ z \qquad x\ w\ z\ y \qquad x\ y\ w\ z \qquad w\ x\ z\ y \qquad x\ z\ w\ y$$

Figure 16

All the scales of Figure 15 are equally compatible with $x\,y\,z\,w$;[10] all those of Figure 16 are incompatible with $x\,y\,z\,w$.

Consider the second preference scale: $z\,y\,x\,w$. This can generate a large family of spatial arrays; but of those compatible with the first ordering, only 15(a) and (g) are compatible with the second as well. Consider the third: $y\,z\,w\,x$. Of these latter two, only (a) in Figure 15 is compatible with $y\,z\,w\,x$ and therefore with all three. Our rules for generating spatial arrays are identical with the requirement for single-peakedness. We find here that only (a) is consistent with all three individual orderings. It is the uniquely appropriate array to describe these orderings.[11] For any one of the orderings, "preference betweenness" (i.e., y is "between" x and z, if and only if, either $x\,y\,z$ or $z\,y\,x$) is fixed, while "spatial betweenness" can take on the pattern of any compatible array. For all three orderings together, however, "preference betweenness" varies for the different orderings, but "spatial betweenness" is fixed. The contrast is not complete, however. "Spatial betweenness" between any two alternatives on this "group array" takes on the interpretation of "preference betweenness" for whichever ordering of the two alternatives occur on the same side of the most preferred alternative. Group spatial betweenness therefore represents a contingent "preference betweenness."

We see that the assumption of single-peakedness fixes a set of spatial betweenness relationships among the alternatives which is consistent with the orderings of all individuals, i.e., consistent with the existence of a spatial array of alternatives on which all individuals can be "located."[12] Thus, in any vote, say between x and y, if x is spatially arrayed to the left of y, *every* individual who has his "peak" to the right of y and prefers that

---

[10]Note, however, that in Figure 15, (a) (and (b)) alone of all enable us to deduce the complete ordering. Each of the others makes a different set of alternative pairs non-comparable.

[11]If we add $z\,x\,y\,w$ to the group, there is no array which is compatible with all. The group violates single-peakedness.

[12]It is a necessary but not a sufficient condition for similarity. If an individual *has* a betweenness relationship among a given three alternatives (say x, y, z), then it must not be inconsistent with the betweenness among the same three alternatives for any other individual. But he may *not* have a betweenness for x, y, z. Thus, he may be indifferent between two of the three or all three.

peak alternative to y, will also prefer y to x (and, indeed, to any alternative to the left of y) since y will be between that peak and x for every individual. Thus, a knowledge of the distribution of preference peaks suffices to determine the socially most preferred alternative in the manner described above.

We may now generalize the social choice procedure which selected y. What is the distinguishing characteristic of this alternative? It is not that y is the median alternative, as might be thought at first glance. This is immediately demonstrable. Suppose we enlarge our population by two, both of whom have their preference peaks at w.[13] Now, alternative x can defeat y as well as every other alternative. So with no change in the number of alternatives the first choice of the group may nonetheless change. It is evident that the alternative getting first choice will be the median *preference peak*.[14] In the situation of Figure 14, two individuals had preference peaks to the left of y, two to the right of y, and one at y. Alternative y was the median peak. In the modified situation with seven individuals, three had peaks to the left of x (all at w), three to the right of x and one at x. x is the median peak.[15]

Up to now we have indicated only how the first choice is made, not how the entire social ordering can be derived. In one sense, for policy implementation, only this is relevant. But there is something to be gained from an examination of the entire ordering. For one thing, one can discover whether the first choice is a true first choice by testing for transitivity. For another, one more clearly understands the nature of the Social Welfare Function by comparing the social ordering with the individual orderings that determined it.

In order to derive the complete social ordering, we must specify the complete orderings of our individuals.

From the data of Figure 14 let us suppose the orderings are as follows:[16]

---

[13]For simplicity we assume that neither individual is indifferent between any two alternatives.

[14]"Median preference peak" and "median alternative" are meaningful terms only because single-peakedness imposes a uniform arrangement of alternatives for all individuals. Without the assumption of single-peakedness, "median" is without meaning.

[15]It can now be seen why the acceptability of majority rule under single-peakedness as a Social Welfare Function depends on the number of voters being odd. When there is an even number of voters there *may* be no median peak and hence no alternative which is capable of securing majority support against every other alternative.

Black gives a solution to the case of an even number of voters. But it depends upon the somewhat different context of his model. He is elaborating an abstract model of a committee where, in addition to voting committee members, there is a committee chairman who is allowed to vote only when there is otherwise a tie. In effect, then, his model guarantees an odd number of voters when needed and, consequently, guarantees the existence of a median peak.

[16]It will be noticed that they are all single-peaked, i.e., compatible with the "betweenness" relationship in the context of the particular arrangement of alternatives w-x-y-z-t.

Individual	Set 1	Set 2
Number 1	$w\,x\,y\,z\,t$	$w\,x\,z\,t$
Number 2	$x\,w\,y\,z\,t$	$x\,w\,z\,t$
Number 3	$y\,z\,x\,t\,w$	$z\,x\,t\,w$
Number 4	$z\,y\,t\,x\,w$	$z\,t\,x\,w$
Number 5	$t\,z\,y\,x\,w$	$t\,z\,x\,w$

From this set of orderings (set 1), the alternative y was chosen. To determine second choice, let us assume that y is no longer available. In effect we now have the orderings of set 2. It is crucial to note that if set 1 obeys the assumption of single-peakedness then so too will set 2 (for the same arrangement of available alternatives). We may therefore proceed with this set to select a first choice by the method of majority rule exactly as we did when y was available. Alternative z is now the median peak and will be chosen; z is second in the social ordering. Similarly, x will be third, t will be fourth, w fifth. Our social order is consequently $y\,z\,x\,t\,w$.

It is easy to see that this ordering is transitive. y was chosen over z, and z over x, and also y over x; z was chosen over x, x over t, and also z over t, etc. This is no accident. The majority rule ordering under single-peakedness will always be transitive.[17]

The dependence of transitivity on single-peakedness can be seen again by a slight modification in set 1. Assume that individual number 4's ordering is $z\,x\,y\,t\,w$ instead of $z\,y\,t\,x\,w$; it is no longer single-peaked. Now, x can defeat y despite the fact that y remains the median peak; x can get a 3:2 majority vote over y. x is socially preferred to y. Similarly, y can defeat z by a 3:2 majority; y is socially preferred to z. But z can still defeat x in a direct vote, 3:2; z is socially preferred to x. Consequently we have here *no* social rank ordering; majority rule gives rise to an intransitive relation.

This example does not assert that every possible set of individual orderings in which there is a single departure from single-peakedness will give rise to intransitivity. Indeed, such an assertion would be incorrect. Thus, for example, if our violation of single-peakedness had resulted from changing individual number 1's ordering from $w\,x\,y\,z\,t$ to $w\,t\,x\,y\,z$, then the social ordering would have changed to $y\,z\,t\,x\,w$, but would remain transitive.[18] What our example above does signify is that, since no other restrictions of individual orderings are imposed on the model, any departure from single-peakedness *might* lead to intransitivity. As soon as we relax our assumption we are no longer guaranteed that majority rule will give rise to a transitive social ordering.

Under single-peakedness we are guaranteed a transitive ordering rela-

---

[17]For a general proof, see Arrow, *Social Choice*, 77-79.
[18]This can be checked by inspection.

tion. This relation, moreover, will be connex so long as there is an odd number of voters. And Arrow has shown that majority rule under all circumstances, e.g., without single-peakedness and with an even number of voters, will always fulfill Conditions 2 through 5.[19] Indeed, this would appear intuitively evident. The ordering does not respond negatively to individual ordering changes, it is obviously neither imposed nor dictatorial, and the social ordering between any two alternatives depends only on the individual orderings of these two (since the social ordering derives from a direct vote between them and the outcome of this vote depends only on individual preferences between the two.[20] But of course single-peakedness does violate Condition 1. There can be no free triple of admissible alternatives. The generally unique (but always possessing restrictive power) spatial betweenness relationship imposed by single-peakedness will always make some individual orderings incompatible with them and be therefore inadmissible. Single-peakedness succeeds in guaranteeing that majority rule will generate transitive social orderings, but at the cost of Condition 1.

11-2. Voting Sequence and the Social Ordering

In the last section we noted that the procedure through which the social orderings was to be derived from majority rule was a placing of each alternative against every other, a total of $m(m - 1) \div 2$ votes in all, when the number of alternatives is m. Black argues that the assumption of single-peakedness enables us to dispense with so cumbersome a procedure. We can obtain the same ordering with a simplified procedure. Take any alternative and put it against any other for a vote. Consider the alternative which is defeated as eliminated from further consideration. Place the victorious alternative against some other. Now one of these will be eliminated. Place the victorious alternative, whichever it is, against another alternative, etc. After all alternatives have been voted on at least once, all but one will have been eliminated. The alternative remaining is the first choice of the community. This procedure requires only $m - 1$ votes, which is considerably less than $m(m - 1) \div 2$ when m is appreciably greater than 2.

That the first choice under this procedure is the same as under the extended vote of the last section follows easily from the transitivity of the social ordering. At some point in the voting, given the individual orderings of set 1, alternative y will be introduced. At whatever point this is, it will thenceforth fail to be displaced, since it can defeat every other alternative. Hence, it will be first choice under the simplified voting procedure as well.

---

[19]Arrow, *Social Choice*, 46-48.
[20]However, see below for a qualification of this.

The same is true of second, third, fourth, etc., choices. The social ordering will be identical under both procedures.[21]

To illustrate the dependence of this result on the transitivity of the original social ordering, let us assume that alternative y can defeat x, x can defeat z, and z can defeat y. Which of the alternatives will be chosen under the simplified "challenge" voting procedure depends on the order in which they are introduced into the voting. If x is put against y, y will eliminate x but will in turn be eliminated by z. If x is put against z, z will be eliminated, and then y will eliminate x. If y is put against z, y will be eliminated, and z will be eliminated by x. Under intransitivity the two voting procedures will not necessarily give rise to equivalent social choices. In particular, the choice under "challenge" voting is a function of the specific sequence of challenges employed.

Despite the foregoing, an important qualification must be made even under single-peakedness, to guarantee that the two procedures will render identical choices. It is not enough that individual orderings be single-peaked. In addition, the individuals must actually vote in accordance with their orderings! But do individuals ever have incentives to vote in any way other than according to their orderings? The answer is that they do, if a different voting strategy seems to promise an *outcome* closer to their preferences. In other words, an individual may vote at odds with his preferences for the sole purpose of bringing about an outcome in accordance with his preferences! Strategic masking or distorting of preferences would appear to be far more likely under the "challenge" voting procedure than under the first, full vote sequence. This can be seen in the following illustration. Assume three individuals have the following orderings:

Individual	*Ordering*
Number 1	$x\ y\ z$
Number 2	$y\ z\ x$
Number 3	$z\ y\ x$

If each individual voted in accordance with his ordering, alternative y would defeat both x and z (it is the median peak). In this circumstance individual number 3 has the incentive and may have the opportunity to make z the chosen alternative. If z is put against either alternative to start the voting, this is not possible since it will sooner or later be defeated by y. But if the first vote opposes x and y, then number 3 has the incentive to vote, not for y as his ordering suggests, but for x! By masking his true preferences he enables x to defeat y *if everyone else votes according to his preferences*, and then z will go on to defeat x to become the first choice. Not everyone else has the incentive to vote according to his preferences on the

[21]Black, *op. cit.*, 29-30.

first round, however, if number 3's intentions are suspected. Thus, if number 1 guesses number 3's plan, he will in turn vote *against* x on the first vote, thereby insuring the loss to y but in this way guaranteeing that his second choice and not his third will finally win.[22]

Strategic masking of preferences can result, then, in an alternative other than the median peak being chosen, even though individual orderings are single-peaked. This difficulty should not be overestimated. Strategic considerations of the sort mentioned are important only when two conditions are met:

 (1) each voter or group of voters whose voting policies are coordinated, can (or feel that he or they can) significantly influence voting outcomes;

 (2) alternatives can be easily eliminated.

As to the first, our context is a voting procedure for the total population of the community. So the number of voters is quite large; it is not likely that individuals will often feel that their vote "counts" for so much. Of course, when there is substantial common information about probable voting direction for large groups of people, members adhering to some particular preferences may employ strategic masking under the belief that others with the same preferences will act similarly. We sometimes see this kind of situation in primaries. Or again, at some levels of public policy formation, voter groups are important, increasing the likelihood that voting strategies will be employed.

As to the second, challenge voting makes the carrying out of voting strategies feasible by enabling the single-stage elimination of alternatives; a single vote can eliminate an alternative.[23] However, the $m(m-1) \div 2$ votes of the first procedure do not lend themselves to strategic masking because they make elimination of alternatives much more cumbersome. First, intentional misrepresentation here requires voting in not one but a number of instances, and the desired misrepresentation must achieve a much more complicated goal — an entire *interrelated pattern* of distorted preferences. This is a difficult task. Second, and perhaps even more important, since the distortion is not accomplished except piecemeal over a sequence of votes, the strategic intentions of the distorter may be guessed by others who will then have incentives to change their own voting pattern, like individual number 1 in the example given above, thus, in large measure, offsetting the original strategy.

The conclusion to be drawn from this discussion of the second precondition for effective voting strategies is that our two procedures of

---

[22]Cf. Arrow, *Social Choice*, 80-81, fn. 8.

[23]Unless the method incorporates the possibility of voting to reconsider an alternative previously eliminated.

majority rule are apt to present substantially different incentives for intentional distortions of individual orderings and so are apt in actual practice to lead to non-equivalent voting outcomes. To resolve this is either to insist on the exclusive use of the first procedure or, if the experimental means should exist, to obtain knowledge of the individual orderings, and from these directly to calculate the social ordering, thereby by-passing completely any actual voting. We have already commented on the difficulty of performing this latter feat in an earlier chapter.[24]

11-3. Single-Peakedness and Consensus

What in effect are we committed to under the assumption of single-peakedness? The most striking fact would seem to be that all individuals order the alternatives of choice in such a way that a particular arrangement of these alternatives on a one-dimensioned scale becomes peculiarly meaningful. This arrangement is, indeed, a geometrical projection of preference uniformities among all the individuals, uniformities defined by the concept of "betweenness." Since it holds for all individuals, whatever their preferences, it seems reasonable to infer that, in the given community at least, the various alternatives themselves are interrelated in a way which is independent of individual orderings of these alternatives.

Consider the nature of the "arrangement" of alternatives (Figure 17).

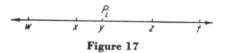

Figure 17

No matter what an individual's preferences may be, they are "consistent" with this arrangement. There would appear to be some given way in which the alternatives must be perceived for purposes of evaluating preferences. The spatial characteristics of the arrangement strongly suggest that the perceptual frame of reference is of a single underlying attribute possessed in varying degrees by the different alternatives. The spatial arrangement of alternatives is a uni-dimensional scale of some single "latent attribute"[25] calibrated by the particular alternatives. The multiple dimensions of each alternative social state *reduce* to one, a given degree of some single attribute. An individual preference scale is therefore only an ordering of different degrees of this attribute. And the problem of social

---

[24]See Chapter 4 on the Compensation principle.

[25]Cf. Clyde H. Coombs, "Psychological Scaling Without a Unit of Measurement," *Psychological Review*, Vol. 57, No. 3 (May, 1950), 145-158; also his "Theory and Methods of Social Measurement," in *Research Methods in the Behavioral Sciences*, (eds. Festinger, Leon and Katz, Daniel) (New York: Dryden Press, 1953).

choice becomes one of finding that degree which seems in some way representative of the community. In a real sense, both individual and social orderings appear to involve different quantities of a single abstract "commodity." That the problem of defining an acceptable social welfare function is solved for the case of one commodity[26] apparently has its analogue here.

The foregoing suggests a further development of the model. Consider Figure 17 again. From the spatial properties of the attribute scale as described above we may infer a concept of "distance." That the interval $\overline{xz}$ is greater than the interval $\overline{xy}$ implies either xyz or zyx for some individual, i.e., it implies that the preference intensity between x and y or y and z is less than the preference intensity between x and z. Distance represents a preference intensity on this scale even as it did on our preference continuum of Chapter 7. There is an important restriction, however. Since only the spatial betweenness in any one direction from the most favored alternative possesses a preference interpretation, similarly only distances on the same side of the individual "location" can be compared.

The assumption of single-peakedness fixes only the order in which alternatives are arranged on this scale of all individuals: it does not fix the distances between these alternatives. So each individual may possess a different scale. Consider Figure 17 as representing one such scale. The individual's preference system is comprised of his ordering of alternatives and his preference intensity between each pair of alternatives. The latter is given on our scale by the relative magnitudes of different intervals (such as $\overline{wx}$, $\overline{yz}$, etc.). Assume that his ordering is $y\ x\ z\ w\ t$. This is consistent with a scale possessing the relative interval displacements of Figure 17 and the individual "located" at point y (point P_1). The scale on each side of the individual's "location" is similar to what in psychological scaling is called a J-scale, a joint scale of both "stimuli" and "subjects."[27]

We must now examine the concept of the "distance" involved more closely. Single-peakedness involves a restriction only on the array order of alternatives. For a sufficiently large group of individuals satisfying single-peakedness, they will generally satisfy single-peakedness for one and only one spatial array. We have seen that the key relationship enabling us to project any individual preference order onto a one-dimensional space is "betweenness" which employs nothing more than transitivity of preference and is thus amenable to the comparison of preference intensities in terms of the logic of inclusiveness (the calculus of classes). A comparison of distances has implications for preference intensities only when the intervals in

---

[26]The Compensation Principle solution of simultaneous increases or decreases in *all* commodities is analogous. See Chapters 3 and 4. See also Arrow, *Social Choice*, 69-70.

[27]See Coombs, "Psychological Scaling without a Unit of Measurement."

question overlap in the same direction from the individual's most preferred alternative (his "origin"). Thus, given the array:

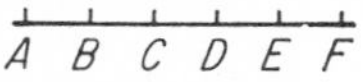

Figure 18

with the individual located at B, we can properly infer:
$$\overline{BC} < \overline{BD} < \overline{BE} < \overline{BF}$$
(with intervals reflecting preference intensities), i.e., the ordering $B\ C\ D\ E\ F$, with A appearing anywhere after B. The comparisons are equivalent to the additivity of intervals in the $B \to F$ direction, e.g.,
$$\overline{BD} = \overline{BC} + \overline{CD}.$$
This additivity is the logical core of the distance concept used here. Assume the ordering is $B\ A\ C\ D\ E\ F$. From this we would infer $\overline{BC} > \overline{AC}$. Yet spatially $\overline{BC} < \overline{AC}$. Spatial distances which straddle the "origin" (B) do not reflect preference intensities, since in terms of preference intensities,
$$\overline{AC} \neq \overline{AB} + \overline{BC}.$$
Only in the same direction from the origin are non-overlapping intervals positively additive. Indeed, in the completely metric type scale to be discussed below, distances in the opposite direction from the origin are negatively additive. But here, because they are not equivalent to inclusiveness, such distances are not comparable.

The same is true of distances on both sides of the origin which do not straddle the origin (and therefore do not overlap either). Suppose an individual is located at C. Can we deduce his whole ordering from this position? If $\overline{CB} < \overline{CD}$, then we could infer $Bp\ D$. But without knowledge about the relative spacing of alternatives, on which no restrictions are placed by single-peakedness, we cannot compare $\overline{CB}$ and $\overline{CD}$, since they are not related by inclusiveness. All we can infer is $Cp\ Dp\ Ep\ F$ and $Cp\ Bp\ A$, two partial orderings instead of one complete ordering. Our spatial continuum is not completely metrical.

By adding restrictions on the spacing of alternatives in our array, we can increase the metricality of the continuum. Consider the ordering CD $(E = B)FA$, to be projected on the array of Figure 18 so that the set of all admissible comparisons will enable us to reinfer the complete ordering. To accomplish this, alternatives must be spaced so that the following non-inclusive comparisons will be satisfied.

(1) $\overline{CE} = \overline{CB}$
(2) $\overline{CB} < \overline{CF}$
(3) $\overline{CF} < \overline{CA}$

A spacing which conforms to these conditions is shown in Figure 19.

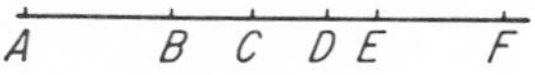

Figure 19

This is not the only scale which satisfies the conditions since the conditions only fix rather wide ranges within which the alternatives may be relatively placed. For an arbitrarily fixed low and high position, the range of indeterminacy of the alternatives' placement decreases as the number of alternatives increases. In the limit, as the number of alternatives approaches infinity, the placement of alternatives becomes uniquely determined. Thus, in the case of infinite alternatives, all distances on the continuum have preference intensity significance, distances from any alternative in one direction being positive, in the other, negative.

Each scale like that in Figure 19 is a projection of only those orderings which possess the preference intensity relationships implied by its relative spacing of alternatives [in this case, (1), (2), and (3)]. For the same number of alternatives, only one ordering does, of course, possess these. But if we had had many more alternatives, yet chose to specify only these three conditions in spacing, many orderings would be compatible. The completely metric scale (fulfilling infinitely many such conditions) is compatible with only one ordering.[27]

These remarks indicate that non-inclusive distances between alternatives on a scale for which spacing restrictions have been made do not reflect

---

[27]It is this more metrical version of the array that psychologists typically use as a J-scale. The main difference of our discussion from Coombs' usage is that ours refers to the projection of an individual ordering while Coombs' refers to that of a composite of individuals. All are assumed to perceive relative spacing of alternatives similarly and to differ only with respect to their preferred "location." In this context Coombs employs what he calls "The Unfolding Technique" to discover simultaneously the location of the individuals and some of the common constraints on spacing. This is accomplished by experimentally discovering the sequence of alternative pair mid-points via preference choices in the group. This technique allows individuals to be located *between* alternatives as well as *at* alternatives. (See Coombs, "Psychological Scaling".)

We have proceeded on the tacit assumption that our J-scales are continuous, but that individuals can be located only *at* alternatives or, at least, only *at* available alternatives. It seems reasonable to continue to require that an individual's location mean his most preferred alternative or, in a different terminology, that his "ideal" on this scale be concretized as an "ideal" conceivable alternative. It would be dangerous to define analytic operations solely in terms of degrees of a disembodied latent attribute (even if we should be convinced, by the way, that the attribute is satisfaction, or utility, itself). See the discussion on this in Chapter 8.

But we clearly need not require that the individual be located at one of the alternatives which we may at some particular time be ordering. In practice we do not always, or indeed, ever, order all the alternatives in *S*. Yet, it is advantageous to employ a single J-scale to describe an individual's preference system (for unchanging tastes) over his orderings of all possible subsets of *S*. If we refer back to Figure 17, this means that in situations where we are ordering only *w*, *x*, *z*, and *t*, we nevertheless wish to show the individual located at *y*, even though we may not know exactly where *y* is.

A slightly different version used is the "equal-appearing interval scale" (See Thurstone, and Chave, *The Measurement of Attitude* (Chicago: University of Chicago Press, 1929), and other works cited in Chapter 7). Here alternatives are defined as equally spaced. The continuum is thereby metrical, and all distances have preference intensity significance. A given location enables one to infer the complete ordering.

preference intensities for all individuals whose orderings are single-peaked with respect to the simple array itself. Any set of spacing restrictions will falsify non-inclusional preference intensities for some of these individuals. The array derived from the assumption of single-peakedness alone will carry, therefore, no implications about non-inclusional intensities held in common.

But we may go even further. If only a common structure of inclusional preference intensities for individuals is implied by single-peakedness, then we know that the concrete intensities reflected by a given array depend on the origins of the several individual orderings for which the array acts as a frame. An individual's location determines which spatially inclusional distance carries preference significance. Now consider the array shown in Figure 18. Since $\overline{BC}$ is included in $\overline{BD}$ ($\overline{BC} < \overline{BD}$), can we infer that every individual with single-peaked preferences relative to this array has an ordering in which either $Bp\ Cp\ D$ or $Dp\ Cp\ B$ (i.e., C is between B and D)? This is true for compatible orderings like $A\ B\ C\ D\ E\ F$ (or its inverse), $B\ C\ A\ D\ E\ F$, $D\ E\ C\ F\ B\ A$, etc., because the relevant comparisons do not straddle the origin. But it is not true for the compatible ordering $C\ D\ B\ E\ A\ F$ (here $Cp\ Dp\ B$), for the usual reason: $\overline{BD}$ straddles the origin C. If we have a large group of individuals, with varied tastes, it is likely that *every* inclusive interval will cross some individual's origin. Under such circumstances (and Duncan Black's illustrations all show at least one individual located at every alternative), the consensual array implied by single-peakedness will demonstrate no single relationship between concrete preference intensities which is true for the whole group.

Distances along the array do not reflect unique preference intensities for the group as a whole. Thus, the spatial locating of the vote winner at the median peak does not imply anything about *group* preference intensities. Furthermore, it does not imply anything about the "aggregate" of individual intensities, even if one should be willing to assume the preference intensities of different individuals comparable. If voting decided the outcome at the *mean* peak, for example, this would minimize the total absolute deviations of voters' positions from the chosen alternative, i.e., minimize the group's total interpersonally comparable "disappointment" in the outcome. However, the median outcome has the property of minimizing only the *number of individuals* who are disappointed in the chosen outcome over any other possible outcome. It does not compare or balance the *amounts* of disappointments of different individuals. Given the special "regularization" of *individual* preference intensities through the constraints of single-peakedness (betweenness relations), this minimization is determined solely by the frequency distribution of first choices in the group. Individual preference orderings are thus permitted but one, an *idiosyncratic*, degree of freedom to influence social choice. The assumption of single-peakedness furnishes the whole of whatever social *consensus* is required to guarantee acceptable social choice.

11-4. Evaluation

Our examination of the assumption of single-peakedness indicates how very restrictive an assumption it is. It does no less than simplify the problem of social choice to one dimension. Individuals, with an amazing perceptual similitude, see reflected in the highly multi-dimensional social state alternatives which we are imagining them to evaluate, one against the other, the same underlying principle of order. In the context of welfare economics this would appear to be a highly unrealistic assumption.

This is not to suggest that single-peakedness is *per se* unrealistic. Indeed, it is almost obviously highly realistic in the orderings of certain kinds of entities, e.g., European pre-war political parties,[28] statements reflecting different degrees of prejudice, etc. But it is apt to be realistic only where the underlying attribute is itself well-known to the subjects. It would be difficult to imagine what single entity all individuals seized upon as being reflected in the various social state alternatives in the set of all alternatives $\overline{S}$.

Consider a simple illustration. We are interested in the arrangement of four alternatives w, x, y, z by two individuals. Alternatives w, x, and y give the first individual the same commodity bundle; z gives him slightly more of all commodities. Alternatives w, x, and y are the same for the second individual as well, except that w gives him a very large house and two pairs of shoes, x gives him a mud hut but very many pairs of shoes, and y gives him a moderate-sized dwelling and four pairs of shoes; z gives him slightly more of all commodities than y. Out of the many possible ways individual number 1 might order these alternatives, $z\ w\ y\ x$ is not an unreasonable ordering. He himself obtains most commodities, and he believes individual number 2, to whom he is sympathetic, to be slightly best off in z; he believes the possibility of more lavish housing for number 2 in w more than offsets the loss of two pairs of shoes in y. At least, modest housing is more important for balanced civilized living than a plethora of shoes. However, if individual number 2 were extremely fond of the open country, loved to walk, was particularly hard on shoes, he might well give the following ordering: $x\ z\ y\ w$. The orderings of the two individuals are not compatible with the same arrangement of alternatives; single-peakedness is violated.

This is not by any means a surprising result. Nor was it artificially rigged. The discrepancy in arrangements stems from the fact that the two

---

[28]Arrow, *Social Choice*, 75-76.

individuals have different values with respect to, at least, individual number 2's standard of living. In a more realistic situation, moreover, the diversity would be even more obvious since if the alternatives differed more appreciably in terms of number 1's consumption, his ordering might have even less in common with number 2's ordering. The violation of single-peakedness stems then, both from a diversity of values with respect to the myriad living patterns possible *because each social state has innumerable dimensions,* and also, within this context, from the diversity of points of reference of the judging individuals. It has nothing to do with fanaticism, or minding other people's business.[29] Differences in values (tastes) should lead us to expect this very diversity in evaluating styles of life. It means that one man's values are another's fanaticisms. When there is a pervasively acknowledged single attribute in question, differences in values need not violate single-peakedness. But when there is no such obvious attribute, and each alternative has many non-reducible dimensions, then differences in values will almost surely express themselves in conflicting evaluations of living styles mixed with conflicting points of reference; there will be no such consensus as single-peakedness describes. To put it differently, the restrictions imposed on individual orderings by single-peakedness, given the interrelatedness of an individual's several evaluations, may empirically be far stronger than the assumption makes explicit. Conversely, if we do not find about us these "attendant" additional restrictions, then we are very likely not to have the restrictions explicitly imposed by single-peakedness as well.

The argument may be made a bit more systematically. I have discussed this fully elsewhere,[29a] so I shall give only a brief summary here. The individual's value system is a composite of three different elements: (1) his tastes for items of his own consumption, (2) external effects of others' consumption on him, and (3) his concern for the well-being of others, for the overall distribution of wealth, and other such "ethical" concerns. In order that there be some presumption that single-peakedness exists, there must be some concordance in the way the various individuals perceive the alternatives; they must have the same *structure* of betweenness relation-

---

[29]If individual number 1 "minded his own business," his ordering would be:

$$z \begin{bmatrix} w \\ x \\ y \end{bmatrix} (w, x, \text{ and } y \text{ indifferent}).$$

But now we can force the violation by having w give individual number 1 the same commodity bundle as z. So his ordering would be:

$$\begin{bmatrix} z \\ w \end{bmatrix} \begin{bmatrix} x \\ y \end{bmatrix}.$$

This ordering and individual number 2's, still $x\, z\, y\, w$, violate single-peakedness.

[29a]*The Theory of Economic and Political Decision-Making as a Single System,* forthcoming, Chapter 10.

ships, even if not the same relations themselves (because of differences in admissible comparisons).

Insofar as their well-being is affected by what they themselves consume, they will have no concordance of values whatever. Each individual pays attention to just those aspects of any given social state that nobody else gives any attention to. That different individuals will perceive different alternatives in some critically similar way would be due to the sheerest chance, or else, to the fact that a particular very small sub-set of the alternatives are constituted in such a way as to make single-peakedness hold trivially for just that sub-set. There is always a small sub-set which will fulfill single-peakedness for a group of individuals in terms of their own consumption, almost utterly independently of individual orderings, because the alternatives represent specially constructed monotonic changes in all commodities for each individual. But this concordance has nothing to do with constraints on individual orderings, and it holds only for a handful of trivial comparisons.

Insofar as specific external effects are concerned, some prospect of concordant values is conceivable since secondary consumers are likely to have their evaluations tied directly or inversely to those of the primary consumer for single items of consumption. But these partial concordances are not likely to be preserved in aggregate because the commodity bundles of our problem are so heterogeneously constituted of numerous items whose external relations go criss-cross, with many very different primary consumers. In effect, the multi-dimensionality of our alternatives and the varying points of reference we spoke of above in connection with which, say, individuals want to help particular others, are key factors in making single-peakedness unlikely.

Concern for over-all distribution of well-being is most likely to lead to single-peakedness, but here too, differences in over-all point of view as to what sorts of things are good for others, differences aggravated by the multi-dimensionality of the social state matrices, will decrease the likelihood substantially. Idiosyncratic principles of equity decrease the chance of concordance. In this context, the conditions under which single-peakedness is most likely to be satisfied are: (1) the "concern [of the individuals of the group] about equitable distributions is so strong that it outweighs their concern for the idiosyncratic character of their own wants; (2) the principles by which they judge equity are shared by groups of varying sizes," and individuals (including oneself) are treated in these principles as conventional ciphers with standardized wants rather than as unique creatures with idiosyncratic wants; (3) "a single method for classifying benefits and their recipients, and the relative degrees of nearness of these recipients to one another, comes to be employed by the adherents of all the various points of view. Essentially, these conditions characterize a situation in which ideologies are of great importance and are polarized; they take direct issue with one·another."[30] The underlying dimension along which the alternatives are arrayed is in effect "ideological advantage."

Thus, ideologies must exist which concern most or all types of consumption by most or all individuals in the population, they must be extremely important to almost everybody, and they must speak in the same terms, differing, for the most part, only in the determination of the sector of the commonly perceived array of benefit groups from which the hierarchy of "friends and enemies" should be calculated. It is not difficult to assert that these conditions most favorable to single-peakedness do not always occur everywhere, probably do not even occur often anywhere, but do probably occur sometimes in some societies. They are probably quite unlikely in the United States today, but may be somewhat more likely in some European and perhaps in some less developed societies at the present time.

The discussion above attempted to cite conditions under which all individuals would evaluate the alternatives of choice as though they represented simply different degrees of some single underlying attribute. Our discussion strongly suggested that the behavioral constraints on the population which correspond to these conditions are not lightly to be assumed. It should, of course, be said that the pessimism of this argument is not to be bypassed by interpreting the attribute underlying individual preferences as satisfaction or utility. Surely utility is by definition the yardstick criterion for desirability. But this is no solution at all. It begs the very problem of the preceding paragraphs: Why is it that these particular alternatives bring about just those degrees of satisfaction or utility for every individual so that the alternatives *can* be arranged in the special way fulfilling single-peakedness?

In summary, I have suggested that although single-peakedness is not *per se* an unreasonable characteristic to expect of some preference orderings, it does seem highly unrealistic as a general assumption about preference orderings in welfare economics where the alternatives of choice are complex, multi-dimensional entities. Differing individual values toward these alternatives would seem to bring about the kind of conflicting orientations by different individuals which would violate single-peakedness. The assumption of single-peakedness as being typically operative is, of course, a matter of fact; empirical observation of the kind of orderings we speak about could refute or verify it. My argument in this section is that a consideration of relevant factors leads me to expect that an empirical confrontation would refute it.

---

[30]These quotes are from J. Rothenberg, *op. cit.*, Chapter 10.

Part V

THE CRITERION

OF RELEVANCE

CHAPTER 12

Individual Choice or Social Choice?

The Condition of Nondictatorship

12-1. Introduction

Our search in this inquiry for a useful welfare analysis has, in effect, centered largely around our ability to formulate a welfare criterion which possesses these properties:

(1) it is internally consistent;

(2) it enables us to obtain a social ordering of at least an important sub-set of the set of all choice alternatives before us;

(3) it is in accordance with the values prevailing in the community concerned.

In Parts II, III, and IV, the important place given to Arrow's Paradox, at least as point of departure, bespoke our concern with the problem of consistency. It will be recalled, furthermore, that our chief standard for appraising the models which we considered was the ability to obtain from them an ordering of usefully many alternatives.[1]

We did not entirely eschew in these sections the third property cited. But we nowhere systematically raised the question: How does one discover whether or not a given set of values *is* in accordance with values prevailing in the community? (Alternatively, how does one discover *to what degree* a set of values corresponds to prevailing values?) Our treatment entailed operating throughout with two major

---

[1] Our empirical "testing" of cardinal utility models falls into this category, since the ability to use the models for obtaining social orders of alternatives depended importantly on the operational justification of the individual scaling units.

value judgments. These were consumer's sovereignty and rationality (with content modified in Part III). They were introduced not after an explicit correlation with "prevailing values" but rather *a priori* on the basis of seemingly plausible conjecture. Modifications in the content of "rationality" and "consumer's sovereignty," and value judgments concerning interpersonal comparisons of utility, were similarly appraised by incidental conjecture based on fragmentary empirical evidence. Certainly a choice among welfare functions would seem to require a more clear-cut standard of relevance than this. As we have noted above, such a standard may not be obtainable. But it is worth confronting the problem directly, at any rate. Part V is devoted to this task.

12-2. Social Choice or Individual Choice?

Our ability to gauge the correspondence of a model with prevailing community values depends crucially on our ability to state what those prevailing values are. This, of course, is the great difficulty. If the values of all individuals in the community were identical, there would be no problem, but individual systems of values differ. What "prevailing" values *are* in such a situation is problematic. First, they might be interpreted as a "highest common factor," those values which *are* held unanimously. Second, they might be interpreted as an "average," some central tendency from which more "extreme" values can be considered to radiate. The problem here would be formally akin to that of index number theory. Third, they might be interpreted as a "least common denominator," that core of values which appears to have a functionally strategic status, a kind of value matrix in the community.

Which of these interpretations, if any, one believes justifiable, would seem to depend on one's own values. But these values, it seems reasonable to suppose, ought to be influenced by certain concrete matters of fact. For example, how numerous and important are values which are held unanimously? How strong is the "central tendency" for "average" values? Is there a value-generative, community-integrative function played by some discoverable values? In the absence of systematic exploration to secure such facts, the determining values will be based upon a smattering of evidence and much conjecture.

It is not difficult to foresee that a presumption of considerable diversity of individual values, without direct confrontation, might lead one to reject all three interpretations. Such a presumption could spring from generalization of cursorily observed, diverse styles of living. The rejection of the suggested interpretations would very likely be followed by a denial that "representative" values can meaningfully be discovered.[2] We cannot

---

[2] One does not logically entail the other, of course. Other interpretations of prevailing values or "consensus" than the three cited are possible.

meaningfully speak of prevailing social values, so we cannot speak of social choices either. There is no such thing as social choice. The best the economist can do, then, is to interpret the Social Welfare Function, our welfare criterion, as the system of values of some individual or group of individuals; we cannot identify it as the values of the community. Thus,

> The so-called 'Social Welfare Function,' postulated by welfare economists, should on my view be regarded as a social ordering only in the sense that it orders states of society . . . . The essential point here is that none of the advantages claimed for theoretical welfare economics, as a result of using such a function, depends in the least on the ordering of economic states being an ordering by society. Instead of writing $W = W(U^1, \ldots, U^m)$, we can write $W^i = W^i(U^1, \ldots, U^m)$, (where $i = 1, \ldots, m$) . . . . We can deduce the whole effective corpus from, say $W^{10} = W^{10}(U^1, \ldots, U^m)$ — remembering only to put 'in the opinion of individual No. 10' after 'welfare' whenever we use the term.[3]

It is true that the completely unrestricted conditions for maximizing W^{10} are of the same form as those for maximizing W which we presented in Chapter 1. But these conditions are of little use for policy recommendations without further restriction. The formulation suggested here has significantly different implications for the problem of adopting "relevant" restrictions than the formulation we have heretofore employed without systematic examination.[4] It is worth inspecting these implications. The formulation is not an unusual one. Indeed, in an age where ethical relativism is influential, it may well be a most popular, perhaps *the* most popular, position.

12-3. Nondictatorship

Perhaps the most revealing implications are those which can be classified as focusing on the Nondictatorship Condition of Arrow's model. These implications have been cogently developed by I. M. D. Little in the work from which the preceding quotation was taken. It will be convenient to follow his argument.

Little paraphrases Arrow's condition as follows: "The collective order must not coincide with the order of any one chooser, regardless of the orders of the other choosers."[5] He is led to criticize this condition. His criticism is twofold. First, the definition of dictatorship is misleading; second, the

---

[3]I. M. D. Little, "Social Choice and Individual Values," *Journal of Political Economy*, Vol. LX, No. 5 (October, 1952), 424, a review of Arrow's book.

[4]The formal relationship between the two can be succinctly put as follows. In effect, the latter function is $W = W(W^1, W^2, \ldots, W^i, \ldots, W^m)$. The former is some W^i which we previously considered a component factor of the latter. But the former conception denies that the functional relationship W exists.

[5]Little, *op. cit.*, 422.

condition of nondictatorship is in general contradictory with the meaning of the Social Welfare Function.

As to the first, Little distinguishes between defining dictatorship as a situation in which one individual's rank ordering coincides with that of the Social Welfare Function, and no change in the ordering of the other members of the community can alter this coincidence; and dictatorship as a situation where a particular social judgment is in opposition to that of all individuals in the community save one. Little is willing to accept the former definition as reasonable, but the latter, he claims is misleading. He offers the following illustration.

In a three-man community, with each man's preferences determined only by what he himself receives, Dick and Harry prefer A to B, Tom prefers B to A, yet B is *socially* preferred to A. But if the third man is much the poorer of the three,

> might not then [the ranking B is socially preferred to A] be *desirable?* Use of the word 'dictatorship' suggests that Tom's preference for [B over A] somehow *causes* society to choose [B]. But, in fact, the coincidence of Tom's and the master-order may be a result of his poverty and not of his power.[6]

Thus, Little is asserting that we may deem nondictatorship a reasonable condition where otherwise the social judgment might be coerced by one man. However, where coincidence does not reflect coercion, it is not so obviously a condition which we would wish all acceptable social welfare functions to fulfill.

This criticism hinges on Little's suggestion that B socially preferred to A may be *desirable.* Desirable to whom? On the basis of Little's conception of the Social Welfare Function, this must mean desirable "in the opinion of individual number x." But who is individual number x? It cannot be Dick or Harry or else they would not have preferred A to B. If it is Tom, then the social judgment is certainly *caused* by Tom; it is nothing but an extrapolation of Tom's private preference scale, and Tom is a dictator in the strong sense. If individual number x is someone else, then he must be someone outside the community postulated in the example.[7] But if he can judge from outside that B preferred to A is desirable *for the community,* then *he* is making the social decision; he is the Social Welfare Function irrespective of the individual preference scales. The Social Welfare Function in this case is "imposed" in Arrow's sense, and since Little elsewhere accepts as reasonable the condition that an "acceptable" Social Welfare Function is not imposed, he can not without contradiction argue acceptance of this notion of "desirability."

---

[6] *Ibid.*, 426, italics mine.
[7] Moreover, he must be judging the social states on a basis other than that of what he himself receives.

It may, of course, be that Little means the evaluation of desirability to come from elsewhere *within* the hypothesized community, that the community in reality contains more than three individuals. In this case, it becomes trivially true that Tom is not a dictator; his is not the sole ranking to coincide with the social ranking. And here again we have a clue as to the source of the social ranking. To be consistent with his conception of the Social Welfare Function, it cannot be a "social judgment" but must be the judgment of some other member of the community. This individual is saying, in effect, "I prefer B to A," not necessarily, of course, solely on the basis of what he himself gets in each alternative, but partly on what the other members of the community obtain. In our own previous analysis we would have treated such a judgment as nothing other than the preference scale of individual x (his ranking of alternatives on the basis of what others get as well as himself). If the social judgment is what x says it is, then he *is* a dictator in the strong sense.

It is hardly surprising, then, to find Little suspicious of the nondictatorship condition. The Social Welfare Function in his conception is by definition dictatorial or imposed. This point is brought out even more clearly by his second criticism of the nondictatorship condition, in the course of which he in effect proves the proposition.

Little asks us to consider the Social Welfare Function momentarily as a machine (like a modern electronic computer) into which one "feeds" the individual preference rankings of any two alternatives x and y, and from which is produced a punch card social ranking of x and y. This, of course, is not Little's true conception; the difference will become apparent in the following. Now, asks Little,

> What would it mean to call the machine a social welfare function? One would be asserting, in effect, that if the machine decided in favor of x rather than in favor of y, then x would produce more social welfare than y or simply be more desirable than y. This is clearly a value judgment, but it is, of course, a value judgment made by the person who calls the machine a social welfare function. Thus, in general, to call the machine a social welfare function is to assert that x is better than y whenever the machine writes the sentence 'x is better than y'. Now we may suppose that the individual who calls the machine a social welfare function is one of those who has fed his own value order into it. It is clear that this person must be contradicting himself unless the 'master' — order coincides with his own value ordering. It follows that if the machine is to be called a social welfare function, then anyone who is called upon to accept or reject the principles on which it is built (i.e., the conditions of correspondence) must refuse to accept any principle which insures that the 'master'-order will necessarily not coincide with his own. This is because the conditions of correspondence determine the 'master'-order and because by calling the machine a social welfare function the person in question has accepted the 'master'-order. (It should be noted that accepting or rejecting a value sentence entails agreement or disagreement with the corresponding value

judgment.) In other words, it is inconsistent both to call the machine a social welfare function and to accept the condition of non-dictatorship . . . . No one can consistently accept the condition of 'non-dictatorship'. At all events, it is sheer nonsense to say, 'A is better than B, but everybody else claims B is better than A; therefore, since I don't want to be a dictator, B is better than A'. [8]

In the passage just quoted, Little is combining two different conceptions of the Social Welfare Function; one, where it is some objective function of individual preference scales (the machine), and two, his basic conception of social judgments as being only judgments by an individual about social states. The crucial assumption he is tacitly making appears, it would seem, toward the end of his passage: "It is sheer nonsense to say 'A is better than B, but everybody else claims B is better than A; therefore, since I don't want to be a dictator, B is better than A'." Little couches the value judgment in isolated absolute terms: "A is better than B," "B is better than A." There is no reference to the authority making the judgment. It is clear from the rest of his article that Little does not intend us to postulate an absolute value authority. We may, consistent with the context, follow modern philosophical analysis and translate these propositions to mean simply: "I believe that A is better than B," "I believe that B is better than A." [9] This is, evidently, the essence of Little's conception of social valuation. Given this conception, it *is* inconsistent for an individual to hold both propositions simultaneously. (Besides, it is also inconsistent for him to hold that A is no better, no worse than B, but everybody else claims B is better than A; therefore B is better than A.)

As a result of the foregoing, one can say that it is, in general, inconsistent for anyone to consider as social preference any ordering differing from his own. Each person is a dictator with regard to what he allows to be the social ordering. If all individuals are treated symmetrically on this, the only judgments which will be deemed social judgments by all are those which are identical with the rankings of every individual, i.e., unanimity judgments. We can have a universally acknowledged Social Welfare Function as conceived by Little only if everyone's preference scales are similar.

12-4. Conclusions

The denial that social values can be discovered in the welter of individual values leads to a position where no welfare criterion has any more justification for policy recommendations than any other. Each is justified only as

---

[8] *Ibid.*, 427, 429.

[9] This formulation does not, of course, preclude justification for private belief stemming from outside the individual.

the "opinions" of some individual or group of individuals. And moreover, no one will "accept" a criterion different from his own even if the criterion is supported by a large group of individuals, a majority, for example, since the lack of sufficient consensus *means* that the opinions of the (majority) group do not merit any special recognition from individuals outside the group. Indeed, the suggestion that the opinions of such groups may possess some special significance, aside from coercive influence, for non-members, is a suggestion that some opinions may be additionally justified by a value consensus not itself pertaining to the content of the particular opinions.

Adherence to Little's interpretation is incompatible with the assumption of consumer's sovereignty. What the rejection of non-dictatorship signifies is that the values of other individuals in the community do not *count* in the welfare function of some person unless *he* wants them to and then only in the way *he* wants them to. Others have no final say in suggesting how their own values ought to influence the shape of his welfare criterion. The welfare criterion is a private criterion, and it can be as exclusive as the evaluator wishes.

It is quite clear that under this interpretation the quest of the present work is for all practical purposes meaningless. We can have a uniquely relevant Social Welfare Function only if it should be universally accepted. Universal acceptance follows only from an identicality of every individual's values. Such a solution is trivial.

We have noted earlier in this chapter that the kind of interpretation which a person gives to the notion of a social value consensus is itself a value judgment. At this different level of discourse[10] concerning the choice of definitions for the welfare criterion, Little's choice is but one of many held by different individuals. At this level, too, we may speak of value consensus, and all the possible interpretations of consensus, whether mentioned here or not, are again appropriate. It is interesting to note that if on our present second level of discourse we should adopt the interpretation which Little applies to our original level of discourse, then Little's actual interpretation would itself possess no justification except as Little's opinion; he could not *demonstrate* the correctness of his position but only hope to *persuade* us to adopt it. Little could *prove* the correctness of his approach only by being able to appeal to more anterior judgments which he believes to be commonly held in the community. Yet on close inspection such beliefs are not supported by unanimity any more than judgments about consensus on our original level of discourse. Little's case, then, is strongest on the original level when he is willing to admit the violation of his case on a higher level. On a still higher level of discourse, however, such a discrepancy

---

[10]In philosophic terms, a *metalanguage*.

in the criteria by which individual values, on each of the several levels of discourse, are "aggregated," might be unanimously, or with near unanimity, rejected.

Be this as it may, we are not forced to accept the kind of interpretation advanced by Little. But whether we can persuasively adopt a kind which asserts the meaningfulness of "value-aggregation" depends on the facts about community-held values. It will be the task of the following chapter to sketch some such facts which may persuade us that, even in the absence of unanimity, we may discover the content of social, in addition to individual, choice.

CHAPTER 13

Social Choice of a
Social Welfare Function*

13-1. Introduction

We have argued that a criterion of relevance depends fundamentally on our ability to specify what comprises the community's prevailing values. This necessitates the social scientist "aggregating" or "resolving" the several systems of values held by individuals in the community. No suggested method of aggregation, short of unanimity, renders a *demonstrably* "correct" resolution. The "correctness" of its solution is to be understood only in terms of the willingness of other scientists to accept it as a reasonable interpretation of "the community's prevailing values."[1]

The method discussed in the preceding chapter insists that only unanimity is satisfactory. The hallmark of this approach is that when an individual identifies certain values as the community's values, he is deemed to be himself embracing these values.[2] In this chapter I shall suggest a

---

*Some of the substance of this chapter appears in the author's "Conditions for a Social Welfare Function," *Journal of Political Economy*, Vol. LXI, No. 5 (October, 1953), 389-405.

[1] This is not an unusual predicament for scientists. The theory of induction, e.g., is an assumed operating rule which enables scientists to choose between different empirical hypotheses. But it has no *demonstrable* validity since to test it empirically involves ultimately an empirical test of the assumption of the uniformity of nature. It is, rather, accepted as reasonable in terms of fundamental unprovable assumptions.

[2] We may recall that Little says that if one were to call a certain "machine" a Social Welfare Function, "one would be asserting . . . that if the machine decided in favor of x rather than in favor of y, then x would . . . be more desirable than y. This is clearly a value judgment . . . made by the person who calls the machine a Social Welfare Function . . . . This person must be contradicting himself unless the 'master'-order coincides with his own value ordering."

method of aggregation which does not call for unanimity. I shall attempt to persuade the reader that it may be reasonable to call the values aggregated in this manner the values *prevailing in the community*. I shall argue that it is not inconsistent for an individual to assert that certain values appear to be the *prevailing* values while he himself opposes them.

The reasonableness of the approach to be presented is not meant to be self-evident. What plausibility it may have is due solely to the empirical reflections which suggested it as a possible approach. More specifically, I shall suggest: (1) that there exists an empirically demonstrable regularity in the pattern of values held by the individuals within any "going society"; (2) that this regularity centers about attitudes toward central decision-making processes in the community; (3) that this consensus toward decision-making processes has deep functional significance for the continued existence of the community in its own distinctive style. My argument, then, is that there is discoverable for a given community a set of values intimately related to the basic characteristics of the community when viewed as a whole. I shall suggest that these values be considered the prevailing values dealing with economic choice in the community.[3] It is against these values that we should place suggested welfare standards for judgment.

13-2. Group Choice

In order to explain the nature of the regularity in "going societies" which I shall discuss below, i.e., the nature of *social choice*, it will be helpful to examine more closely the principles by which it may be meaningful to speak of prevailing values. If social choice exists, it must refer in some sense to the composite choice or preferences[4] of a group. We may consider it a kind of group choice. In what sense, then, can a group be said to have a set of preferences? This may be clarified by considering a suggestive classification of groups proposed by Marschak.[5] Marschak classifies groups as teams, foundations, and coalitions.

A team is a group in which every member has the same group-oriented interests. A team has solidarity. We can identify the preferences of a particular team as the team's goals or purposes. Moreover, since the team comes into existence solely for the purpose of realizing these common

---

[3] In the terminology of the last chapter, our method of aggregating values is an example of a "least common denominator," i.e., finding a matrix set of values.

[4] Throughout this work I have been using the term "choice" in two senses, one the narrow sense of a preference which has been revealed through controlled experimental, or uncontrolled but observed, choosing behavior, and second, the broader sense of a preference itself. Where the distinction is important I have tried to specify the meaning intended.

[5] Jacob Marschak, "Towards an Economic Theory of Organization and Information," *Decision Processes* (eds. R. M. Thrall, C. H. Coombs, and R. L. Davis) (New York: John Wiley & Sons, Inc., 1954), Chapter 14.

goals, they can usually be inferred without difficulty from the organization of the team, from the allocation of roles, etc., and from its coherent functioning in concrete situations. Group choice would appear to have real content when referring to teams.

A foundation is a group set up to achieve a certain purpose, but it is a group in which the individual members have their own interests. Although in a team each member feels that the goal of the group is *his* goal too, members of a foundation do not identify themselves with the purpose of the foundation. By serving to realize the foundation's goals they will be rewarded in a way that will enable them independently to realize their own goals.

A rather crude illustration of the difference between the two kinds of groups is given by a partnership manufacturing firm. The firm as a whole partakes closely of the character of a foundation, since if the employees have no strong loyalties to the particular firm, and if they can fairly easily obtain comparable employment elsewhere, their employment here is in the nature of an impersonal exchange relationship; by performing services useful to the firm, they can obtain rewards with which to achieve fulfillment of their own interests. For the most part, their satisfactions come from outside, and there is a general postponement of satisfaction while on the job. In contrast, the partner owners of the firm comprise a team. They identify their success with the success of the firm. Although their fulfillment generally comes from successful monetary operations by the firm, which enable them to satisfy outside interests, a significant consequence of their identification with and resultant loyalty to the firm is that their harmonious and efficient performance within the firm becomes in itself an important source of gratification.

It should be pointed out that in the case of both the foundation and the team it is meaningful to speak of the group's purposes or preferences. In the team it is somewhat easier to infer these purposes since they inform, more or less obviously, the behavior of the members. In the foundation, the group purposes are not so easily inferred by observing a small sub-set of the group. The group purposes are inferable almost exclusively through a comprehension of the organizational structure and its functioning. Group activities as a system (self-correcting and self-directing) is the key to such inferences.

The coalition is a group in which there is no such obvious group goal. Moreover, the interests of the members are not similar. But there are advantages to be gained by entering a coalition in that various arrangements whereby members adopt mutually modified patterns of behavior vis-à-vis one another and the outside world redound in various ways to the benefit of the respective members of the coalition, depending on the interplay of preferences and the particular arrangements chosen. These arrangements need not be permanent and may give way to one another either systematically or without particular pattern. The fact that advantages are to be gained in the coalition does help to define the notion of group purpose. Given the commitment of individual interest patterns to greater fulfillment through the coalition, the perpetuation of the coalition in a state in which these commitments are not pervasively regretted, is a subject of consensus by the members. And this consensus, whether explicit or implicit, is the source from which inferences as to group preferences must be made. It should not be thought that for our purposes there is necessarily a crucial difference between a coalition and a team or foundation insofar as the stability of the consensus is concerned. In all types of groups widespread frustration of expectations about rewards is a diremptive force. Some teams have little cohesiveness, and some coalitions have strong cohesiveness. The difference that is important for our purposes is the greater ease in characterizing the content of the consensus for teams and foundations, in describing their group goals, than for coalitions.

Any concrete group is apt to partake of elements of all three types. The practical problem of classification in this case is met in terms of the relative importance of loyalty and identification behavior, or affectively neutral exchange relationships (usually contractual) within an organized, highly directed structure, or conditional arrangements for reciprocally patterned behavior, designed to be mutually beneficial. This hybridity may somewhat complicate the attempt to discover the content of group choice in any particular instance, but it sometimes can simplify this attempt, as when noticeable elements of identification clarify an otherwise ambiguous coalition.

In summary, we have suggested the sense in which it would be proper to speak about group choice for different kinds of groups. But this possibility should not lead us to over-optimism about our particular quest. We are seeking to determine whether it is possible to observe social choice, and if so, whether this social choice is such that we may infer from it unambiguous evaluations from a usefully large sub-set of alternatives. Nothing in the foregoing guarantees that this will be possible. For one thing, a society will not fit into any of the classes discussed above if it lacks the coherence of even a coalition. Even if it should be classifiable, say as a coalition, the integration present may well bespeak only a partial ordering of very narrow range, and vague besides.

13-3. A Digression on Family Choice

We may now approach more closely our concept of social choice by briefly considering the nature of choices made in contemporary American families.[6]

---

[6] I am indebted to Professor A. G. Hart for emphasizing the importance of family choice in welfare economics.

In consumer preference theory we proceed on the assumption that market decisions made by consumers reflect their underlying preference scales, indeed, that these choice decisions in principle *reveal* their underlying preferences. Strictly speaking, many such decisions, perhaps the majority of them, are made by some persons *on behalf of others*. It is said, for example, that women spend 70 per cent of the national income. Certainly, we are familiar with the fact that, in every family unit, decisions about expenditures on goods and services are frequently made by one individual *for* another. The implication of this is one or more of the following.

(1) The choices are "errand" choices; each individual transmits his own preferences to an individual whose market decisions represent simply a carrying-out of "instructions." Here, no modification is required for the assumption that consumer market choices reflect the individual preferences of the actual consumers.

(2) The choices are dictatorial; when the decider decides, he is substituting his own preferences for those of the individuals on whose behalf his decisions are being made. Here in the relevant market decisions, some actual consumers are not expressing their preferences (they are being disenfranchised).

(3) The choices are group choices; the choices made by the "decider" are approved by the individual decided for because they are approved by the group itself on the basis of a consensus which need not extend to prior agreement on the content of the choices. Here, a slight modification is required to the assumption that market choices reflect actual consumer preferences, namely that as members of family groups consumer preferences are expressed through family choices.

Undoubtedly, "errand" choices occur sometimes in families, but they do not exhaust all the "proxy" choices within the family we are referring to. When the wife plans the menus for the week, and the husband buys a particular fire insurance policy on the house, neither is necessarily carrying out specific instructions from the other members of the family. Similarly, there may occasionally be dictatorial choices made, but these cannot be too frequent in any family or refer to really significant issues because the lack of consensus which dictatorship implies would, in the event of serious conflict, tear the family apart. Since the external obstacles to family *dismemberment* are by no means insuperable and, on the less radical level, in modern society external obstacles to family *disharmony* or disorganization are almost non-existent, the existence of widespread, harmonious family life suggests some minimum consensus on operating decisions.

The foregoing suggests that observation of family life will disclose group choice operative over important issues. Various characteristics of such choice are relevant to our study. First, many family choices reflect interpersonal comparisons of utility. On the simple level of, e.g., what should the family do on a given Sunday, the decision would seem to involve comparing preference intensities of different members of the family, and oftentimes differentially weighting these preference intensities by the importance of the particular member to the group. What radio or television program should be listened to (in cases where scarcity still operates here to make impossible the simultaneous satisfaction of several conflicting desires); which member's marginal "need" should complete the budgetary allocations: braces for Susie's teeth, Billy's new train, Mother's new coat, Father's new tool chest, these questions typify a kind of choice which the welfare economist has regarded with both longing and repulsion. If we can be persuaded that *social* choice also acts on issues like these, we will have laid to rest a troublesome ambivalence in the methodology of welfare analysis.[7]

A second characteristic of many family choices is that the proxy element arises out of formal or informal delegation of decision-making authority. The wife is implicitly expected to plan menus; her own discretion over such matters is approved in advance by the other members of the family. Specific choices may be complained about, but her right to have made them is not challenged; they are accepted as the *legitimate* group choices. Only after frequent gross "blunders" is complaint likely to take on the complexion of challenge to the prevailing decision-making rules of the game. But this is only to say that there are limits to the consensus in the group; these limits are also the limits of stable functioning of the family unit. The concept of *family choice* refers to the solidarity which exists *within* these limits.

The fact of delegation is important because it suggests functional differentiation in the family, and this in turn suggests notions about direction or purpose. It would be difficult, indeed, to define *a* purpose, or even a hierarchy of purposes, to the family. One would be close to defining a purpose or hierarchy of purposes to life itself. This is one reason for stressing a similarity with social choice (whereas a baseball team would not be comparable). Yet the understanding of functional limits to working stability, which comes from isolating challenge to the legitimatization of delegated decision making, helps disclose the content of the loyalty to the group.[8]

A third characteristic of family choice is the temporal development of a

---

[7]To say that this family makes a certain interpersonal comparison of utility is only to call attention to the existence of an evaluational procedure used by one group of people; it does not raise the question of how valid such a procedure is. Indeed, although probably couched in a terminology suggesting matters of fact, the procedure will most likely be a set of value judgments without refutable content for which the question of validity is meaningless.

[8]The loyalty elements and ambiguity of purpose of the family suggest a mixture of the team and the coalition.

common evaluational orientation on basic issues. This orientation is the product of behavior patterns come upon by historical interactions among the members of the family and with the outside world, and in turn it recommits the future even more tightly into the continuing pattern. This orientation is most revealing for our study because it indicates the content of the gratifications and deprivations,[9] to which the personalities of the family members become quite firmly committed; it is the matrix of their scale of values.[10]

13-4. An Hypothesis on Social Choice

The description above of family choice has been presented because it resembles in rather striking fashion a concept of *social choice* which is being developed by social psychologists, anthropologists and sociologists.[11] The concept describes an important degree of value consensus in any going society. In fact, such consensus is discovered to be a functional requirement for the going-ness of the society. It is this consensus that integrates the several institutional networks in the society to avoid conflict. But these values are not imposed from outside onto a system of social institutions; rather, values and institutions are mutually engendering, mutually reinforcing, mutually sustaining. A rough analogy of mutual reinforcement from economics is to be found in the chain as follows: expectation of price increase induces advance buying, which results in price increase, which reinforces expectation of price increase, which induces further advance buying, which results in further price increase, etc. A closer analogy is from individual psychology, where a person's orientation leads to the kind of experience of the world which resupports his original orientation. Thus, suppose a person, perhaps because of past traumas, believes the world to be hostile. His resulting mode of behavior in interpersonal interactions, suspicious, defensive and/or aggressive, will most likely prevent him from attaining non-hostile relations with others, thereby reinforcing his original

---

[9]Cf. Talcott Parsons, and Edward Shils, "Values, Motives and Systems of Action," *Toward a General Theory of Action* (eds. Parsons and Shils) (Cambridge: Harvard University Press, 1951), Chapter 2.

[10]This, again, is not to suggest complete similarity of preference scales within a family. Sometimes major differences, and always minor differences, are to be found. But family cohesiveness does involve similarity in basic ways of looking at things, from the point of view of the welfare of the person. Furthermore, these are the structural foci of individual scales of values.

[11]For example, see the treatments of Theodore Newcomb, *Social Psychology* (New York: Dryden Press, 1949); Talcott Parsons, *The Social System* (Glencoe, Ill.: The Free Press, 1952); T. Parsons, and E. Shils, *Toward a General Theory of Action*; Solomon E. Asch, *Social Psychology* (Englewood Cliffs, N. J.: Prentice-Hall, Inc., 1952). My exposition of this concept to follow leans most heavily on the first three sources.

beliefs and, very likely, committing him deeper and deeper to this pattern of behavior in the future.

The value consensus is not mystical, like that of Rousseau's "general will"; it is a value scale possessed pervasively *by individuals* but maintained and fostered and passed on to succeeding generations within and through a particular "social system." Like the individual in the last paragraph, everyone born into a society is socialized into that society; he is taught a particular orientation on basic issues. The orientation is reinforced because the expectations about others' behavior which it engenders (the "reciprocally modified" behavior patterns of our coalitional arrangements above) are generally realized due to the fact that the others' are similarly conditioned to the rules of this game of complementary role patterns. And realization of these expectations brings satisfaction because the process of socialization teaches the person to find his gratifications in the "correct" acting out of his social roles. His value orientation develops as a kind of learning process along with trial and error interactions in the world. In a going society, the established, highly structured complementarity of roles furnishes the easiest channel along which to pursue gratifying interactions. The individual's value orientation comes to reflect the relative desirability of these established channels.

It is then an acceptance of the organized differentiation of role contents and their patterned juxtaposition that is reflected in basic value consensus. But this differentiation and juxtaposition, this structure of *system*, is given content by certain strategic decision-making institutions in the society. As in the family, solidarity exists side by side with, and in a real sense is evidenced by, the delegation (whether explicit or implicit) of authority to make some decisions for the group as a whole. These decision-making processes are approved as the rules of the game and their decisions are approved in advance. Such decisions are legitimized articulations of the group's values. Since socialization in a going society commits most individuals so deeply to established values in seeking to fulfill their desires, acceptance of these strategic social processes is a most important means by which these individuals uphold their own values. These processes become themselves important values. And they create by their functioning other social values. Since they are choice mechanisms they separate chosen from rejected alternatives. In this way they differentiate, and define by this very differentiation, socially desirable and socially undesirable alternatives, or, more generally, they rank alternatives as to the degree of social desirability. Within the going society there may be different levels of legitimized valuation.[12] But what is important for us is that the basic consensus extends to

---

[12] For example, there may be social choice of alternative methods of choosing among alternative social welfare criteria, or of alternative welfare criteria, or of alternative social states, etc.

social validation of decision processes whose choices concern the social state alternatives of welfare economics; the consensus extends to choice of an "official" Social Welfare Function.

This is a brief description of the related concepts of social consensus and social valuation which have been gaining adherents in the social sciences mentioned. They are inductive theories, empirical hypotheses about observable phenomena. They have not been definitively verified. In fact, much of the preparatory work of studying their concrete empirical implications is still being carried on. They have not yet been satisfactorily formalized. In short, these are not well-established, highly precise concepts to which we turn: they are, or seem, attractive rough generalizations from a number of the highly diverse, but important, recent findings in these fields. They represent a pulling together of distinctive accumulating insights in cultural anthropology, learning theory, psychoanalysis, individual and group field theory, political theory, and sociological theory.[13] I cannot claim, therefore, that if we should desire to employ these concepts in welfare economics we should be standing solidly on established fact. Rather, we should be standing on a heuristic program of continued study in related social sciences.

I have attempted to indicate above that a welfare economics which does not possess concepts such as these is severely crippled. Let us now examine some of the characteristics of a welfare economics which does possess these concepts.

13-5. The Social Welfare Function as Empirical Consensus

In the preceding chapter, we have seen that under Little's interpretation, when a person says "*A* is socially preferred to *B*" he means only, "I prefer *A* to *B*." If we should adopt as the Social Welfare Function the empirical generalization of values discussed above, then we may alternatively interpret "*A* is socially preferred to *B*" as "There is a social process of evaluation by which *A* has been declared preferable to *B*." Clearly, a particular individual may on this view himself prefer *B* to *A* and simultaneously recognize that the judgment, "*A* is preferred to *B*" has been socially validated. This interpretation of social judgment avoids Little's foregoing criticism of the nondictatorship condition. It is not logically restricted to unanimity situations.

Little recognizes the possibility of this conception. He refers to the "social process of evaluation" as a "decision-making process," but insists that such a process is not what we mean by a Social Welfare Function.

---

[13]The closest formulation for our purposes which I know is that in Parsons and Shils, *Toward a General Theory of Action*, and Parsons, *The Social System*.

The importance of the distinction between a value order and a decision order, for our purposes is as follows: In a given community, or committee, as many value orderings as there are individuals may coexist. *On the other hand*, as between two alternatives there can be only one effective decision. Thus we may all have our conflicting opinions as to whether we ought to go to war or not. But the decision to do so or not to do so is unique and binding for everyone. Where values are concerned, everyone must be a 'dictator' (i.e., the logic of value judgments is such that one cannot consistently *accept* any value ordering which differs from one's own); where decisions are in question, everyone cannot be a dictator, in Arrow's sense, unless there is unanimity.[14]

Little's distinction diverges, of course, from our conception. A large if not major portion of all social valuation occurs only within the context of institutionalized decision-making processes. A conception of social valuation as independent of real social decision-making processes has little empirical content.[15] It quite understandably leads Little to a fruitless hypothetical consideration of the Social Welfare Function as an arbitrary scrambling machine with no social justification outside the machinist's (economist's?) preference scale. It must be recognized that what is wrong with this conception is not only that it is too abstract but that it is empirically misleading.

My alternative conception of social valuation gives content to the notion of prevailing values. But we may go further. As a way of achieving for it the utmost relevance, we may consider treating the Social Welfare Function for a particular society as the very same values embodied in those strategic social decision-making processes within the society which valuate the kinds of social states pertinent to the economic problem, and thus that we con-consider treating the social ordering (or social preference scale) as the ordering of social states which results from the operation of those processes. This approach would define the content of the Social Welfare Function as a generalization of something observable in the real world. The uniquely relevant Social Welfare Function, as interpreted here, would not, then, be my valuational rule, nor the rule of all (or almost all) economists, nor even the rule of all (or almost all) members of the population at large. It would be only an empirical generalization *about* the valuational rule of the population at large. It could be a good generalization only if there really existed a strategic value consensus within the given society, and if this consensus were unambiguously discoverable. My presentation of this conception is prompted by the belief that current work in the allied social sciences lends preliminary support to the contention that these conditions can be met.

---

[14]I. M. D. Little, "Social Choice and Individual Values," 430-431.

[15]This is not to imply that definitive empirical studies for any society do already exist. But the direction for such studies seems pretty clearly indicated.

But being a good generalization is one thing and serving as foundation for a useful welfare analysis is another. How useful an analysis would we obtain if we adopted as a welfare criterion the empirical generalization of "matrix values" described above? As we may remember from Chapter 1, the elements of any welfare analysis consist of: (1) the agents whose welfare is involved, (2) the concept of welfare, (3) the alternatives to be compared, and (4) the rule by which the alternatives can be compared in accordance with the definition of welfare. Given the interpretation of (2) and (4) (the Social Welfare Function) suggested here, will the analysis yield consistent results? Will it enable us to appraise sufficiently many of the alternatives which we consider important? Will its conclusions be relevant to the agents whose opinions we believe ought to count?

1. Consistency. The consistency of the results depends partly on the consistency of the concept of welfare itself and partly on the consistency of the valuational rule. Since we have defined the welfare of the group in terms of the welfare of individuals, and assumed an individual's welfare to be appraisable by means of his system of values (his ends), consistency of the first type would seem to be founded on the existence of individual value scales which are not self-contradictory.[16]

Although most *single* ends are to some extent contradictory,[17] it is the individual's *system* or *hierarchy* of ends by which we appraise his welfare. The extent of inconsistency in the hierarchical patterns of ends is a question beyond the scope of the present work. The question is closely related to the intransitivity of individual choices, but, as Appendix 2 of Chapter 7 suggests, the two may not be equivalent,[18] even though we have only a doubtful ability to discover the content of an individual's system of ends apart from his ranking of alternatives. We can expect that an inconsistent system of ends will give rise to an intransitive ordering of alternatives and probably to outright contradictions, such that in one situation some alternative x will be preferred to y, while in another, with ends presumably unchanged, y will be preferred to x. Any policy recommendations deriving from a series of comparisons with these characteristics are highly ambiguous.

In Chapters 7 and 10 we noted that no convincing evidence had been adduced to lead us to question the pervasiveness of *transitive* individual

---

[16]Examples of contradictory values are the simultaneous desires for a quiet life *and* unusual business achievement, or the desire for a slim figure *and* a craving for rich foods. (Professor Albert G. Hart in a personal communication.)

[17]See Chapter 9, p. 200, fn. 1.

[18]The moral of Appendix 2 is that we may have intransitivity in the ranking of alternatives without having an inconsistent welfare criterion. The lack of equivalence between the two may consist in this: that an inconsistent criterion always leads to an intransitive ordering of alternatives, not a *true* ordering, and perhaps to outright contradictions, whereas an intransitive ordering may, but need not, stem from an inconsistent criterion.

orderings. Be this as it may, it is important for our purposes here that whatever the extent of intransitivity should·in fact be, such intransitivity would equally tend to weaken any welfare model based upon consumer's sovereignty.[19]

As for the consistency of the valuational rule, the case is different. In the present model this rule is the functioning of the central decision-making processes in the given community. Without specifying further the characteristics of the particular social processes we can give no judgment about consistency. But this is itself revealing. Our inability to make a blanket judgment stems from the fact that the choices of some decision-making processes are apt to be inconsistent. This is especially likely where strategic considerations are important in the process by which decisions are reached. The form in which the inconsistency appears is that in any two situations where the initial conditions are identical to the greatest degree practicable, the decisions reached may differ; there is an indeterminacy of outcome.[20] A game of chess illustrates the principle involved. More pertinent examples are the behavior of an oligopolistic industry, or the passage of legislation through the United States Congress.[21] When we adopt as the content of the Social Welfare Function those values generalized as being embedded in the community's central decision-making processes, we may, depending upon the determinateness of the decision processes actually involved, be employing an inconsistent welfare criterion (even where individual values are consistent). Since conjecture as to the specific decision processes which may be properly incorporated into Social Welfare Function models is beyond the scope of the present work we cannot appraise the seriousness of this possible defect. Clearly, however, the seriousness should not be prematurely overstated. There are greatly differing degrees of inconsistency conceivable. The usefulness of an approach which explicitly seeks to make welfare analysis relevant may not be vitally harmed if the analysis is obtained at the cost of limited pockets of inconsistency.

2. *Power.* The power of our suggested model, its ability to appraise enough of the alternatives that interest us, is likewise not free from possible criticism. It must be admitted that, as so far substantiated by empirical findings, there is no evidence that all, or nearly all, the social states which

---

[19]Except that in some models, the valuational rule itself may be fashioned to "resolve" value inconsistencies, typically by *imposing* consistency on the social choices resulting from inconsistent individual choices. The significance of such resolution is dubious.

[20]The mathematical analogy to this is a many valued function of certain variables.

[21]The strategic jockeying for advantage by a few influential interest group coalitions and the resulting compromises (a form of misrepresentation of preferences such as we mentioned in Chapter 9), make the description of Congressional activities in terms of a game of strategy quite revealing. I have explored some of the characteristics of such a description as part of a model of the social welfare function for the United States.

the economist would like appraised are explicitly differentiated in terms of the pervasive values. Many of these can clearly be conceived of as chosen or rejected in terms of the outcomes of the central social decision-making processes under changing initial conditions. As such, the appraisals implicit in these outcomes will be legitimized; they will be accepted within the society as portions of the social ordering.[22] But there are two foci in which we may possibly discover significant limitations on the range of alternatives which can be compared in the model.

First, if the welfare function should give rise to intransitive or inconsistent choices, this would make ambiguous both some comparisons actually "carried out" and also many comparisons not actually, or easily, "carried out" but which are inferred from comparisons which *were* "carried out." The consistency and analytic power of a model are often closely related.[23]

Second, the valuation rule may systematically prevent consideration of some types of alternatives. As an illustration, consider the market system. The market system, the economic activities of the population as oriented around and systematically interrelated by market relationships, can be considered a social decision-making process. Given a certain set of initial conditions, tastes, technological knowledge and distribution of productive resources, we can expect, by notable simplification, a particular social state outcome to result, i.e., a general equilibrium. With a different set of initial conditions, a different outcome can be expected.[24] If we were to consider the market system as the valuational rule in a welfare model, then we would be interpreting the general equilibrium outcome as the social state alternative which is preferred to all others that are technologically possible (i.e., with given community endowment of productive resources and technological knowledge).

But we have reason to believe that there are some alternatives that would very likely not have been considered by the market process because the individual preferences for such alternatives would very likely not have been expressed in market activities. These preferences concern external

---

[22]See the following sections for a more extensive discussion of the acceptance of such outcomes as social welfare judgments.

[23]Inconsistency perhaps always leads to some loss of power, but a loss of power need not be due to inconsistency.

[24]Some of the problem areas assumed away are:

(1) Economic theory cannot predict a unique outcome even under static assumptions; the most it can do is to predict a range of outcomes within which the unique outcome will probably occur.

(2) No general equilibrium may result, the "outcome" being systematic or irregular oscillations without strong convergence tendencies.

(3) The operation of the decision process itself induces changes in the initial conditions, so that even if there were strong equilibrium tendencies, these would be swamped by considerable "endogenous change" in the parameters.

economies and diseconomies, both in production and consumption. A consumer, for example, is unable through the market mechanism to control consumption activities of others which affect him. Moreover, in his own activities he is often unable to trace their effects on others, and the market gives him little opportunity to try. An inference from this is that, if each consumer were apprised of these interrelationships, he might well prefer to change his behavior.[25] The frequency with which individual market action is by-passed, or even superseded, by cooperative or collective action (e.g., the activities of government) testifies to the truth of this inference.

There are other institutional decision-making processes which systematically lessen the chances for certain kinds of alternatives to be considered. For any such process which does in fact embed the crucially accepted prevailing values of the community, the practical exclusion of these alternatives is not necessarily to be taken as an indication that the population *really* would have preferred an outcome other than the one which resulted. If the population understood which outcomes were being excluded from contention by the very nature of the social welfare function *and still accepted that function* as final criterion, then this would indicate that an attachment to the decision process itself outweighed relatively small annoyance over some specific choices. It is only if the structural exclusions were not understood, if, in other words, there was systematic *ignorance*, that we might extrapolate the judgment that social choice might *really* be other than what our model reveals.[26] It is this case that pertains to the power of our analysis.

As with the question of the consistency of the particular welfare model being investigated, documentation of the criticisms relating to its power waits upon more elaborate empirical studies oriented around the present notion of value consensus than is yet available. We therefore admit the *possibility* that the present notion of value consensus may not yield a powerful welfare analysis, but we have no conclusive evidence about the *actuality* of such a contention.

3. *Relevance.* The relevance of the analysis depends upon the relevance of the welfare concept and of the valuational rule. For the first, we have assumed consumer sovereignty; the individual's own conception of his welfare is to be accepted as the criterion of his welfare. As we have noted in passing, this has been frequently subject to criticism. Consumer sovereignty has been rejected as a trustworthy index of individual welfare by such

---

[25]It is sometimes suggested that the exploration and publicity of external relationships is one of the most important functions of the welfare economist. Professor A. G. Hart has made this point strongly in personal communication. Also, see Baumol, *Welfare Economics and the Theory of the State.*

[26]See below for a further discussion of ignorance.

notable economists as Frank Knight and J. M. Clark (and, of course, by the whole school of depth psychology), largely, it might be added, on grounds that it is scientifically known to misinterpret the psychological needs of the organism. In addition to our argument in Chapter 2 that consumer's sovereignty be accepted because of the absence of any empirically demonstrable alternative criterion, it is arguable that so long as the existing institutional framework of society and its accompanying value orientations remain unchanged, rejection on these psychological grounds is beside the point because there may well exist no way of translating the unfulfilled needs into gratifying modes of behavior. If this is so, then those values which currently pervade the society can be viewed as the closest representation of evaluative norms to point up the desirable and the undesirable for members of the society. Since these values are held by individuals, they presumably are consulted when relevant choices are in the offing. Consumer sovereignty may be tolerably accepted as an indication of individual welfare for choices informed by the central value orientation of society.

The valuational rule in our model is the operation of the central decision-making processes in the community. It has been introduced expressly for the purpose of achieving a relevant welfare analysis. Indeed, the only distinctive virtue which the model can claim over others in the literature *is* relevance. Nonetheless, it is one thing to seek to achieve relevance, another to achieve it. It is worth considering possible criticisms about the relevance of our valuational rule. They raise important issues.

One possible criticism is that the value consensus we point to is insufficient to warrant being characterized as the community's prevailing values. It might be claimed that the consensus so far revealed in the social sciences is actually only a weak tendency which conceptualization has concretized into something that looks substantial. Such a tendency would scarcely deserve exclusive attention as *the* socially accepted decision rule. This criticism can be largely refuted if empirical investigations should show strong consensus. The current state of knowledge suggests more than a minor "tendency," but, in all fairness, nothing more definitive than this can be offered at the present time.[27] However, even in the event that such conforming evidence be found, the force of the criticism is not entirely spent, since whatever the degree of consensus found, the critic may still regard it as "not enough" to serve as an index of *welfare*. Ultimately, of

---

[27]It is, of course, not enough that the consensus be strong. It must also be such that relatively unambiguous evaluations can be read off from it. The answer as of now, with incomplete understanding of the phenomenon, seems to be that societies differ in their "goingness," in the strength and decision stages of their consensus, in the uniqueness of their content, in their coherence or consistency. For our purposes in welfare economics, an empirical concept of social choice is most useful if it reflects strong consensus on an approved Social Welfare Function level, and if this consensus has a determinate, coherent content.

course, the criticism is a value judgment about what an index of welfare ought to be when more than one person is involved.

Because this criticism cannot ultimately be avoided, we must be quite precise about what our procedure entails. We are labeling an empirical congeries of individual behavior as a process of social choice and defining social welfare as that which is ordered by this process of social choice.

Another possible criticism is that, however strong the consensus may be, the particular values involved, only a small subset of all the values relating to welfare which are held in the community, have no especial justification to be considered *the* prevailing values relating to welfare. Here too, no definitive refutation is even in principle possible. But the characteristics of the values which our concept of social choice selects would seem to be of such unique significance in the community as to persuade one strongly to relinquish this objection. I have attempted to describe a value consensus which is perhaps the chief motivational support for the continued functioning of those institutions which are fundamental in the structure of the given community. These values are intimately interrelated with what is most distinctive in the society. They color the general orientation to the world which individuals socialized within that community tend to develop. They are, then, in this sense, basic as a kind of common frame of reference within which individual differences are perceived.

At this point our description of the hypothesis of social choice and the important part played by actual decision-making functions might well lead to complaint that we are asserting only that what is, is right.[28] Our resulting welfare analysis would seem to lose all possibility of *evaluating*, as opposed to simply accepting, a prevailing social state. We apparently have to exclude room for policy recommendations stemming from familiar economic analyses of monopolistic restriction, external economies, economic stabilization, and the like. Moreover, if the analysis really allows no opportunity to evaluate the actual, is it really a *welfare* analysis at all?[29]

This objection is warranted if our schema is such that every prevailing social state is deemed to have been brought about by a social choice, or, what has the same effect for us, if we can discover the content of social choice only through what social states actually come about. In these cases, whatever social state prevails is optimal by definition. Therefore, evaluation is trivial. I do not think my approach necessarily entails such a schema. For one thing, the social decision-making processes with which I have identified the Social Welfare Function are not bound to be institutions

---

[28]Or, perhaps, that which is voted is right.

[29]I am indebted to Professor A. G. Hart for his sharp formulation of this objection. He has made his criticism even more precise by defining welfare economics itself as "a *search for biases* in the procedures of social decision, such that we may find ourselves rejecting alternatives we 'really' prefer."

which have the power to transform the existing social state into the preferred alternative. In a particular society, the strategic decision-making process may be an institution which simply articulates evaluations of alternatives on the verbal or literary level alone, e.g., the clergy in a quasi-medieval environment.[30]

It is true that when we come to societies in which popular representative government is granted a strong socially integrative allegiance, it may be more difficult to distinguish between socially expressed preferences and the public policy attempts to change existing conditions in accordance with them. But this is not the fault of a welfare analysis based on our interpretation. Inasmuch as the valid employment of the concept of social choice as described here implies pervasive integration of value orientations among the population, it is quite possible that in employing the concept for welfare economics, the dispersion from optimality of prevailing social states may be found to be less than what was believed under purely *a priori* formulations about social preference. This means not that welfare economics is the poorer, but that our understanding of group choice is the richer.[31]

---

[30]An only partly comparable, but quite dramatic symbolization of articulation without conclusive transforming power is the Oracle at Delphi in Ancient Greece. In a real sense, the role of the High Priest Nathan in the biblical story of King David, partook of elements of social valuation.

As a contemporary example, let us say we take the formulation of public policy by Congress as the relevant Social Welfare Function for American society. Then, among "social decisions" made would be congressional legislation, or resolutions expressing a desire that certain states of affairs be brought about but without the implementation of adequate machinery to enforce them.

[31]Two related issues brought up in connection with this objection can be answered as follows. First is the implication that positive economic analysis alone gives rise to specific policy recommendations, and that a model of the Social Welfare Function in which these recommendations are not incorporable is thereby deficient. What is implied here is the claim that knowledge about social preference can be obtained without reference to any particular social preference scale. Actually, it can be shown for any of the aforementioned analytic insights, — e.g. monopolistic restriction, that, because of conceptual proscription against the distinction between "productive efficiency" and "distribution of real income," no non-subjective welfare conclusions do strictly follow, except through specific reference to the social state ordering of a social preference scale. (Cf. Samuelson, *Foundations of Economic Analysis*, 225; discussions by William J. Baumol, and J. N. Morgan of T. Scitovsky, "Recent Developments in Welfare Economics," *Econometrica*, Vol. 19, No. 3 (July, 1951), 350; Little, *A Critique of Welfare Economics*, 60-62; and especially, Arrow, "Little's Critique of Welfare Economics," *American Economic Review*, Vol. XLI, No. 5 (December, 1951), 927-8). These insights, then, do not enable us to obtain welfare conclusions independently of some conception about the nature of social choice. Consequently, there is neither reason to expect nor desire that they carry similar recommendations in different models. This particularity carries no criticism of the respective models.

The second issue concerns the assertion in footnote 29 that "we" reject alternatives which "we" really prefer. Here it is claimed that we possess information about social preference other than — and sometimes contradictory to — what is embedded in the choices of social decision-making processes. This does involve a criticism of our model; but it is not by any means obviously justified criticism, since it seems only to assert

Moreover, even in these latter situations, there are senses in which one can distinguish social preference (or choice) from social action (or "decision," when taken in the sense of action). We may introduce the notions of distortion, error and ignorance.

Distortion. Three forms of distortion may be pointed out: (1) bias, (2) "window-dressing," and (3) gross misrepresentation.

(1) Despite strong approval of the central decision-making processes (for example, representative government) there may well be general recognition that these processes have defects (correspondingly, for example, favoritism, bribery, pork-barreling). The system is widely understood to be "biassed" so the alternatives which are considered by the public at large to be legitimized are not those which actually are "chosen" by the decision processes but those which the public believes would have come about if the bias had not been present. No strong attempts are actually made to reform the decision processes, since it is usually felt that "tinkering" could seriously damage the processes. The acceptance of the processes by the public makes them unwilling to tinker, and at the same time willing to bear the annoyance of decisions which diverge somewhat from what is really wanted.

(2) In their role as arbiters of the "public welfare," citizens may wish to feel that "something is being done" about certain of their own behavior in which they would like themselves to be persuaded to desist. They favor social action (e.g., legislation) based on welfare standards that they do not now favor, but might like to be educated to favor. The social decision is legitimized as a symbolic, educative choice. It is window dressing in two respects. It is ostensive action which is not fully desired, and it may be "on the books" but is actually "enforced" in only a token manner due to the pervasive present opposition. The distortion involved here derives from a widespread conflict between individuals' short-run and long-run values. The social decision diverges from what is "really" wanted insofar as the long-run values (the desire to be "reformed") do not strongly override the conflicting short-run values. Prevailing values are thus inconsistent and a decision favoring one set of values does not reflect the contemporaneous contradictory set.

(3) The decision process itself may be considered to be so defective by a substantial minority of the population that they refuse to accept it as the reflection of prevailing values; they feel that the social decisions grossly misrepresent the community's "real" desires. In this situation, of course,

---

that there is some (unspecified) different ordering of social states which (for some unspecified reason) better deserves to be considered *the* social ordering than the one here presented. The case has yet to be made.

I shall, however, discuss some biases which are consistent with the present interpretation in the text immediately below.

we are perilously close simply not to having the matrix value consensus of which our welfare function consists. Such situations in the real world typically result after a time in institutional change tending toward a new reintegration of values where the consensus is firmer.[32]

The welfare economist has a critical function to perform in situations representing each kind of distortion. He may make policy recommendations calling for a revision of the prevailing social state. With regard to the first, his function would appear to be to suggest reforms of the accepted decision process which would eliminate the biases without damaging what is fundamentally approved in them. With regard to the second, his function would appear to be to seek to resolve the inconsistency in values. It is again an educative function. He may expose the full force of the existing discrepancy; he may make clear the consequences of either set of values; he may suggest some common ground between the conflicting values. With regard to the last type of distortion he may seek to suggest reforms of the decision-making process which would be widely accepted. The content of these reforms could conceivably stem from predictions by the social scientist as to what institutional change which *might* occur would probably lead to a new stable value consensus (and "going society").[33]

Error. Some choices concretized in action may well be reversed or modified within a relatively short time. The scientist's delineation of social consensus is necessarily crude, his inferences from particular choices imprecise. We must interpret our ability to infer social preferences from social decisions only in a "long-run" sense, where, after observing a sequence of oscillating positions taken, we may predict the direction of apparently desirable social change. The functions of welfare analysis here are to criticize short-run deviations from the inferred direction of desirable change, to forestall erroneous formulation of social choice by schematizing the decision-making process or in the case of bias by suggesting structural reforms; to forestall erroneous implementation of social choice by publicizing the consequences of different policies (this, of course, is related to ignorance).

Ignorance. On the operational evidence that when consequences are understood which were previously unknown or wrongly known, or more narrowly known, social decisions are changed, we infer that, given identical individual preferences, social structure and external data, different states and

---

[32]If the social scientist could predict the characteristics of the new integration, the economist might reformulate his welfare analysis in light of these predictions.

[33]In effect, this last would have the economist favor a particular institutional change merely because it may lead to a new consensus. It is not justified on the basis of *current* values held by individuals, however, since on this basis there might be more agreement in favor of a certain institutional change which would not soon lead to a new stable consensus. Social fragmentation may sometimes be more widely favored than social cohesion.

distributions of knowledge about causal relationships would lead to different choices. Hence, a particular decision will not be optimal unless supported by maximum information. One function of welfare analysis here is to evaluate alternative methods of minimizing ignorance within the basic framework of the decision process (including various degrees of delegation of authority to "experts" so long as such delegation can be accomplished without changing the basic rationale of the decision-making process). Another is to publicize the vital specific information about cause and effect without which social decisions are uninformed, hence inefficient, decisions. This involves the introduction of the familiar causal chains of positive economics, e.g., the consequences of monopoly versus those of competition. I have argued above that these chains do not themselves enable us to make policy recommendations. They must be referred to a social preference scale. The act of referring in our approach is the concrete process by which the fruits of positive economic theory are made available to the public or at least, to the relevant social decision-making agents.[34] A last function of welfare analysis is to make known the alternatives which, as previously noted, the decision-making function may systematically suppress from consideration or even from consciousness of the population. Such a confrontation, together with information about institutional changes designed to include consideration of the neglected alternatives, give additional scope to the full preferences of the population.

One important qualification must be reaffirmed. In each case, the value commitment to existing decision processes, for all their demonstrable distortion, inducement to error, and proliferation of ignorance, might well exceed the anticipated advantages of institutional change or even the advantages of *ex post correction* to social decisions without institutional change. The welfare economist must be prepared to find that the validated *ways* of obtaining things are often more prized than the supposedly ultimately prized things to be obtained.[35] This is a consequence of the fact, already noted, that it is often the decision-making processes which define for an individual what his ultimate goals should be, and also of the fact that stable organization of role interrelationships in a society results in the satisfactions attached to "ultimate" goals becoming attached to the more proximate *means* of obtaining those goals, thereby reinforcing the original approval of the decision-making processes. The valuation of ways of getting things is not more "artificial" than the things themselves, as can be

---

[34]It is, of course, possible that if the economist has evidence as to what relevant knowledge the public lacked in making its choices, he may himself estimate, on the basis of a knowledge of individual preferences, what the social decision would have been if individuals had possessed more information.

I am indebted to Professor Hart for this suggestion.

[35]For example, government subsidies to farmers.

seen by attempting to specify which of the million or so derived "needs" for things is not artificial, which satisfy only direct organismic needs without any social content whatsoever. If in fact it should be widely found that fundamental means are substantially more prized than ends, then it would become almost impossible to distinguish between a prevailing and a preferred social state. But, once again, this failure is not a defect of welfare economics but rather, if a defect at all, of our initial value judgment to measure social welfare in terms of the group's own scale of values instead of imposing some other scale from outside. It is, in less negative words, an insight into social valuation.

13-6. Acceptability of the Social Welfare Function

In order to proceed further, it is important to consider the structure of the analysis in our enquiry so far. Our basic criteria for judging Social Welfare Functions are (1) consistency, (2) power, and (3) relevance. An "acceptable" Social Welfare Function is one which fulfills these criteria to a high degree. Acceptability in these general terms is not an all or nothing proposition. Arrow's five conditions can be taken roughly as an attempt at giving content to these criteria; consumer sovereignty (Conditions 2, 4 and 5) is to be the content of relevance; Arrow's conception of rationality (Conditions 1 and 3) is to be roughly the content of power and consistency.[36] The acceptability of a Social Welfare Function in Arrow's treatment is, then, similarly its fulfillment of our criteria, but now the fulfillment is an all or nothing affair due to the greater specificity of the criteria. In early sections of this chapter I have focused on the attempt to give a different, and potentially more concrete, content to the criterion of relevance. In these terms we may return to the spirit of Arrow's treatment and, — admittedly roughly, — conceive of at least one welfare function which *completely fulfills* the criterion. It will be convenient to refer to less successful functions as *failing to fulfill* the criterion.[37] Because of the importance of the relevancy criterion in formulating a useful welfare analysis, I have proceeded to examine the characteristics of welfare functions which do fulfill this criterion. Employing the results of this examination, we may add some further notions to the question of acceptability.

Suppose we should at least require that an acceptable Social Welfare

---

[36]To paraphrase Condition 1 from this point of view, we require that the social ordering be complete (power), and a "true," transitive, ordering (power and consistency). Paraphrasing Condition 3, we require that the social ordering be unchanged so long as all the determinants of that ordering are unchanged (consistency).

[37]Just as in Arrow's treatment a welfare function fulfilling Conditions 2 through 5 and generating only a single intransitive triplet would still be said to have failed to fulfill Condition 1 and therefore to be unacceptable.

Function must fulfill our newly defined criterion of relevance. Then the function must necessarily embody the prevailing values of the community as understood by our hypothesis on social choice. From this, two facts follow:

(1) its content reflects on existing value consensus;

(2) it assumes a form peculiar to the specific society.

Our hypothesis submits that the pertinent value consensus, when it exists in a community, is empirically observable and amenable to scientific generalization. Hence, to require that a welfare function fulfill the criterion of relevance is to stipulate only that its content represent an *accurate* generalization of the pertinent value consensus. The structural conditions which this imposes on the welfare function are not *a priori* analytic (i.e., purely formal) requirements. They are *a posteriori* synthetic requirements; they are "conditions of correspondence"[38] between the generalization and the real world. Conditions of this sort, then, are not value judgments; they are demonstrably true or false, and not "reasonable" or "unreasonable." All that can be characterized as "reasonable" or "unreasonable" are the scientific procedures by which we discover the nature of the social consensus.[39]

These facts, together with our discussion of the last section, suggest that if we require a particular welfare function to fulfill the criterion of relevance it may be unable to fulfill the criteria of consistency and power. The first requirement allows us no freedom to shape the function to the demands of the other two criteria; the degree to which the function is consistent or powerful depends only on the substance of the particular value consensus generalized.[40]

Although we may stress the importance of having a welfare standard which is relevant, we may not wish thereby to be completely unconcerned about its consistency and power. Considerable inconsistency in such a standard, for example, would hinder our ability to make predictions about social choices. Moreover, actual choices would be highly ambiguous and therefore difficult to interpret.[41] In such a situation we would be very unlikely to be able to secure unambiguous appraisals of many of the alternatives that interest us. It is doubtful that we should term such a welfare function useful.

This suggests that we drop the all or nothing character of the test for

---

[38]Little, "Social Choice and Individual Values," 421.

[39]To judge these characterizations we would have to have recourse to such operating rules as the rules of induction, etc.

[40]This situation is similar to one which we discussed in Chapter 2. At that point we noted that an acceptance of Bergson's hypothetical value consensus as the Social Welfare Function made Arrow's conditions simply irrelevant.

[41]Ambiguous in the same sense that the outcome of a majority voting process would be ambiguous if the rankings of alternatives by the voters were intransitive.

relevance. Evaluation of different welfare functions would then be carried on in terms of *the relative degrees* to which they fulfilled our three criteria. This is not itself an unambiguous rule, however, since we have had intimations that the criteria may not render similar verdicts with regard to any pair of functions being compared (a kind of situation quite familiar to us by now!). How then would we make over-all appraisals of different welfare functions? Which criterion is most important? Which least important? Or perhaps we ought to ask (without unduly maddening the reader): By what decision function of these criteria can we obtain an ordering of Social Welfare Function models? I do not pretend to know the answer.

My own predilections are to weight relevance heavily, and to ask for a close approximation to this criterion unless it must be paid for by a heavy loss of analytic power. Moderate, if isolated, inconsistencies may be more tolerable than a standard which diverges in some important respects from the values which matter to the individuals concerned.

An important qualification is required. Our criterion of relevance is based on a generalization of *currently* prevailing values. But we are none of us entirely satisfied with where our own or our neighbor's pathways have led us. The search for a useful welfare economics should nowhere criticize the far more urgent search for better paths.[42]

13-7. Acceptance of the Social Welfare Function

It is enlightening to compare the substance of the last section with the different conception of the acceptability of a Social Welfare Function as derived from the approach of Chapter 12. I do this not to disparage Little, his criteria are quite appropriate for his different conception of the social welfare function and decision-making processes, but to throw further light on the conception developed in this chapter. In the absence of empirical delineation of the particular value consensus we may be interested in, and, consequently, in the absence of information about consistency and analytic power, we may proceed in the present section to require that the Social Welfare Function fulfill the criterion of relevance. Our own model, then, will consist in identifying the content of the Social Welfare Function as reflecting the central social decision-making process (or processes) in the community (our procedure in Section 13-5). As noted in Section 13-6, the

---

[42] The distinction is very important. Anyone is free to criticize currently prevailing values. The welfare economist is neither uniquely nor even especially qualified for such a task. Ethical criticism is an attempt to persuade individuals to *change* their values and their institutions. If it succeeds, the welfare economist's competence is called on only to help reconstruct institutions in accordance with the newly formed values or to evaluate how well newly fashioned institutions accord with the new values. The welfare economist, *qua* welfare economist, is not concerned with criticizing either the old or the new values themselves.

acceptability of such a model consists in its representing an accurate generalization of the pertinent value consensus, an accurate generalization of the pertinent decision-processes.

In Little's view, the "reasonableness" of the conditions to be imposed on acceptable welfare functions depends on whether or not it is reasonable for particular individuals to "accept" them as part of some social decision-making function.

After showing that it is not in general inconsistent for an individual to prefer A to B and yet "accept" the judgment of a decision-making process that B is preferred *to* A, he continues:

> Thus, the individual will often be prepared to accept a decision which goes against him, because the same decision-making process (or 'procedure', for short) will be used for making many other decisions between other alternatives, some of which will go in his favor. This is, of course, true; but it is not an answer to the problem of why acceptance of Arrow's conditions does not imply inconsistency. I may be prepared, of course, to accept decisions which go against me because it is unwise to rebel against an established procedure with established sanctions. But this does not explain why, when I am free and still without my chains, I should accept certain *a priori* conditions to which any social contract must conform — *a priori* conditions which rule out all procedures which would decide in my favor against everyone else. To explain this, we require, I think, the hypothesis that, among the very limited number of procedures which would stand any chance of being established, none would make me dictatorial in Arrow's sense, together with the hypothesis that all such procedures would determine social states higher on my valuation than anarchy.[43]

We may examine this from the point of view of our own approach. Two kinds of "acceptance" by the individual are discussed in this passage: (1) "acceptance" of particular social decisions running counter to the individual's own valuation; (2) "acceptance" of decision-making processes themselves. According to Little, an individual *may* "accept" a specific judgment running counter to his own because he expects that "the same decision-making process will [result in] other decisions which will go in his favor." But the implication cannot be denied that the same individual may, nonetheless, not "accept," i.e., "reject," the same specific judgment. In both cases, the individual recognizes the social decision-making process. Yet, in one he accepts, in the other rejects, its specific judgment. In the interpretation given in this chapter, however, (identifying the decision process with the Social Welfare Function) the possibility of "rejection," given recognition of the decision process, must be denied. For what does this "rejection" mean?

We must first suggest that the distinction made by Little about situa-

---

[43]Little, *op. cit.*, 431.

tions in which the individual is faced by an "established procedure" and situations in which he is "free and still without . . . chains" is not meaningful. Criticism of this distinction is, indeed, one of the important fruits of the approach developed in this chapter. The individual, whether as social scientist or citizen, is always faced by "established procedure." He exists within a social system and already has developed basic preconceptions which are not independent of his social context. He is never in this sense free and without chains. So his appraisal of any decision process, whether established or hypothetical, is grounded on his saturation in community values.

Suppose now the individual is faced with a decision by what we should consider the central decision-making process (an "established procedure"). If "rejection" of this decision is taken to mean that the individual disagrees with the decision and refuses to abandon his own opposite judgment, then such disagreement does not logically entail his denying that the social decision was nevertheless the outcome of the decision process, and that this decision process may embody matrix values for the community; he is not denying that it *is* the social welfare judgment. Even if "rejection" is taken to mean active opposition to the social judgment—the individual acts in a "socially disapproved" way—he is not thereby necessarily questioning that the social decision was rendered through the proper channels and thereby represents the social welfare judgment. Real rejection follows only if: (1) he believes the particular decision was not the outcome of the decision process in question (figuratively, "Ignorance of the law"); (2) he does not accept the decision process as a Social Welfare Function.

We must not deny that some social structures may make "ignorance" substantial, and in such cases, the very concept of social valuation will be ambiguous. But sociological studies give us hope that in many societies that interest us as economists, there is sufficient institutional articulation of social value decisions to minimize the importance of "ignorance." Practically speaking, then, we may summarize this section so far by stating that "acceptance" of particular social decisions entails "acceptance" of the decision-making process as a Social Welfare Function; "rejection" of particular social decisions entails "rejection" of the decision-making process as a Social Welfare Function.[44]

---

[44]An interesting treatment of this issue is given, though within a different context and with notably different terminology, by Yves Simon in *Philosophy of Democratic Government* (Chicago: University of Chicago Press, 1951). He quotes Thomas Aquinas (*Summa Theologica*) as saying: "Thus a judge has a good will in willing a thief to be put to death, because this is just; while the will of another (e.g., the thief's wife or son) who wishes him not to be put to death, inasmuch as killing is a natural evil, is also good." (p. 40) He summarizes his views on public and private judgments as follows:

"1. That virtue implies love for the common good, willingness to sacrifice one's own advantage to its requirements.

"Acceptance" or "rejection" of social decision-making processes is clearly of importance for Little's interpretation and for the one developed in this chapter (identifying the welfare function as a decision-making process). In Little's view the problem (with respect to the nondictatorship condition especially) can be expressed: "[Why should I] accept certain *a priori* conditions which rule out all procedures which would ever decide in my favor against everyone else?"

He envisages the very process by which parties to the "social contract" choose which social decision-making process shall be established. For each individual, choosing among decision processes is quite analogous to ordering social states; it depends solely upon his own preference scale (where he orders social states on the basis of the distribution of goods and services to others as well as to himself) since each decision process suggests a particular future sequence of social states (or a particular probability distribution of future social states). And the difficulty again, as seen above, is that no one can logically accept the unique decision process chosen as representing a Social Welfare Function unless he agrees with the choice.

Little's way of looking at the acceptance or rejection of social decision-making processes may be formally correct, but its abstractness blurs over a most important fact about such acceptance in the real world. The interpretation of social welfare functions developed in ·this chapter is on a lower level of abstraction and so cannot avoid dealing with this fact. It is certainly true that a decision-making process subject to heavy popular disapproval could not be usefully considered a Social Welfare Function. But this is exactly the point. The decision-making process which *can* be considered a Social Welfare Function, and it is of this that contemporary social science

---

"2. That the common good may be intended formally without being intended materially.

"3. That the virtue of the private person guarantees the intention of the common good formally considered, not the intention of the common good materially considered.

"4. That society would be harmed if everyone intended the common good not only formally but also materially; that, in a material sense, particular persons and groups ought to intend particular goods.

"5. That the intention of the common good, materially considered, is the business of a public reason and a public will.

"6. That the intention of the common good by the public reason and will necessarily develops into a direction of society, by the public reason and will, toward the common good, considered not only formally but also materially; which is the same as to say that the intention of the common good, materially considered, demands the operation of authority." (p. 48)

It should be noted that his formulation avoids the Rousseauean totalitarian mysticism that Little rightly criticizes. Thus, in our terms, given some institutional social decision-making process proclaiming the "socially desirable" (the "common good"), a disagreement by an individual with a particular judgment neither involves logical contradiction, nor does it necessarily involve his rejection of the social decision-making process.

speaks, *is* so highly institutionalized, so pervasively and deeply *accepted*, that this acceptance involves individuals interiorizing it as a personal value. Only misleadingly can such acceptance be described by Little's fiction of a conscious rational evaluating of future consequences. Acceptance or rejection of basic institutional decision functions is actually part of the gradual process by which each individual is socialized into his society. It is within this same process, moreover, that the individual develops all his values, his whole orientation for future behavior. Within any stable social system (and the economic system is a part of this social system) the stability is given *only* by such widespread interiorization of the values implicit in accepting the major social decision-making processes. These values, this acceptance, persists for the most part independently of rational calculation. One could say, in fact, that it is they that provide the goals for each individual which define the direction rational calculation must take.

Thus, we may summarize the previous argument concerning acceptability of the Social Welfare Function by saying that, when Little's criteria about acceptance or rejection of social decisions and decision-making processes are examined in the light of the empirical content of the interpretation of the present chapter, they are applicable only when they reduce to the proposition presented above, namely; a Social Welfare Function is acceptable only when it accurately describes a social decision-making process for which there exists in the observable real world a matrix-value consensus supporting it.[45]

Value standards like those relevant to the economic welfare problem do change over time. Minor standards, those not deeply engaged in the social framework or the personality,[46] may change frequently. But changes in those values which sustain the basic decision-making processes occur only in the course of significant changes in the structure of society itself. For periods of relative stability in the structure of society, it may be assumed that there exists the requisite general approval of those social decision-making processes which I have defined as the content of the Social Welfare Function. Few tools in modern economic analysis claim applicability under any assumption other than that of an essentially unchanged social structure. If I have argued correctly, therefore, the invariance of the combinatorial rule known as the Social Welfare Function is founded empirically on as extended a time scale as almost any concept in economic theory.[47]

---

[45]Only a necessary condition is appropriate here. Sufficient conditions, of course, involve, in addition, specifying which decision processes are relevant for the economist's problems.

[46]One interesting insight of modern sociology seems to me to be the close correspondence between the degree of "ego-involvement" and "social involvement."

[47]Hence my argument in Chapter 2 that the rule is independent of individual taste orderings.

13-8. SUMMARY

In this chapter I have suggested how to give empirical content to the notion of a community's prevailing values. The method suggested is based on a refutable hypothesis recently developed in the allied social sciences concerning the existence of a uniquely important value consensus in the going society. I have broadly sketched the outlines of this hypothesis. Our willingness to employ the hypothesis as a criterion of relevance in appraising Social Welfare Function models certainly depends in part on its empirical verification, but no conclusive testing of the hypothesis has as yet been achieved.

In addition to my purpose of constructing a criterion of relevance, I have examined some of the implications for welfare analysis of a model of the Social Welfare Function in which the content of the function consists of the above empirical generalization of a community's prevailing values. The crucial assumption is that the ordering derivable from this function is widely accepted as an expression of social choice. At the current, still rudimentary stage of enquiry we must interpret the acceptance and indeed, the underlying generalization of the value consensus, in only a very rough way, e.g., as a long-run tendency in a stable society. Moreover, we must leave as open questions the degree to which any concrete generalization will generate inconsistent or in other respects ambiguous choices, and the range of policy issues which can be arbitered through its use. This is unfortunate for our purposes, but not fatal; tentative adoption of an incomplete and imprecise formulation on these lines today is only the setting out of a frame of reference whereby welfare economics can share the fruits of advances in the mainstream of neighboring social sciences.

A final word. Adoption of the approach suggested here either for the construction of a relevance criterion by which to judge social welfare functions or as giving the content of a Social Welfare Function itself, does not transform welfare economics into a value-free discipline. In neither case can it be *empirically demonstrated* that our approach tells us what we ought to mean by relevancy or social welfare. In both cases, adoption of the approach requires making the unverifiable value judgment that it does tell us this.

Bibliography

Alchian, Armen, "Uncertainty, Evolution and Economic Theory," *The Journal of Political Economy*, Vol. LVIII, No. 3 (June, 1950), 211-221.

_____ "The Meaning of Utility Measurement," *American Economic Review*, Vol. XLIII, No. 1 (March, 1953), 26-50.

Allais, M., "Le Comportement de l'Homme Rationnel devant le Risque: Critique des Postulats et Axiomes de l'Ecole Americaine," *Econometrica*, Vol. 21, No. 4 (October, 1953), 503–546.

_____ "L'Extension des Theories de l'Equilibre economique general et de Rendement social au Cas du Risque," *Econometrica*, Vol. 21, No. 2 (April, 1953), 269–90.

_____ "La Psychologie de l'Homme Rationnel devant le Risque," *Journal of Social Statistics*, Vol. 94 (1953), 47–73.

Allen, R. G. D., "A Note on the Determinateness of the Utility Function," *Review of Economic Studies*, Vol. II (1935), 155–158.

_____ "The Economic Theory of Index Numbers," *Economica*, New Series, Vol. XVI (May, 1949), 197–203.

Ames, Edward, *Induction and Probability Theories in Economics*, unpublished Ph. D. dissertation, Harvard University, 1950.

Andrews, Tom Gaylord, *Methods of Psychology*, New York: John Wiley & Sons, Inc., 1948.

Archibald, G. C., "Utility, Risk and Linearity," *The Journal of Political Economy*, Vol. LXVII, No. 5 (October, 1959), 437–450.

_____ "Welfare Economics, Ethics and Essentialism," *Economica*, New Series, Vol. XXVI (November, 1959), 316–327.

Archimedes, *The Works of Archimedes* (ed. by T. L. Heath), New York: Dover Publications.

Armstrong, W. E., "The Determinateness of the Utility Function," *Economic Journal*, Vol. XLIX (1939).

_____ "Uncertainty and the Utility Function," *Economic Journal*, Vol. LVIII (1945).

_____ "A Note on the Theory of Consumer's Behavior," *Oxford Economic Papers*, New Series, Vol. 2, No. 1 (January, 1950).

_____ "Utility and the Theory of Welfare," *Oxford Economic Papers*, New Series, Vol. 3, No. 3 (October, 1951).

_____ "A Reply to 'Marginal Preference and the Theory of Welfare'," *Oxford Economic Papers*, Vol. 5, No. 3 (October, 1953), 264–271.

Arrow, Kenneth J., "Alternative Approaches to the Theory of Choice in Risk-Taking Situations," *Econometrica*, Vol. 19, No. 4 (October, 1951).

_____ "A Difficulty in the Concept of Social Welfare," *The Journal of Political Economy*, Vol. LVIII, No. 4 (August, 1950), 328–346.

_____ "An Extension of the Basic Theorems of Classical Welfare Economics," in *Proceedings of the Second Berkeley Symposium on Mathematical Statistics and Probability*. Berkeley, Calif.: University of California Press, 1951, 507–532.

_____ "Little's Critique of Welfare Economics," *American Economic Review*, Vol. XLI, No. 5 (December, 1951), 923–934.

_____ *Social Choice and Individual Values*. New York: John Wiley & Sons, Inc., 1951.

_____ "The Work of Ragnar Frisch, Econometrician," *Econometrica*, Vol. 28, No. 2 (April, 1960), 175–192.

Asch, Solomon E., *Social Psychology*. Englewood Cliffs, N. J.: Prentice-Hall, Inc., 1952.

Bailey, M. J., "The Interpretation and Application of the Compensation Principle," *Economic Journal*, Vol. LXIV, No. 253 (March, 1954), 39–52.

Baldwin, Robert E., "A Comparison of Welfare Criteria," *Review of Economic Studies*, Vol. XXI (2), No. 5 (1954), 154–161.

Barone, Enrico, "The Ministry of Production in a Socialist State," *Giornale degli Economisti* (1908); collected in *Collectivist Economic Planning* (ed. Friedrich A. von Hayek). London: Routledge & Sons, 1935, 245–290.

Bator, F. M., "The Simple Analytics of Welfare Maximization," *American Economic Review*, Vol. XLVII, No. 1 (March, 1957), 22–59.

Baumol, W. J., "The Cardinal Utility which is Ordinal," *The Economic Journal*, Vol. LXVII, No. 272 (December, 1958), 665–672.

_____ "Community Indifference," *Review of Economic Studies*, Vol. 14, No. 1 (1946–1947).

_____ "The Community Indifference Map: A Construction," *Review of Economic Studies*, Vol. XVII (3), No. 44 (1950), 189–197.

_____ "Discussion of Scitovsky's 'Recent Developments in Welfare Economics'," *Econometrica*, Vol. 19, No. 3 (July, 1951), 350.

_____ "The von Neumann-Morgenstern Utility Index — An Ordinalist View," *The Journal of Political Economy*, Vol. LIX, No. 1 (February, 1951), 61–66.

_____ *Welfare Economics and the Theory of the State*. Cambridge: Harvard University Press, 1952.

Beckwith, Burnham P., *Marginal Cost Output Control*. New York: Columbia University Press, 1955.

Bergson, Abram, "On the Concept of Social Welfare," *The Quarterly Journal of Economics*, Vol. LXVIII, No. 2 (May, 1954), 233–252.

⸻ "A Reformulation of Certain Aspects of Welfare Economics," *Quarterly Journal of Economics* (February, 1938), 310–334.

⸻ "Socialist Economics." In *A Survey of Contemporary Economics* (ed. Howard S. Ellis). Philadelphia: Blakiston, 1948.

Bernoulli, Daniel, *Specimen Theoriae Novae de Mensura Sortis*. English Translation by Louise Sommer, "Exposition of a New Theory on the Measurement of Risk," *Econometrica*, Vol. 22, No. 1 (January, 1954), 23–36.

Black, Duncan, "On the Rationale of Group Decision-Making," *The Journal of Political Economy*, Vol. LVI, No. 1 (February, 1948), 23–34.

⸻ *The Theory of Committees and Elections*. Cambridge: Cambridge University Press, 1958.

⸻ "The Decisions of a Committee Using a Special Majority," *Econometrica*, Vol. 16, No. 3 (July, 1948), 245–270.

⸻ "The Elasticity of Committee Decisions with an Altering Size of Majority," *Econometrica*, Vol. 16, No. 3 (July, 1948), 262–270.

Blau, Julian H., "The Existence of Social Welfare Functions," *Econometrica*, Vol. 25, No. 2 (April, 1957), 302–313.

Boulding, Kenneth E., "Welfare Economics," in *A Survey of Contemporary Economics*, Vol. II (ed. Bernard F. Haley). New York: Blakiston, 1952.

Buchanan, J. M., "Individual Choice in Voting and the Market," *The Journal of Political Economy*, Vol. LXII, No. 4 (August, 1954), 334–343.

⸻ "Social Choice, Democracy and Free Markets," *The Journal of Political Economy*, Vol. LXII, No. 2 (April, 1954), 114–123.

Carnap, Rudolf, *Logical Foundations of Probability*. Chicago: The University of Chicago Press, 1950.

⸻ "The Two Concepts of Probability," in *Essays in Philosophic Analysis* (eds. Herbert Feigl and Wilfrid Sellars). New York: Appleton-Century-Crofts, Inc., 1949.

Chatalian, George, "Probability: Inductive vs. Deductive," *Philosophical Studies*, Vol. III, No. 4 (June, 1952).

Chipman, John S., "The Foundations of Utility," *Econometrica*, Vol. 28, No. 2 (April, 1960), 193–224.

Clark, John M., *Alternative to Serfdom*. New York: Alfred A. Knopf, Inc., 1948.

———— "Realism and Relevance in the Theory of Demand," *The Journal of Political Economy*, Vol. LIV, No. 4 (August, 1945), 347–353.

Coase, R. H., "The Marginal Cost Controversy," *Economica*, New Series, Vol. XIII, No. 51 (August, 1946), 169–182.

———— "The Marginal Cost Controversy, Some Further Comments," *Economica* (1947), 150.

Committee on Public Finance, *Public Finance*. Chapter 2: "The Role of Government in a Market Economy," by Nelson McClung, Jerome Rothenberg and Angel Rugina. New York: Pitman & Co., 1959.

Coombs, Clyde H., "Psychological Scaling without a Unit of Measurement," *Psychological Review*, Vol. 57, No. 3 (May, 1950), 145–158.

———— "Theory and Methods of Social Measurement," in *Research Methods in the Behavioral Sciences* (eds. Leon Festinger and Daniel Katz). New York: Dryden Press, 1953.

———— and J. E. Milholland, "Testing the 'Rationality' of an Individual's Decision Making under Uncertainty," *Psychometrica*, (1954).

Dahl, Robert A., and Charles E. Lindblom, *Politics, Economics and Welfare*. New York: Harper & Brothers, Publishers, 1953.

Davidson, Donald, and Patrick Suppes, in collaboration with Sidney Siegel, *Decision Making: An Experimental Approach*. Stanford, Calif.: Stanford University Press, 1957.

Davis, Harold T., *The Theory of Econometrics*. Bloomington, Ind.: The Principia Press, 1941.

Davis, R. G., "Comment on Arrow and the 'New Welfare' Economics," *Economic Journal*, Vol. 68, No. 272 (December, 1958), 834–835.

Debreu, Gerard, "The Coefficient of Resource Utilization," *Econometrica*, Vol. 19, No. 3 (July, 1951), 273–292.

DeFinetti, Bruno, "Recent Suggestions for the Reconciliation of Theories of Probability," in *Proceedings of the Second Berkeley Symposium on Mathematical Statistics and Probability*. Berkeley, Calif.: University of California Press, 1951.

Dobb, Maurice H., "A Note on Index Numbers and Compensation Criteria," *Oxford Economic Papers*, Vol. 8, No. 1 (February, 1956), 78–79.

Duesenberry, James S., *Income, Saving and the Theory of Consumer Behavior*. Cambridge: Harvard University Press, 1949.

Dworetsky, Aryeh, "Decision Functions," *Econometrica*, Vol. 18 (1950), 181–182.

Eckstein, Otto, "Investment Criteria for Economic Development and the Theory of Intertemporal Welfare Economics," *The Quarterly Journal of Economics*, Vol. LXXI, No. 1 (February, 1957), 56–85.

Edgeworth, Francis Y., *Mathematical Psychics*. London: C. Kegan Paul & Co., 1881.

Edwards, Ward, "Experiments on Economic Decision-Making in Gambling Situations," *Econometrica*, Vol. 21, No. 2 (April, 1953), 349–350 (abstract).

_____ "Probability Preferences Among Bets with Differing Expected Values," *American Journal of Psychology*, Vol. 67 (1954), 56–57.

_____ "Probability-Preferences in Gambling," *American Journal of Psychology*, Vol. LXVI (1953), 349–364.

_____ "The Reliability of Probability Preferences," *American Journal of Psychology*, Vol. 67 (1954), 68-95.

_____ "The Theory of Decision Making," *Psychological Bulletin*, Vol. 51, No. 4 (1954), 380–417.

Ellsberg, Daniel, "Classic and Current Notions of 'Measurable Utility'," *Economic Journal*, Vol. LXIV, No. 255 (September, 1954), 528–556.

_____ "The Theory of the Reluctant Duelist," *American Economic Review*, Vol. XLVI, No. 5 (December, 1956), 909–923.

Farrell, M. J., "In Defence of Public-Utility Price Theory," *Oxford Economic Papers*, New Series, Vol. X, No. 1 (February, 1958), 109–123.

_____ "Mr. Lancaster on Welfare and Choice," *Economic Journal*, Vol. LXIX, No. 275 (September, 1959), 588.

Fisher, Franklin M., "Income Distribution, Value Judgments, and Welfare," *The Quarterly Journal of Economics*, Vol. LXX (August, 1956) 380–424.

_____ and Jerome Rothenberg, "How Income Ought to Be Distributed: Paradox Lost," *The Journal of Political Economy*, Vol. LXIX, No. 2 (April, 1961).

Fisher, Irving, "A Statistical Measure for Measuring 'Marginal Utility' and Testing the Justice of a Progressive Income Tax," in *Economic Essays Contributed in Honor of John Bates Clark* (ed. Hollander). New York: The Macmillan Company, 1927.

Fleming, Marcus, "Cardinal Welfare and Individualistic Ethics, a Comment," *The Journal of Political Economy*, Vol. LXV, No. 4 (August, 1957), 355–357.

_____ "A Cardinal Concept of Welfare," *The Quarterly Journal of Economics*, Vol. LXIV, No. 3 (August, 1952), 366-384.

Flood, M. M., *A Preference Experiment*, P-256, P-258, P-263. Santa Monica, Calif.: The Rand Corporation, November, 1951–January, 1952.

Frankel, S. H., " 'Psychic' and 'Accounting' Concepts of Income and Welfare," *Oxford Economic Papers*, New Series, Vol. 4, No. 1 (February, 1952), 1–17.

Friedman, Milton, *Essays in Positive Economics*. Chicago: The University of Chicago Press, 1953.

_____ "The Expected-Utility Hypothesis and the Measurability of Utility," *The Journal of Political Economy*, Vol. LX, No. 6 (December, 1952), 463–474.

_____ "Lerner on the Economics of Control," *The Journal of Political Economy*, Vol. LV, No. 5 (October, 1947), 405–416.

_____ "What all is Utility?" *Economic Journal*, Vol. LXV, No. 259 (September, 1955), 405–409.

_____ and L. J. Savage, "The Utility Analysis of Choices Involving Risk," *The Journal of Political Economy*, Vol. LVI, No. 4 (August, 1948), 279–304.

Frisch, Ragnar, *New Methods of Measuring Marginal Utility*. Tuebingen, 1932.

Fromm, Erich, *Man for Himself*. New York: Rinehart & Company, Inc., 1949.

Georgescu-Roegen, Nicholas, "Choice, Expectations, and Measurability," *The Quarterly Journal of Economics*, Vol. 68, No. 4 (November, 1954), 503–534.

_____ "The Pure Theory of Consumer's Behavior," *The Quarterly Journal of Economics*, Vol. I (August, 1936), 545–593.

_____ "The Theory of Choice and the Constancy of Economic Laws," *The Quarterly Journal of Economics*, Vol. LXIV (February, 1950), 125–138.

Gorman, W. M., "Are Social Indifference Curves Convex?" *The Quarterly Journal of Economics*, Vol. LXXIII, No. 3 (August, 1959), 485–496.

_____ "Community Preference Fields," *Econometrica*, Vol. 21, No. 1 (January, 1953), 63–80.

_____ "The Intransitivity of Certain Criteria Used in Welfare Economics," *Oxford Economic Papers*, New Series, Vol. 7, No. 1 (February, 1955), 25–35.

Graaff, J. deV., "On Optimum Tariff Structures," *Review of Economic Studies*, Vol. XVII, No. 1 (1949), 47–59.

_____ *Theoretical Welfare Economics*. Cambridge: Cambridge University Press, 1957.

_____ and W. J. Baumol, "Three Notes on 'Expectation in Economics', II," *Economica*, New Series, Vol. 16 (November, 1949), 338–342.

Guilford, J. P., *Fundamental Statistics in Psychology and Education*. New York: McGraw-Hill Book Company, Inc., 1950.

_____ Psychometric Methods. New York: McGraw-Hill Book Company, Inc., 1936.

Harsanyi, John C., "Cardinal Utility in Welfare Economics and in the Theory of Risk-Taking," *The Journal of Political Economy*, Vol. LXI, No. 5 (October, 1953), 434–435.

_____ "Cardinal Welfare, Individualistic Ethics, and Interpersonal Comparisons of Utility," *The Journal of Political Economy*, Vol. XLIII, No. 4 (August, 1955), 309–321.

_____ "Welfare Economics of Variable Tastes," *Review of Economic Studies*, Vol. XXI (3), No. 56 (1954), 204–213.

Hart, Albert G., *Anticipation, Uncertainty and Dynamic Planning*. Chicago: University of Chicago Press, 1940.

_____ "Risk, Uncertainty, and the Unprofitability of Compounding Probabilities," in *Studies in Mathematical Economics and Econometrics, in Memory of Henry Schultz* (eds. O. Lange, F. McIntyre, and T. O. Yntema). Chicago: University of Chicago Press, 1942, 110–118.

_____ and Stephen W. Rousseas, "Experimental Verification of a Composite Indifference Map," *The Journal of Political Economy*, Vol. LIX, No. 4 (August, 1951), 288–318.

Hicks, John R., "Consumers' Surplus and Index Numbers," *Review of Economic Studies*, Vol. IX, No. 2 (1942), 126–137.

_____ "The Foundations of Welfare Economics," *Economic Journal*, Vol. XLIX, No. 196 (December, 1939), 696–712.

_____ "The Four Consumers' Surpluses," *Review of Economic Studies*, Vol. XI, No. 1 (1944), 31–41.

_____ "The Generalized Theory of Consumers' Surplus," *Review of Economic Studies*, Vol. XIII, No. 34 (1946), 68–74.

_____ "The Rehabilitation of Consumer Surplus," *Review of Economic Studies*, Vol. VIII, No. 2 (February, 1941), 108–116.

Hildreth, Clifford, "Alternative Conditions for Social Orderings," *Econometrica*, Vol. 21, No. 1 (January, 1953), 81–91.

_____ "Measurable Utility and Social Welfare," *Economics*, Cowles Commission Discussion Paper, No. 2002 (December, 1950).

Hotelling, Harold, "The General Welfare in Relation to Problems of Taxation and of Railway and Utility Rates," *Econometrica*, Vol. 6, No. 3 (July, 1938), 242–269.

Houthakker, H. S., "Revealed Preference and the Utility Function," *Economica*, Vol. 17, No. 66 (May, 1950), 159–174.

Hunter, Alex, "Product Differentiation and Welfare Economics," *The Quarterly Journal of Economics*, Vol. LXIX, No. 4 (November, 1955), 533-552.

Inada, K., "Alternative Incompatible Conditions for a Social Welfare Function," *Econometrica*, Vol. 23, No. 4 (October, 1955), 396–399.

Irwin, F., "Psychological Measurement Methods," *Psychological Bulletin*, Vol. 32 (1953), 140–171.

James, S. F., and W. Beckerman, "Interdependence of Consumers' Preferences in the Theory of Income Distribution," *Economic Journal*, Vol. LXIII, No. 249 (March, 1953), 70–82.

Johannsen, Dorothy, *The Principles of Psychophysics with Laboratory Exercises*. Saratoga Springs, N. Y.: the Author, 1941.

Kahn, R. F., "Some Notes on Ideal Output," *Economic Journal*, Vol. XLV (March, 1935), 1–35.

Kaldor, Nicholas, "A Comment on 'Community Indifference'," *Review of Economic Studies*, Vol. XIV, No. 1 (1946–1947), 49.

—— "Welfare Propositions in Economics," *Economic Journal*, Vol. XLIX (1939), 549–552.

Kardiner, Abram, *The Individual and His Society*. New York: Columbia University Press, 1941.

—— *Psychological Frontiers of Society*. New York: Columbia University Press, 1945.

Kemp, Murray C., "Arrow's General Possibility Theorem," *Review of Economic Studies*, Vol. XXI (3), No. 56 (1934), 240–243.

—— "The Efficiency of Competition as an Allocator of Resources," Parts I and II, *Canadian Journal of Economics and Political Science*, Vol. 21, No. 1 (February, 1955), 30–42, and Vol. 21, No. 2 (May, 1955), 217–227.

—— "Welfare Economics: A Stocktaking," *Economic Record*, Vol. XXX, No. 59 (November, 1954), 245–251.

Kenen, Peter B., and F. M. Fisher, "Income Distribution, Value Judgments and Welfare: a Correction," *The Quarterly Journal of Economics*, Vol. LXX (May, 1957), 322–324.

Kennedy, C. M., "The Economic Welfare Function and Dr. Little's Criterion," *Review of Economic Studies*, Vol. XX(2), No. 52 (1953), 137–142.

—— "The Common Sense of Indifference Curves," *Oxford Economic Papers*, New Series, Vol. 2, No. 1 (January, 1950).

Knight, Frank H., *The Economic Order and Religion*. New York: Harper & Brothers, Publishers, 1945.

—— *The Economic Organization*. New York: Augustus M. Kelley, 1951.

—— *The Ethics of Competition*. London: Allen & Unwin, 1935.

_____ *Freedom and Reform.* New York: Harper & Brothers, Publishers, 1947.

_____ "Realism and Relevance in the Theory of Demand," *The Journal of Political Economy,* Vol. LII, No. 6 (December, 1944), 289–318.

Koopmans, Tjalling, "Efficient Allocation of Resources," *Econometrica,* Vol. 19, No. 4 (October, 1951), 455–466.

_____ "Utility Analysis of Decisions Affecting Future Well-being," *Econometrica,* Vol. 18, No. 2 (April, 1950), 175–177.

Lancaster, Kelvin, "Welfare Propositions in Terms of Consistency and Expanded Choice," *Economic Journal,* Vol. LXVIII, No. 271 (September, 1958), 464–470.

_____ and R. G. Lipsey, "The General Theory of Second Best," *Review of Economic Studies,* Vol. XXIV(1), No. 63 (1957), 11–32.

_____ and R. G. Lipsey, "McManus on Second Best," *Review of Economic Studies,* Vol. XXVI(3), No. 71 (1959), 225–226.

Lange, Oskar, "The Determinateness of the Utility Function," *Review of Economic Studies,* Vol. 1 (June, 1934), 218–225.

_____ "The Foundations of Welfare Economics," *Econometrica,* Vol. 10, No. 3 (July–October, 1942), 215–238.

_____ "The Scope and Method of Economics," *Review of Economic Studies,* Vol. XIII, No. 1 (1945–1946), 19–32.

Leibenstein, Harvey, "Bandwagon, Snob and Veblen Effects in the Theory of Consumers' Demand," *The Quarterly Journal of Economics,* Vol. LXIV, No. 2 (May, 1950), 183–207.

Lerner, Abba P., "The Concept of Monopoly and the Measurement of Monopoly Power," *Review of Economic Studies,* Vol. 1 (June, 1934), 157–175.

_____ *The Economics of Control.* New York: The Macmillan Company, 1944.

Leys, Wayne A. R., *Ethics for Policy Decisions: The Art of Asking Deliberative Questions.* Englewood Cliffs, N. J.: Prentice-Hall, Inc., 1952.

Little, Ian M. D., *A Critique of Welfare Economics.* Oxford: Oxford University Press, 1949.

_____ "The Foundations of Welfare Economics," *Oxford Economic Papers,* New Series, Vol. 1, No. 2 (June, 1949), 227–246.

_____ "A Reformulation of the Theory of Consumers' Behavior," *Oxford Economic Papers,* Vol. 1 (1949), 90–99.

_____ "Social Choice and Individual Values," *The Journal of Political Economy,* Vol. LX, No. 5 (October, 1952).

Luce, R. Duncan, "A Probabilistic Theory of Utility," *Econometrica,* Vol. 20, No. 2 (April, 1958), 193–224.

Majumdar, Tapas, "Armstrong and the Utility Measurement Controversy," *Oxford Economic Papers*, New Series, Vol. 9, No. 1 (February, 1957), 30–40.

———— *The Measurement of Utility.* London: The Macmillan Company, 1958.

Malinvaud, Edmond, "Capital Accumulation and Efficient Allocation of Resources," *Econometrica*, Vol. 21, No. 2 (April, 1953), 233–268.

———— "Note on von Neumann-Morgenstern's Strong Independence Axiom," *Econometrica*, Vol. 20, No. 4 (October, 1951), 680.

Manne, Allan S., "The Strong Independence Assumption — Gasoline Blends and Probability Mixtures," (with note by A. Charnes), *Econometrica*, Vol. 20, No. 4 (October, 1952), 665–669.

Margolis, Julius, "Welfare Criteria, Pricing and Decentralization of Public Services," *The Quarterly Journal of Economics*, Vol. LXXI, No. 3 (August, 1957), 448–463.

Markowitz, Harry, "The Utility of Wealth," *The Journal of Political Economy*, Vol. LX, No. 2 (April, 1952), 151–158.

———— and Leo A. Goodman, "Social Welfare Functions Based on Individual Rankings," *The American Journal of Sociology*, Vol. LVII, No. 3 (November, 1952), 257–262.

Marschak, Jacob, "Basic Problems in the Economic Theory of Teams," paper read at the December, 1952 meeting of the Econometric Society in Chicago.

———— "Rational Behavior, Uncertain Prospects and Measurable Utility," *Econometrica*, Vol. 18, No. 2 (April, 1950), 111–141.

———— "Towards an Economic Theory of Organization and Information," in *Decision Processes* (eds. R. M. Thrall, C. H. Coombs, and R. L. Davis). New York: John Wiley & Sons, Inc., 1954, Chapter 14.

———— "Why 'Should' Statisticians and Businessmen Maximize 'Moral Expectation'?" *Proceedings of the Second Berkeley Syposium on Mathematical Statistics and Probability*. Berkeley: University of California Press, 1951, 493–505.

Marshall, Alfred, *Principles of Economics*. London: The Macmillan Company, 1946.

May, Kenneth O., "The Intransitivity of Individual Preferences," paper read at the December, 1952 meeting of the Econometric Society in Chicago.

———— "Intransitivity, Utility and Aggregation in Preference Patterns," *Econometrica*, Vol. 22, No. 1 (January, 1954), 1–13.

———— "A Note on the Complete Independence of the Conditions for Simple Majority Decision," *Econometrica*, Vol. 21, No. 1 (January, 1953), 172–173.

———— "A Set of Independent, Necessary and Sufficient Conditions for Simple Major Decision," *Econometrica,* Vol. 20, No. 4 (October, 1952), 680–684.

McGarvey, D. C., "A Theorem in the Construction of Voting Paradoxes," *Econometrica*, Vol. 21, No. 4 (October, 1953), 608–610.

McManus, Maurice, "Comments on the General Theory of Second Best," *Review of Economic Studies*, Vol. XXVI(3), No. 71 (1959), 209–224.

Menger, Karl, "Das Unsicherleitsmoment in der Wertlehre," *Zeitschrift fuer Nationaloekonomie*, Vol. 5 (1934), 459–485.

Mishan, E. J., "Arrow and the 'New Welfare' Economics, a Restatement," *Economic Journal*, Vol. LXVIII, No. 271 (September, 1958), 595–596.

———— "An Investigation into some Alleged Contradictions in Welfare Economics," *Economic Journal*, Vol. LXVII, No. 267 (September, 1957), 445–454.

———— "Mr Lancaster's Welfare Definitions. A Comment," *Economic Journal*, Vol. LXIX, No. 274 (June, 1959,) 395–396.

———— "The Principle of Compensation Reconsidered," *The Journal of Political Economy*, Vol. LX, No. 4 (August, 1952), 312–322.

———— "Realism and Relevance in the Theory of Consumers' Surplus," *Review of Economic Studies*, Vol. XV(1), No. 37 (1948), 27–33.

———— "A Reappraisal of the Principles of Resource Allocation," *Economica*, New Series, Vol. XXIV, No. 96 (November, 1957), 324–342.

———— "A Survey of Welfare Economics, 1939–1959," *The Economic Journal*, Vol. LXX, No. 278 (June, 1960), 197–265.

Modigliani, Franco, "The Measurement of Expectations," *Econometrica*, Vol. 20, No. 3 (July, 1952), 481–483.

Morgan, J. N., "Discussion of Scitovsky's 'Recent Developments in Welfare Economics'," *Econometrica*, Vol. 19, No. 3 (July, 1951), 350.

Mosteller, Frederick, and Philip Nogee, "An Experimental Measurement of Utility," *The Journal of Political Economy*, Vol. LIX, No. 5 (October, 1951), 371–404.

Myint, Hla, *Theories of Welfare Economics*. Cambridge: Harvard University Press, 1948.

Nagel, Ernest, "Wholes, Sums, and Organic Unities," *Philosophical Studies*, Vol. III, No. 2 (February, 1952).

Nash, John J., "The Bargaining Problem," *Econometrica*, Vol. 18, No. 2 (April, 1950).

Newcomb, Theodore, *Social Psychology*. New York: Dryden Press, 1949.

Newman, P., "Mr. Lancaster on Welfare and Choice," *Economic Journal*, Vol. LXIX, No. 275 (September, 1959), 588–590.

Osgood, Charles E., *Method and Theory in Experimental Psychology*. New York: Oxford University Press, 1953.

Papandreou, A. G., "Experimental Testing of a Postulate on the Theory of Choice," paper read at the December, 1952 meeting of the Econometric Society in Chicago.

Pareto, Vilfredo, *Cours d'Economie politique.* Lausanne, 1897.

Parsons, Talcott, *Essays in Sociological Theory, Pure and Applied.* Glencoe, Ill.: The Free Press, 1949.

―――― *The Social System.* Glencoe, Ill.. The Free Press, 1952.

―――― and Edward Shils, *Toward a General Theory of Value.* Cambridge: Harvard University Press, 1951.

Pigou, A. C., *The Economics of Welfare.* London. The Macmillan Company, 1920.

―――― "Real Income and Economic Welfare," *Oxford Economic Papers,* New Series, Vol. 3, No. 1 (February, 1951), 16–20.

―――― "Some Aspects of Welfare Economics," *American Economic Review,* Vol. XLI, No. 3 (June, 1951), 303–315.

Pole, D., "Pareto on the Compensating Principle," *Economic Journal,* Vol. LXV, No. 257 (March, 1955), 156–157.

Radomysler, A., "Welfare Economics and Economic Policy," *Economica,* New Series. Vol. XIII, No. 51 (August, 1946), 190–204

Ramsey, Frank, *The Foundation of Mathematics and Other Logical Essays.* New York: The Humanities Press, 1950.

Reder, M. W., *Studies in the Theory of Welfare Economics.* New York: Columbia University Press, 1947.

―――― "Theories of Welfare Economics," *The Journal of Political Economy,* Vol. LVIII, No. 2 (April, 1950), 158–161.

Reichenbach, Hans, *Experience and Prediction.* Chicago: University of Chicago Press, 1938.

―――― "On the Justification of Induction," in *Readings in Philosophical Analysis* (eds. Feigl and Sellars). New York: Appleton-Century-Crofts, Inc., 1949.

―――― "Philosophical Foundations of Probability," in *Proceedings of the First Berkeley Symposium on Mathematical Statistics and Probability.* Berkeley, Calif.: University of California Press, 1951.

―――― *The Rise of Scientific Philosophy.* Berkeley, Calif.: University of California Press, 1951.

Robbins, Lionel, *An Essay on the Nature and Significance of Economic Science.* London: The Macmillan Company, 1932.

―――― "Robertson on Utility and Scope," *Economica,* New Series. Vol. XX, No. 78 (May, 1953).

Robertson, D. H., "Utility, A Rejoinder," *Economic Journal,* Vol. LXV, No. 259 (September, 1955), 410.

———— "Utility and all What?" *Economic Journal,* Vol. LXIV, No. 256 (December, 1954), 665–678.

Rolph, E. R., and G. F. Break, "The Welfare Aspects of Excise Taxes," *The Journal of Political Economy,* Vol. LVII, No. 1 (February, 1949).

Rose, Arnold M., "A Study of Irrational Judgments," *The Journal of Political Economy,* Vol. LXV, No. 5 (October, 1957), 394–402.

Rothenberg, Jerome, "Conditions for a Social Welfare Function," *The Journal of Political Economy,* Vol. LXI, No. 5 (October, 1953), 389–405.

———— "Marginal Preference and the Theory of Welfare," *Oxford Economic Papers,* New Series, Vol. 5, No. 3 (October, 1953), 248–263.

———— "Non-Convexity, Aggregation and Pareto Optimality," *The Journal of Political Economy,* Vol. LXVIII, No. 5 (October, 1960), 435–468.

———— "Reconsideration of a Group-Welfare Index," *Oxford Economic Papers,* New Series, Vol. 6, No. 1 (February, 1954), 164–180.

———— "The Theory of Economic and Political Decision Making as a Single System." Unpublished manuscript.

———— "Welfare Comparisons and Changes in Tastes," *American Economic Review,* Vol. XLIII, No. 5 (December, 1953).

Rothschild, K. W., "The Meaning of Rationality: A Note on Prof. Lange's Article," *Review of Economic Studies,* Vol. XIV, No. 1 (1946–1947), 50–52.

Ruggles, Nancy, "Recent Developments in the Theory of Marginal Cost Pricing," *Review of Economic Studies,* Vol. XVII(2), No. 43 (1950), 107–126.

———— "The Welfare Basis of Marginal Cost Pricing," *Review of Economic Studies,* Vol. XVII, No. 42 (1949–1950).

Samuelson, Paul A., "Empirical Implications of Utility Analysis," *Econometrica,* Vol. 6 (1938), 344–356.

———— "A Note on the Pure Theory of Consumer's Behaviour," *Economica,* New Series, Vol. V, No. 17 (February, 1938), 61–71, 353–354.

———— "Welfare Economics and Foreign Trade," *American Economic Review,* Vol. XXVIII (June, 1938), 261–266.

———— "The Gains from International Trade," *Canadian Journal of Economics and Political Science,* Vol. V (May, 1939), 195–205.

———— "A Further Comment on Welfare Economics," *American Economic Review,* Vol. XXXIII, No. 4 (September, 1943), 604–607.

———— *Foundations of Economic Analysis.* Cambridge: Harvard University Press, 1947.

—————— "Consumption Theory in Terms of Revealed Preference," *Economica*, New Series, Vol. 15 (1948), 243–253.

—————— "Evaluation of Real National Income," *Oxford Economic Papers*, New Series, Vol. 2, No. 1 (January, 1950), 1–40.

—————— "The Problem of Integrability in Utility Theory," *Economica*, New Series, Vol. XVII, No. 68 (May, 1950), 355–385.

—————— "Probability, Utility and the Independence Axiom," *Econometrica*, Vol. 20, No. 4 (October, 1952), 670–678.

—————— "Utility, Preference and Probability." Hectographed abstract of paper read at conference of Les Fondements et Applications de la Theorie du Risque en Econometrie, March 15, 1952. Referred to by Manne, *Econometrica* (October, 1952), 667.

—————— "Consumption Theorems in Terms of Overcompensation rather than Indifference Comparisons," *Economica*, New Series, Vol. XX, No. 77 (February, 1953), 1–9.

—————— "Social Indifference Curves," *The Quarterly Journal of Economics*, Vol. LXX, No. 1 (February, 1956), 1–22.

Savage, Leonard J., "The Role of Personal Probability in Statistics," *Econometrica*, Vol. 18 (1950), 183.

—————— "The Theory of Statistical Decision," *Journal of American Statistical Association*, Vol. XLVI (March, 1951), 55–68.

—————— "Note on the Strong Independence Assumption," *Econometrica*, Vol. 20, No. 4 (October, 1952), 663–664.

—————— *The Foundations of Statistics.* New York: John Wiley & Sons, Inc., 1954.

Schoeffler, Sidney, "A Note on Modern Welfare Economics," *American Economic Review*, Vol. XLII, No. 5 (December, 1952), 880–886.

Scitovsky, Tibor, "A Note on Welfare Propositions in Economics," *Review of Economic Studies*, Vol. 9 (November, 1941), 77–88.

—————— "A Reconsideration of the Theory of Tariffs," *Review of Economic Studies*, Vol. 9 (November, 1941).

—————— "The State of Welfare Economics," *American Economic Review*, Vol. XLI, No. 3 (June, 1951), 303–315.

Shackle, G. L. S., *Expectation in Economics.* London: The Macmillan Company, 1949.

—————— "A Non-Additive Measure of Uncertainty," *Review of Economic Studies*, Vol. XVII, No. 42 (1949–1950).

—————— "Note on the Strong Independence Assumption," *Econometrica*, Vol. 20, No. 4 (October, 1952).

Shils, Edward A., and E. C. Banfield, "Individual Ends and the Structure of Social Choice," paper read at the December, 1952 meeting of the Econometric Society in Chicago.

Simon, Yves, *Philosophy of Democratic Government*. Chicago: University of Chicago Press, 1951.

Smith, T. V., and Eduard Lindeman, *The Democratic Way of Life*. New York: New American Library, 1952 (reprint).

Stevens, S. S., "Mathematics, Measurement and Psychophysics," in *Handbook of Experimental Psychology*, (ed. S. Stevens). New York: John Wiley & Sons, Inc., 1951.

Stevenson, C. L., "The Nature of Ethical Disagreement," *Readings in Philosophical Analysis* (eds. Herbert Feigl and Wilfrid Sellars), New York: Appleton-Century-Crofts, Inc., 1949.

Stigler, George J., "A Note on the New Welfare Economics," *American Economic Review*, Vol. 33, No. 2 (June, 1943), 355–359.

―――― "The Development of Utility Theory," *The Journal of Political Economy*, Vol. LVIII, Nos. 4–5 (August–October, 1950).

Streeten, Paul, "Economics and Value Judgments," *The Quarterly Journal of Economics*, Vol. LXIV, No. 4 (November, 1950).

Strotz, Robert H., "How Income Ought to be Distributed: A Paradox in Distributive Ethics," *The Journal of Political Economy*, Vol. LXVI, No. 3 (June, 1958), 189–205.

Suppes, Patrick, and Muriel Winet, "An Axiomatization of Utility Based on the Notion of Utility Differences," *Management Science*, (1955), 259–270.

Suranyi-Unger, Theo, "Individual and Collective Wants," *The Journal of Political Economy*, Vol. XLVI, No. 1 (February, 1948).

Thrall, R. M., D. H. Coombs, and R. L. Davis, eds., *Decision Processes*. New York: John Wiley & Sons, Inc., 1954.

Thurstone, L. L., "A Law of Comparative Judgment," *Psychological Review*, Vol. 34 (1927), 273–280.

―――― "Attitudes Can Be Measured," *American Journal of Sociology*, Vol. 33 (1928), 529–554.

―――― "The Measurement of Opinion," *Journal of Abnormal and Social Psychology*, Vol. 22 (1928), 415–430.

―――― "Fechner's Law and the Method of Equal Appearing Intervals," *Journal of Experimental Psychology*, Vol. 12 (1929), 214–224.

―――― "Psychophysical Methods," in *Methods of Psychology* (ed. T. G. Andrews), New York: John Wiley & Sons, Inc., 1948.

Thurstone, L. L., and E. J. Chave, *The Measurement of Attitude*. Chicago: University of Chicago Press, 1929.

Tintner, Gerhard, "A Contribution to the Non-static Theory of Choice," *The Quarterly Journal of Economics*, Vol. LVI, No. 1 (February, 1942).

———— "A Note on Welfare Economics," *Econometrica*, Vol. 14, No. 1 (January, 1946).

———— "Foundations of Probability and Statistical Inference," *Journal of Royal Statistical Society*, Vol. CXII (1949), Part III, 251–279.

Vickrey, William S., "Measuring Marginal Utility by Reaction to Risk," *Econometrica*, Vol. XIII (1945), 319–333.

———— "Some Objections to Marginal Cost Pricing," *The Journal of Political Economy*, Vol. LVI, No. 3 (June, 1948), 218–238.

———— "Utility, Strategy, and Social Decision Rules," *The Quarterly Journal of Economics*, Vol. LXXIV, No. 4 (November, 1960), 507–535.

Ville, Jean, "The Existence Conditions of a Total Utility Function," *Review of Economic Studies*, Vol. XIX (2), No. 49 (1951), 123–128.

Von Mises, Richard, *Wahrscheinlichkeit Statistik und Wahrheit*, third edition, Wein: J. Springer, 1951.

Von Neumann, John, and Oskar Morgenstern, *The Theory of Games and Economic Behavior*. Princeton: Princeton University Press, 1947.

Wagner, Harvey, "An Eclectic Approach to the Pure Theory of Consumer Behavior," *Econometrica*, Vol. 24, No. 4 (October, 1956), 451–466.

———— "A Note in Testing the Transitivity Axiom," *Southern Economic Journal*, Vol. 22, No. 4 (1956), 493–494.

———— "The Case for 'Revealed Preference'," *Review of Economic Studies*, Vol. XXVI, No. 3 (1959), 178–189.

Wald, Abram, "Some Recent Results in the Theory of Decision Functions," *Econometrica*, Vol. 18 (1950), 182–183.

Wallis, W. A., and Milton Friedman, "The Empirical Derivation of Indifference Functions," *Studies in Mathematical Economics and Econometrics*, Chicago: University of Chicago Press, 1942, 175–189.

Weckstein, Richard S., "On the Use of the Theory of Probability in Economics," *Review of Economic Studies*, Vol. XX (3), No. 53 (1952–1953), 191–198.

Weldon, J. C., "On the Problem of Social Welfare Functions," *Canadian Journal of Economics and Political Science*, Vol. 18, No. 4 (November, 1952), 452–463.

Wold, Herman, "Ordinal Preferences or Cardinal Utility," *Econometrica*, Vol. 20, No. 4 (October, 1952), 661–663.

Index

A

Admissibility, 19, 28, 29, 70, 100–101, 103, 201
Alchian, A., 217, 218, 240, 253–254
Allais, M., 215, 242, 247
Allen, R. G. D., 145
Andrews, T. G., 231
Aquinas, T., 333
Archibald, G. C., 257
Archimedean postulate, 232–234
Archimedes, 232
Armstrong, W. E., 134, 146–179, 230
Arrow, K., 15, 17–58, 33, 62, 65, 68, 70, 71, 73, 78, 89, 102, 131, 146, 155, 159, 178–179, 181, 204, 234–236, 262–267, 281–283, 286, 287, 289, 295, 303, 325, 330, 332
Asch, Solomon E., 315
Attitudes toward gambling (or Risk), 207, 222–224, 236–250, 251

B

Bailey, M., 25, 61, 81, 94, 97
Bare preference (*see also* Threshold preference and Marginal preference), 146, 148–179, 230–231
Barone, E., 8
Basic personality, 56, 57
Bator, F. M., 91, 114
Baumol, W. J., 8, 52, 62, 65, 73, 77, 95, 150, 205, 215, 263, 273, 322, 325
Bergson, A., 8, 11, 12, 13, 14, 15, 21, 30–36, 27, 45–52, 62, 84, 200–201, 264, 330
"Bergson frontier," 109
Bernoulli, D., 203–205
"Betweenness," preference and spatial, 137, 156, 283–287
Black, D., 178–179, 280–287, 294
Blau, J., 24, 26–30

C

Cannan, E., 9
Carnap, R., 259
Certainty equivalent, 205
Charnes, A., 236
Chave, E. J., 189, 293
Chipman, J., 232–233
Citizen's sovereignty (*see* Consumer's sovereignty)
Clark, J. M., 73, 145, 174, 323
Coalition, 310, 311, 312
Community indifference curves, 91, 109
Compensation:
  payment of, 61–79, 192–193
  possibility of, 80–103
"Compensation Principle," 8, 61–79, 80–103, 108, 117, 123, 192, 290
Complete ordering (*see* Connexity)
Condition 1 (Arrow's), 19–21, 28, 29, 30, 44, 70, 99, 287, 329
Condition 2 (Arrow's), 20, 25, 27, 28, 44, 70, 181, 184, 282, 287, 329
Condition 3 (Arrow's) ("Independence of Irrelevant Alternatives"), 21–22, 25, 44, 45, 70, 71, 81, 99, 100, 127–144, 181, 183, 205, 282, 287, 329
Conditions 3′ and 3″ ("Modified Independence of Irrelevant Alternatives"), 143
Condition 4 (Arrow's) ("Imposition"), 22–23, 24, 27, 44, 71, 141, 282, 287, 304, 329
Condition 5 (Arrow's) ("Dictatorship"), 23, 24, 26, 29, 44, 71, 141, 282, 287, 301–308, 313–314, 317, 318, 329
Conditions of correspondence, 330
Connexity (or connectedness), 19, 20, 23, 219, 227–229, 282
Consensus of preferences (values), 46–51, 72, 290–295, 296–298, 301–308, 312–336

DATE DUE

HIGHSMITH 45-102   PRINTED IN U.S.A.